Norbert Hornstein, Howard Lasnik, Pritty Patel-Grosz, Charles Yang (Eds.)
Syntactic Structures after 60 Years

Studies in Generative Grammar

Editors
Norbert Corver
Harry van der Hulst
Roumyana Pancheva

Founding editors
Jan Koster
Henk van Riemsdijk

Volume 129

Syntactic Structures after 60 Years

Edited by
Norbert Hornstein
Howard Lasnik
Pritty Patel-Grosz
Charles Yang

DE GRUYTER
MOUTON

ISBN 978-1-5015-1465-4
e-ISBN (PDF) 978-1-5015-0692-5
e-ISBN (EPUB) 978-1-5015-0686-4
ISSN 0167-4331

Library of Congress Cataloging-in-Publication Data
A CIP catalog record for this book has been applied for at the Library of Congress.

Bibliographic information published by the Deutsche Nationalbibliothek
The Deutsche Nationalbibliothek lists this publication in the Deutsche Nationalbibliografie;
detailed bibliographic data are available on the Internet at http://dnb.dnb.de.

© 1957, 2018 Walter de Gruyter GmbH, Berlin/Boston
Printing and binding: CPI books GmbH, Leck
♾ Printed on acid-free paperr
Printed in Germany

www.degruyter.com

Contents

Part I: *Syntactic Structures*

Preface —— 5

Table of Contents —— 9

Part II: *Syntactic Structures* after 60 Years

Acknowledgements —— 121

Norbert Hornstein, Howard Lasnik, Pritty Patel-Grosz and Charles Yang
Introduction —— 123

Noam Chomsky
Syntactic Structures. Some retrospective comments —— 131

Howard Lasnik
Syntactic Structures: Formal Foundations —— 137

David Adger
The Autonomy of Syntax —— 153

Robert C. Berwick
Revolutionary New Ideas Appear Infrequently —— 177

Jon Sprouse
Acceptability judgments and grammaticality, prospects and challenges —— 195

Jeffrey Lidz
The explanatory power of linguistic theory —— 225

Heidi Harley
Kernel sentences, phrase structure grammars, and theta roles —— 241

Mamoru Saito
Transformations in the Quest for a Simpler, more Elegant Theory —— 255

Gillian Ramchand
Grammatical vs. Lexical Formatives —— 283

Bronwyn Moore Bjorkman
***Syntactic Structures* and Morphology** —— 301

Henk C. van Riemsdijk
Constructions —— 317

Paul M. Pietroski
Meanings via Syntactic Structures —— 331

Omer Preminger
***Back to the Future*: Non-generation, filtration, and the heartbreak of interface-driven minimalism** —— 355

Mark Aronoff
English verbs in *Syntactic Structures* —— 381

Artemis Alexiadou, Elena Anagnostopoulou and Florian Schäfer
Passive —— 403

Martina Wiltschko
Discovering syntactic variation —— 427

Part I: *Syntactic Structures*

PREFACE

This study deals with syntactic structure both in the broad sense (as opposed to semantics) and the narrow sense (as opposed to phonemics and morphology). It forms part of an attempt to construct a formalized general theory of linguistic structure and to explore the foundations of such a theory. The search for rigorous formulation in linguistics has a much more serious motivation than mere concern for logical niceties or the desire to purify well-established methods of linguistic analysis. Precisely constructed models for linguistic structure can play an important role, both negative and positive, in the process of discovery itself. By pushing a precise but inadequate formulation to an unacceptable conclusion, we can often expose the exact source of this inadequacy and, consequently, gain a deeper understanding of the linguistic data. More positively, a formalized theory may automatically provide solutions for many problems other than those for which it was explicitly designed. Obscure and intuition-bound notions can neither lead to absurd conclusions nor provide new and correct ones, and hence they fail to be useful in two important respects. I think that some of those linguists who have questioned the value of precise and technical development of linguistic theory may have failed to recognize the productive potential in the method of rigorously stating a proposed theory and applying it strictly to linguistic material with no attempt to avoid unacceptable conclusions by *ad hoc* adjustments or loose formulation. The results reported below were obtained by a conscious attempt to follow this course systematically. Since this fact may be obscured by the informality of the presentation, it is important to emphasize it here.

Specifically, we shall investigate three models for linguistic structure and seek to determine their limitations. We shall find that a certain very simple communication theoretic model of language and a more powerful model that incorporates a large part of what is now generally known as "immediate constituent analysis" cannot properly serve the purposes of grammatical description. The investigation and application of these models brings to light certain facts about linguistic structure and exposes several gaps in linguistic theory; in particular, a failure to account for such relations between sentences as the active-passive relation. We develop a third, *transformational* model for linguistic structure which is more powerful than the immediate constituent model in certain important respects and which does account for such relations in a natural way. When we formulate the theory of transformations carefully and apply it freely to English, we find that it provides a good deal of insight into a wide range of phenomena beyond those for which it was specifically designed. In short, we find that formalization can, in fact, perform both the negative and the positive service commented on above.

During the entire period of this research I have had the benefit of very frequent and lengthy discussions with Zellig S. Harris. So many of his ideas and suggestions are incorporated in the text below and in the research on which it is based that I will make no attempt to indicate them by special reference. Harris' work on transformational structure, which proceeds from a somewhat different point of view from that taken below, is developed in items 15, 16, and 19 of the bibliography (p. 115). In less obvious ways, perhaps, the course of this research has been influenced strongly by the work of Nelson Goodman and W. V. Quine. I have discussed most of this material at length with Morris Halle, and have benefited very greatly from his comments and suggestions. Eric Lenneberg, Israel Scheffler, and Yehoshua Bar-Hillel have read earlier versions of this manuscript and have made many valuable criticisms and suggestions on presentation and content.

The work on the theory of transformations and the transformational structure of English which, though only briefly sketched below, serves as the basis for much of the discussion, was largely carried out in 1951 – 55 while I was a Junior Fellow of the Society of Fellows, Harvard University. I would like to express my gratitude to the Society of Fellows for having provided me with the freedom to carry on this research.

This work was supported in part by the U.S.A. Army (Signal Corps), the Air Force (Office of Scientific Research, Air Research and Development Command), and the Navy (Office of Naval Research); and in part by the National Science Foundation and the Eastman Kodak Corporation.

Massachusetts Institute of Technology,   NOAM CHOMSKY
Department of Modern Languages and
Research Laboratory of Electronics,
Cambridge, Mass.

August 1, 1956.

TABLE OF CONTENTS

Preface 5
1. Introduction 11
2. The Independence of Grammar 13
3. An Elementary Linguistic Theory 18
4. Phrase Structure 26
5. Limitations of Phrase Structure Description 34
6. On the Goals of Linguistic Theory 49
7. Some Transformations in English 61
8. The Explanatory Power of Linguistic Theory 85
9. Syntax and Semantics 92
10. Summary 106
11. Appendix I: Notations and Terminology 109
12. Appendix II: Examples of English Phrase Structure and
    Transformational Rules 111
Bibliography 115

INTRODUCTION

Syntax is the study of the principles and processes by which sentences are constructed in particular languages. Syntactic investigation of a given language has as its goal the construction of a grammar that can be viewed as a device of some sort for producing the sentences of the language under analysis. More generally, linguists must be concerned with the problem of determining the fundamental underlying properties of successful grammars. The ultimate outcome of these investigations should be a theory of linguistic structure in which the descriptive devices utilized in particular grammars are presented and studied abstractly, with no specific reference to particular languages. One function of this theory is to provide a general method for selecting a grammar for each language, given a corpus of sentences of this language.

The central notion in linguistic theory is that of "linguistic level." A linguistic level, such as phonemics, morphology, phrase structure, is essentially a set of descriptive devices that are made available for the construction of grammars; it constitutes a certain method for representing utterances. We can determine the adequacy of a linguistic theory by developing rigorously and precisely the form of grammar corresponding to the set of levels contained within this theory, and then investigating the possibility of constructing simple and revealing grammars of this form for natural languages. We shall study several different conceptions of linguistic structure in this manner, considering a succession of linguistic levels of increasing complexity which correspond to more and more powerful modes of grammatical description; and we shall attempt to show that linguistic theory must contain at least these levels if it is to provide, in particular, a satisfactory grammar of English. Finally, we shall suggest that this purely formal investigation of the structure of language has certain interesting implications for semantic studies.[1]

---

[1] The motivation for the particular orientation of the research reported here is discussed below in § 6.

2

THE INDEPENDENCE OF GRAMMAR

2.1 From now on I will consider a *language* to be a set (finite or infinite) of sentences, each finite in length and constructed out of a finite set of elements. All natural languages in their spoken or written form are languages in this sense, since each natural language has a finite number of phonemes (or letters in its alphabet) and each sentence is representable as a finite sequence of these phonemes (or letters), though there are infinitely many sentences. Similarly, the set of 'sentences' of some formalized system of mathematics can be considered a language. The fundamental aim in the linguistic analysis of a language L is to separate the *grammatical* sequences which are the sentences of L from the *ungrammatical* sequences which are not sentences of L and to study the structure of the grammatical sequences. The grammar of L will thus be a device that generates all of the grammatical sequences of L and none of the ungrammatical ones. One way to test the adequacy of a grammar proposed for L is to determine whether or not the sequences that it generates are actually grammatical, i.e., acceptable to a native speaker, etc. We can take certain steps towards providing a behavioral criterion for grammaticalness so that this test of adequacy can be carried out. For the purposes of this discussion, however, suppose that we assume intuitive knowledge of the grammatical sentences of English and ask what sort of grammar will be able to do the job of producing these in some effective and illuminating way. We thus face a familiar task of explication of some intuitive concept — in this case, the concept "grammatical in English," and more generally, the concept "grammatical."

Notice that in order to set the aims of grammar significantly it is sufficient to assume a partial knowledge of sentences and non-sentences. That is, we may assume for this discussion that certain sequences of phonemes are definitely sentences, and that certain other sequences are definitely non-sentences. In many intermediate cases we shall be prepared to let the grammar itself decide, when the grammar is set up in the simplest way so that it includes the clear sentences and excludes the clear non-sentences. This is a familiar feature of explication.[1] A certain number of clear cases, then, will provide us with a criterion of adequacy for any particular grammar. For a single language, taken in isolation, this provides only a weak test of adequacy, since many different grammars may handle the clear cases properly. This can be generalized to a very strong condition, however, if we insist that the clear cases be handled properly for *each* language by grammars all of which are constructed by the same method. That is, each grammar is related to the corpus of sentences in the language it describes in a way fixed in advance for all grammars by a given linguistic theory. We then have a very strong test of adequacy for a linguistic theory that attempts to give a general explanation for the notion "grammatical sentence" in terms of "observed sentence," and for the set of grammars constructed in accordance with such a theory. It is furthermore a reasonable requirement, since we are interested not only in particular languages, but also in the general nature of Language. There is a great deal more that can be said about this crucial topic, but this would take us too far afield. Cf. § 6.

2.2 On what basis do we actually go about separating grammatical sequences from ungrammatical sequences? I shall not attempt to

---

[1] Cf., for example, N. Goodman, *The structure of appearance* (Cambridge, 1951), pp. 5–6. Notice that to meet the aims of grammar, given a linguistic theory, it is sufficient to have a partial knowledge of the sentences (i.e., a corpus) of the language, since a linguistic theory will state the relation between the set of observed sentences and the set of grammatical sentences; i.e., it will define "grammatical sentence" in terms of "observed sentence," certain properties of the observed sentences, and certain properties of grammars. To use Quine's formulation, a linguistic theory will give a general explanation for what 'could' be in language on the basis of "what *is* plus *simplicity* of the laws whereby we describe and extrapolate what is". (W. V. Quine, *From a logical point of view* [Cambridge, 1953], p. 54). Cf. § 6.1.

give a complete answer to this question here (cf. §§ 6.7), but I would like to point out that several answers that immediately suggest themselves could not be correct. First, it is obvious that the set of grammatical sentences cannot be identified with any particular corpus of utterances obtained by the linguist in his field work. Any grammar of a language will *project* the finite and somewhat accidental corpus of observed utterances to a set (presumably infinite) of grammatical utterances. In this respect, a grammar mirrors the behavior of the speaker who, on the basis of a finite and accidental experience with language, can produce or understand an indefinite number of new sentences. Indeed, any explication of the notion "grammatical in L" (i.e., any characterization of "grammatical in L" in terms of "observed utterance of L") can be thought of as offering an explanation for this fundamental aspect of linguistic behavior.

2.3 Second, the notion "grammatical" cannot be identified with "meaningful" or "significant" in any semantic sense. Sentences (1) and (2) are equally nonsensical, but any speaker of English will recognize that only the former is grammatical.

(1) Colorless green ideas sleep furiously.
(2) Furiously sleep ideas green colorless.

Similarly, there is no semantic reason to prefer (3) to (5) or (4) to (6), but only (3) and (4) are grammatical sentences of English.

(3) have you a book on modern music?
(4) the book seems interesting.
(5) read you a book on modern music?
(6) the child seems sleeping.

Such examples suggest that any search for a semantically based definition of "grammaticalness" will be futile. We shall see, in fact, in § 7, that there are deep structural reasons for distinguishing (3) and (4) from (5) and (6); but before we are able to find an explanation for such facts as these we shall have to carry the theory of syntactic structure a good deal beyond its familiar limits.

2.4 Third, the notion "grammatical in English" cannot be identified in any way with the notion "high order of statistical approximation to English." It is fair to assume that neither sentence (1) nor (2) (nor indeed any part of these sentences) has ever occurred in an English discourse. Hence, in any statistical model for grammaticalness, these sentences will be ruled out on identical grounds as equally 'remote' from English. Yet (1), though nonsensical, is grammatical, while (2) is not. Presented with these sentences, a speaker of English will read (1) with a normal sentence intonation, but he will read (2) with a falling intonation on each word; in fact, with just the intonation pattern given to any sequence of unrelated words. He treats each word in (2) as a separate phrase. Similarly, he will be able to recall (1) much more easily than (2), to learn it much more quickly, etc. Yet he may never have heard or seen any pair of words from these sentences joined in actual discourse. To choose another example, in the context "I saw a fragile—," the words "whale" and "of" may have equal (i.e., zero) frequency in the past linguistic experience of a speaker who will immediately recognize that one of these substitutions, but not the other, gives a grammatical sentence. We cannot, of course, appeal to the fact that sentences such as (1) 'might' be uttered in some sufficiently far-fetched context, while (2) would never be, since the basis for this differentiation between (1) and (2) is precisely what we are interested in determining.

Evidently, one's ability to produce and recognize grammatical utterances is not based on notions of statistical approximation and the like. The custom of calling grammatical sentences those that "can occur", or those that are "possible", has been responsible for some confusion here. It is natural to understand "possible" as meaning "highly probable" and to assume that the linguist's sharp distinction between grammatical and ungrammatical[2] is motivated by a feeling that since the 'reality' of language is too complex to be described completely, he must content himself with a schematized

[2] Below we shall suggest that this sharp distinction may be modified in favor of a notion of levels of grammaticalness. But this has no bearing on the point at issue here. Thus (1) and (2) will be at different levels of grammaticalness even if (1) is assigned a lower degree of grammaticalness than, say, (3) and (4); but they will be at the same level of statistical remoteness from English. The same is true of an indefinite number of similar pairs.

version replacing "zero probability, and all extremely low probabilities, by *impossible*, and all higher probabilities by *possible*."[3] We see, however, that this idea is quite incorrect, and that a structural analysis cannot be understood as a schematic summary developed by sharpening the blurred edges in the full statistical picture. If we rank the sequences of a given length in order of statistical approximation to English, we will find both grammatical and ungrammatical sequences scattered throughout the list; there appears to be no particular relation between order of approximation and grammaticalness. Despite the undeniable interest and importance of semantic and statistical studies of language, they appear to have no direct relevance to the problem of determining or characterizing the set of grammatical utterances. I think that we are forced to conclude that grammar is autonomous and independent of meaning, and that probabilistic models give no particular insight into some of the basic problems of syntactic structure.[4]

[3] C. F. Hockett, *A manual of phonology* (Baltimore, 1955), p. 10.
[4] We return to the question of the relation between semantics and syntax in §§ 8, 9, where we argue that this relation can only be studied after the syntactic structure has been determined on independent grounds. I think that much the same thing is true of the relation between syntactic and statistical studies of language. Given the grammar of a language, one can study the use of the language statistically in various ways; and the development of probabilistic models for the use of language (as distinct from the syntactic structure of language) can be quite rewarding. Cf. B. Mandelbrot, "Structure formelle des textes et communication: deux études," *Word* 10.1-27 (1954); H. A. Simon, "On a class of skew distribution functions," *Biometrika* 42.425-40 (1955).

One might seek to develop a more elaborate relation between statistical and syntactic structure than the simple order of approximation model we have rejected. I would certainly not care to argue that any such relation is unthinkable, but I know of no suggestion to this effect that does not have obvious flaws. Notice, in particular, that for any n, we can find a string whose first n words may occur as the beginning of a grammatical sentence S_1 and whose last n words may occur as the ending of some grammatical sentence S_2, but where S_1 must be distinct from S_2. For example, consider the sequences of the form "the man who ... are here," where ... may be a verb phrase of arbitrary length. Notice also that we can have new but perfectly grammatical sequences of word classes, e.g., a sequence of adjectives longer than any ever before produced in the context "I saw a — house." Various attempts to explain the grammatical-ungrammatical distinction, as in the case of (1), (2), on the basis of frequency of sentence type, order of approximation of word class sequences, etc., will run afoul of numerous facts like these.

AN ELEMENTARY LINGUISTIC THEORY

3.1 Assuming the set of grammatical sentences of English to be given, we now ask what sort of device can produce this set (equivalently, what sort of theory gives an adequate account of the structure of this set of utterances). We can think of each sentence of this set as a sequence of phonemes of finite length. A language is an enormously involved system, and it is quite obvious that any attempt to present directly the set of grammatical phoneme sequences would lead to a grammar so complex that it would be practically useless. For this reason (among others), linguistic description proceeds in terms of a system of "levels of representations." Instead of stating the phonemic structure of sentences directly, the linguist sets up such 'higher level' elements as morphemes, and states separately the morphemic structure of sentences and the phonemic structure of morphemes. It can easily be seen that the joint description of these two levels will be much simpler than a direct description of the phonemic structure of sentences.

Let us now consider various ways of describing the morphemic structure of sentences. We ask what sort of grammar is necessary to generate all the sequences of morphemes (or words) that constitute grammatical English sentences, and only these.

One requirement that a grammar must certainly meet is that it be finite. Hence the grammar cannot simply be a list of all morpheme (or word) sequences, since there are infinitely many of these. A familiar communication theoretic model for language suggests a way out of this difficulty. Suppose that we have a machine that can be in any one of a finite number of different internal states, and suppose that this machine switches from one state to another by producing a certain symbol (let us say, an English word). One of these states is an *initial state*; another is a *final state*. Suppose that the machine begins in the initial state, runs through a sequence of states (producing a word with each transition), and ends in the final state. Then we call the sequence of words that has been produced a "sentence". Each such machine thus defines a certain language; namely, the set of sentences that can be produced in this way. Any language that can be produced by a machine of this sort we call a *finite state language*; and we can call the machine itself a *finite state grammar*. A finite state grammar can be represented graphically in the form of a "state diagram".[1] For example, the grammar that produces just the two sentences "the man comes" and "the men come" can be represented by the following state diagram:

(7)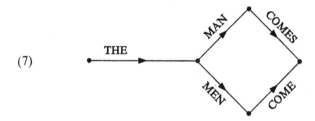

We can extend this grammar to produce an infinite number of sentences by adding closed loops. Thus the finite grammar of the subpart of English containing the above sentences in addition to "the old man comes", "the old old man comes", ..., "the old men come", "the old old men come", ..., can be represented by the following state diagram:

(8)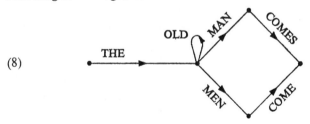

---

[1] C. E. Shannon and W. Weaver, *The mathematical theory of communication* (Urbana, 1949), pp. 15f.

Given a state diagram, we produce a sentence by tracing a path from the initial point on the left to the final point on the right, always proceeding in the direction of the arrows. Having reached a certain point in the diagram, we can proceed along any path leading from this point, whether or not this path has been traversed before in constructing the sentence in question. Each node in such a diagram thus corresponds to a state of the machine. We can allow transition from one state to another in several ways, and we can have any number of closed loops of any length. The machines that produce languages in this manner are known mathematically as "finite state Markov processes." To complete this elementary communication theoretic model for language, we assign a probability to each transition from state to state. We can then calculate the "uncertainty" associated with each state and we can define the "information content" of the language as the average uncertainty, weighted by the probability of being in the associated states. Since we are studying grammatical, not statistical structure of language here, this generalization does not concern us.

This conception of language is an extremely powerful and general one. If we can adopt it, we can view the speaker as being essentially a machine of the type considered. In producing a sentence, the speaker begins in the initial state, produces the first word of the sentence, thereby switching into a second state which limits the choice of the second word, etc. Each state through which he passes represents the grammatical restrictions that limit the choice of the next word at this point in the utterance.[2]

In view of the generality of this conception of language, and its utility in such related disciplines as communication theory, it is important to inquire into the consequences of adopting this point of view in the syntactic study of some language such as English or a formalized system of mathematics. Any attempt to construct a finite state grammar for English runs into serious difficulties and complications at the very outset, as the reader can easily convince himself. However, it is unnecessary to attempt to show this by

[2] This is essentially the model of language that Hockett develops in *A manual of phonology* (Baltimore, 1955), 02.

example, in view of the following more general remark about English:

(9) English is not a finite state language.

That is, it is *impossible*, not just difficult, to construct a device of the type described above (a diagram such as (7) or (8)) which will produce all and only the grammatical sentences of English. To demonstrate (9) it is necessary to define the syntactic properties of English more precisely. We shall proceed to describe certain syntactic properties of English which indicate that, under any reasonable delimitation of the set of sentences of the language, (9) can be regarded as a theorem concerning English. To go back to the question asked in the second paragraph of § 3, (9) asserts that it is not possible to state the morphemic structure of sentences directly by means of some such device as a state diagram, and that the Markov process conception of language outlined above cannot be accepted, at least for the purposes of grammar.

3.2 A language is defined by giving its 'alphabet' (i.e., the finite set of symbols out of which its sentences are constructed) and its grammatical sentences. Before investigating English directly, let us consider several languages whose alphabets contain just the letters *a*, *b*, and whose sentences are as defined in (10i–iii):

(10) (i) *ab, aabb, aaabbb,* ..., and in general, all sentences consisting of *n* occurrences of *a* followed by *n* occurrences of *b* and only these;
    (ii) *aa, bb, abba, baab, aaaa, bbbb, aabbaa, abbbba,* ..., and in general, all sentences consisting of a string X followed by the 'mirror image' of X (i.e., X in reverse), and only these;
    (iii) *aa, bb, abab, baba, aaaa, bbbb, aabaab, abbabb,* ..., and in general, all sentences consisting of a string X of *a*'s and *b*'s followed by the identical string X, and only these.

We can easily show that each of these three languages is not a finite state language. Similarly, languages such as (10) where the *a*'s and *b*'s in question are not consecutive, but are embedded in other strings, will fail to be finite state languages under quite general conditions.³

But it is clear that there are subparts of English with the basic form of (10i) and (10ii). Let $S_1, S_2, S_3, \ldots$ be declarative sentences in English. Then we can have such English sentences as:

(11) (i) If S_1, then S_2.
    (ii) Either S_3, or S_4.
    (iii) The man who said that S_5, is arriving today.

In (11i), we cannot have "or" in place of "then"; in (11ii), we cannot have "then" in place of "or"; in (11iii), we cannot have "are" instead of "is". In each of these cases there is a dependency between words on opposite sides of the comma (i.e., "if"–"then", "either"–"or", "man"–"is"). But between the interdependent words, in each case, we can insert a declarative sentence S_1, S_3, S_5, and this declarative sentence may in fact be one of (11i–iii). Thus if in (11i) we take S_1 as (11ii) and S_3 as (11iii), we will have the sentence:

(12)   if, either (11iii), or S_4, then S_2,

and S_5 in (11iii) may again be one of the sentences of (11). It is clear, then, that in English we can find a sequence $a + S_1 + b$, where there is a dependency between a and b, and we can select as S_1 another sequence containing $c + S_2 + d$, where there is a dependency between c and d, then select as S_2 another sequence of this form, etc. A set of sentences that is constructed in this way (and we see from (11) that there are several possibilities available for such construction—(11) comes nowhere near exhausting these possibilities) will have all of the mirror image properties of (10ii) which exclude (10ii) from the set of finite state languages. Thus we can find various kinds of non-

---

³ See my "Three models for the description of language," *I.R.E. Transactions on Information Theory*, vol. IT-2, Proceedings of the symposium on information theory, Sept., 1956, for a statement of such conditions and a proof of (9). Notice in particular that the set of well-formed formulas of any formalized system of mathematics or logic will fail to constitute a finite state language, because of paired parentheses or equivalent restrictions.

finite state models within English. This is a rough indication of the lines along which a rigorous proof of (9) can be given, on the assumption that such sentences as (11) and (12) belong to English, while sentences that contradict the cited dependencies of (11) (e.g., "either S_1, then S_2," etc.) do not belong to English. Note that many of the sentences of the form (12), etc., will be quite strange and unusual (they can often be made less strange by replacing "if" by "whenever", "on the assumption that", "if it is the case that", etc., without changing the substance of our remarks). But they are all grammatical sentences, formed by processes of sentence construction so simple and elementary that even the most rudimentary English grammar would contain them. They can be understood, and we can even state quite simply the conditions under which they can be true. It is difficult to conceive of any possible motivation for excluding them from the set of grammatical English sentences. Hence it seems quite clear that no theory of linguistic structure based exclusively on Markov process models and the like, will be able to explain or account for the ability of a speaker of English to produce and understand new utterances, while he rejects other new sequences as not belonging to the language.

3.3 We might arbitrarily decree that such processes of sentence formation in English as those we are discussing cannot be carried out more than n times, for some fixed n. This would of course make English a finite state language, as, for example, would a limitation of English sentences to length of less than a million words. Such arbitrary limitations serve no useful purpose, however. The point is that there are processes of sentence formation that finite state grammars are intrinsically not equipped to handle. If these processes have no finite limit, we can prove the literal inapplicability of this elementary theory. If the processes have a limit, then the construction of a finite state grammar will not be literally out of the question, since it will be possible to list the sentences, and a list is essentially a trivial finite state grammar. But this grammar will be so complex that it will be of little use or interest. In general, the assumption that languages are infinite is made in order to simplify the description of these languages. If a grammar does not have recursive devices (closed loops, as in (8), in the finite state grammar) it will be prohibitively complex. If it does have recursive devices of some sort, it will produce infinitely many sentences.

In short, the approach to the analysis of grammaticalness suggested here in terms of a finite state Markov process that produces sentences from left to right, appears to lead to a dead end just as surely as the proposals rejected in § 2. If a grammar of this type produces all English sentences, it will produce many non-sentences as well. If it produces only English sentences, we can be sure that there will be an infinite number of true sentences, false sentences, reasonable questions, etc., which it simply will not produce.

The conception of grammar which has just been rejected represents in a way the minimal linguistic theory that merits serious consideration. A finite state grammar is the simplest type of grammar which, with a finite amount of apparatus, can generate an infinite number of sentences. We have seen that such a limited linguistic theory is not adequate; we are forced to search for some more powerful type of grammar and some more 'abstract' form of linguistic theory. The notion of "linguistic level of representation" put forth at the outset of this section must be modified and elaborated. At least one linguistic level *cannot* have this simple structure. That is, on some level, it will not be the case that each sentence is represented simply as a finite sequence of elements of some sort, generated from left to right by some simple device. Alternatively, we must give up the hope of finding a *finite* set of levels, ordered from high to low, so constructed that we can generate all utterances by stating the permitted sequences of highest level elements, the constituency of each highest level element in terms of elements of the second level, etc., finally stating the phonemic constituency of elements of the next-to-lowest level.[4] At the outset of § 3, we

---

[4] A third alternative would be to retain the notion of a linguistic level as a simple linear method of representation, but to generate at least one such level from left to right by a device with more capacity than a finite state Markov process. There are so many difficulties with the notion of linguistic level based on left to right generation, both in terms of complexity of description and lack

proposed that levels be established in this way in order to *simplify* the description of the set of grammatical phoneme sequences. If a language can be described in an elementary, left-to-right manner in terms of a single level (i.e., if it is a finite state language) then this description may indeed be simplified by construction of such higher levels; but to generate non-finite state languages such as English we need fundamentally different methods, and a more general concept of "linguistic level".

---

of explanatory power (cf. § 8), that it seems pointless to pursue this approach any further. The grammars that we discuss below that do not generate from left to right also correspond to processes less elementary than finite state Markov processes. But they are perhaps less powerful than the kind of device that would be required for direct left-to-right generation of English. Cf. my "Three models for the description of language" for some futher discussion.

4

PHRASE STRUCTURE

4.1 Customarily, linguistic description on the syntactic level is formulated in terms of constituent analysis (parsing). We now ask what form of grammar is presupposed by description of this sort. We find that the new form of grammar is *essentially* more powerful than the finite state model rejected above, and that the associated concept of "linguistic level" is different in fundamental respects.

As a simple example of the new form for grammars associated with constituent analysis, consider the following:

(13) (i)   *Sentence* → *NP* + *VP*
   (ii) *NP* → *T* + *N*
  (iii) *VP* → *Verb* + *NP*
  (iv) *T* → *the*
   (v) *N* → *man, ball*, etc.
  (vi) *Verb* → *hit, took*, etc.

Suppose that we interpret each rule $X \to Y$ of (13) as the instruction "rewrite X as Y". We shall call (14) a *derivation* of the sentence "the man hit the ball." where the numbers at the right of each line of the derivation refer to the rule of the "grammar" (13) used in constructing that line from the preceding line.[1]

---

[1] The numbered rules of English grammar to which reference will constantly be made in the following pages are collected and properly ordered in § 12, *Appendix II*. The notational conventions that we shall use throughout the discussion of English structure are stated in § 11, *Appendix I*.

In his "Axiomatic syntax: the construction and evaluation of a syntactic calculus," *Language* 31.409-14 (1955), Harwood describes a system of word class analysis similar in form to the system developed below for phrase structure. The system he describes would be concerned only with the relation between $T + N + Verb + T + N$ and *the + man + hit + the + ball* in the example discussed

(14) *Sentence*
    NP + VP   (i)
    T + N + VP   (ii)
    T + N + Verb + NP   (iii)
    the + N + Verb + NP   (iv)
    the + man + Verb + NP   (v)
    the + man + hit + NP   (vi)
    the + man + hit + T + N   (ii)
    the + man + hit + the + N   (iv)
    the + man + hit + the + ball   (v)

Thus the second line of (14) is formed from the first line by rewriting *Sentence* as $NP + VP$ in accordance with rule (i) of (13); the third line is formed from the second by rewriting NP as $T + N$ in accordance with rule (ii) of (13); etc. We can represent the derivation (14) in an obvious way by means of the following diagram:

(15)

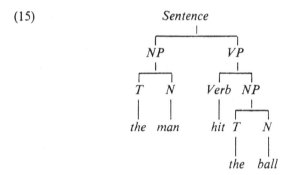

The diagram (15) conveys less information than the derivation (14), since it does not tell us in what order the rules were applied in (14).

---

in (13)–(15); i.e., the grammar would contain the "initial string" $T + N + Verb + T + N$ and such rules as (13 iv–vi). It would thus be a weaker system than the elementary theory discussed in § 3, since it could not generate an infinite language with a finite grammar. While Harwood's formal account (pp. 409–11) deals only with word class analysis, the linguistic application (p. 412) is a case of immediate constituent analysis, with the classes $C_{i..m}$ presumably taken to be classes of word sequences. This extended application is not quite compatible with the formal account, however. For example, none of the proposed measures of goodness of fit can stand without revision under this reinterpretation of the formalism.

Given (14), we can construct (15) uniquely, but not vice versa, since it is possible to construct a derivation that reduces to (15) with a different order of application of the rules. The diagram (15) retains just what is essential in (14) for the determination of the phrase structure (constituent analysis) of the derived sentence "the man hit the ball." A sequence of words of this sentence is a constituent of type Z if we can trace this sequence back to a single point of origin in (15), and this point of origin is labelled Z. Thus "hit the ball" can be traced back to VP in (15); hence "hit the ball" is a VP in the derived sentence. But "man hit" cannot be traced back to any single point of origin in (15); hence "man hit" is not a constituent at all.

We say that two derivations are *equivalent* if they reduce to the same diagram of the form (15). Occasionally, a grammar may permit us to construct nonequivalent derivations for a given sentence. Under these circumstances, we say that we have a case of "constructional homonymity",[2] and if our grammar is correct, this sentence of the language should be ambiguous. We return to the important notion of constructional homonymity below.

One generalization of (13) is clearly necessary. We must be able to limit application of a rule to a certain context. Thus T can be rewritten *a* if the following noun is singular, but not if it is plural; similarly, *Verb* can be rewritten "hits" if the preceding noun is *man*, but not if it is *men*. In general, if we wish to limit the rewriting of X as Y to the context $Z - W$, we can state in the grammar the rule

(16) $Z + X + W \rightarrow Z + Y + W$.

For example, in the case of singular and plural verbs, instead of having $Verb \rightarrow hits$ as an additional rule of (13), we should have

(17) $NP_{sing} + Verb \rightarrow NP_{sing} + hits$

indicating that *Verb* is rewritten *hits* only in the context $NP_{sing}-$.

---

[2] See § 8.1 for some examples of constructional homonymity. See my *The logical structure of linguistic theory* (mimeographed); "Three models for the description of language" (above, p. 22, fn. 3); C. F. Hockett, "Two models of grammatical description," *Linguistics Today, Word* 10.210–33 (1954); R. S. Wells, "Immediate constituents," *Language* 23.81–117 (1947) for more detailed discussion.

Correspondingly, (13ii) will have to be restated to include NP_{sing} and NP_{pl}.[3] This is a straightforward generalization of (13). One feature of (13) must be preserved, however, as it is in (17): only a single element can be rewritten in any single rule; i.e., in (16), X must be a single symbol such as T, *Verb*, and not a sequence such as $T + N$. If this condition is not met, we will not be able to recover properly the phrase structure of derived sentences from the associated diagrams of the form (15), as we did above.

We can now describe more generally the form of grammar associated with the theory of linguistic structure based upon constituent analysis. Each such grammar is defined by a finite set Σ of initial strings and a finite set F of 'instruction formulas' of the form $X \to Y$ interpreted: "rewrite X as Y." Though X need not be a single symbol, only a single symbol of X can be rewritten in forming Y. In the grammar (13), the only member of the set Σ of initial strings was the single symbol *Sentence*, and F consisted of the rules (i) – (vi); but we might want to extend Σ to include, for example, *Declarative Sentence, Interrogative Sentence*, as additional symbols. Given the grammar [Σ, F], we define a *derivation* as a finite sequence of strings, beginning with an initial string of Σ, and with each string in the sequence being derived from the preceding string by application of one of the instruction formulas of F. Thus (14) is a derivation, and the five-termed sequence of strings consisting of the first five lines of (14) is also a derivation. Certain derivations are *terminated* derivations, in the sense that their final string cannot be rewritten any further by the rules F. Thus (14) is a terminated derivation, but the sequence consisting of the first five

---

[3] Thus in a more complete grammar, (13ii) might be replaced by a set of rules that includes the following:

$NP \to \begin{Bmatrix} NP_{sing} \\ NP_{pl} \end{Bmatrix}$
$NP_{sing} \to T + N + \emptyset \ (+ Prepositional\ Phrase)$
$NP_{pl} \to T + N + S \ (+ Prepositional\ Phrase)$

where S is the morpheme which is singular for verbs and plural for nouns ("comes," "boys"), and $\emptyset$ is the morpheme which is singular for nouns and plural for verbs ("boy," "come"). We shall omit all mention of first and second person throughout this discussion. Identification of the nominal and verbal number affix is actually of questionable validity.

lines of (14) is not. If a string is the last line of a terminated derivation, we say that it is a *terminal* string. Thus *the + man + hit + the + ball* is a terminal string from the grammar (13). Some grammars of the form [Σ, F] may have no terminal strings, but we are interested only in grammars that do have terminal strings, i.e., that describe some language. A set of strings is called a *terminal language* if it is the set of terminal strings for some grammar [Σ, F]. Thus each such grammar defines some terminal language (perhaps the 'empty' language containing no sentences), and each terminal language is produced by some grammar of the form [Σ, F]. Given a terminal language and its grammar, we can reconstruct the phrase structure of each sentence of the language (each terminal string of the grammar) by considering the associated diagrams of the form (15), as we saw above. We can also define the grammatical relations in these languages in a formal way in terms of the associated diagrams.

4.2 In § 3 we considered languages, called "finite state languages", which were generated by finite state Markov processes. Now we are considering terminal languages that are generated by systems of the form [Σ, F]. These two types of languages are related in the following way

Theorem: Every finite state language is a terminal language, but there are terminal languages which are not finite state languages.[4]

The import of this theorem is that description in terms of phrase structure is essentially more powerful than description in terms of the elementary theory presented above in § 3. As examples of terminal languages that are not finite state languages we have the languages (10i), (10ii) discussed in § 3. Thus the language (10i), consisting of all and only the strings *ab, aabb, aaabbb*, ... can be produced by the [Σ, F] grammar (18).

(18)   Σ: Z
        F: $Z \to ab$
            $Z \to aZb$

[4] See my "Three models for the description of language" (above, p. 22, fn. 3) for proofs of this and related theorems about relative power of grammars.

This grammar has the initial string Z (as (13) has the initial string *Sentence*) and it has two rules. It can easily be seen that each terminated derivation constructed from (18) ends in a string of the language (10i), and that all such strings are produced in this way. Similarly, languages of the form (10ii) can be produced by [Σ, F] grammars (10iii), however, cannot be produced by a grammar of this type, unless the rules embody contextual restrictions.[5]

In § 3 we pointed out that the languages (10i) and (10ii) correspond to subparts of English, and that therefore the finite state Markov process model is not adequate for English. We now see that the phrase structure model does not fail in such cases. We have not proved the adequacy of the phrase structure model, but we have shown that large parts of English which literally cannot be described in terms of the finite-state process model can be described in terms of phrase structure.

Note that in the case of (18), we can say that in the string *aaabbb* of (10i), for example, *ab* is a Z, *aabb* is a Z, and *aaabbb* itself is a Z.[6] Thus this particular string contains three 'phrases,' each of which is a Z. This is, of course, a very trivial language. It is important to observe that in describing this language we have introduced a symbol Z which is not contained in the sentences of this language. This is the essential fact about phrase structure which gives it its 'abstract' character.

Observe also that in the case of both (13) and (18) (as in every system of phrase structure), each terminal string has many different representations. For example, in the case of (13), the terminal string "the man hit the ball" is represented by the strings *Sentence*, $NP + VP$, $T + N + VP$, and all the other lines of (14), as well as by such strings as $NP + Verb + NP$, $T + N + hit + NP$, which would occur in other derivations equivalent to (14) in the sense there defined. On the level of phrase structure, then, each sentence of the language is represented by a *set* of strings, not by a single string as it

---

[5] See my "On certain formal properties of grammars", *Information and Control* 2.133–167 (1959).

[6] Where "is a" is the relation defined in § 4.1 in terms of such diagrams as (15).

is on the level of phonemes, morphemes, or words. Thus phrase structure, taken as a linguistic level, has the fundamentally different and nontrivial character which, as we saw in the last paragraph of § 3, is required for some linguistic level. We cannot set up a hierarchy among the various representations of "the man hit the ball"; we cannot subdivide the system of phrase structure into a finite set of levels, ordered from higher to lower, with one representation for each sentence on each of these sublevels. For example, there is no way of ordering the elements *NP* and *VP* relative to one another. Noun phrases are contained within verb phrases, and verb phrases within noun phrases, in English. Phrase structure must be considered as a single level, with a set of representations for each sentence of the language. There is a one-one correspondence between the properly chosen sets of representations, and diagrams of the form (15).

4.3 Suppose that by a $[\Sigma, F]$ grammar we can generate all of the grammatical sequences of morphemes of a language. In order to complete the grammar we must state the phonemic structure of these morphemes, so that the grammar will produce the grammatical phoneme sequences of the language. But this statement (which we would call the *morphophonemics* of the language) can also be given by a set of rules of the form "rewrite X as Y", e.g., for English,

(19) (i) *walk* → /wɔk/
   (ii) *take* + *past* → /tuk/
  (iii) *hit* + *past* → /hit/
  (iv) /...D/ + *past* → /...D/ + /ɪd/ (where D = /t/ or /d/)
  (v) /...C_{unv}/ + *past* → /...C_{unv}/ + /t/ (where C_{unv} is an unvoiced consonant)
  (vi) *past* → /d/.
 (vii) *take* → /teyk/
    etc.

or something similar. Note, incidentally, that order must be defined among these rules — e.g., (ii) must precede (v) or (vii), or we will derive such forms as /teykt/ for the past tense of *take*. In these morphophonemic rules we need no longer require that only a single symbol be rewritten in each rule.

We can now extend the phrase structure derivations by applying (19), so that we have a unified process for generating phoneme sequence from the initial string *Sentence*. This makes it appear as though the break between the higher level of phrase structure and the lower levels is arbitrary. Actually, the distinction is not arbitrary. For one thing, as we have seen, the formal properties of the rules $X \to Y$ corresponding to phrase structure are different from those of the morphophonemic rules, since in the case of the former we must require that only a single symbol be rewritten. Second, the elements that figure in the rules (19) can be classified into a finite set of levels (e.g., phonemes and morphemes; or, perhaps, phonemes, morphophonemes, and morphemes) each of which is elementary in the sense that a single string of elements of this level is associated with each sentence as its representation on this level (except in cases of homonymity), and each such string represents a single sentence. But the elements that appear in the rules corresponding to phrase structure cannot be classified into higher and lower levels in this way. We shall see below that there is an even more fundamental reason for marking this subdivison into the higher level rules of phrase structure and the lower level rules that convert strings of morphemes into strings of phonemes.

The formal properties of the system of phrase structure make an interesting study, and it is easy to show that further elaboration of the form of grammar is both necessary and possible. Thus it can easily be seen that it would be quite advantageous to order the rules of the set F so that certain of the rules can apply only after others have applied. For example, we should certainly want all rules of the form (17) to apply before any rule which enables us to rewrite *NP* as *NP* + *Preposition* + *NP*, or the like; otherwise the grammar will produce such nonsentences as "the men near the truck begins work at eight." But this elaboration leads to problems that would carry us beyond the scope of this study.

5

LIMITATIONS OF
PHRASE STRUCTURE DESCRIPTION

5.1 We have discussed two models for the structure of language, a communication theoretic model based on a conception of language as a Markov process and corresponding, in a sense, to the minimal linguistic theory, and a phrase structure model based on immediate constituent analysis. We have seen that the first is surely inadequate for the purposes of grammar, and that the second is more powerful than the first, and does not fail in the same way. Of course there are languages (in our general sense) that cannot be described in terms of phrase structure, but I do not know whether or not English is itself literally outside the range of such analysis. However, I think that there are other grounds for rejecting the theory of phrase structure as inadequate for the purpose of linguistic description.

The strongest possible proof of the inadequacy of a linguistic theory is to show that it literally cannot apply to some natural language. A weaker, but perfectly sufficient demonstration of inadequacy would be to show that the theory can apply only clumsily; that is, to show that any grammar that can be constructed in terms of this theory will be extremely complex, *ad hoc*, and 'unrevealing', that certain very simple ways of describing grammatical sentences cannot be accommodated within the associated forms of grammar, and that certain fundamental formal properties of natural language cannot be utilized to simplify grammars. We can gather a good deal of evidence of this sort in favor of the thesis that the form of grammar described above, and the conception of linguistic theory that underlies it, are fundamentally inadequate.

The only way to test the adequacy of our present apparatus is to attempt to apply it directly to the description of English sentences.

As soon as we consider any sentences beyond the simplest type, and in particular, when we attempt to define some order among the rules that produce these sentences, we find that we run into numerous difficulties and complications. To give substance to this claim would require a large expenditure of effort and space, and I can only assert here that this can be shown fairly convincingly.[1] Instead of undertaking this rather arduous and ambitious course here, I shall limit myself to sketching a few simple cases in which considerable improvement is possible over grammars of the form [Σ, F]. In § 8 I shall suggest an independent method of demonstrating the inadequacy of constituent analysis as a means of describing English sentence structure.

5.2 One of the most productive processes for forming new sentences is the process of conjunction. If we have two sentences $Z + X + W$ and $Z + Y + W$, and if X and Y are actually constituents of these sentences, we can generally form a new sentence $Z - X + and + Y - W$. For example, from the sentences (20a-b) we can form the new sentence (21).

(20) (a) the scene – of the movie – was in Chicago
      (b) the scene – of the play – was in Chicago
(21) the scene – of the movie and of the play – was in Chicago.

If X and Y are, however, not constituents, we generally cannot do this.[2] For example we cannot form (23) from (22a-b).

---

[1] See my *The logical structure of linguistic theory* for detailed analysis of this problem.

[2] (21) and (23) are extreme cases in which there is no question about the possibility of conjunction. There are many less clear cases. For example, it is obvious that "John enjoyed the book and liked the play" (a string of the form $NP - VP + and + VP$) is a perfectly good sentence, but many would question the grammaticalness of, e.g., "John enjoyed and my friend liked the play" (a string of the form $NP + Verb + and + Verb - NP$). The latter sentence, in which conjunction crosses over constituent boundaries, is much less natural than the alternative "John enjoyed the play and my friend liked it", but there is no preferable alternative to the former. Such sentences with conjunction crossing constituent boundaries are also, in general, marked by special phonemic features such as extra long pauses (in our example, between "liked" and "the"), contrastive stress and intonation, failure to reduce vowels and drop final consonants in

(22) (a) the – liner sailed down the – river
 (b) the – tugboat chugged up the – river
(23) the – liner sailed down the and tugboat chugged up the – river.

Similarly, if X and Y are both constituents, but are constituents of different kinds (i.e., if in the diagram of the form (15) they each have a single origin, but this origin is labelled differently), then we cannot in general form a new sentence by conjunction. For example, we cannot form (25) from (24a-b).

(24) (a) the scene – of the movie – was in Chicago
 (b) the scene – that I wrote – was in Chicago
(25) the scene – of the movie and that I wrote – was in Chicago

In fact, the possibility of conjunction offers one of the best criteria for the initial determination of phrase structure. We can simplify the description of conjunction if we try to set up constituents in such a way that the following rule will hold:

(26) If S_1 and S_2 are grammatical sentences, and S_1 differs from S_2 only in that X appears in S_1 where Y appears in S_2 (i.e., $S_1 = ..X..$ and $S_2 = ..Y..$), and X and Y are constituents of the same type in S_1 and S_2, respectively, then S_3 is a sentence, where S_3 is the result of replacing X by $X + and + Y$ in S_1 (i.e., $S_3 = ..X + and + Y..$).

---

rapid speech, etc. Such features normally mark the reading of non-grammatical strings. The most reasonable way to describe this situation would seem to be by a description of the following kind: to form fully grammatical sentences by conjunction, it is necessary to conjoin single constituents; if we conjoin pairs of constituents, and these are major constituents (i.e., 'high up' in the diagram (15)), the resulting sentences are semi-grammatical; the more completely we violate constituent structure by conjunction, the less grammatical is the resulting sentence. This description requires that we generalize the grammatical-ungrammatical dichotomy, developing a notion of degree of grammaticalness. It is immaterial to our discussion, however, whether we decide to exclude such sentences as "John enjoyed and my friend liked the play" as ungrammatical, whether we include them as semi-grammatical, or whether we include them as fully grammatical but with special phonemic features. In any event they form a class of utterances distinct from "John enjoyed the play and liked the book," etc., where constituent structure is preserved perfectly; and our conclusion that the rule for conjunction must make explicit reference to constituent structure therefore stands, since this distinction will have to be pointed out in the grammar.

LIMITATIONS OF PHRASE STRUCTURE DESCRIPTION   37

Even though additional qualification is necessary here, the grammar is enormously simplified if we set up constituents in such a way that (26) holds even approximately. That is, it is easier to state the distribution of "and" by means of qualifications on this rule than to do so directly without such a rule. But we now face the following difficulty: we cannot incorporate the rule (26) or anything like it ir a grammar [Σ, F] of phrase structure, because of certain fundamental limitations on such grammars. The essential property of rule (26) is that in order to apply it to sentences S_1 and S_2 to form the new sentence S_3 we must know not only the actual form of S_1 and S_2 but also their constituent structure — we must know not only the final shape of these sentences, but also their 'history of derivation.' But each rule $X \to Y$ of the grammar [Σ, F] applies or fails to apply to a given string by virtue of the actual substance of this string. The question of how this string gradually assumed this form is irrelevant. If the string contains X as a substring, the rule $X \to Y$ can apply to it; if not, the rule cannot apply.

We can put this somewhat differently. The grammar [Σ, F] can also be regarded as a very elementary process that generates sentences not from "left to right" but from "top to bottom". Suppose that we have the following grammar of phrase structure:

(27)   Σ: *Sentence*
       F: $X_1 \to Y_1$
          $\vdots$
          $X_n \to Y_n$.

Then we can represent this grammar as a machine with a finite number of internal states, including an initial and a final state. In its initial state it can produce only the element *Sentence*, thereby moving into a new state. It can then produce any string Y_i such that *Sentence* $\to Y_i$ is one of the rules of F in (27), again moving into a new state. Suppose that Y_i is the string ... X_j ... Then the machine can produce the string ... Y_j ... by "applying" the rule $X_j \to Y_j$. The machine proceeds in this way from state to state until it finally produces a terminal string; it is now in the final state. The machine thus produces derivations, in the sense of §4. The important point is that the state of the machine is completely determined by the string it has just produced (i.e., by the last step of the derivation); more specifically, the state is determined by the subset of 'left-hand' elements X_i of F which are contained in this last-produced string. But rule (26) requires a more powerful machine, which can "look back" to earlier strings in the derivation in order to determine how to produce the next step in the derivation.

Rule (26) is also fundamentally new in a different sense. It makes essential reference to two distinct sentences S_1 and S_2, but in grammars of the [Σ, F] type, there is no way to incorporate such double reference. The fact that rule (26) cannot be incorporated into the grammar of phrase structure indicates that even if this form for grammar is not literally inapplicable to English, it is certainly inadequate in the weaker but sufficient sense considered above. This rule leads to a considerable simplification of the grammar; in fact, it provides one of the best criteria for determining how to set up constituents. We shall see that there are many other rules of the same general type as (26) which play the same dual role.

5.3 In the grammar (13) we gave only one way of analyzing the element *Verb*, namely, as *hit* (cf. (13 vi)). But even with the verbal root fixed (let us say, as *take*), there are many other forms that this element can assume, e.g., *takes, has + taken, will + take, has + been + taken, is + being + taken*, etc. The study of these "auxiliary verbs" turns out to be quite crucial in the development of English grammar. We shall see that their behavior is very regular and simply describable when observed from a point of view that is quite different from that developed above. though it appears to be quite complex if we attempt to incorporate these phrases directly into a [Σ, F] grammar.

Consider first the auxiliaries that appear unstressed; for example, "has" in "John has read the book" but not "does" in "John *does* read books."[3] We can state the occurrence of these auxiliaries in declarative sentences by adding to the grammar (13) the following rules:

[3] We return to the stressed auxiliary "do" below, in § 7.1 (45)–(47).

(28) (i) $Verb \to Aux + V$
 (ii) $V \to hit, take, walk, read$, etc.
 (iii) $Aux \to C(M) (have + en) (be + ing) (be + en)$
 (iv) $M \to will, can, may, shall, must$

(29) (i) $C \to \begin{cases} S \text{ in the context } NP_{sing}- \\ \emptyset \text{ in the context } NP_{pl}- \\ past \end{cases}$ [4]

 (ii) Let *Af* stand for any of the affixes *past, S, Ø, en, ing*. Let *v* stand for any *M* or *V*, or *have* or *be* (i.e., for any non-affix in the phrase *Verb*). Then:
 $Af + v \to v + Af \#$,
 where $\#$ is interpreted as word boundary.[5]

 (iii) Replace $+$ by $\#$ except in the context $v - Af$. Insert $\#$ initially and finally.

The interpretation of the notations in (28 iii) is as follows: we must choose the element *C*, and we may choose zero or more of the parenthesized elements in the given order. In (29 i) we may develop *C* into any of three morphemes, observing the contextual restrictions given. As an example of the application of these rules, we construct a derivation in the style of (14), omitting the initial steps.

(30) the + man + Verb + the + book   from (13 i-v)
    the + man + Aux + V + the + book   (28 i)
    the + man + Aux + read + the + book   (28 ii)
    the + man + C + have + en + be + ing + read + the + book
                                           (28 iii) – we select the elements *C*, *have + en* and *be + ing*.
    the + man + S + have + en + be + ing + read + the + book
                                           (29 i)

[4] We assume here that (13 ii) has been extended in the manner of fn. 3, above, p. 29, or something similar.
[5] If we were formulating the theory of grammar more carefully, we would interpret $\#$ as the concatenation operator on the level of words, while $+$ is the concatention operator on the level of phrase structure. (29) would then be part of the definition of a mapping which carries certain objects on the level of phrase structure (essentially, diagrams of the form (15)) into strings of words. See my *The logical structure of linguistic theory* for a more careful formulation.

the + *man* + *have* + *S* # *be* + *en* # *read* + *ing* # *the* + *book*
(29ii) – three times.
the # *man* # *have* + *S* # *be* + *en* # *read* + *ing* # *the* # *book*
(29iii)

The morphophonemic rules (19), etc., will convert the last line of this derivation into:

(31)   the man has been reading the book

in phonemic transcription. Similarly, every other auxiliary verb phrase can be generated. We return later to the question of further restrictions that must be placed on these rules so that only grammatical sequences can be generated. Note, incidentally, that the morphophonemic rules will have to include such rules as: *will* + *S* → *will*, *will* + *past* → *would*. These rules can be dropped if we rewrite (28 iii) so that either *C* or *M*, but not both, can be selected. But now the forms *would*, *could*, *might*, *should* must be added to (28 iv), and certain 'sequence of tense' statements become more complex. It is immaterial to our further discussion which of these alternative analysesis iadopted. Several other minor revisions are possible.

Notice that in order to apply (29 i) in (30) we had to use the fact that *the* + *man* is a singular noun phrase NP_{sing}. That is, we had to refer back to some earlier step in the derivation in order to determine the constituent structure of *the* + *man*. (The alternative of ordering (29 i) and the rule that develops NP_{sing} into *the* + *man* in such a way that (29 i) must precede the latter is not possible, for a variety of reasons, some of which appear below). Hence, (29 i), just like (26), goes beyond the elementary Markovian character of grammars of phrase structure, and cannot be incorporated within the [Σ, F] grammar.

Rule (29 ii) violates the requirements of [Σ, F] grammars even more severely. It also requires reference to constituent structure (i.e., past history of derivation) and in addition, we have no way to express the required inversion within the terms of phrase structure. Note that this rule is useful elsewhere in the grammar, at least in the case where *Af* is *ing*. Thus the morphemes *to* and *ing* play a very similar role within the noun phrase in that they convert verb phrases into noun phrases, giving, e.g.,

(32) $\begin{Bmatrix} \text{to prove that theorem} \\ \text{proving that theorem} \end{Bmatrix}$ was difficult.

etc. We can exploit this parallel by adding to the grammar (13) the rule

(33) $NP \rightarrow \begin{Bmatrix} ing \\ to \end{Bmatrix} VP$

The rule (29 ii) will then convert *ing + prove + that + theorem* into *proving # that + theorem*. A more detailed analysis of the *VP* shows that this parallel extends much further than this, in fact.

The reader can easily determine that to duplicate the effect of (28 iii) and (29) without going beyond the bounds of a system [Σ, F] of phrase structure, it would be necessary to give a fairly complex statement. Once again, as in the case of conjunction, we see that significant simplification of the grammar is possible if we are permitted to formulate rules of a more complex type than those that correspond to a system of immediate constituent analysis. By allowing ourselves the freedom of (29 ii) we have been able to state the constituency of the auxiliary phrase in (28 iii) without regard to the interdependence of its elements, and it is always easier to describe a sequence of independent elements than a sequence of mutually dependent ones. To put the same thing differently, in the auxiliary verb phrase we really have discontinuous elements – e.g., in (30), the elements *have..en* and *be..ing*. But discontinuities cannot be handled within [Σ, F] grammars.[6] In (28 iii) we treated these

---

[6] We might attempt to extend the notions of phrase structure to account for discontinuities. It has been pointed out several times that fairly serious difficulties arise in any systematic attempt to pursue this course. Cf. my "System of syntactic analysis," *Journal of Symbolic Logic* 18.242-56 (1953); C. F. Hockett, "A formal statement of morphemic analysis," *Studies in Linguistics* 10.27-39 (1952); idem, "Two models of grammatical description," *Linguistics Today*, *Word* 10.210-33 (1954). Similarly, one might seek to remedy some of the other deficiencies of [Σ, F] grammars by a more complex account of phrase structure. I think that such an approach is ill-advised, and that it can only lead to the development of *ad hoc* and fruitless elaborations. It appears to be the case that the notions of phrase structure are quite adequate for a small

elements as continuous, and we introduced the discontinuity by the very simple additional rule (29 ii). We shall see below, in § 7, that this analysis of the element *Verb* serves as the basis for a far-reaching and extremely simple analysis of several important features of English syntax.

5.4 As a third example of the inadequacy of the conceptions of phrase structure, consider the case of the active-passive relation. Passive sentences are formed by selecting the element *be + en* in rule (28 iii). But there are heavy restrictions on this element that make it unique among the elements of the auxiliary phrase. For one thing, *be + en* can be selected only if the following V is transitive (e.g., *was + eaten* is permitted, but not *was + occurred*); but with a few exceptions the other elements of the auxiliary phrase can occur freely with verbs. Furthermore, *be + en* cannot be selected if the verb V is followed by a noun phrase, as in (30) (e.g., we cannot in general have $NP + is + V + en + NP$, even when V is transitive — we cannot have "lunch is eaten John"). Furthermore, if V is transitive and is followed by the prepositional phrase $by + NP$, then we *must* select *be + en* (we can have "lunch is eaten by John" but not "John is eating by lunch," etc.). Finally, note that in elaborating (13) into a full-fledged grammar we will have to place many restrictions on the choice of V in terms of subject and object in order to permit such sentences as: "John admires sincerity," "sincerity frightens John," "John plays golf," "John drinks wine," while excluding the 'inverse' non-sentences[7] "sincerity admires John," "John frightens sincerity,"

---

part of the language and that the rest of the language can be derived by repeated application of a rather simple set of transformations to the strings given by the phrase structure grammar. If we were to attempt to extend phrase structure grammar to cover the entire language directly, we would lose the simplicity of the limited phrase structure grammar and of the transformational development. This approach would miss the main point of level construction (cf. first paragraph of § 3.1), namely, to rebuild the vast complexity of the actual language more elegantly and systematically by extracting the contribution to this complexity of several linguistic levels, each of which is simple in itself.

[7] Here too we might make use of a notion of levels of grammaticalness as suggested in footnote 2, p. 35. Thus "sincerity admires John," though clearly less grammatical than "John admires sincerity," is certainly more grammatical

"golf plays John," "wine drinks John". But this whole network of restrictions fails completely when we choose $be + en$ as part of the auxiliary verb. In fact, in this case the same selectional dependencies hold, but in the opposite order. That is, for every sentence $NP_1 - V - NP_2$ we can have a corresponding sentence $NP_2 - is + Ven - by + NP_1$. If we try to include passives directly in the grammar (13), we shall have to restate all of these restrictions in the opposite order for the case in which $be + en$ is chosen as part of the auxiliary verb. This inelegant duplication, as well as the special restrictions involving the element $be + en$, can be avoided only if we deliberately exclude passives from the grammar of phrase structure, and reintroduce them by a rule such as:

(34) If S_1 is a grammatical sentence of the form
$$NP_1 - Aux - V - NP_2,$$
then the corresponding string of the form
$$NP_2 - Aux + be + en - V - by + NP_1$$
is also a grammatical sentence.

For example, if $John - C - admire - sincerity$ is a sentence, then $sincerity - C + be + en - admire - by + John$ (which by (29) and (19) becomes "sincerity is admired by John") is also a sentence.

We can now drop the element $be + en$, and all of the special restrictions associated with it, from (28 iii). The fact that $be + en$ requires a transitive verb, that it cannot occur before $V + NP$, that it must occur before $V + by + NP$ (where V is transitive), that it inverts the order of the surrounding noun phrases, is in each case an automatic consequence of rule (34). This rule thus leads to a considerable simplification of the grammar. But (34) is well beyond the limits of $[\Sigma, F]$ grammars. Like (29 ii), it requires reference to the constituent structure of the string to which it applies and it carries out an inversion on this string in a structurally determined manner.

---

than "of admires John," I believe that a workable notion of degree of grammaticalness can be developed in purely formal terms (cf. my *The logical structure of linguistic theory*), but this goes beyond the bounds of the present discussion. See § 7.5 for an even stronger demonstration that inversion is necessary in the passive.

5.5 We have discussed three rules ((26), (29), (34)) which materially simplify the description of English but which cannot be incorporated into a [Σ, F] grammar. There are a great many other rules of this type, a few of which we shall discuss below. By further study of the limitations of phrase structure grammars with respect to English we can show quite conclusively that these grammars will be so hopelessly complex that they will be without interest unless we incorporate such rules.

If we examine carefully the implications of these supplementary rules, however, we see that they lead to an entirely new conception of linguistic structure. Let us call each such rule a "grammatical transformation." A grammatical transformation T operates on a given string (or, as in the case of (26), on a set of strings) with a given constituent structure and converts it into a new string with a new derived constituent structure. To show exactly *how* this operation is performed requires a rather elaborate study which would go far beyond the scope of these remarks, but we can in fact develop a certain fairly complex but reasonably natural algebra of transformations having the properties that we apparently require for grammatical description.[8]

From these few examples we can already detect some of the essential properties of a transformational grammar. For one thing, it is clear that we must define an order of application on these transformations. The passive transformation (34), for example, must apply *before* (29). It must precede (29i), in particular, so that the verbal element in the resulting sentence will have the same number as the new grammatical subject of the passive sentence. And it must precede (29ii) so that the latter rule will apply properly to the new inserted element *be + en*. (In discussing the question of whether or not (29i) can be fitted into a [Σ, F] grammar, we mentioned that this rule could not be required to apply before the rule

---

[8] See my "Three models for the description of language" (above, p. 22, fn. 3) for a brief account of transformations, and *The logical structure of linguistic theory* and *Transformational Analysis* for a detailed development of transformational algebra and transformational grammars. See Z. S. Harris, "Cooccurrence and Transformations in linguistic structure," *Language* 33.283-340 (1957), for a somewhat different approach to transformational analysis.

analyzing NP_{sing} into *the* + *man*, etc. One reason for this is now obvious — (29i) must apply after (34), but (34) must apply after the analysis of NP_{sing}, or we will not have the proper selectional relations between the subject and verb and the verb and 'agent' in the passive.)

Secondly, note that certain transformations are *obligatory*, whereas others are only *optional*. For example, (29) must be applied to every derivation, or the result will simply not be a sentence.[9] But (34), the passive transformation, may or may not be applied in any particular case. Either way the result is a sentence. Hence (29) is an obligatory transformation and (34) is an optional transformation.

This distinction between obligatory and optional transformations leads us to set up a fundamental distinction among the sentences of the language. Suppose that we have a grammar G with a [Σ, F] part and a transformational part, and suppose that the transformational part has certain obligatory transformations and certain optional ones. Then we define the *kernel* of the language (in terms of the grammar G) as the set of sentences that are produced when we apply obligatory transformations to the terminal strings of the [Σ, F] grammar. The transformational part of the grammar will be set up in such a way that transformations can apply to kernel sentences (more correctly, to the forms that underlie kernel sentences — i.e., to terminal strings of the [Σ, F] part of the grammar) or to prior transforms. Thus every sentence of the language will either belong to the kernel or will be derived from the strings underlying one or more kernel sentences by a sequence of one or more transformations.

From these considerations we are led to a picture of grammars as possessing a natural tripartite arrangement. Corresponding to the level of phrase structure, a grammar has a sequence of rules of the form $X \rightarrow Y$, and corresponding to lower levels it has a sequence of

---

[9] But of the three parts of (29i), only the third is obligatory. That is, *past* may occur after NP_{sing} or NP_{pl}. Whenever we have an element such as C in (29i) which must be developed, but perhaps in several alternative ways, we can order the alternatives and make each one but the last optional, and the last, obligatory.

morphophonemic rules of the same basic form. Linking these two sequences, it has a sequence of transformational rules. Thus the grammar will look something like this:

(35) Σ: *Sentence*:

$$F: \left.\begin{matrix} X_1 \to Y_1 \\ \vdots \\ X_n \to Y_n \end{matrix}\right\} \text{Phrase structure}$$

$$\left.\begin{matrix} T_1 \\ \vdots \\ T_j \end{matrix}\right\} \text{Transformational structure}$$

$$\left.\begin{matrix} Z_1 \to W_1 \\ \vdots \\ Z_m \to W_m \end{matrix}\right\} \text{Morphophonemics}$$

To produce a sentence from such a grammar we construct an extended derivation beginning with *Sentence*. Running through the rules of F we construct a terminal string that will be a sequence of morphemes, though not necessarily in the correct order. We then run through the sequence of transformations $T_1, \ldots T_j$, applying each obligatory one and perhaps certain optional ones. These transformations may rearrange strings or may add or delete morphemes. As a result they yield a string of words. We then run through the morphophonemic rules, thereby converting this string of words into a string of phonemes. The phrase structure segment of the grammar will include such rules as those of (13), (17) and (28). The transformational part will include such rules as (26), (29) and (34), formulated properly in the terms that must be developed in a full-scale theory of transformations. The morphophonemic part will include such rules as (19). This sketch of the process of generation of sentences must (and easily can) be generalized to allow for proper functioning of such rules as (26) which operate on a set of sentences, and to allow transformations to reapply to transforms so that more and more complex sentences can be produced.

When we apply only obligatory transformations in the generation of a given sentence, we call the resulting sentence a kernel sentence. Further investigation would show that in the phrase structure and morphophonemic parts of the grammar we can also extract a skeleton of obligatory rules that *must* be applied whenever we reach them in the process of generating a sentence. In the last few paragraphs of § 4 we pointed out that the phrase structure rules lead to a conception of linguistic structure and "level of representation" that is fundamentally different from that provided by the morphophonemic rules. On each of the lower levels corresponding to the lower third of the grammar an utterance is, in general, represented by a single sequence of elements. But phrase structure cannot be broken down into sublevels: on the level of phrase structure an utterance is represented by a set of strings that cannot be ordered into higher or lower levels. This set of representing strings is equivalent to a diagram of the form (15). On the transformational level, an utterance is represented even more abstractly in terms of a sequence of transformations by which it is derived, ultimately from kernel sentences (more correctly, from the strings which underlie kernel sentences). There is a very natural general definition of "linguistic level" that includes all of these cases,[10] and as we shall see later, there is good reason to consider each of these structures to be a linguistic level.

When transformational analysis is properly formulated we find that it is essentially more powerful than description in terms of phrase structure, just as the latter is essentially more powerfull than description in terms of finite state Markov processes that generate sentences from left to right. In particular, such languages as (10iii) which lie beyond the bounds of phrase structure description with context-free rules can be derived transformationally.[11] It is important to observe that the grammar is materially simplified when we add a transformational level, since it is now necessary to provide phrase structure directly only for kernel sentences — the terminal strings of the [Σ, F] grammar are just those which underlie kernel

---

[10] Cf. *The logical structure of linguistic theory* and *Transformational Analysis*.

[11] Let G be a [Σ, F] grammar with the initial string *Sentence* and with the set of all finite strings of a's and b's as its terminal output. There is such a grammar. Let G' be the grammar which contains G as its phrase structure part, supplemented by the transformation T that operates on any string K which is a *Sentence*, converting it into $K + K$. Then the output of G' is (10iii). Cf. p. 31.

sentences. We choose the kernel sentences in such a way that the terminal strings underlying the kernel are easily derived by means of a [Σ, F] description, while all other sentences can be derived from these terminal strings by simply statable transformations. We have seen, and shall see again below, several examples of simplifications resulting from transformational analysis. Full-scale syntactic investigation of English provides a great many more cases.

One further point about grammars of the form (35) deserves mention, since it has apparently led to some misunderstanding. We have described these grammars as devices for generating sentences. This formulation has occasionally led to the idea that there is a certain asymmetry in grammatical theory in the sense that grammar is taking the point of view of the speaker rather than the hearer; that it is concerned with the process of producing utterances rather than the 'inverse' process of analyzing and reconstructing the structure of given utterances. Actually, grammars of the form that we have been discussing are quite neutral as between speaker and hearer, between synthesis and analysis of utterances. A grammar does not tell us how to synthesize a specific utterance; it does not tell us how to analyze a particular given utterance. In fact, these two tasks which the speaker and hearer must perform are essentially the same, and are both outside the scope of grammars of the form (35). Each such grammar is simply a description of a certain set of utterances, namely, those which it generates. From this grammar we can reconstruct the formal relations that hold among these utterances in terms of the notions of phrase structure, transformational structure, etc. Perhaps the issue can be clarified by an analogy to a part of chemical theory concerned with the structurally possible compounds. This theory might be said to generate all physically possible compounds just as a grammar generates all grammatically 'possible' utterances. It would serve as a theoretical basis for techniques of qualitative analysis and synthesis of specific compounds, just as one might rely on a grammar in the investigation of such special problems as analysis and synthesis of particular utterances.

6

ON THE GOALS OF LINGUISTIC THEORY

6.1 In §§ 3, 4 two models of linguistic structure were developed: a simple communication theoretic model and a formalized version of immediate constituent analysis. Each was found to be inadequate, and in § 5 I suggested a more powerful model combining phrase structure and grammatical transformations that might remedy these inadequacies. Before going on to explore this possiblity, I would like to clarify certain points of view that underlie the whole approach of his study.

Our fundamental concern throughout this discussion of linguistic structure is the problem of justification of grammars. A grammar of the language L is essentially a theory of L. Any scientific theory is based on a finite number of observations, and it seeks to relate the observed phenomena and to predict new phenomena by constructing general laws in terms of hypothetical constructs such as (in physics, for example) "mass" and "electron." Similarly, a grammar of English is based on a finite corpus of utterances (observations), and it will contain certain grammatical rules (laws) stated in terms of the particular phonemes, phrases, etc., of English (hypothetical constructs). These rules express structural relations among the sentences of the corpus and the indefinite number of sentences generated by the grammar beyond the corpus (predictions). Our problem is to develop and clarify the criteria for selecting the correct grammar for each language, that is, the correct theory of this language.

Two types of criteria were mentioned in § 2.1. Clearly, every grammar will have to meet certain *external conditions of adequacy*; e.g., the sentences generated will have to be acceptable to the native speaker. In § 8 we shall consider several other external conditions of this sort. In addition, we pose a *condition of generality* on grammars; we require that the grammar of a given language be constructed in accordance with a specific theory of linguistic structure in which such terms as "phoneme" and "phrase" are defined independently of any particular language.[1] If we drop either the external conditions or the generality requirement, there will be no way to choose among a vast number of totally different 'grammars,' each compatible with a given corpus. But, as we observed in § 2.1, these requirements jointly give us a very strong test of adequacy for a general theory of linguistic structure and the set of grammars that it provides for particular languages.

Notice that neither the general theory nor the particular grammars are fixed for all time, in this view. Progress and revision may come from the discovery of new facts about particular languages, or from purely theoretical insights about organization of linguistic data — that is, new models for linguistic structure. But there is also no circularity in this conception. At any given time we can attempt to formulate as precisely as possible both the general theory and the set of associated grammars that must meet the empirical, external conditions of adequacy.

We have not yet considered the following very crucial question: What is the relation between the general theory and the particular grammars that follow from it? In other words, what sense can we give to the notion "follow from," in this context? It is at this point that our approach will diverge sharply from many theories of linguistic structure.

The strongest requirement that could be placed on the relation between a theory of linguistic structure and particular grammars is that the theory must provide a practical and mechanical method for

---

[1] I presume that these two conditions are similar to what Hjelmslev has in mind when he speaks of the *appropriateness* and *arbitrariness* of linguistic theory. Cf. L. Hjelmslev, *Prolegomena to a theory of language = Memoir 7, Indiana University Publications Antropology and Linguistics* (Baltimore, 1953), p. 8. See also Hockett's discussion of "metacriteria" for linguistics ("Two models of grammatical description," *Linguistics Today, Word* 10.232-3) in this connection.

ON THE GOALS OF LINGUISTIC THEORY

actually constructing the grammar, given a corpus of utterances. Let us say that such a theory provides us with a *discovery procedure* for grammars.

A weaker requirement would be that the theory must provide a practical and mechanical method for determining whether or not a grammar proposed for a given corpus is, in fact, the best grammar of the language from which this corpus is drawn. Such a theory, which is not concerned with the question of *how* this grammar was constructed, might be said to provide a *decision procedure* for grammars.

An even weaker requirement would be that given a corpus and given two proposed grammars G_1 and G_2, the theory must tell us which is the better grammar of the language from which the corpus is drawn. In this case we might say that the theory provides an *evaluation procedure* for grammars.

These theories can be represented graphically in the following manner.

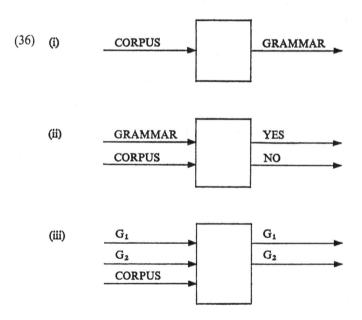

Figure (36i) represents a theory conceived as a machine with a corpus as its input and a grammar as its output; hence, a theory that provides a discovery procedure. (36ii) is a device with a grammar and a corpus as its inputs, and the answers "yes" or "no" as its outputs, as the grammar is or is not the correct one; hence, it represents a theory that provides a decision procedure for grammars. (36iii) represents a theory with grammars G_1 and G_2 and a corpus as inputs, and the more preferable of G_1 and G_2 as output; hence a theory that provides an evaluation procedure for grammars.[2]

The point of view adopted here is that it is unreasonable to demand of linguistic theory that it provide anything more than a practical evaluation procedure for grammars. That is, we adopt the weakest of the three positions described above. As I interpret most of the more careful proposals for the development of linguistic theory,[3] they attempt to meet the strongest of these three requirements. That is, they attempt to state methods of analysis that an investigator might actually use, if he had the time, to construct a grammar of a language directly from the raw data. I think that it is very questionable that this goal is attainable in any interesting way,

---

[2] The basic question at issue is not changed if we are willing to accept a small set of correct grammars instead of a single one.

[3] For example, B. Bloch, "A set of postulates for phonemic analysis," *Language* 24.3-46 (1948); N. Chomsky, "Systems of syntactic analysis," *Journal of Symbolic Logic* 18.242-56 (1953); Z. S. Harris, "From phoneme to morpheme," *Language* 31.190-222 (1955); idem, *Methods in structural linguistics* (Chicago, 1951); C. F. Hockett, "A formal statement of morphemic analysis," *Studies in Linguistics* 10.27-39 (1952); idem, "Problems of morphemic analysis," *Language* 23.321-43 (1947); R. S. Wells, "Immediate constituents," *Language* 23.81-117 (1947); and many other works. Although discovery procedures are the explicit goal of these works, we often find on careful examination that the theory that has actually been constructed furnishes no more than an evaluation procedure for grammars. For example, Hockett states his aim in "A formal statement of morphemic analysis" as the development of "formal procedures by which one can work from scratch to a complete description of the pattern of a language" (p. 27); but what he actually does is describe some of the formal properties of a morphological analysis and then propose a "criterion whereby the relative efficiency of two possible morphic solutions can be determined; with that, we can choose the maximally efficient possibility, or, arbitrarily, any one of those which are equally efficient but more efficient than all others" (p. 29).

and I suspect that any attempt to meet it will lead into a maze of more and more elaborate and complex analytic procedures that will fail to provide answers for many important questions about the nature of linguistic structure. I believe that by lowering our sights to the more modest goal of developing an evaluation procedure for grammars we can focus attention more clearly on really crucial problems of linguistic structure and we can arrive at more satisfying answers to them. The correctness of this judgment can only be determined by the actual development and comparison of theories of these various sorts. Notice, however, that the weakest of these three requirements is still strong enough to guarentee significance for a theory that meets it. There are few areas of science in which one would seriously consider the possibility of developing a general, practical, mechanical method for choosing among several theories, each compatible with the available data.

In the case of each of these conceptions of linguistic theory we have qualified the characterization of the type of procedure by the word "practical". This vague qualification is crucial for an empirical science. Suppose, for example, that we were to evaluate grammars by measuring some such simple property as length. Then it would be correct to say that we have a practical evaluation procedure for grammars, since we could count the number of symbols they contain; and it would also be literally correct to say that we have a discovery procedure, since we can order all sequences of the finite number of symbols from which grammars are constructed in terms of length, and we can test each of these sequences to see if it is a grammar, being sure that after some finite amount of time we shall find the shortest sequence that qualifies. But this is not the type of discovery procedure that is contemplated by those who are attempting to meet the strong requirement discussed above.

Suppose that we use the word "simplicity" to refer to the set of formal properties of grammars that we shall consider in choosing among them. Then there are three main tasks in the kind of program for linguistic theory that we have suggested. First, it is necessary to state precisely (if possible, with operational, behavioral tests) the external criteria of adequacy for grammars. Second, we must characterize the form of grammars in a general and explicit way so that we can actually propose grammars of this form for particular languages. Third, we must analyze and define the notion of simplicity that we intend to use in choosing among grammars all of which are of the proper form. Completion of the latter two tasks will enable us to formulate a general theory of linguistic structure in which such notions as "phoneme in L", "phrase in L", "transformation in L" are defined for an arbitrary language L in terms of physical and distributional properties of utterances of L and formal properties of grammars of L.[4] For example, we shall define the set of phonemes of L as a set of elements which have certain physical and distributional properties, and which appear in the simplest grammar for L. Given such a theory, we can attempt to construct grammars for actual languages, and we can determine whether or not the simplest grammars that we can find (i.e., the grammars that the general theory compels us to choose) meet the external conditions of adequacy. We shall continue to revise our notions of simplicity and out characterization of the form of grammars until the grammars selected by the theory do meet the external conditions.[5] Notice that this theory may not tell us, in any practical way, how to actually go about constructing the grammar of a given language from a corpus. But it must tell us how to evaluate such a grammar; it must thus enable us to choose between two proposed grammars.

In the preceding sections of this study we have been concerned with the second of these three tasks. We have assumed that the set of grammatical sentences of English is given and that we have some notion of simplicity, and we have tried to determine what sort of grammar will generate exactly the grammatical sentences in some simple way. To formulate this goal in somewhat different terms,

---

[4] Linguistic theory will thus be formulated in a metalanguage to the language in which grammars are written — a metametalanguage to any language for which a grammar is constructed.

[5] We may in fact revise the criteria of adequacy, too, in the course of research. That is, we may decide that certain of these tests do not apply to grammatical phenomena. The subject matter of a theory is not completely determined in advance of investigation. It is partially determined by the possibility of giving an organized and systematic account of some range of phenomena.

we remarked above that one of the notions that must be defined in general linguistic theory is "sentence in L." Entering into the definitions will be such terms as "observed utterance in L", "simplicity of the grammar of L," etc. This general theory is accordingly concerned with clarifying the relation between the set of grammatical sentence and the set of observed sentences. Our investigation of the structure of the former set is a preparatory study, proceeding from the assumption that before we can characterize this relation clearly, we will have to know a great deal more about the formal properties of each of these sets.

In § 7 below, we shall continue to investigate the relative complexity of various ways of describing English structure. In particular, we shall be concerned with the question of whether the whole grammar is simplified if we consider a certain class of sentences to be kernel sentences or if we consider them to be derived by transformation. We thus arrive at certain decisions about the structure of English. In § 8 we shall argue that there is independent evidence in favor of our method for selecting grammars. That is, we shall try to show that the simpler grammars meet certain external conditions of adequacy while the more complex grammars that embody different decisions about assignment of sentences to the kernel, etc., fail these conditions. These results can be no more than suggestive, however, until we give a rigorous account of the notion of simplicity employed. I think that such an account can be given, but this would go beyond the scope of the present monograph. Nevertheless, it should be fairly clear that under any reasonable definition of "simplicity of grammar", most of the decisions about relative complexity that we reach below will stand.[6]

Notice that simplicity is a *systematic* measure; the only ultimate

---

[6] See my *The logical structure of linguistic theory* for discussion of methods for evaluating grammars in terms of formal properties of simplicity.

We are not, incidentally, denying the usefullness of even partially adequate discovery procedures. They may provide valuable hints to the practicing linguist or they may lead to a small set of grammars that can then be evaluated. Our main point is that a linguistic theory should not be identified with a manual of useful procedures, nor should it be expected to provide mechanical procedures for the discovery of grammars.

criterion in evaluation is the simplicity of the whole system. In discussing particular cases, we can only indicate how one or another decision will affect the over-all complexity. Such validation can only be tentative, since by simplifying one part of the grammar we may complicate other parts. It is when we find that simplification of one part of the grammar leads to corresponding simplification of other parts that we feel that we are really on the right track. Below, we shall try to show that the simplest transformational analysis of one class of sentences does quite frequently clear the way to a simpler analysis of other classes.

In short, we shall never consider the question of how one might have arrived at the grammar whose simplicity is being determined; e.g., how one might have discovered the analysis of the verb phrase presented in § 5.3. Question of this sort are not relevant to the program of research that we have outlined above. One may arrive at a grammar by intuition, guess-work, all sorts of partial methodological hints, reliance on past experience, etc. It is no doubt possible to give an organized account of many useful procedures of analysis, but it is questionable whether these can be formulated rigorously, exhaustively and simply enough to qualify as a practical and mechanical discovery procedure. At any rate, this problem is not within the scope of our investigations here. Our ultimate aim is to provide an objective, non-intuitive way to evaluate a grammar once presented, and to compare it with other proposed grammars. We are thus interested in describing the form of grammars (equivalently, the nature of linguistic structure) and investigating the empirical consequences of adopting a certain model for linguistic structure, rather than in showing how, in principe, one might have arrived at the grammar of a language.

6.2 Once we have disclaimed any intention of finding a practical discovery procedure for grammars, certain problems that have been the subject of intense methodological controversy simply do not arise. Consider the problem of interdependence of levels. It has been correctly pointed out that if morphemes are defined in terms of phonemes, and, simultaneously, morphological considerations are considered relevant to phonemic analysis, then linguistic theory may be nullified by a real circularity. However, interdependence of levels does not necessarily lead to circularity. In this case, for example, we can define "tentative phoneme set" and "tentative morpheme set" independently and we can develop a relation of compatibility that holds between tentative phoneme sets and tentative morpheme sets. We can then define a pair of a phoneme set and a morpheme set for a given language as a compatible pair of a tentative phoneme set and a tentative morpheme set. Our compatibility relation may be framed partially in terms of simplicity considerations; that is, we may define the phonemes and morphemes of a language as the tentative phonemes and morphemes which, among other things, jointly lead to the simplest grammar. This gives us a perfectly straightforward way to define interdependent levels with no circularity. Of course, it does not tell us how to *find* the phonemes and morphemes in a direct, mechanical way. But no other phonemic or morphological theory really meets this strong requirement either, and there is little reason to believe that it can be met significantly. In any event, when we lower our aims to the development of an evaluation procedure, there remains little motivation for any objection to mixing of levels, and there is no difficulty in avoiding circularity in the definition of interdependent levels.[7]

---

[7] See Z. S. Harris, *Methods in structural linguistics* (Chicago, 1951) (e.g., *Appendix to 7.4, Appendix to 8.2*, chapters 9, 12) for examples of procedures which lead to interdependent levels. I think that Fowler's objections to Harris' morphological procedures (cf.. *Language* 28.504-9 [1952]) can be met without difficulty by a noncircular formulation of the type just proposed. Cf. C. F. Hockett, *A manual of phonology* = *Memoir 11, Indiana University Publications in Anthropology and Linguistics* (Baltimore, 1955); idem, "Two fundamental problems in phonemics," *Studies in Linguistics* 7.33 (1949); R. Jakobson, "The phonemic and grammatical aspects of language and their interrelation," *Proceedings of the Sixth International Congress of Linguists* 5-18 (Paris, 1948); K. L. Pike, "Grammatical prerequisites to phonemic analysis," *Word* 3.155-72 (1947); idem, "More on grammatical prerequisites," *Word* 8.106-21 (1952), for further discussion on interdependence of levels. Also N. Chomsky, M. Halle, F. Lukoff, "On accent and juncture in English," *For Roman Jakobson* ('s-Gravenhage, 1956), 65-80.

Bar-Hillel has suggested in "Logical syntax and semantics", *Language* 30.230-7 (1954) that Pike's proposals can be formalized without the circularity

Many problems of morphemic analysis also receive quite simple solutions if we adopt the general framework outlined above. In attempting to develop discovery procedures for grammars we are naturally led to consider morphemes as classes of sequences of phonemes, i.e., as having actual phonemic 'content' in an almost literal sense. This leads to trouble in such well-known cases as English "took" /tuk/, where it is difficult without artificiality to associate any part of this word with the past tense morpheme which appears as /t/ in "walked" /wɔkt/, as /d/ in "framed" /freymd/, etc. We can avoid all such problems by regarding morphology and phonology as two distinct but interdependent levels of representation, related in the grammar by morphophonemic rules such as (19). Thus "took" is represented on the morphological level as *take + past* just as "walked" is represented as *walk + past*. The morphophonemic rules (19 ii), (19 v), respectively, carry these strings of morphemes into /tuk/, /wɔkt/. The only difference between the two cases is that (19 v) is a much more general rule than (19 ii).[8] If we give up the idea that higher levels are literally constructed out of

---

that many sense in them by the use of recursive definitions. He does not pursue this suggestion in any detail, and my own feeling is that success along these lines is unlikely. Moreover, if we are satisfied with an evaluation procedure for grammars, we can construct interdependent levels with only direct definitions, as we have just seen.

The problem of interdependence of phonemic and morphemic levels must not be confused with the question of whether morphological information is required to read a phonemic transcription. Even if morphological considerations are considered relevant to determining the phonemes of a language, it may still be the case that the phonemic transcription provides complete 'reading' rules with no reference to other levels. Cf. N. Chomsky, M. Halle, F. Lukoff, "On accent and juncture in English," *For Roman Jakobson* ('s-Gravenhage, 1956), 65–80, for discussion and examples.

[8] Hockett gives a very clear presentation of this approach to levels in *A manual of phonology* (1955), p. 15. In "Two models of grammatical description," *Linguistics Today*, *Word* 10.210–33 (1954), Hockett rejected a solution very much like the one we have just proposed on the grounds that "*took* and *take* are partly similar in phonemic shape just as are *baked* and *bake*, and similar in meaning also in the same way; this fact should not be obscured" (p. 224). But the similarity in meaning is not obscured in our formulation, since the morpheme *past* appears in the morphemic representation of both "took" and "baked." And the similarity in phonemic shape can be brought out in the actual

lower level elements, as I think we must, then it becomes much more natural to consider even such abstract systems of representation as transformational structure (where each utterance is represented by the sequence of transformations by which it is derived from a terminal string of the phrase structure grammar) as constituting a linguistic level.

We are not actually forced to give up hope of finding a practical discovery procedure by adopting either the view that levels are interdependent, or the conception of linguistic levels as abstract systems of representation related only by general rules. Nevertheless, I think it is unquestionable that opposition to mixing levels, as well as the idea that each level is literally constructed out of lower level elements, has its origin in the attempt to develop a discovery procedure for grammars. If we renounce this goal and if we distinguish clearly between a manual of suggestive and helpful procedures and a theory of linguistic structure, then there is little reason for maintaining either of these rather dubious positions.

There are many other commonly held views that seem to lose much of their appeal if we formulate our goals in the manner suggested above. Thus it is sometimes argued that work on syntactic theory is premature at this time in view of the fact that many of the problems that arise on the lower levels of phonemics and morphology are unsolved. It is quite true that the higher levels of linguistic description depend on results obtained at the lower levels. But there is also a good sense in which the converse is true. For example, we have seen above that it would be absurd, or even hopeless, to state principles of sentence construction in terms of phonemes or morphemes, but only the development of such higher levels as phrase structure indicates that this futile task need not be

---

formulation of the morphophonemic rule that carries $take + past$ into /tuk/. We will no doubt formulate this rules as

$$ey \rightarrow u \text{ in the context } t - k + past$$

in the actual morphophonemic statement. This will allow us to simplify the grammar by a generalization that will bring out the parallel between "take"-"took," "shake"-"shook," "forsake"-"forsook," and more generally, "stand"-"stood," etc.

undertaken on lower levels.[9] Similarly, we have argued that description of sentence structure by constituent analysis will be unsuccessful, if pushed beyond certain limits. But only the development of the still more abstract level of transformations can prepare the way for the development of a simpler and more adequate technique of constituent analysis with narrower limits. The grammar of a language is a complex system with many and varied interconnections between its parts. In order to develop one part of grammar thoroughly, it is often useful, or even necessary, to have some picture of the character of a completed system. Once again, I think that the notion that syntactic theory must await the solution of problems of phonology and morphology is completely untenable whether or not one is concerned with the problem of discovery procedures, but I think it has been nurtured by a faulty analogy between the order of development of linguistic theory and the presumed order of operations in discovery of grammatical structure.

---

[9] See N. Chomsky, M. Halle, F. Lukoff, "On accent and juncture in English," *For Roman Jakobson* ('s-Gravenhage, 1956), 65–80, for a discussion of the possibility that considerations on all higher levels, including morphology, phrase structure, and transformations, are relevant to the selection of a phonemic analysis.

7

SOME TRANSFORMATIONS IN ENGLISH

7.1 After this digression, we can return to the investigation of the consequences of adopting the transformational approach in the description of English syntax. Our goal is to limit the kernel in such a way that the terminal strings underlying the kernel sentences are derived by a simple system of phrase structure and can provide the basis from which all sentences can be derived by simple transformations: obligatory transformations in the case of the kernel, obligatory *and* optional transformations in the case of non-kernel sentences.

To specify a transformation explicitly we must describe the analysis of the strings to which it applies and the structural change that it effects on these strings.[1] Thus, the passive transformation applies to strings of the form $NP - Aux - V - NP$ and has the effect of interchanging the two noun phrases, adding *by* before the final noun phrase, and adding $be + en$ to *Aux* (Cf. (34)). Consider now the introduction of *not* or *n't* into the auxiliary verb phrase. The simplest way to describe negation is by means of a transformation which applies before (29 ii) and introduces *not* or *n't* after the second morpheme of the phrase given by (28 iii) if this phrase contains at least two morphemes, or after the first morpheme of this phrase if it contains only one. Thus this transformation T_{not} operates on strings that are analyzed into three segments in one of the following ways:

(37) (i) $NP - C - V...$

---

[1] For a more detailed discussion of the specification of transformations in general and of specific transformations, see the references cited in footnote 8, p. 44.

(ii) $NP - C + M - \ldots$
(iii) $NP - C + have - \ldots$
(iv) $NP - C + be - \ldots$

where the symbols are as in (28), (29), and it is immaterial what stands in place of the dots. Given a string analyzed into three segments in one of these ways, T_{not} adds *not* (or *n't*) after the second segment of the string. For example, applied to the terminal string *they* $\emptyset + can - come$ (an instance of (37ii)), T_{not} gives *they* $- \emptyset + can + n't - come$ (ultimately, "they can't come"); applied to *they* $- \emptyset + have - en + come$ (an instance of (37iii)), it gives *they* $- \emptyset + have + n't - en + come$ (ultimately, "they haven't come"); applied to *they* $- \emptyset + be - ing + come$ (an instance of (37iv)), it gives *they* $- \emptyset + be + n't - ing + come$ (ultimately, "they aren't coming") The rule thus works properly when we select the last three cases of (37).

Suppose, now, that we select an instance of (37i), i e., a terminal string such as

(38) $John - S - come.$

which would give the kernel sentence "John comes" by (29ii). Applied to (38), T_{not} yields

(39) $John - S + n't - come.$

But we specified that T_{not} applies before (29ii), which has the effect of rewriting $Af + v$ as $v + Af \#$. However, we see that (29ii) does not apply at all to (39) since (39) does not now contain a sequence $Af + v$. Let us now add to the grammar the following obligatory transformational rule which applies *after* (29):

(40) $\# Af \rightarrow \# do + Af$

where *do* is the same element as the main verb in "John does his homework". Cf. (29iii) for introduction of $\#$.) What (40) states is that *do* is introduced as the 'bearer' of an unaffixed affix. Applying (40) and morphological rules to (39) we derive "John doesn't come." The rules (37) and (40) now enable us to derive all and only the grammatical forms of sentence negation.

As it stands, the transformational treatment of negation is somewhat simpler than any alternative treatment within phrase structure.

The advantage of the transformational treatment (over inclusion of negatives in the kernel) would become much clearer if we could find other cases in which the same formulations (i.e., (37) and (40)) are required for independent reasons. But in fact there are such cases.

Consider the class of 'yes-or-no' questions such as "have they arrived", "can they arrive," "did they arrive". We can generate all (and only) these sentences by means of a transformation T_q that operates on strings with the analysis (37), and has the effect of interchanging the first and second segments of these strings, as these segments are defined in (37). We require that T_q apply *after* (29i) and *before* (29ii). Applied to

(41) (i)   *they − Ø − arrive*
  (ii)   *they − Ø + can − arrive*
 (iii)   *they − Ø + have − en + arrive*
 (iv)   *they − Ø + be − ing + arrive*

which are of the forms (37i − iv), T_q yields the strings

(42) (i)   *Ø − they − arrive*
  (ii)   *Ø + can − they − arrive*
 (iii)   *Ø + have − they − en + arrive*
 (iv)   *Ø + be − they − ing + arrive.*

Applying to these the obligatory rules (29ii, iii) and (40), and then the morphophonemic rules, we derive

(43) (i)   do they arrive
  (ii)   can they arrive
 (iii)   have they arrived
 (iv)   are they arriving

in phonemic transcription. Had we applied the obligatory rules directly to (41), with no intervening T_q, we would have derived the sentences

(44) (i)   they arrive
  (ii)   they can arrive
 (iii)   they have arrived
 (iv)   they are arriving.

Thus (43i − iv) are the interrogative counterparts to (44i − iv).

In the case of (42i), *do* is introduced by rule (40) as the bearer of the unaffixed element $\emptyset$. If C had been developed into S or *past* by rule (29i), rule (40) would have introduced *do* as a bearer of these elements, and we would have such sentences as "does he arrive," "did he arrive." Note that no new morphophonemic rules are needed to account for the fact that $do + \emptyset \rightarrow$ /duw/, $do + S \rightarrow$ /dəz/, $do + past \rightarrow$ /did/; we need these rules anyway to account for the forms of *do* as a main verb. Notice also that T_q must apply after (29i), or number will not be assigned correctly in questions.

In analyzing the auxiliary verb phrase in rules (28), (29), we considered S to be the morpheme of the third person singular and $\emptyset$ to be the morpheme affixed to the verb for all other forms of the subject. Thus the verb has S if the noun subject has $\emptyset$ ("the boy arrives") and the verb has $\emptyset$ if the subject has S ("the boys arrive"). An alternative that we did not consider was to eliminate the zero morpheme and to state simply that *no* affix occurs if the subject is not third person singular. We see now that this alternative is not acceptable. We must have the $\emptyset$ morpheme or there will be no affix in (42i) for *do* to bear, and rule (40) will thus not apply to (42i). There are many other cases where transformational analysis provides compelling reasons for or against the establishment of zero morphemes. As a negative case, consider the suggestion that intransitive verbs be analyzed as verbs with zero object. But then the passive transformation (34) would convert, e.g., "John − slept − $\emptyset$" into the non-sentence "$\emptyset$ − was slept − by John" → "was slept by John." Hence this analysis of intransitives must be rejected. We return to the more general problem of the role of transformations in determining constituent structure in § 7.6.

The crucial fact about the question transformation T_q is that almost nothing must be added to the grammar in order to describe it. Since both the subdivision of the sentence that it imposes and the rule for appearance of *do* were required independently for negation, we need only describe the inversion effected by T_q in extending the grammar to account for yes-or-no questions. Putting it differently, transformational analysis brings out the fact that negatives and interrogatives have fundamentally the same 'structure', and it can make use of this fact to simplify the description of English syntax.

In treating the auxiliary verb phrase we left out of consideration forms with the heavy stressed element *do* as in "John *does* come," etc. Suppose we set up a morpheme A of contrastive stress to which the following morphophonemic rule applies.

(45) $..V..+A \rightarrow ..\grave{V}..$, where " indicates extra heavy stress.

We now set up a transformation T_A that imposes the same structural analysis of strings as does T_{not} (i.e., (37)), and adds A to these strings in exactly the position where T_{not} adds *not* or *n't*. Then just as T_{not} yields such sentences as

(46) (i) John doesn't arrive (from *John # S + n't # arrive*, by (40))
  (ii) John can't arrive (from *John # S + can + n't # arrive*)
  (iii) John hasn't arrived (from *John # S + have + n't # en + arrive*)

T_A yields the corresponding sentences

(47) (i) John *does* arrive (from *John # S + A # arrive*, by (40))
  (ii) John *can* arrive (from *John # S + can + A # arrive*)
  (iii) John *has* arrived (from *John # S + have + A # en + arrive*).

Thus T_A is a transformation of 'affirmation' which affirms the sentences "John arrives", "John can arrive", "John has arrived," etc., in exactly the same way as T_{not} negates them. This is formally the simplest solution, and it seems intuitively correct as well.

There are still other instances of transformations that are determined by the same fundamental syntactic analysis of sentences, namely (37). Consider the transformation T_{so} that converts the pairs of strings of (48) into the corresponding strings of (49):

(48) (i) John − S − arrive, I − Ø − arrive
  (ii) John − S + can − arrive, I − Ø + can − arrive
  (iii) John − S + have − en + arrive, I − Ø + have − en + arrive
(49) (i) John − S − arrive − and − so − Ø − I
  (ii) John − S + can − arrive − and − so − Ø + can − I
  (iii) John − S + have − en + arrive − and − so − Ø + have − I.

Applying rules (29 ii, iii), (40), and the morphophonemic rules, we ultimately derive

(50) (i) John arrives and so do I
   (ii) John can arrive and so can I
   (iii) John has arrived and so have I.

T_{so} operates on the second sentence in each pair in (48), first replacing the third segment of this sentence by *so*, and then interchanging the first and third segment. (The element *so* is thus a pro-*VP*, in much the same sense in which *he* is a pronoun). The transformation T_{so} combines with the conjunction transformation to give (49). While we have not described this in anywhere near sufficient detail, it is clear that both the analysis (37) of sentences and the rule (40) again are fundamental. Thus almost nothing new is required in the grammar to incorporate such sentences as (50), which are formed on the same underlying transformational pattern as negatives, questions, and emphatic affirmatives.

There is another remarkable indication of the fundamental character of this analysis that deserves mention here. Consider the kernel sentences

(51) (i) John has a chance to live
   (ii) John is my friend.

The terminal strings that underly (51) are

(52) (i) *John + C + have + a + chance + to + live*
   (ii) *John + C + be + my + friend*

where *have* in (52i) and *be* in (52ii) are main verbs, not auxiliaries. Consider now how the transformations T_{not}, T_q and T_{so} apply to these underlying strings. T_{not} applies to any string of the form (37), adding *not* or *n't* between the second and the third segments, as given in (37). But (52i) is, in fact, an instance of both (37i) and (37iii). Hence T_{not} applied to (52i) will give either (53i) or (53ii):

(53) (i) *John − C + n't − have + a + chance + to + live*
       (→ "John doesn't have a chance to live")
   (ii) *John − C + have + n't − a + chance + to + live*
       (→ "John hasn't a chance to live").

But in fact both forms of (53) are grammatical. Furthermore *have* is the only transitive verb for which this ambiguous negation is possible, just as it is the only transitive verb that can be ambiguously analyzed in terms of (37). That is, we have "John doesn't read books" but not "John readsn't books".

Similarly, T_q applied to (52i) will give either form of (54), and T_{so} will give either form of (55), since these transformations are also based on the structural analysis (37).

(54) (i) does John have a chance to live?
    (ii) has John a chance to live?
(55) (i) Bill has a chance to live and so does John.
    (ii) Bill has a chance to live and so has John.

But in the case of all other transitive verbs such forms as (54ii), (55ii) are impossible. We do not have "reads John books?" or "Bill reads books and so reads John". We see, however, that the apparently irregular behavior of "have" is actually an automatic consequence of our rules. This solves the problem raised in § 2.3 concerning the grammaticalness of (3) but not (5).

Now consider (52ii). We have not shown this, but it is in fact true that in the simplest phrase structure grammar of English there is never any reason for incorporating "be" into the class of verbs; i.e., it will not follow from this grammar that *be* is a V. Just as one of the forms of the verb phrase is $V + NP$, one of the forms is *be + Predicate*. Hence, even though *be* is not an auxiliary in (52ii), it is nevertheless the case that of the analyses permitted by (37), only (37iv) holds of (52ii). Therefore the transformations T_{not}, T_q, and T_{so}, applied to (52ii), yield, respectively (along with (29i)),

(56) (i) $John - S + be + n't - my + friend$ ($\to$ "John isn't my friend")
    (ii) $S + be - John - my + friend$ ($\to$ "is John my friend")
    (iii) $Bill - S + be - my + friend - and - so - S + be - John$
            ($\to$ "Bill is my friend and so is John").

Again, the analogous forms (e.g., "John readsn't books," etc.) are impossible with actual verbs. Similarly, T_A gives "John *is* here" instead of "John *does* be here", as would be the case with actual verbs.

If we were to attempt to describe English syntax wholly in terms of phrase structure, the forms with "be" and "have" would appear as glaring and distinct exceptions. But we have just seen that exactly these apparently exceptional forms result automatically from the simplest grammar constructed to account for the regular cases. Hence, this behavior of "be" and "have" actually turns out to be an instance of a deeper underlying regularity when we consider English structure from the point of view of transformational analysis.

Notice that the occurrence of *have* as an auxiliary in such terminal strings as $John + C + have + en + arrive$ (underlying the kernel sentence "John has arrived") is not subject to the same ambiguous analysis. This terminal string is an instance of (37iii), but not of (37i). That is, it can be analyzed as in (57i), but not (57ii).

(57) (i) $John - C + have - en + arrive$ ($NP - C + have - ...$, i.e., (37iii))

(ii) $John - C - have + en + arrive$ ($NP - C - V...$, i.e., (37i))

This string is not an instance of (37i) since *this occurrence* of *have* is not a V, even though certain other occurrences of *have* (e.g., in (52i)) are V's. The phrase structure of a terminal string is determined from its derivation, by tracing segments back to node points in the manner described in § 4.1. But *have* in (57) is not traceable to any node point labelled V in the derivation of this string. (52i) is ambiguously analyzable, however, since the occurrence of *have* in (52i) is traceable back to a V, and of course, is traceable back to a *have* (namely, itself), in the diagram corresponding to the derivation of the string (52i). The fact that (57ii) is not a permissible analysis prevents us from deriving such non-sentences as "John doesn't have arrived", "does John have arrived", etc.

In this section we have seen that a wide variety of apparently distinct phenomena all fall into place in a very simple and natural way when we adopt the viewpoint of transformational analysis and that, consequently, the grammar of English becomes much more simple and orderly. This is the basic requirement that any conception of linguistic structure (i.e., any model for the form of grammars) must meet. I think that these considerations give ample justification for our earlier contention that the conceptions of phrase structure are fundamentally inadequate and that the theory of linguistic structure must be elaborated along the lines suggested in this discussion of transformational analysis.

7.2 We can easily extend the analysis of questions given above to include such interrogatives as

(58) (i) what did John eat
(ii) who ate an apple

which do not receive yes-or-no answers. The simplest way to incorporate this class of sentences into the grammar is by setting up a new optional transformation T_w which operates on any string of the form

(59) $X - NP - Y$

where X and Y stands for any string (including, in particular, the 'null' string — i.e., the first or third position may be empty). T_w then operates in two steps:

(60) (i) T_{w1} converts the string of the form $X - NP - Y$ into the corresponding string of the form $NP - X - Y$; i.e., it inverts the first and second segments of (59). It thus has the same transformational effect as T_q (cf. (41)–(42)).
(ii) T_{w2} converts the resulting string $NP - X - Y$ into *who* $- X - Y$ if NP is an animate NP or into *what* $- X - Y$ if NP is inanimate.[2]

We now require that T_w can apply only to strings to which T_q has already applied. We specified that T_q must apply after (29 i) and before (29 ii). T_w applies after T_q and before (29 ii), and it is conditional upon T_q in the sense that it can only apply to forms given by T_q. This conditional dependence among transformations is a generalization of the distinction between obligatory and optional transformations which we can easily build into the grammar, and

---

[2] More simply, we can limit application of T_w to strings $X - NP - Y$ where NP is *he, him,* or *it,* and we can define T_{w2} as the transformation that converts any string Z into $wh + Z$, where *wh* is a morpheme. In the morphophonemics of English we shall have rules: $wh + he \rightarrow$ /huw/, $wh + him \rightarrow$ /huwm/, $wh + it \rightarrow$ /wat/.

which proves essential. The terminal string underlying both (58 i) and (58 ii) (as well as (62), (64)) is

(61)   *John − C − eat + an + apple (NP − C − V...)*,

where the dashes indicate the analysis imposed by T_q. Thus (61) is a case of (37 i), as indicated. If we were to apply only obligatory transformations to (61), choosing *past* in developing *C* by (29 i), we would derive

(62)   # *John* # *eat + past* # *an* # *apple* # (→ "John ate an apple")

If we apply (29 i) and T_q to (61), we derive

(63)   *past − John − eat + an + apple*,

where *C* is taken as *past*. If we were now to apply (40) to (63), introducing *do* as the bearer of *past*, we would have the simple interrogative

(64)   did John eat an apple

If we apply T_w to (63), however, we derive first (65), by T_{w1}, and then (66), by T_{w2}.

(65)   *John − past − eat + an + apple*
(66)   *who − past − eat + an + apple*.

Rule (29 ii) and the morphophonemic rules then convert (66) into (58 ii). To form (58 ii), then, we apply first T_q and then T_w to the terminal string (61) that underlies the kernel sentence (62). Note that in this case T_{w1} simply undoes the effect of T_q, which explains the absence of inversion in (58 ii).

To apply T_w to a string, we first select a noun phrase and then invert this noun phrase with the string that precedes it. In forming (58 ii), we applied T_w to (63), choosing the noun phrase *John*. Suppose now that we apply T_w to (63), choosing the noun phrase *an + apple*. Thus for the purposes of this transformation we now analyze (63) as

(67)   *past + John + eat − an + apple*,

a string of the form (59), where *Y* in this case is null. Applying T_w to (67) we derive first (68), by T_{w1}, and then (69), by T_{w2}.

(68)   *an + apple − past + John + eat*

(69)   what − past + John + eat.

(29ii) does not now apply to (69), just as it did not apply to (39) or (42i), since (69) does not contain a substring of the form $Af+v$. Hence (40) applies to (69), introducing *do* as a bearer of the morpheme *past*. Applying the remaining rules, we finally derive (58i).

T_w as formulated in (59)–(60) will also account for all such *wh*-questions as "what will he eat", "what has he been eating". It can easily be extended to cover interrogatives like "what book did he read", etc.

Notice that T_{w1} as defined in (60i) carries out the same transformation as does T_q; that is, it inverts the first two segments of the string to which it applies. We have not discussed the effect of transformations on intonation. Suppose that we set up two fundamental sentence intonations: falling intonations, which we associate with kernel sentences, and rising intonations, which we associate with yes-or-no questions. Then the effect of T_q is in part to convert the intonation from one of these to the other; hence, in the case of (64), to convert a falling intonation into a rising one. But we have seen that T_{w1} applies only after T_q, and that its transformational effect is the same as that of T_q. Hence T_{w1} will convert the rising intonation back into a falling one. It seems reasonable to put this forth as an explanation for the fact that the interrogatives (58i-ii) normally have the falling intonation of declaratives. There are many problems in extending our discussion to intonational phenomena and this remark is too sketchy to carry much weight, but it does suggest that such an extension may be fruitful.

To summarize, we see that the four sentences

(70) (i)   John ate an apple   (= (62))
     (ii) did John eat an apple   (= (64))
     (iii) what did John eat   (= (58i))
     (iv) who ate an apple   (= (58ii))

are all derived from the underlying terminal string (61). (70i) is a kernel sentence, since only obligatory transformations enter into its 'transformational history.' (70ii) is formed from (61) by applying

T_q. (70iii) and (70iv) are even more remote from the kernel, since they are formed from (61) by applying first T_q and then T_w. We shall refer to this analysis briefly in § 8.2.

7.3 In § 5.3 we mentioned that there are certain noun phrases of the form *to* + *VP*, *ing* + *VP* ("to prove that theorem," "proving that theorem"— cf. (32)–(33)). Among these we will have such phrases as "to be cheated," "being cheated", which are derived from passives. But passives have been deleted from the kernel. Hence noun phrases of the type *to* + *VP*, *ing* + *NP* can no longer be introduced within the kernel grammar by such rules as (33). They must therefore be introduced by a 'nominalizing transformation' which converts a sentence of the form *NP* − *VP* into a noun phrase of the form *to* + *VP* or *ing* + *VP*.[3] We shall not go into the structure of this very interesting and ramified set of nominalizing transformations except to sketch briefly a transformational explanation for a problem raised in § 2.3.

One of the nominalizing transformations will be the transformation T_{adj} which operates on any string of the form

(71) *T* − *N* − *is* − *Adj* (i.e., article − noun − is − adjective)

and converts it into the corresponding noun phrase of the form *T* + *Adj* + *N*. Thus, it converts "the boy is tall" into "the tall boy," etc. It is not difficult to show that this transformation simplifies the grammar considerably, and that it must go in this, not the opposite direction. When we formulate this transformation properly, we find that it enables us to drop all adjective-noun combinations from the kernel, reintroducing them by T_{Adj}.

In the phrase structure grammar we have a rule

(72) *Adj* → *old, tall, …*

---

[3] This nominalizing transformation will be given as a generalized transformation such as (26). It will operate on a pair sentences, one of which it converts from *NP* − *VP* into *to* + *VP* (or *ing* + *VP*), which it then substitutes for an *NP* of the other sentence. See my *The logical structure of linguistic theory* and *Transformational analysis* for a detailed discussion. – For a fuller and more adequate analysis of the material in this subsection, see my "A transformational approach to syntax," *Proceedings of the University of Texas Symposium of 1958* (to appear).

which lists all of the elements that can occur in the kernel sentences of the form (71). Words like "sleeping", however, will not be given in this list, even though we have such sentences as

(73) the child is sleeping.

The reason for this is that even when "sleeping" is not listed in (72), (73) is generate by the transformation (29 ii) (that carries $Af + v$ into $v + Af \#$) form the underlying terminal string

(74) $the + child + C + be - ing - sleep$,

where $be + ing$ is part of the auxiliary verb (cf. (28 iii)). Alongside of (73), we have such sentences as "the child will sleep," "the child sleeps," etc., with different choices for the auxiliary verb.

Such words as "interesting", however, will have to be given in the list (73). In such sentences as

(75) the book is interesting,

"interesting" is an *Adj*, not part of the *Verb*, as can be seen from the fact that we do not have "the book will interest," "the book interests," etc.

An independent support for this analysis of "interesting" and "sleeping" comes from the behavior of "very," etc., which can occur with certain adjectives, but not others. The simplest way to account for "very" is to put into the phrase structure grammar the rule

(76) $Adj \rightarrow very + Adj$.

"very" can appear in (75), and in general with "interesting"; but it cannot appear in (73) or with other occurrences of "sleeping." Hence, if we wish to preserve the simplest analysis of "very," we must list "interesting" but not "sleeping" in (72) as an *Adj*.

We have not discussed the manner in which transformations impose constituent structure, although we have indicated that this is necessary; in particular, so that transformations can be compounded. One of the general conditions on derived constituent structure will be the following:

(77) If X is a Z in the phrase structure grammar, and a string Y formed by a transformation is of the same structural form as X, then Y is also a Z.

In particular, even when passives are deleted from the kernel we will want to say that the *by*-phrase (as in "the food was eaten — by the man") is a prepositional phrase (*PP*) in the passive sentence. (77) permits this, since we know from the kernel grammar that *by* + *NP* is a *PP*. (77) is not stated with sufficient accuracy, but it can be elaborated as one of a set of conditions on derived constituent structure.

But now consider (73). The word "sleeping" is formed by transformation (i.e., (29 ii)) and it is of the same form as "interesting" (i.e., it is a *V* + *ing*), which, as we know from the phrase structure grammar, is an *Adj*. Hence, by (77), "sleeping" is also an *Adj* in the transform (73). But this means that (73) can be analyzed as a string of the form (71) so that T_{Adj} applies to it, forming the noun phrase

(78)   the sleeping child

just as it forms "the interesting book" from (75). Thus even though "sleeping" is excluded from (72), it will appear as an adjective modifying nouns.

This analysis of adjectives (which is all that we are required to give to account for the actually occurring sentences) will not introduce the word "sleeping," however, into all the adjective positions of such words as "interesting" which remained in the kernel. For example, it will never introduce "sleeping" into the context "very —." Since "very" never modifies verbs, "very" will not appear in (74) or (73), and all occurences of "sleeping" as a modifier are derived from its occurrence as a verb in (74), etc. Similarly, there will be phrase structure rules that analyze the verb phrase into

(79)   *Aux* + *seem* + *Adj*

just as other rules analyze *VP* into *Aux* + *V* + *NP*, *Aux* + *be* + *Adj*. etc. But "sleeping" will never be introduced into the context "seems —" by this grammar, which is apparently the simplest one constructible for the actually occurring sentences.

When we develop this sketchy argument more carefully, we reach the conclusion that the simplest transformational grammar for the occurring sentences will exclude (80) while generating (81).

(80) (i) the child seems sleeping
   (ii) the very sleeping child
(81) (i) the book seems interesting
   (ii) the very interesting book.

We see, then, that the apparently arbitrary distinctions noted in § 2.3 between (3) (= "have you a book on modern music?") and (4) (= (81 i)) on the one hand, and (5) (= "read you a book on modern music?") and (6) (= (80 i)) on the other, have a clear structural origin, and are really instances of higher level regularity in the sense that they are consequences of the simplest transformational grammar. In other words, certain linguistic behavior that seems unmotivated and inexplicable in terms of phrase structure appears simple and systematic when we adopt the transformational point of view. To use the terminology of § 2.2, if a speaker were to project his finite linguistic experience by using phrase structure and transformations in the simplest possible way, consistent with his experience, he would include (3) and (4) as grammatical while rejecting (5) and (6).

7.4 In (28), § 5.3, we analyzed the element *Verb* into $Aux + V$, and then simply listed the verbal roots of the class V. There are, however, a large number of productive subcontructions of V that deserve some mention, since they bring to light some basic points in a rather clear way. Consider first such verb + particle $(V + Prt)$ constructions as "bring in," "call up," "drive away." We can have such forms as (82) but not (83).

(82) (i) the police brought in the criminal
   (ii) the police brought the criminal in
   (iii) the police brought him in
(83)   the police brought in him.

We know that discontinuous elements cannot be handled readily within the phrase structure grammar. Hence the most natural way of analyzing these constructions is to add to (28 ii) the following possibility:

(84) $V \rightarrow V_1 + Prt$

along with a set of supplementary rules to indicate which V_1 can go with which *Prt*. To allow for the possibility of (82ii) we set up an optional transformation T_{sep}^{op} which operates on strings with the structural analysis

(85) $X - V_1 - Prt - NP$

and has the effect of interchanging the third and fourth segments of the string to which it applies. It thus carries (82i) into (82ii). To provide for (82iii) while excluding (83), we must indicate that this transformation is obligatory when the *NP* object is a pronoun (*Pron*). Equivalently, we can set up an obligatory transformation T_{sep}^{ob} which has the same structural effect as T_{sep}^{op} but which operates on strings with the structural analysis

(86) $X - V_1 - Prt - Pron$

We know that the passive transformation operates on any string of the form $NP - Verb - NP$. If we specify that the passive transformation applies before T_{sep}^{op} or T_{sep}^{ob}, then it will form the passives

(87) (i) the criminal was brought in by the police
   (ii) he was brought in by the police

from (82), as it should.

Further investigation of the verb phrase shows that there is a general verb + complement ($V + Comp$) construction that behaves very much like the verb + particle construction just discussed. Consider the sentences

(88) everyone in the lab considers John incompetent
(89) John is considered incompetent by everyone in the lab.

If we wish to derive (89) from (88) by the passive transformation we must analyze (88) into the structure $NP_1 - Verb - NP_2$, where $NP_1 = everyone + in + the + lab$ and $NP_2 = John$. That is, we must apply the passive not to (88), but to a terminal string (90) that underlies (88):

(90) everyone in the lab — considers incompetent — John.

We can now form (88) from (90) by a transformation analogous to T_{sep}^{ob}. Suppose that we add to the phrase structure grammar the rule (91), alongside (84).

(91) $V \rightarrow V_a + Comp$

We now extend T^{ob}_{sep} permitting it to apply to strings of the form (92) as well as to strings of the form (86), as before.

(92) $X - V_a - Comp - NP$.

This revised transformation T^{ob}_{sep} will convert (90) into (88). Thus, the treatment of the verb + complement and verb + particle constructions are quite similar. The former, in particular, is an extremely well-developed construction in English.[4]

7.5   We have barely sketched the justification for the particular form of each of the transformations that we have discussed, though it is very important to study the question of the uniqueness of this system. I think it can be shown that in each of the cases considered above, and in many other cases, there are very clear and easily generalizable considerations of simplicity that determine which set of sentences belong to the kernel and what sorts of transformations are required to account for the non-kernel sentences. As a paradigmatic instance, we shall briefly review the status of the passive transformation.

In § 5.4 we showed that the grammar is much more complex if it contains both actives and passives in the kernel than if the passives are deleted and reintroduced by a transformation that interchanges the subject and object of the active, and replaces the verb V by $is + V + en + by$. Two questions about uniqueness immediately suggest themselves. First, we ask whether it is necessary to inter-

---

[4]   Further study shows that most of the verb + complement forms introduced by rule (91) should themselves be excluded from the kernel and derived transformationally from "John is incompetent," etc. But this is a complex matter that requires a much more detailed development of transformational theory than we can give here. Cf. my *The logical structure of linguistic theory*, *Transformational analysis* and "A transformational approach to syntax".

There are several other features of these constructions that we have passed over far too briefly. It is not at all clear that this is an obligatory transformation. With long and complex objects we can have, e.g., "they consider incompetent anyone who is unable to..." Hence we might extend T^{op}_{sep}, rather than T^{ob}_{sep}, to take care of this case. It is interesting to study those features of the grammatical object that necessitate or preclude this transformation. Much more than length is involved. There are also other possibilities for the passive that we shall not consider here, for lack of space, though they make an interesting study.

change the noun phrases to form the passive. Second, we ask whether passives could have been chosen as the kernel, and actives derived from them by an 'active' transformation.

Consider first the question of the interchange of subject and object. Is this interchange necessary, or could we describe the passive transformation as having the following effect:

(93) $NP_1 - Aux - V - NP_2$ is rewritten $NP_1 - Aux + be + en - V - by + NP_2$.

In particular, the passive of "John loves Mary" would be "John is loved by Mary."

In § 5.4 we argued against (93) and in favor of inversion on the basis of the fact that we have such sentences as (94) but not (95).

(94) (i)   John admires sincerity — sincerity is admired by John
    (ii) John plays golf — golf is played by John
    (iii) sincerity frightens John — John is frightened by sincerity
(95) (i)   sincerity admires John — John is admired by sincerity
    (ii) golf plays John — John is played by golf
    (iii) John frightens sincerity — sincerity is frightened by John.

We pointed out, however, that this approach requires that a notion of "degree of grammaticalness" be developed to support this distinction. I believe that this approach is correct, and that there is a clear sense in which the sentences of (94) are more grammatical than those of (95), which are themselves more grammatical than "sincerity admires eat," etc. Any grammar that distinguishes abstract from proper nouns would be subtle enough to characterize the difference between (94i, iii) and (95i, iii), for example, and surely linguistic theory must provide the means for this distinction. However, since we have not gone into the question of category analysis in this discussion, it is interesting to show that there is even a stronger argument against (93). In fact, any grammar that can distinguish singular from plural is sufficiently powerful to enable us to prove that the passive requires inversion of noun phrases.

To see this, consider the verb + complement construction discussed in § 7.4. Alongside (88), (89) we have such sentences as:

(96) all the people in the lab consider John a fool
(97) John is considered a fool by all the people in the lab.

In § 7.4 we saw that (96) is formed by the transformation T_{sep}^{ob} from the underlying string

(98) all the people in the lab – consider a fool – John (*NP – Verb – NP*),

with the *Verb* "consider a fool" being an instance of (91). We also saw that the passive transformation applies directly to (98). If the passive interchanges subject and object, it will correctly form (97) from (98) as the passive of (96). If, however, we take (93) as the definition of the passive, we will derive the non-sentence.

(99) all the people in the lab are considered a fool by John

by application of this transformation to (98).

The point is that we have found a verb — namely, "consider a fool" — which must agree in number both with its subject and its object.[5] Such verbs prove quite conclusively that the passive must be based on an inversion of subject and object.

Consider now the question of whether passives could be taken as the kernel sentences instead of actives. It is quite easy to see that this proposal leads to a much more complex grammar. With actives as kernel sentences, the phrase structure grammar will include (28) with *be + en* dropped from (28 iii). But if passives are taken as kernel sentences, *be + en* will have to be listed in (28 iii), along with all the other forms of the auxiliary, and we will have to add special rules indicating that if *V* is intransitive, it cannot have the auxiliary *be + en* (i.e., we cannot have "is occurred"), whereas if *V* is transitive it must have *be + en* (i.e., we cannot have "lunch eats by John"). Comparing the two alternatives, there is no doubt as to relative complexity; and we are forced to take actives, not passives, as the kernel sentences.

Notice that if passives were chosen as kernel sentences instead of actives we would run into certain difficulties of quite a different sort.

---

[5] The agreement between "a fool" and "John" in (98) is of course one support for the futher transformational analysis of the verb + complement + noun phrase constructions mentioned in footnote 4 on p. 77.

The active transformation would have to apply to strings of the form

(100) $NP_1 - Aux + be + en - V - by + NP_2$,

converting them to $NP_2 - Aux - V - NP_1$. For example, it would convert

(101)   the wine was drunk by the guests

into "the guests drank the wine," where "drunk" in (101) originates from $en + drink$. But there is also an adjective "drunk" that must be listed in (72) along with "old," "interesting," etc., since we have "he is very drunk," "he seems drunk," etc. (cf. § 7.3), and this adjective will also originate from $en + drink$. It thus appears that in the simplest system of phrase structure for English, the sentence

(102)   John was drunk by midnight

is also based on an underlying terminal string that can be analyzed in accordance with (100). In other words, there is no structural way to differentiate properly between (101) and (102), if both are taken as kernel sentences. But application of the 'active' transformation to (102) does not give a grammatical sentence.

When we actually try to set up, for English, the simplest grammar that contains a phrase structure and transformational part, we find that the kernel consist of simple, declarative, active sentences (in fact, probably a finite number of these), and that all other sentences can be described more simply as transforms. Each transformation that I have investigated can be shown to be irreversible in the sense that it is much easier to carry out the transformation in one direction than in the other, just as in the case of the passive transformation discussed above. This fact may account for the traditional practice of grammarians, who customarily begin the grammar of English, for example, with the study of simple 'actor-action' sentences and simple grammatical relations such as subject-predicate or verb-object. No one would seriously begin the study of English constituent structure with such a sentence as "whom have they nominated," attempting to analyze it into two parts, etc.; and while some very detailed considerations of English structure (e.g., reference [33]) do not mention interrogatives, none fails to include simple declaratives. Transformational analysis provides a rather simple explanation for this assymmetry (which is otherwise formally unmotivated) on the assumption that grammarians have been acting on the basis of a correct intuition about the language.[6]

7.6 One other point deserves some mention before we leave the topic of English transformations. At the outset of § 5 we noted that the rule for conjunction provides a useful criterion for constituent analysis in the sense that this rule is greatly simplified if constituents are set up in a certain way. Now we are interpreting this rule as a transformation. There are many other cases in which the behavior of a sentence under transformations provides valuable, even compelling evidence as to its constituent structure.

Consider for example the pair of sentences

(103) (i) John knew the boy studying in the library.
     (ii) John found the boy studying in the library.

It is intuitively obvious that these sentences have different grammatical structure (this becomes clear, for example, when we attempt to add "not running around in the streets" to (103)), but I do not believe that within the level of phrase structure grounds can be found for analyzing them into different constituents. The simplest analysis in both cases is as $NP - Verb - NP - ing + VP$. But consider the behavior of these sentences under the passive transformation. We have the sentences (104) but not (105).[7]

---

[6] In determining which of two related forms is more central, we are thus following the reasoning outlined by Bloomfield for morphology: "...when forms are partially similar, there may be a question as to which one we had better take as the underlying form... the structure of the language may decide this question for us, since, taking it one way, we get an unduly complicated description, and taking it the other way, a relatively simple one," (*Language* [New York, 1933], p. 218). Bloomfield continues by pointing out that "this same consideration often leads us to *set up* an artificial underlying form." We have also found this insight useful in transformational analysis, as, e.g., when we set up the terminal string $John - C - have + en - be + ing - read$ underlying the kernel sentence "John has been reading."

[7] The sentences of (104) without the parenthesized expression are formed by a second 'elliptical' transformation that converts e.g., "the boy was seen by John" into "the boy was seen."

(104) (i)   the boy studying in the library was known (by John)
     (ii) the boy studying in the library was found (by John)
     (iii) the boy was found studying in the library (by John)
(105)   the boy was known studying in the library (by John)

The passive transformation applies only to sentences of the form $NP - Verb - NP$. Hence, to yield (104 ii), (103 ii) must be analyzable as

(106)   John — found — the boy studying in the library,

with the noun phrase object "the boy studying in the library," (103 i) will have a corresponding analysis, since we have the passive (104 i).

But (103 ii) also has the passive (104 iii). From this we learn that (103 ii) is a case of the verb + complement construction studied in § 7.4; i.e., that it is derived by the transformation T_{sep}^{ob} from the underlying string

(107)   John — found studying in the library — the boy,

with the verb "found" and the complement "studying in the library." The passive transformation will convert (107) into (104 iii), just as it converts (90) into (89). (103 i), however, is not a transform of the string "John — knew studying in the library — the boy" (the same form as (107)), since (105) is not a grammatical sentence.

By studying the grammatical passives, then, we determine that "John found the boy studying in the library" (=(103 ii) is analyzable ambiguously as either $NP - Verb - NP$, with the object "the boy studying in the library," or as $NP - Aux + V - NP - Comp$, a transform of the string (107 which has the complex *Verb* "found studying in the library." "John knew the boy studying in the library" (=(103 i)), however, has only the first of these analyses. The resulting description of (103) seems quite in accord with intuition.

As another example of a similar type, consider the sentence

(108)   John came home.

Although "John" and "home" are *NP*'s, and "came" is a *Verb*, investigation of the effect of transformations on (108) shows that it cannot be analyzed as a case of *NP — Verb — NP*. We cannot have "home was come by John" under the passive transformation, or "what did John come" under the question transformation T_w. We must therefore analyze (108) in some other way (if we are not to complicate unduly the description of these transformations), perhaps as *NP — Verb — Adverb*. Apart from such considerations as these, there do not appear to be very strong reasons for denying to (108) the completely counterintuitive analysis *NP — Verb — NP*, with "home" the object of "came".

I think it is fair to say that a significant number of the basic criteria for determining constituent structure are actually transformational. The general principle is this: if we have a transformation that simplifies the grammar and leads from sentences to sentences in a large number of cases (i.e., a transformation under which the set of grammatical sentences is very nearly closed), then we attempt to assign constituent structure to sentences in such a way that this transformation always leads to grammatical sentences, thus simplifying the grammar even further.

The reader will perhaps have noted a certain circularity or even apparent inconsistency in our approach. We define such transformations as the passive in terms of particular phrase structure analyses, and we then consider the behavior of sentences under these transformations in determining how to assign phrase structure to these sentences. In § 7.5 we used the fact that "John was drunk by midnight" (= (102)) does not have a corresponding 'active' as an argument against setting up a passive-to-active transformation. In § 7.6 we have used the fact that "John came home" (= (108)) does not have a passive as an argument against assigning to it the constituent structure *NP — Verb — NP*. However, if the argument is traced carefully in each case it will be clear that there is no circularity or inconsistency. In each case our sole concern has been to decrease the complexity of the grammar, and we have tried to show that the proposed analysis is clearly simpler than the rejected alternatives. In some cases the grammar becomes simpler if we reject a certain transformation: in some cases reassignment of constituent structure is preferable. We have thus been following the course outlined in § 6. Making use of phrase structure and transformations, we are trying to construct a grammar of English that will be simpler than any proposed alternative; and we are giving no thought to the question of how one might actually arrive at this grammar in some mechanical way from an English corpus, no matter how extensive. Our weaker goal of evaluation instead of discovery eliminates any fear of vicious circularity in the cases discussed above. The intuitive correspondences and explanations of apparent irregularities seem to me to offer important evidence for the correctness of the approach we have been following. Cf. § 8.

8

THE EXPLANATORY POWER OF LINGUISTIC THEORY

8.1 So far we have considered the linguist's task to be that of producing a device of some sort (called a grammar) for generating all and only the sentences of a language, which we have assumed were somehow given in advance. We have seen that this conception of the linguist's activities leads us naturally to describe languages in terms of a set of levels of representation, some of which are quite abstract and non-trivial. In particular, it leads us to establish phrase structure and transformational structure as distinct levels of representation for grammatical sentences. We shall now proceed to formulate the linguist's goals in quite different and independent terms which, however, lead to very similar notions of linguistic structure.

There are many facts about language and linguistic behavior that require explanation beyond the fact that such and such a string (which no one may ever have produced) is or is not a sentence. It is reasonable to expect grammars to provide explanations for some of these facts. For example, for many English speakers the phoneme sequence /əneym/ can be understood ambiguously as either "a name" or "an aim". If our grammar were a one-level system dealing only with phonemes, we would have no explanation for this fact. But when we develop the level of morphological representation, we find that, for quite independent reasons, we are forced to set up morphemes "a", "an", "aim" and "name", associated with the phonemic shapes /ə/, /ən/, /eym/ and /neym/. Hence, as an automatic consequence of the attempt to set up the morphology in the simplest possible way we find that the phoneme sequence /əneym/ is ambiguously represented on the morphological level. In general, we say that we have a case of *constructional homonymity* when a certain phoneme sequence is analyzed in more than one way on some level. This suggests a criterion of adequacy for grammars We can test the adequacy of a given grammar by asking whether or not each case of constructional homonymity is a real case of ambiguity and each case of the proper kind of ambiguity is actually a case of constructional homonymity.[1] More generally, if a certain conception of the form of grammar leads to a grammar of a given language that fails this test, we may question the adequacy of this conception and the linguistic theory that underlies it. Thus, a perfectly good argument for the establishment of a level of morphology is that this will account for the otherwise unexplained ambiguity of /əneym/.

We have a case of constructional homonymity when some phoneme sequence is ambiguously represented. Suppose that on some level two distinct phoneme sequences are similarly or identically analyzed. We expect that these sequences should somehow be 'understood' in a similar manner, just as cases of dual representation are 'understood' in more than one way. For example, the sentences

(109) (i) John played tennis
     (ii) my friend likes music

are quite distinct on phonemic and morphemic levels. But on the level of phrase structure they are both represented as *NP – Verb – NP*; correspondingly, it is evident that in some sense they are similarly understood. This fact could not be explained in terms of a grammar that did not go beyond the level words or morphemes, and such instances offer a motivation for establishing the level of phrase structure that is quite independent of that advanced in § 3. Note that considerations of structural ambiguity can also be brought

---

[1] Obviously, not all kinds of ambiguity will be analyzable in syntactic terms. For example, we would not expect a grammar to explain the referential ambiguity of "son"-"sun", "light" (in color, weight), etc.

In his "Two models of grammatical description," *Linguistics Today, Word* 10.210–33 (1954), Hockett uses notions of structural ambiguity to demonstrate the independence of various linguistic notions in a manner very similar to what we are suggesting here.

forth as a motivation for establishing a level of phrase structure. Such expressions as "old men and women" and "they are flying planes" (i.e., "those specks on the horizon are ...", "my friends are ...") are evidently ambiguous, and in fact they are ambiguously analyzed on the level of phrase structure, though not on any lower level. Recall that the analysis of an expression on the level of phrase structure is provided not by a single string but by a diagram such as (15) or, equivalently, by a certain *set* of representing strings.[2]

What we are suggesting is that the notion of "understanding a sentence" be explained in part in terms of the notion of "linguistic level". To understand a sentence, then, it is first necessary to reconstruct its analysis on each linguistic level; and we can test the adequacy of a given set of abstract linguistic levels by asking whether or not grammars formulated in terms of these levels enable us to provide a satisfactory analysis of the notion of "understanding." Cases of higher level similarity of representation and higher level dissimilarity (constructional homonymity) are simply the extreme cases which, if this framework is accepted, prove the existence of higher levels. In general, we cannot understand any sentence fully unless we know at least how it is analyzed on all levels, including such higher levels as phrase structure, and, as we shall see, transformational structure.

We were able to show the inadequacy of a theory of linguistic structure that stopped short of phrase structure by exhibiting cases of ambiguity and similarity of understanding that were unexplained on lower levels. But it turns out that there is still a large residue of unexplained cases even after the level of phrase structure is established and applied to English. Analysis of these cases demonstrates the

---

[2] That is, by what is called a "phrase marker" in my *The logical structure of linguistic theory* and "Three models for the description of language" (above, p. 22, fn. 1). See "Three models..." for discussion of the constructional homonymity of "they are flying planes" within a phrase structure grammar. When we adjoin a transformational grammar to the phrase structure grammar, this sentence is, however, an example of transformational ambiguity, not constructional homonymity within phrase structure. In fact, it is not clear that there are *any* cases of constructional homonymity purely within the level of phrase structure once a transformational grammar is developed.

necessity for a still 'higher' level of transformational analysis in a manner independent of §§ 5, 7. I shall mention only a few representative instances.

8.2 In § 7.6 we came across an example of a sentence (i.e., "I found the boy studying in the library" = (103 ii)) whose ambiguity of representation could not be demonstrated without bringing transformational criteria to bear. We found that under one interpretation this sentence was a transform under T_{sep}^{ob} of "I — found studying in the library — the boy," and that under another interpretation it was analyzed into an $NP - Verb - NP$ construction with the object "the boy studying in the library." Further transformational analysis would show that in both cases the sentence is a transform of the pair of terminal strings that underlie the simple kernel sentences

(110) (i) I found the boy
     (ii) the boy is studying in the library.

Hence this is an interesting case of a sentence whose ambiguity is the result of alternative transformational developments from the same kernel strings. This is quite a complicated example, however, requiring a fairly detailed study of the way in which transformations assign constituent structure, and simpler examples of ambiguity with a transformational origin are not hard to find.

Consider the phrase (111), which can be understood ambiguously with "hunters" as the subject, analogously to (112i), or as the object, analogously to (112ii).

(111) the shooting of the hunters
(112) (i) the growling of lions
     (ii) the raising of flowers.

On the level of phrase structure there is no good way to explain this ambiguity; all of these phrases are represented as *the* $- V + ing -$ *of* $+ NP$.[3] In transformational terms, however, there is a clear and

---

[3] It is true that (111) may be represented ambiguously with *shoot* taken either as a transitive or an intransitive verb, but the essential fact here is that the

automatic explanation. Careful analysis of English shows that we can simplify the grammar if we strike such phrases as (111) and (112) out of the kernel and reintroduce them by transformation. To account for such phrases as (112i), we will set up a transformation that carries any sentence of the form $NP - C - V$ into the corresponding phrase of the form $the - V + ing - of + NP$; and this transformation will be designed in such a way that the result is an NP.[4] To account for (112ii), we will set up a transformation which carries any sentence of the form $NP_1 - C - V - NP_2$ into the corresponding NP of the form $the - V + ing - of + NP_2$. Thus the first of these transformations will carry "lions growl" into "the growling of lions," and the second will carry "John raises flowers" into "the raising of flowers." But both "the hunters shoot" and "they shoot the hunters" are kernel sentences. Hence (111) = "the shooting of the hunters" will have two distinct transformational origins; it will be ambiguously represented on the transformational level. The ambiguity of the grammatical relation in (111) is a consequence of the fact that the relation of "shoot" to "hunters" differs in the two underlying kernel sentences. We do not have this ambiguity in (112), since neither "they growl lions" nor "flowers raise" are grammatical kernel sentences.

Similarly, consider such pairs as

(113) (i) the picture was painted by a new technique
(ii) the picture was painted by a real artist.

These sentences are understood quite differently, though identically represented as $NP - was + Verb + en - by + NP$ on the level of phrase structure. But their transformational history is quite different. (113ii) is the passive of "a real artist painted the picture". (113i) is

---

grammatical relation in (111) is ambiguous (i.e., "hunters" may be subject or object). Grammatical relations can be defined within phrase structure in terms of the shape of the diagrams (15), etc. But in these terms there will be no grounds for the assertion that *either* the subject-verb *or* the verb-object relation is to be found in (111). If we analyze verbs into three classes, transitive, intransitive and either transitive or intransitive, then even this (in itself insufficient) distinction disappears.

[4] Cf. footnote 3 on p. 72.

formed from, e.g., "John painted the picture by a new technique" by a double transformation; first the passive, then the elliptical transformation (mentioned in fn. 7 on p. 81) that drops the 'agent' in the passive. An absolute homonym on the model of (113) is not hard to find. For example,

(114)   John was frightened by the new methods.

may mean either that John is a conservative — new methods frighten him; or that new methods of frightening people were used to frighten John (an interpretation that would be the more normal one if "being" were inserted after "was"). On the transformational level, (114) has both the analysis of (113i) and (113ii), which accounts for its ambiguity.

8.3 We can complete the argument by presenting an example of the opposite extreme; namely, a case of sentences which are understood in a similar manner, though they are quite distinct in phrase structure and lower level representation. Consider the following sentences, discussed in § 7.2.

(115) (i) John ate an apple   — declarative
      (ii) did John eat an apple — yes-or-no-question ⎫
      (iii) what did John eat   ⎫   ⎬ interrogative
      (iv) who ate an apple   ⎬ — *wh*-question   ⎭
                                 ⎭

It is intuitively obvious that (115) contains two types of sentences, declaratives (115i) and interrogatives (115ii–iv). Furthermore, the interrogatives are intuitively subdivided into two types, the yes-or-no-question (115ii), and the *wh*-questions (115iii, iv). It is difficult, however, to find a formal basis for this classification that is not arbitrary and *ad hoc*. If, for example, we classify sentences by their 'normal' intonation, then (115i), (115iii) and (115iv), with the normal declarative (falling) intonation, will be opposed to (115ii), with rising intonation. If we classify sentences on the basis of word order, then (115i) and (115iv), with normal *NP – Verb – NP* order, will be opposed to (115ii) and (115iii), which have inversion of subject and auxiliary. Nevertheless, any grammar of English will classify these sentences in the manner indicated in (115), and any speaker of English will understand these sentences according to this pattern. Certainly a linguistic theory that fails to provide grounds for this classification must be judged inadequate.

The representation of a string on the level of transformations is given by the terminal string (or strings) form which it originates and the sequence of transformations by which it is derived from this underlying string. In §§ 7.1–2 we came to the following conclusions about the sentences (115) (=(70)). Each of these sentences originates from the underlying terminal string.

(116)   *John C − eat + an + apple* (=(61)),

which is derived within the phrase structure grammar. (115i) is derived from (116) by applying obligatory transformations only; hence, it is by definition a kernel sentence. (115ii) is formed from (116) by applying the obligatory transformations and T_q. Both (115iii) and (115iv) are formed by applying obligatory transformations, T_q, and T_w. They differ from one another only in the choice of the noun phrase to which T_w applies. Suppose that we determine sentence types in general in terms of transformational history, i.e., representation on the transformational level. Then the major subdivisions of (115) are the kernel sentence (115i) on the one hand, and (115ii–iv), all of which have T_q in their transformational representation, on the other. Thus (115ii–iv) are all interrogatives. (115iii–iv) form a special subclass of interrogatives, since they are formed by the additional subsidiary transformation T_w. Thus when we formulate the simplest transformational grammar for (115), we find that the intuitively correct classification of sentences is given by the resulting transformational representations.

9

SYNTAX AND SEMANTICS

9.1 We have now found cases of sentences that are understood in more than one way and are ambiguously represented on the transformational level (though not on other levels) and cases of sentences that are understood in a similar manner and are similarly represented on the transformational level alone. This gives an independent justification and motivation for description of language in terms of transformational structure, and for the establishment of transformational representation as a linguistic level with the same fundamental character as other levels. Furthermore it adds force to the suggestion that the process of "understanding a sentence" can be explained in part in terms of the notion of linguistic level. In particular, in order to understand a sentence it is necessary to know the kernel sentences from which it originates (more precisely, the terminal strings underlying these kernel sentences) and the phrase structure of each of these elementary components, as well as the transformational history of development of the given sentence from these kernel sentences.[1] The general problem of analyzing the process of "understanding" is thus reduced, in a sense, to the problem of explaining how kernel sentences are understood, these being considered the basic 'content elements' from which the usual, more complex sentences of real life are formed by transformational development.

---

[1] When transformational analysis is more carefully formulated, we find that knowledge of the transformational representation of a sentence (which incorporates the phrase structure of the kernel strings from which the sentence originates) is all that is necessary to determine the derived phrase structure of the transform.

In proposing that syntactic structure can provide a certain insight into problems of meaning and understanding we have entered onto dangerous ground. There is no aspect of linguistic study more subject to confusion and more in need of clear and careful formulation than that which deals with the points of connection between syntax and semantics. The real question that should be asked is: "How are the syntactic devices available in a given language put to work in the actual use of this language?" Instead of being concerned with this very important problem, however, the study of interconnections between syntax and semantics has largely been dominated by a side issue and a misformulated question. The issue has been whether or not semantic information is required for discovering or selecting a grammar; and the challenge usually posed by those who take the affirmative in this dispute is: "How can you construct a grammar with no appeal to meaning?"

The remarks in § 8 about possible semantic implications of syntactic study should not be misinterpreted as indicating support for the notion that grammar is based on meaning. In fact, the theory outlined in §§ 3–7 was completely formal and non-semantic. In § 8, we have indicated briefly some ways in which the actual use of available syntactic devices can be studied. Perhaps this problem can be elucidated somewhat further by a purely negative discussion of the possibility of finding semantic foundations for syntactic theory

9.2.1 A great deal of effort has been expended in attempting to answer the question: "How can you construct a grammar with no appeal to meaning?" The question itself, however, is wrongly put, since the implication that obviously one can construct a grammar *with* appeal to meaning is totally unsupported. One might with equal justification ask: "How can you construct a grammar with no knowledge of the hair color of speakers?" The question that should be raised is: "How can you construct a grammar?" I am not acquainted with any detailed attempt to develop the theory of grammatical structure in partially semantic terms or any specific and rigorous proposal for the use of semantic information in constructing or evaluating grammars. It is undeniable that "intuition about linguistic form" is very useful to the investigator of linguistic form (i.e., grammar). It is also quite clear that the major goal of grammatical theory is to replace this obscure reliance on intuition by some rigorous and objective approach. There is, however, little evidence that "intuition about meaning" is at all useful in the actual investigation of linguistic form. I believe that the inadequacy of suggestions about the use of meaning in grammatical analysis fails to be apparent only because of their vagueness and because of an unfortunate tendency to confuse "intuition about linguistic form" with "intuition about meaning," two terms that have in common only their vagueness and their undesirability in linguistic theory. However, because of the widespread acceptance of such suggestion, it may be worthwhile to investigate some of them briefly, even though the burden of proof in this case rests completely on the linguist who claims to have been able to develop some grammatical notion in semantic terms.

9.2.2 Among the more common assertions put forth as supporting the dependence of grammar on meaning we have the following:

(117) (i) two utterances are phonemically distinct if and only if they differ in meaning;
 (ii) morphemes are the smallest elements that have meaning;
 (iii) grammatical sentences are those that have semantic significance;
 (iv) the grammatical relation subject-verb (i.e., $NP - VP$ as an analysis of *Sentence*) corresponds to the general 'structural meaning' actor-action;
 (v) the grammatical relation verb-object (i.e., $Verb - NP$ as an analysis of VP) corresponds to the structural meaning action-goal or action-object of action;
 (vi) an active sentence and the corresponding passive are synonymous.

9.2.3 A great many linguists have expressed the opinion that phonemic distinctness must be defined in terms of differential meaning (synonymity, to use a more familiar term), as proposed in

(117i). However, it is immediately evident that (117i) cannot be accepted, as it stands, as a definition of phonemic distinctness.² If we are not to beg the question, the utterances in question must be tokens, not types. But there are utterance tokens that are phonemically distinct and identical in meaning (synonyms) and there are utterance tokens that are phonemically identical and different in meaning (homonyms). Hence (117i) is false in both directions. From left to right it is falsified by such pairs as "bachelor" and "unmarried man," or, even more seriously, by such absolute synonyms as /ekɪnámiks/ and /iykɪnámiks/ ("economics"), "ádult" and "adúlt," /rǽšɪn/ and /réyšɪn/, ("ration"), and many others, which may coexist even within one style of speech. From right to left, (117i) is falsified by such pairs as "bank" (of a river) and "bank" (for savings),³ "metal" and "medal" (in many dialects), and numerous other examples. In other words, if we assign two utterance tokens to the same utterance type on the basis of (117i), we will simply get the wrong classification in a large number of cases.

A weaker claim than (117i) might be advanced as follows. Suppose that we have an absolute phonetic system given in advance of the analysis of any language, and guaranteed to be detailed enough so that every two phonemically distinct utterances in any language will be differently transcribed. It may now be the case that certain different tokens will be identically transcribed in this phonetic transcription. Suppose that we define the "ambiguous meaning" of an utterance token as the set of meanings of all tokens transcribed identically with this utterance token. We might now revise (117i), replacing "meaning" by "ambiguous meaning." This might provide an approach to the homonymity problem, if we had an immense corpus in which we could be fairly sure that each of the

---

² See my "Semantic considerations in grammar," *Monograph no. 8*, pp. 141–53 (1955), for a more detailed investigation of (117i).

³ Note that we cannot argue that "bank" in "the river bank" and "bank" in "the savings bank" are two occurrences of the same word, since this is precisely the question under investigation. To say that two utterance tokens are occurrences of the same word is to say that they are not phonemically distinct, and presumably this is what the synonymity criterion (117i) is supposed to determine for us.

phonetically distinct forms of a given word occurred with each of the meanings that this word might have. It may be possible to elaborate this approach even further to cope with the problem of synonyms. In such a way one might hope to determine phonemo distinctness by laborious investigation of the meanings of phonetically transcribed items in a vast corpus. The difficulty of determining in any precise and realistic manner how many meanings several items may have in common, however, as well as the vastness of the undertaking, make the prospect for any such approach appear rather dubious.

9.2.4 Fortunately, we do not have to pursue any such far-fetched and elaborate program in order to determine phonemic distinctness. In practice, every linguist uses much more simple and straightforward non-semantic devices. Suppose that a linguist is interested in determining whether or not "metal" and "medal" are phonemically distinct in some dialect of English. He will not investigate the meanings of these words, since this information is clearly irrelevant to his purpose. He knows that the meanings are different (or he is simply not concerned with the question) and he is interested in determining whether or not the words are phonemically distinct. A careful field worker would probably use the pair test,[4] either with two informants or with an informant and a tape recorder. For example, he might make a random sequence of copies of the utterance tokens that interest him, and then determine whether or not the speaker can consistently identify them. If there is consistent identification, the linguists may apply an even stricter test, asking the speaker to repeat each word several times, and running the pair test over again on the repetitions. If consistent distinguishability is maintained under repetition, he will say that the words "metal" and "medal" are phonemically distinct. The pair test with its variants

---

[4] Cf. my "Semantic considerations of grammar," *Monograph no. 8*, pp. 141–54 (1955); M. Halle, "The strategy of phonemics," *Linguistics Today, Word* 10.197–209 (1954); Z. S. Harris, *Methods in structural linguistics* (Chicago, 1951), pp. 32f.; C. F. Hockett, *A manual of phonology* = *Memoir 11, Indiana University Publications in Anthropology and Linguistics* (Baltimore, 1955), p. 146.

and elaborations provides us with a clear operational criterion for phonemic distinctness in completely non-semantic terms.[5]

It is customary to view non-semantic approaches to grammar as possible alternatives to semantic approaches, and to criticize them as too complex, even if possible in principle. We have found, however, that in the case of phonemic distinctness, at least, exactly the opposite is true. There is a fairly straightforward and operational approach to the determination of phonemic distinctness in terms of such non-semantic devices as the pair test. It may be possible in principle to develop some semantically oriented equivalent to the pair test and its elaborations, but it appears that any such procedure will be quite complex, requiring exhaustive analysis of an immense corpus, and involving the linguists in the rather hopeless attempt to determine how many meanings a given phone sequence might have.

---

[5] Lounsbury argues in his "A semantic analysis of the Pawnee kinship usage," *Language* 32.158–94 (1956), p. 190, that appeal to synonymity is necessary to distinguish between free variation and contrast: "If a linguist who knows no English records from my lips the word *cat* first with a final aspirated stop and later with a final preglottalized unreleased stop, the phonetic data will not tell him whether these forms contrast or not. It is only when he asks me, his informant, whether the meaning of the first form is different from that of the second, and I say it is not, that he will be able to proceed with his phonemic analysis." As a general method, this approach is untenable. Suppose that the linguist records /ekɪnamiks/ and /iykɪnamiks/, /viksɪn/ and /fiymeyl #faks/, etc., and asks whether or not they are different in meaning. He will learn that they are not, and will incorrectly assign them the same phonemic analysis, if he takes this position literally. On the other hand, there are many speakers who do not distinguish "metal" from "medal," though if asked, they may be quite sure that they do. The responses of such informants to Lounsbury's direct question about meaning would no doubt simply becloud the issue.

We can make Lounsbury's position more acceptable by replacing the question "do they have the same meaning?" with "are they the same word?" This will avoid the pitfalls of the essentially irrelevant semantic question, but it is hardly acceptable in this form, since it amounts to asking the informant to do the linguist's work; it replaces an operational test of behavior (such as the pair test) by an informant's judgment about his behavior. The operational tests for linguistic notions may require the informant to respond, but not to express his opinion about his behavior, his judgment about synonymy, about phonemic distinctness, etc. The informant's opinions may be based on all sorts of irrelevant factors. This is an important distinction that must be carefully observed if the operational basis for grammar is not be trivialized.

9.2.5 There is one further difficulty of principle that should be mentioned in the discussion of any semantic approach to phonemic distinctness. We have not asked whether the meanings assigned to distinct (but phonemically identical) tokens are identical, or merely very similar. If the latter, then all of the difficulties of determining phonemic distinctness are paralleled (and magnified, because of the inherent obscurity of the subject matter) in determining sameness of meaning. We will have to determine when two distinct meanings are sufficiently similar to be considered 'the same.' If, on the other hand, we try to maintain the position that the meanings assigned are always identical, that the meaning of a word is a fixed and unchanging component of each occurrence, then a charge of circularity seems warranted. It seems that the only way to uphold such a position would be to conceive of the meaning of a token as "the way in which tokens of this type are (or can be) used," the class of situations in which they can be used, the type of response that they normally evoke, or something of this sort. But it is difficult to make any sense at all out of such a conception of meaning without a prior notion of utterance type. It would appear, then, that even apart from our earlier objections, any approach to phonemic distinctness in semantic terms is either circular or is based on a distinction that is considerably more difficult to establish than the distinction it is supposed to clarify.

9.2.6 How, then, can we account for the widespread acceptance of some such formulation as (117i)? I think that there are two explanations for this. In part, it is a consequence of the assumption that semantic approaches are somehow immediately given and are too simple to require analysis. Any attempt to provide a careful description, however, quickly dispels this illusion. A semantic approach to some grammatical notion requires as careful and detailed a development as is justly required of any non-semantic approach. And as we have seen, a semantic approach to phonemic distinctness is beset by quite considerable difficulties.

A second source for such formulations as (117i), I believe, is a confusion of "meaning" with "informant's response." We thus find such comments on linguistic method as the following: "In linguistic analysis we define contrast among forms operationally in terms of difference in meaning responses."[6] We have observed in § 9.2.3 that if we were to determine contrast by 'meaning response' in any direct way we would simply make the wrong decision in a great many places; and if we try to avoid the difficulties that immediately arise, we are led to a construction that is so elaborate and has such intolerable assumptions that it can be hardly taken as a serious proposal. And we saw in § 9.2.5 that there are apparently even more fundamental difficulties of principle. Hence, if we interpret the quoted assertion literally, we must reject it as incorrect.

If we drop the word "meaning" from this statement, however, we have a perfectly acceptable reference to such devices as the pair test. But there is no warrant for interpreting the responses studied in the pair test as semantic in any way.[7] One might very well develop an operational test for rhyme that would show that "bill" and "pill" are related in a way in which "bill" and "ball" are not. There would be nothing semantic in this test. Phonemic identity is essentially complete rhyme, and there is no more reason for postulating some unobserved semantic reaction in the case of "bill" and "bill" than in the case of "bill" and "pill."

It is strange that those who have objected to basing linguisitc theory on such formulations as (117i) should have been accused of disregard for meaning. It appears to be the case, on the contrary, that those who propose some variant of (117i) must be interpreting "meaning" so broadly that any response to language is called "meaning." But to accept this view is to denude the term "meaning" of any interest or significance. I think that anyone who wishes to save the phrase "study of meaning" as descriptive of an important

---

[6] F. Lounsbury, "A semantic analysis of the Pawnee kinship usage", *Language* 32.158–94 (1956), p. 191.

[7] One should not be confused by the fact that the subject in the pair test may be asked to identify the utterance tokens by meaning. He might just as well be asked to identify them by arbitrarily chosen numbers, by signs of the zodiac, etc. We can no more use some particular formulation of the pair test as an argument for dependence of grammatical theory on meaning than as an argument that linguistics is based on arithmetic or astrology.

aspect of linguistic research must reject this identification of "meaning" with "response to language," and along with it, such formulations as (117i).

9.2.7 It is, of course, impossible to prove that semantic notions are of no use in grammar, just as it is impossible to prove the irrelevance of any other given set of notions. Investigation of such proposals, however, invariably seems to lead to the conclusion that only a purely formal basis can provide a firm and productive foundation for the construction of grammatical theory. Detailed investigation of each semantically oriented proposal would go beyond the bounds of this study, and would be rather pointless, but we can mention briefly some of the more obvious counterexamples to such familiar suggestion as (117).

Such morphemes as "to" in "I want to go" or the dummy carrier "do" in "did he come?" (cf. § 7.1) can hardly be said to have a meaning in any independent sense, and it seems reasonable to assume that an independent notion of meaning, if clearly given, may assign meaning of some sort to such non-morphemes as *gl-* in "gleam," "glimmer," "glow."[8] Thus we have counterexamples to the suggestion (117ii) that morphemes be defined as minimal meaning-bearing elements. In § 2 we have given grounds for rejecting "semantic significance" as a general criterion for grammaticalness, as proposed in (117iii). Such sentences as "John received a letter" or "the fighting stopped" show clearly the untenability of the assertion (117iv) that the grammatical relation subject-verb has the 'structural meaning' actor-action, if meaning is taken seriously as a concept independent of grammar. Similarly, the assignment (117v) of any such structural meaning as action-goal to the verb-object relation as such is precluded by such sentences as "I will disregard his incompetence" or "I missed the train." In contradiction to (117vi), we can describe circumstances in which a 'quantificational' sentence such as "everyone in the room knows at

---

[8] See L. Bloomfield, *Language* (New York, 1933), p. 156; Z. S. Harris, *Methods in structural linguistics* (Chicago, 1951), p. 177; O. Jespersen, *Language* (New York, 1922), chapter XX, for many further examples.

least two languages" may be true, while the corresponding passive "at least two languages are known by everyone in the room" is false, under the normal interpretation of these sentences — e.g., if one person in the room knows only French and German, and another only Spanish and Italian. This indicates that not even the weakest semantic relation (factual equivalence) holds in general between active and passive.

9.3 These counterexamples should not, however, blind us to the fact that there are striking correspondences between the structures and elements that are discovered in formal, grammatical analysis and specific semantic functions. None of the assertions of (117) is wholly false; some are very nearly true. It seems clear, then, that undeniable, though only imperfect correspondences hold between formal and semantic features in language. The fact that the correspondences are so inexact suggests that meaning will be relatively useless as a basis for grammatical description.[9] Careful analysis of each proposal for reliance on meaning confirms this, and shows, in fact, that important insights and generalizations about linguistic structure may be missed if vague semantic clues are followed too closely. For example, we have seen that the active-passive relation is just one instance of a very general and fundamental aspect of formal linguistic structure. The similarity between active-passive, negation, declarative-interrogative, and other transformational relations would not have come to light if the active-passive relation had been investigated exclusively in terms of such notions as synonymity.

---

[9] Another reason for suspecting that grammar cannot be effectively developed on a semantic basis was brought out in the particular case of phonemic distinctness in § 9.2.5. More generally, it seems that the study of meaning is fraught with so many difficulties even after the linguistic meaningbearing elements and their relations are specified, that any attempt to study meaning independently of such specification is out of the question. To put it differently, given the instrument language and its formal devices, we can and should investigate their semantic function (as, e.g., in R. Jakobson, "Beitrag zur allgemeinen Kasuslehre," *Travaux du Cercle Linguistique de Prague* 6.240-88 (1936)); but we cannot, apparently, find semantic absolutes, known in advance of grammar, that can be used to determine the objects of grammar in any way.

The fact that correspondences between formal and semantic features exist, however, cannot be ignored. These correspondences should be studied in some more general theory of language that will include a theory of linguistic form and a theory of the use of language as subparts. In § 8 we found that there are, apparently, fairly general types of relations between these two domains that deserve more intensive study. Having determined the syntactic structure of the language, we can study the way in which this syntactic structure is put to use in the actual functioning of language. An investigation of the semantic function of level structure, as suggested briefly in § 8, might be a reasonable step towards a theory of the interconnections between syntax and semantics. In fact, we pointed out in § 8 that the correlations between the form and use of language can even provide certain rough criteria of adequacy for a linguistic theory and the grammars to which it leads. We can judge formal theories in terms of their ability to explain and clarify a variety of facts about the way in which sentences are used and understood. In other words, we should like the syntactic framework of the language that is isolated and exhibited by the grammar to be able to support semantic description, and we shall naturally rate more highly a theory of formal structure that leads to grammars that meet this requirement more fully.

Phrase structure and transformational structure appear to provide the major syntactic devices available in language for organization and expression of content. The grammar of a given language must show how these abstract structures are actually realized in the case of the language in question, while linguistic theory must seek to clarify these foundations for grammar and the methods for evaluating and choosing between proposed grammars.

It is important to recognize that by introducing such considerations as those of § 8 into the metatheory that deals with grammar and semantics and their points of connection, we have not altered the purely formal character of the theory of grammatical structure itself. In §§ 3-7 we outlined the development of some fundamental linguistic concepts in purely formal terms. We considered the problem of syntactic research to be that of constructing a device for producing a given set of grammatical sentences and of studying the properties of grammars that do this effectively. Such semantic notions as reference, significance, and synonymity played no role in the discussion. The outlined theory, of course, had serious gaps in it — in particular, the assumption that the set of grammatical sentences is given in advance is clearly too strong, and the notion of "simplicity" to which appeal was made explicitly or tacitly was left unanalyzed. However, neither these nor other gaps in this development of grammatical theory can be filled in or narrowed, to my knowledge, by constructing this theory on a partially semantic basis.

In §§ 3-7, then, we were studying language as an instrument or a tool, attempting to describe its structure with no explicit reference to the way in which this instrument is put to use. The motivation for this self-imposed formality requirement for grammars is quite simple — there seems to be no other basis that will yield a rigorous. effective, and 'revealing' theory of linguistic structure. The requirement that this theory shall be a completely formal discipline is perfectly compatible with the desire to formulate it in such a way as to have suggestive and significant interconnections with a parallel semantic theory. What we have pointed out in § 8 is that this formal study of the structure of language as an instrument may be expected to provide insight into the actual use of language, i.e., into the process of understanding sentences.

9.4 To understand a sentence we must know much more than the analysis of this sentence on each linguistic level. We must also know the reference and meaning[10] of the morphemes or words of

---

[10] Goodman has argued—to my mind, quite convincingly—that the notion of meaning of words can at least in part be reduced to that of reference of expressions containing these words. See N. Goodman, "On likeness of meaning," *Analysis*, vol. 10, no. 1 (1949); idem, "On some differences about meaning," *Analysis*, vol. 13, no. 4 (1953). Goodman's approach amounts to reformulating a part of the theory of meaning in the much clearer terms of the theory of reference, just as much of our discussion can be understood as suggesting a reformulation of parts of the theory of meaning that deal with so-called "structural meaning" in terms of the completely nonsemantic theory of grammatical structure. Part of the difficulty with the theory of meaning is that "meaning"

which it is composed; naturally, grammar cannot be expected to be of much help here. These notions form the subject matter for semantics. In describing the meaning of a word it is often expedient, or necessary, to refer to the syntactic framework in which this word is usually embedded; e.g., in describing the meaning of "hit" we would no doubt describe the agent and object of the action in terms of the notions "subject" and "object", which are apparently best analyzed as purely formal notions belonging to the theory of grammar.[11] We shall naturally find that a great many words or morphemes of a single grammatical category are described semantically in partially similar terms, e.g. verbs in terms of subject and object, etc. This is not surprising; it means that the syntactic devices available in the language are being used fairly systematically. We have seen, however, that so generalize from this fairly systematic use and to assign 'structural meanings' to grammatical categories or constructions just as 'lexical meanings' are assigned to words or morphemes, is a step of very questionable validity.

Another common but dubious use of the notion 'structural meaning' is with reference to the meanings of so-called 'grammatically functioning' morphemes such as *ing*, *ly*, prepositions, etc. The contention that the meanings of these morphemes are fundamentally different from the meanings of nouns, verbs, adjectives, and perhaps other large classes, is often supported by appeal to the fact that these morphemes can be distributed in a sequence of blanks or nonsense syllables so as to give the whole the appearance of a sentence, and in fact, so as to determine the grammatical category of the nonsense elements. For example, in the sequence "Pirots karulize etalically" we know that the three words are noun, verb, and adverb by virtue of the *s*, *ize*, and *ly*, respectively. But this

---

tends to be used as a catch-all term to include every aspect of language that we know very little about. Insofar as this is correct, we can expect various aspects of this theory to be claimed by other approaches to language in the course of their development.

[11] Such a description of the meaning of "hit" would then account automatically for the use of "hit" in such transforms as "Bill was hit by John," "hitting Bill was wrong," etc., if we can show in sufficient detail and generality that transforms are 'understood' in terms of the underlying kernel sentences.

property does not sharply distinguish 'grammatical' morphemes from others, since in such sequences as "the Pirots karul — yesterday" or "give him — water" the blanks are also determined as a variant of past tense, in the first case, and as "the", "some," etc., but not "a," in the second. The fact that in these cases we were forced to give blanks rather than nonsense words is explained by the productivity or 'open-endedness' of the categories Noun, Verb, Adjective, etc., as opposed to the categories Article, Verbal Affix, etc. In general, when we distribute a sequence of morphemes in a sequence of blanks we limit the choice of elements that can be placed in the unfilled positions to form a grammatical sentence. Whatever differences there are among morphemes with respect to this property are apparently better explained in terms of such grammatical notions as productivity, freedom of combination, and size of substitution class than in terms of any presumed feature of meaning.

SUMMARY

In this discussion we have stressed the following points: The most that can reasonably be expected of linguistic theory is that it shall provide an evaluation procedure for grammars. The theory of linguistic structure must be distinguished clearly from a manual of helpful procedures for the discovery of grammars, although such a manual will no doubt draw upon the results of linguistic theory, and the attempt to develop such a manual will probably (as it has in the past) contribute substantially to the formation of linguistic theory. If this viewpoint is adopted, there is little motivation for the objection to mixing levels, for the conception of higher-level elements as being literally constructed out of lower-level elements, or for the feeling that syntactic work is premature until all problems of phonemics or morphology are solved.

Grammar is best formulated as a self-contained study independent of semantics. In particular, the notion of grammaticalness cannot be identified with meaningfulness (nor does it have any special relation, even approximate, to the notion of statistical order of approximation). In carrying out this independent and formal study, we find that a simple model of language as a finite state Markov process that produces sentences from left to right is not acceptable, and that such fairly abstract linguistic levels as phrase structure and transformational structure are required for the description of natural languages.

We can greatly simplify the description of English and gain new and important insight into its formal structure if we limit the direct description in terms of phrase structure to a kernel of basic sentences (simple, declarative, active, with no complex verb or noun phrases), deriving all other sentences from these (more properly, from the strings that underlie them) by transformation, possibly repeated. Conversely, having found a set of transformations that carry grammatical sentences into grammatical sentences, we can determine the constituent structure of particular sentences by investigating their behavior under these transformations with alternative constituent analyses.

We consequently view grammars as having a tripartite structure. A grammar has a sequence of rules from which phrase structure can be reconstructed and a sequence of morphophonemic rules that convert strings of morphemes into strings of phonemes. Connecting these sequences, there is a sequence of transformational rules that carry strings with phrase structure into new strings to which the morphophonemic rules can apply. The phrase structure and morphophonemic rules are elementary in a sense in which the transformational rules are not. To apply a transformation to a string, we must know some of the history of derivation of this string; but to apply non-transformational rules, it is sufficient to know the shape of the string to which the rule applies.

As an automatic consequence of the attempt to construct the simplest grammar for English in terms of the abstract levels developed in linguistic theory we find that the apparently irregular behavior of certain words (e.g., "have," "be," "seem") is really a case of higher level regularity. We also find that many sentences are assigned dual representations on some level, and many pairs of sentences are assigned similar or identical representations on some level. In a significant number of cases, dual representation (constructional homonymity) corresponds to ambiguity of the represented sentence and similar or identical representation appears in cases of intuitive similarity of utterances.

More generally, it appears that the notion of "understanding a sentence" must be partially analyzed in grammatical terms. To understand a sentence it is necessary (though not, of course, sufficient) to reconstruct its representation on each level, including the transformational level where the kernel sentences underlying a given sentence can be thought of, in a sense, as the 'elementary content elements' out of which this sentence is constructed. In other words, one result of the formal study of grammatical structure is that a syntactic framework is brought to light which can support semantic analysis. Description of meaning can profitably refer to this underlying syntactic framework, although systematic semantic considerations are apparently not helpful in determining it in the first place. The notion of "structual meaning" as opposed to "lexical meaning", however, appears to be quite suspect, and it is questionable that the grammatical devices available in language are used consistently enough so that meaning can be assigned to them directly. Nevertheless, we do find many important correlations, quite naturally, between syntactic structure and meaning; or, to put it differently, we find that the grammatical devices are used quite systematically. These correlations could form part of the subject matter for a more general theory of language concerned with syntax and semantics and their points of connection.

Appendix I

NOTATIONS AND TERMINOLOGY

In this appendix we shall present a brief account of the new or less familiar notational and terminological conventions that we have used.

A linguistic level is a method of representing utterances. It has a finite *vocabulary* of symbols (on the phonemic level, we call this vocabulary the *alphabet* of the language) which can be placed in a linear sequence to form *strings* of symbols by an operation called *concatenation* and symbolized by + Thus on the morphemic level in English we have the vocabulary elements *the, boy, S, past, come,* etc., and we can form the string *the + boy + S + come + past* (which would be carried by the morphophonemic rules into the string of elements /ðɪbɔ́yz # kéym./) representing the utterance "the boys came." Apart form the phonemic level, we have used italics or quotes for vocabulary symbols and strings of representing symbols; on the phonemic level we suppress the concatenation symbol + and use the customary slant lines, as in the example just given. We use X, Y, Z, W as variables over strings.

Occasionally we use a hyphen instead of the plus sign, to symbolize concatenation. We do this to call special attention to a subdivision of the utterance with which we happen to be particularly concerned at the moment. Sometimes we use wider spacing for the same purpose. Neither of these notational devices has any systematic significance; they are introduced simply for clarity in exposition. In the discussion of transformations, we use the hyphen to indicate the subdivision of a string that is imposed by a certain transformation. Thus when we assert that the question transformation T_q applies in particular to a string of the form

(118) NP − have − en + V (cf. (37 iii))

inverting the first two segments, we mean that it applies, for example, to

(119) they − have − en + arrive.

since *they* is an NP and *arrive* is a V in this string. The transform in this case will be

(120) have − they − en + arrive,

ultimately, "have they arrived?"

A rule of the form $X \rightarrow Y$ is to be interpreted as the instruction "rewrite X as Y," where X and Y are strings. We use parentheses to indicate that an element may or may not occur, and brackets (or listing) to indicate choice among elements. Thus both the rules (121 i) and (121 ii)

(121) (i) $a \rightarrow b\,(c)$
(ii) $a \rightarrow \begin{Bmatrix} b+c \\ b \end{Bmatrix}$

are abbreviations for the pair of alternatives: $a \rightarrow b+c$, $a \rightarrow b$.

The following list gives the page references for the first occurrence of the special symbols other than those mentioned above.

(122)

NP	p. 26	S	p. 39
VP	p. 26	∅	p. 39
T	p. 26	past	p. 39
N	p. 26	Af	p. 39
NP_{sing}	p. 28	#	p. 39
NP_{pl}	p. 29	A	p. 65
[Σ, F]	p. 29	wh	p. 69, fn. 2
Aux	p. 39	Adj	p. 72
V	p. 39	PP	p. 74
C	p. 39	Prt	p. 75
M	p. 39	Comp	p. 76
en	p. 39		

Appendix II

EXAMPLES OF ENGLISH PHRASE STRUCTURE AND TRANSFORMATIONAL RULES

We collect here for ease of reference the examples of rules of English grammar that played an important role in the discussion. The numbers to the left give the proper ordering of these rules, assuming that this sketch is the outline of a grammar of the form (35). The parenthesized number to the right of each rule is the number of this rule in the text. Certain rules have been modified from their forms in the text in the light of subsequent decision or for more systematic presentation.

Phrase Structure:

Σ: # *Sentence* #

F:	1.	$Sentence \rightarrow NP + VP$	(13 i)
	2.	$VP \rightarrow Verb + NP$	(13 iii)
	3.	$NP \rightarrow \begin{Bmatrix} NP_{sing} \\ NP_{pl} \end{Bmatrix}$	(p. 29, fn. 3)
	4.	$NP_{sing} \rightarrow T + N + \emptyset$	(p. 29, fn. 3)
	5.	$NP_{pl} \rightarrow T + N + S$	(p. 29, fn. 3)
	6.	$T \rightarrow the$	(13 iv)
	7.	$N \rightarrow man, ball,$ etc.	(13 v)
	8.	$Verb \rightarrow Aux + V$	(28 i)
	9.	$V \rightarrow hit, take, walk, read,$ etc.	(28 ii)
	10.	$Aux \rightarrow C(M) (have + en) (be + ing)$	(28 iii)
	11.	$M \rightarrow will, can, may, shall, must$	(28 iv)

Transformational Structure:

A transformation is defined by the structural analysis of the strings to which it applies and the structural change that it effects on these strings.

12. *Passive* – optional:
    Structural analysis: $NP - Aux - V - NP$
    Structural change: $X_1 - X_2 - X_3 - X_4 \to X_4 - X_2 + be + en - X_3 - by + X_1$ \hfill (34)

13. T_{sep}^{ob} – obligatory:
    Structural analysis: $\begin{cases} X - V_1 - Prt - Pronoun \\ X - V_2 - Comp - NP \end{cases}$ \hfill (86) \ (92)
    Structural change: $X_1 - X_2 - X_3 - X_4 \to X_1 - X_2 - X_4 - X_3$

14. T_{sep}^{op} – optional:
    Structural analysis: $X - V_1 - Prt - NP$ \hfill (85)
    Structural change: same as 13

15. *Number Transformation* – obligatory
    Structural analysis: $X - C - Y$
    Structural change: $C \to \begin{cases} S \text{ in the context } NP_{sing} - \\ \emptyset \text{ in other contexts} \\ past \text{ in any context} \end{cases}$ \hfill (29i)

16. T_{not} – optional
    Structural analysis: $\begin{cases} NP - C - V \ldots \\ NP - C + M - \ldots \\ NP - C + have - \ldots \\ NP - C + be - \ldots \end{cases}$ \hfill (37)
    Structural change: $X_1 - X_2 - X_3 \to X_1 - X_2 + n't - X_3$

17. T_A – optional:
    Structural analysis: same as 16 \hfill (cf. (45)–(47))
    Structural change: $X_1 - X_2 - X_3 \to X_1 - X_2 + A - X_3$

18. T_q – optional:
    Structural analysis: same as 16 \hfill (cf. (41)–(43))
    Structural change: $X_1 - X_2 - X_3 \to X_2 - X_1 - X_3$

19. T_w – optional and conditional on T_q:
    T_{w1}: Structural analysis: $X - NP - Y$ (X or Y may be null)
    Structural change: same as 18 \hfill (60i)
    T_{w2}: Structural analysis: $NP - X$ \hfill (60ii)
    Structural change: $X_1 - X_2 \to wh + X_1 - X_2$
    where wh + animate noun $\to who$ \hfill (cf. p. 69, fn. 2)
    wh + animate noun $\to what$

APPENDIX II

20. *Auxiliary Transformation* — obligatory:
    Structural analysis: $X - Af - v - Y$ (where Af is any C or is en or ing; v is any M or V, or $have$ or be) (29ii)
    Structural change: $X_1 - X_2 - X_3 - X_4 \to X_1 - X_3 - X_2 \# - X_4$

21. *Word Boundary Transformation* — obligatory:
    Structural analysis: $X - Y$ (where $X \neq v$ or $Y \neq Af$) (29iii)
    Structural change: $X_1 - X_2 \to X_1 - \# X_2$

21. *do — Transformation* — obligatory:
    Structural analysis: $\# - Af$ (40)
    Structural change: $X_1 - X_2 \to X_1 - do + X_2$

Generalized Transformations:

22. Conjunction (26)
    Structural analysis: of S_1: $Z - X - W$
    of S_2: $Z - X - W$
    where X is a minimal element (e.g., *NP*, *VP*, etc.) and Z, W are segments of terminal strings.
    Structural change: $(X_1 - X_2 - X_3; X_4 - X_5 - X_6) \to X_1 - X_2 + and + X_5 - X_3$

23. T_{so}: (48)–(50)
    Structural analysis: of S_1: same as 16
    of S_2: same as 16
    Structural change: $(X_1 - X_2 - X_3; X_4 - X_5 - X_6) \to X_1 - X_2 - X_3 - and - so - X_5 - X_4$
    T_{so} is actually a compound with the conjunction transformation.

24. Nominalizing Transformation T_{to}: (p. 72, fn. 3)
    Structural analysis: of S_1: $NP - VP$
    of S_2: $X - NP - Y$ (X or Y may be null)
    Structural change: $(X_1 - X_2; X_3 - X_4 - X_5) \to X_3 - to + X_2 - X_5$

25. Nominalizing Transformation T_{ing}: (p. 72, fn. 3)
    Same as 24, with *ing* in place of *to* in Structural change

26. Nominalizing Transformation T_{Adj}: (71)
 Structural analysis: of S_1: $T - N - is - A$
  of S_2: same as 24
 Structural change: $(X_1 - X_2 - X_3 - X_4; X_5 - X_6 - X_7) \rightarrow$
  $X_5 - X_1 + X_4 + X_2 - X_7$

Morphophonemic Structure:

Rules (19); (45); p. 58, fn. 8; p. 69, fn. 2; etc.

We thus have three sets of rules, as in (35): rules of phrase structure, transformational rules (including simple and generalized transformations), and morphophonemic rules. Order of rules is essential, and in a properly formulated grammar it would be indicated in all three sections, along with a distinction between optional and obligatory rules and, at least in the transformational part, a statement of conditional dependence among rules. The result of applying all of these rules is an extended derivation (such as (13)–(30)–(31)) terminating in a string of phonemes of the language under analysis, i.e., a grammatical utterance. This formulation of the transformational rules is meant only to be suggestive. We have not developed the machinery for presenting all these rules in a proper and uniform manner. See the references cited in fn. 8, p. 44, for a more detailed development and application of transformational analysis.

BIBLIOGRAPHY

1. Y. Bar-Hillel, "Logical syntax and semantics," *Language* 30.230–7 (1954).
2. B. Bloch, "A set of postulates for phonemic analysis," *Language* 24.3–46 (1948).
3. L. Bloomfield, *Language* (New York, 1933).
4. N. Chomsky, *The logical structure of linguistic theory* (mimeographed).
5. ——, "Semantic considerations in grammar," *Monograph no. 8*, pp. 141–53 (1955), The Institute of Languages and Linguistics, Georgetown University.
6. ——, "Systems of syntactic analysis," *Journal of Symbolic Logic* 18.242–56 (1953).
7. ——, "Three models for the description of language," *I.R.E.Transactions on Information Theory*, vol. IT-2, Proceedings of the symposium on information theory, Sept., 1956.
8. ——, *Transformational analysis*, Ph. D. Dissertation, University of Pennsylvania (1955).
9. ——, with M. Halle and F. Lukoff, "On accent and juncture in English," *For Roman Jakobson* ('s-Gravenhage, 1956).
10. M. Fowler, Review of Z. S. Harris, *Methods in structural linguistics*, in *Language* 28.504–9 (1952).
11. N. Goodman, *The structure of appearance* (Cambridge, 1951).
12. ——, "On likeness of meaning," *Analysis*, vol. 10, no. 1 (1949).
13. ——, "On some differences about meaning," *Analysis*, vol. 13, no. 4 (1953). Both 12 and 13 are reprinted, with an additional note, in *Philosophy and Analysis*, M. Macdonald, editor (New York, 1954).
14. M. Halle, "The strategy of phonemics," *Linguistics Today, Word* 10.197–209 (1954).
15. Z. S. Harris, "Discourse analysis," *Language* 28.1–30 (1952).
16. ——, "Distributional structure," *Linguistics Today, Word* 10.146–62 (1954).
17. ——, "From phoneme to morpheme," *Language* 31.190–222 (1955).
18. ——, *Methods in structural linguistics* (Chicago, 1951).
19. ——, "Cooccurrence and transformations in linguistic structure," *Language* 33. 283–340 (1957).
20. F. W. Harwood, "Axiomatic syntax; the construction and evaluation of a syntactic calculus," *Language* 31.409–14 (1955).
21. L. Hjelmslev, *Prolegomena to a theory of language* = Memoir 7, Indiana Publications in Anthropology and Linguistics (Baltimore, 1953).
22. C. F. Hockett, "A formal statement of morphemic analysis," *Studies in Linguistics* 10.27–39 (1952).

23. ——, *A manual of phonology* = Memoir 11, Indiana University Publications in Anthropology and Linguistics (Baltimore, 1955).
24. ——, "Problems of morphemic analysis," *Language* 23.321–43 (1947).
25. ——, "Two models of grammatical description," *Linguistics Today, Word* 10.210–33 (1954).
26. ——, "Two fundamental problems in phonemics," *Studies in Linguistics* 7.33 (1949).
27. R. Jakobson, "Beitrag zur allgemeinen Kasuslehre," *Travaux du Cercle Linguistique de Prague* 6.240–88 (1936).
28. ——, "The phonemic and grammatical aspects of language and their interrelation," *Proceedings of the Sixth International Congress of Linguists* 5–18 (Paris, 1948).
29. O. Jespersen, *Language* (New York, 1922).
30. F. Lounsbury, "A semantic analysis of the Pawnee kinship usage," *Language* 32.158–94 (1956).
31. B. Mandelbrot, "Simple games of strategy occurring in communication through natural languages," *Transactions of the I.R.E.*, Professional Group on Information Theory, PGIT-3, 124–37 (1954).
32. ——, "Structure formelle des textes et communication: deux études," *Word* 10.1–27 (1954).
33. E. Nida, *A synopsis of English syntax* (South Pasadena, 1951).
34. K. L. Pike, "Grammatical prerequisites to phonemic analysis," *Word* 3.155–72 (1947).
35. ——, "More on grammatical prerequisites," *Word* 8.106–21 (1952).
36. W. V. Quine, *From a logical point of view* (Cambridge, 1953).
37. C. E. Shannon and W. Weaver, *The mathematical theory of communication* (Urbana, 1949).
38. H. A. Simon, "On a class of skew distribution functions," *Biometrika* 42.425–40 (1955).
39. R. S. Wells, "Immediate constituents," *Language* 23.81–117 (1947).

SOME ADDITIONAL BIBLIOGRAPHY ON GENERATIVE GRAMMAR

Bar-Hillel, Y., C. Gaifman, E. Shamir, "On categorial and phrase-structure grammars", *The Bulletin of the Research Council of Israel*, vol. 9F, 1–16 (1960).
Bar-Hillel, Y., M. Perles, E. Shamir, *On formal properties of simple phrase structure grammars*, Technical report no. 4, U.S. Office of Naval Research, Information Systems Branch (July, 1960).
Chomsky, N., "A transformational approach to syntax", *Proceedings of the 1958 University of Texas Symposium on Syntax* (to appear).
——, "On certain formal properties of grammars", *Information and Control* 2.133–67 (1959).
——, "A note on phrase structure grammars", *Information and Control* 2.393–5 (1959).
——, "On the notion 'rule of grammar'", *Proceedings of the symposium on the structure of language and its mathematical aspects*, American Mathematical Society, vol. 12.6–24 (1961).

——, "Some methodological remarks on generative grammar", *Word* 17. 219-239 (1961).

——, "Explanatory models in Linguistics", *Proceedings of the 1960 International Congress on Logic, Methodology and Philosophy of Science*, P. Suppes, editor, (to appear).

Chomsky, N., and M. Halle, *The sound pattern of English* (to appear).

Gleitman, L., "Pronominals and Stress in English Conjunctions" (to appear in *Language Learning*).

——, "Causative and Instrumental Structures in English" (to appear).

Halle, M., *The sound pattern of Russian* ('s-Gravenhage, 1959).

——, "Questions of linguistics", *Nuovo Cimento* 13.494-517 (1959).

——, "On the role of simplicity in linguistic descriptions", *Proceedings of the symposium on the structure of language and its mathematical aspects*, American Mathematical Society, vol. 12.89-94 (1961).

Halle, M., and K. Stevens, "Analysis by synthesis", in: L. E. Woods and W. Wathen-Dunn, eds., *Proceedings of the Seminar on Speech Compression and Processing*, Dec. 1959, AFCRC-TR-'59-198, vol II, paper D-7.

Householder, F., "On linguistic primes", *Word* 15 (1959).

Klima, E. S., "Negation in English" (to appear).

Lees, R. B., *The grammar of English nominalizations*, Supplement to *International Journal of American Linguistics* 26 (1960).

——, "A multiply ambiguous adjectival construction in English", *Language* 36.207-221 (1960).

——, "The English comparative construction", *Word* 17.171-185 (1961).

——, "O pereformulirovanii transformacionnyx grammatik" (to appear in *Voprosy Jazykoznanija 10 # 6* (1961)).

——, "On the So-called 'Substitution-in-Frames' Technique" (to appear in *General Linguistics*).

——, "On the Constituent-Structure of English Noun-Phrases" (to appear in *American Speech*).

——, "Some Neglected Aspects of Parsing" (to appear in *Language Learning*).

——, "The Grammatical Basis of Some Semantic Notions" (to appear in *Proceedings of the Eleventh Annual Round Table Conference*, Georgetown University Monograph Series).

——, "On the Testability of Linguistic Predicates" (to appear in *Voprosy Jazykoznanija 11* (1962)).

——, *Turkish Phonology* (to be published by *Uralic and Altaic Series*, Indiana University (1962)).

——, "A Compact Analysis for the Turkish Personal Morphemes" (to appear in *American Studies in Altaic Linguistics*, Indiana University, (1962)).

Matthews, G. H., "On Tone in Crow", *IJAL* 25.135-6 (1959).

——, "A grammar of Hidatsa" (to appear).

——, "Analysis by synthesis of sentences of natural languages", *Proceedings of the International Conference on Mechanical Translation and Applied Linguistics*, National Physical Laboratory, Teddington.

Smith, C. S., "A class of complex modifiers in English" (to appear in *Language*).

Stockwell, R. P., "The place of intonation in a generative grammar of English", *Language* 36 (1960).

Part II: *Syntactic Structures* after 60 Years

Acknowledgements

The editors would like to thank Norbert Corver for both initiating this project, helping assemble the editorial team and providing useful input to the process of bringing the project to fruition. We would also like to thank Chris Neufeld for taking the mess that we dropped into his lap and returning camera ready, copy and Bob Freidin for looking over that near final version and making us aware of several typos and other errors.

Norbert Hornstein, Howard Lasnik, Pritty Patel-Grosz and Charles Yang

Introduction

Syntactic Structures (SS) needs no introduction. This makes providing one especially challenging. There are at least two reasons why.

First, works that need no introduction are always historically significant, and this often means that people "know" what's in them without having ever actually read them. It is common for such second hand knowledge to be less well grounded than supposed. And this is fortunate for us for it leaves open a useful function for an anniversary work like this one; to align the common wisdom with what is actually in the text.

Second, even given that SS is an important historical work (*the* founding document of the Generative Enterprise), the question remains: what has it done for us lately? Or to state this point more politely: What SS ideas have *current* relevance? Retrospection invites us to look back so that we can see more clearly where we are *now* and a good part of this evaluative exercise consists in seeing how relevant earlier ideas of apparent importance look to us with 20/20 hindsight. So the second function of an anniversary work is to gauge how far the original motivations for the project remain relevant. And, as regards SS, this resolves itself into three judgments: to estimate how well the problems that launched the Generative Enterprise were initially framed, to judge how far we have come in addressing the identified issues, and to evaluate how many of the leading ideas that framed the effort we currently ignore (or have forgotten) to our detriment.

The essays that follow take up these three tasks concisely and elegantly (the contributors really did an excellent job in our modest opinions and we the editors (plus Norbert Corver (the instigator of this volume) definitely deserve kudos for having chosen as wisely as we did). It is amazing (and at times disheartening) to see how many of the important points SS made have still not been fully appreciated (let alone assimilated). Some of us look forward to the day when SS will be a boring read because all of its insights have been fully integrated into the received wisdom. It is also impressive (and heartening) to see how many of the ambitious goals SS set have been successfully realized, albeit (unsurprisingly) in modified form. As the essays highlight, both the general framework ideas that SS outlines and many of the particular analyses it offers still inspire. It is fair to say, we believe, that despite being 60 years old, SS is still a provocative and clarifying book.

Which brings us back to this introduction. As per editors' prerogative, we here make a few brief comments about what we take some of the significance of SS to be. Many of the themes we touch on are investigated more fully in the excellent contributions, which we encourage you all to read carefully. Consider this short note as appetizer.

SS contains many important insights. Here are five.

The first and most important idea centers on the aims of linguistic theory (ch 6). SS contrasts the study of grammatical *form* and the particular internal (empirically to be determined) "simplicity" principles that inform it with discovery procedures that are "practical and mechanical" (56) methods that "*an investigator* (our emphasis) might actually use, if he had the time, to construct a grammar of the language directly from the raw data" (52). SS argues that a commitment to discovery procedures leads to strictures on *grammatical* analysis (e.g. bans on level mixing) that are methodologically and empirically dubious.

The discussion in SS is reminiscent of the well-known distinction in the philosophy of science between the context of discovery and the context of justification. How one finds one's theory can be idiosyncratic and serendipitous; justifying one's "choice" is another matter entirely. SS makes the same point.[1] It proposes a methodology of research in which grammatical argumentation is more or less the standard of reasoning in the sciences more generally: data plus general considerations of simplicity are deployed to argue for the superiority of one theory over another. SS contrasts this with the far stronger strictures Structuralists endorsed, principles which if seriously practiced would sink most any serious science. In practice then, one of the key features of SS lies in its call to linguists to act like regular scientists (in modern parlance, to reject methodological dualism).

We can be more specific. The structuralism that SS is arguing against took as a methodological dictum that the aim of analysis was to classify a corpus into a hierarchy of categories conditioned by substitution criteria. So understood, grammatical categories are classes of words, which are definable as classes of morphemes, which are definable as classes of phonemes, which are definable as classes of phones. The higher levels are, in effect, simple *generalizations* over lower level entities. The thought was that higher level categories were entirely reducible to lower level distributional patterns. In this sort of analysis, there are no (and can be no) theoretical entities, in the sense of real abstract constructs that have empirical consequences but are not reducible or definable in purely observational terms. By arguing against discovery procedures and in favor of evaluation metrics

---

[1] What follows uses the very helpful and clear discussion of these matters in John Collins in *Chomsky: A guide for the perplexed*, 2008, London: Continuum Publishing Group: 26–7.

SS argues for the legitimacy of *theoretical* linguistics.² Or, more accurately, for the legitimacy of *normal* scientific inquiry into language without methodological constrictions that would cripple physics were it applied.

We can put this another way: Structuralism adopted a strong Empiricist methodology in which theory was effectively a summary of observables. SS argues for the Rationalist conception of inquiry in which theory must make contact with observables, but is not (and cannot) be reduced to them. Given that the Rationalist stance simply reflects common scientific practice, SS is a call for linguists to start treating language scientifically and should not hamstring inquiry by adopting unrealistic, indeed non-scientific, dicta. This is why SS (and Generative Grammar (GG)) is reasonably seen as the start of the modern *science* of linguistics.

Note that the discussion here in SS differs substantially from that in chapter 1 of *Aspects*, though there are important points of contact.³ SS is Rationalist as concerns the research methodology of linguists. Aspects is Rationalist as concerns the structure of human mind/brains. The former concerns research methodology. The latter concerns substantive claims about human neuro-psychology.

That said the two conceptions resonate with each other. For example, if discovery procedures fail methodologically, then this strongly suggests that they will also fail as theories of linguistic mental structures. Syntax, for example, is not *reducible* to properties of sound and/or meaning despite its having observable consequences for both. In other words, the Autonomy of Syntax thesis is just a step away from the rejection of discovery procedures. It amounts to the claim that syntax constitutes a viable G level that is not reducible to the primitives and operations of any other G level.

To beat this horse good and dead: SS makes two important points. First, Gs contain distinct levels that interact with empirically evaluable consequences, but they are not organized so that higher levels are definable in terms of generalizations over lower level entities. Syntax is real. Phonology is real. Semantics is real.

---

2 Here is how SS (51) describes the process: "given a corpus and given two proposed grammars G1 and G2, the theory must tell us which is the better grammar of the language from which the corpus is drawn."

3 Indeed, the view in Aspects is clearly prefigured in SS, though is not as highlighted in SS as it is later on (see discussion p. 15).

> ... a grammar mirrors the behavior of speakers who, on the basis of a finite and accidental experience with language, can produce or understand an indefinite number of new sentences. Indeed, any explication of "grammatical in L" ... can be thought of as offering an explanation for this fundamental aspect of linguistic behavior.

Phonetics is real. These levels have their own primitives and principles of operation. The levels interact (and mappings between them), but are ontologically autonomous. Second, some properties of level X are undiscoverable by analyzing the distributional properties of level X-1. So, for example, the fact that a certain sentence *cannot* carry a certain interpretation (though structurally similar ones can) will be very hard to discern by just inspecting the distributional properties of earlier levels of analysis (c.f. discussion of constructional homonymity below).

Given the contemporary obsession with deep learning and its implicit endorsement of discovery procedures, these two points are worth reiterating and keeping in mind. The idea that Gs are just generalizations over generalizations over generalizations that seems the working hypothesis of Deep Learners and others has a wide following nowadays so it is worth recalling the SS lesson that discovery procedures both don't work and are fundamentally anti-theoretical. It is Empiricism run statistically amok!

Let us add one more point and then move on. How should we understand the SS discussion of discovery procedures from an *Aspects* perspective given that they are not making the same point? Put more pointedly, don't we want to understand how a LAD (aka, kid) goes from PLD (a corpus) to a G? Isn't this the aim of GG research? And wouldn't such a function *be* a discovery procedure?

Yes and no. What we mean is that SS makes a distinction that is important to still keep in mind. Principles of the Faculty of Language/Universal Grammar (FL/UG) are not themselves sufficient to explain how LADs acquire Gs. More is required. Here's a quote from SS (56):

> Our ultimate aim is to provide an objective, non-intuitive way to evaluate a grammar once presented, and to compare it with other proposed grammars (equivalently, the nature of linguistic structure) and investigating the empirical consequences of adopting a certain model for linguistic structure, rather than showing how, in principle, one might have arrived at the grammar of a language.

Put in slightly more modern terms: finding FL/UG does not by itself provide a theory of how the LAD actually acquires a G. More is needed. Among other things, we need accounts of how we find phonemes, and morphemes and many of the other units of analysis the levels require. The full theory will be very complex, with lots of interacting parts. Many mental modules will no doubt be involved. Understanding that there is a peculiarly *linguistic* component to this story does not imply forgetting that it is not the whole story. SS makes this very clear. However, focusing on the larger problem often leads to ignoring the fundamental linguistic aspects of the problem, what SS calls "conditions of generality" (50), many/some of which will be linguistically proprietary.[4]

So, perhaps the most important contribution of SS is that it launched the modern science of linguistics by arguing against discovery procedures (i.e. methodological dualism). And sadly, the ground that SS should have cleared is once again full of toxic weeds. Hence, the continuing relevance of the SS message.

Here are four more ideas of continuing relevance.

First, SS shows that speaker intuitions are a legitimate source of linguistic data. The discussions of G adequacy in the first several chapters are all framed in terms of what speakers know about sentences. Indeed, that Gs are models of human linguistic judgment behavior is quite explicit (15):

> … a grammar mirrors the behavior of speakers who, on the basis of a finite and accidental experience with language, can produce or understand an indefinite number of new sentences. Indeed, any explication of "grammatical in L" can be thought of as offering an explanation for this fundamental aspect of linguistic behavior.

Most of the data presented for choosing one form of G over another involves plumbing a native speaker's sense of what is and isn't natural for his/her language. SS has an elaborate discussion of this in chapter 8 where the virtues of "constructional homonymity" (86) as probes of grammatical adequacy are elaborated. Natural languages are replete with sentences that have the same phonological form but differ thematically (*flying planes can be dangerous*) or that have different phonological forms but are thematically quite similar (*John hugged Mary, Mary was hugged by John*). As SS notes (83): "It is reasonable to expect grammars to provide explanations for some of these facts" and for theories of grammar to be evaluated in terms of their ability to handle them.

Note too that SS focuses on two *kinds* of facts relevant to constructional homonymity: why certain sentences *do* mean what they *do* and, just as important (indeed maybe more so) why they *don't* mean what they *don't*. So for example, whereas *the shooting of the hunters* can be understood with *the hunters* shooting something or being shot by someone, *the growing of the flowers* and *the growling of the lions* cannot be. SS relates such differences to the different kernel sentences that the nominalization transformation operates on to derive the three examples.[5]

---

[4] Of course, the ever hopeful minimalist will hope that not very much will be such.
[5] Thus the ambiguity of *the shooting of the hunters* is related to the fact that *the hunters shot someone* and *someone shot the hunters* are both fine kernel sentences in contrast to *someone grew the flowers* vs *the flowers grew something* and *the lions growled* vs *someone growled the lions*.

The details are interesting and important.⁶ But just as critical is SS's identification of the relevance of this dual kind of data. The observation that both positive data and negative data are linguistically relevant to evaluating proposals is still not fully appreciated. Here's an example of the baleful effects of forgetting this observation.

Facts about constructional homonymity are still relevant to "debates" about structure dependence and the poverty of the stimulus, as has been recently highlighted once again in Berwick, Pietroski, Yankama and Chomsky. Linguistic facts go beyond the observation that "such and such a string ... is or is not a sentence" (85). SS warns against forgetting this by showcasing constructional homonymity, and the world would be a better place (or at least dumb critiques of GG would be less thick on the ground) if this warning 60 years ago had been heeded.

Consider now a second critical contribution. By focusing on constructional homonymity, SS identifies a central aim of linguistics as understanding how Gs relate sound and meaning (viz. more specifically thematic roles (though this term is not used)). This places Gs and their structure at the center of the enterprise. Indeed, this is what makes constructional homonymity such an interesting probe into the structure of Gs. There is an unbounded number of these pairings and the rules that pair them (i.e. Gs) are not "visible." This means the central problem in linguistics is determining the structure of these abstract Gs by examining their products. Most of SS exhibits how to do this and the central arguments in favor of adding transformations to the inventory of syntactic operations involve noting how transformational grammars accommodate such data in simple and natural ways.

This brings us to a third lasting contribution of SS. It makes a particular proposal concerning the *kind* of G natural languages embody. The right G involves Transformations (T). Finite State Gs don't cut it, nor can simple context free PSGs. T-grammars are required. The argument *against* PSGs is particularly important. It is not that they cannot generate the right structures but that they cannot do so *in the right way*, capturing the evident generalizations that Gs embodying Ts can do.

Isolating Ts as grammatically central operations sets the stage for the next 60 years of inquiry: specifying the kinds of Ts required and figuring out how to limit them so that they don't wildly overgenerate or misgenerate.

---

6 The point concerning negative data is made forcefully very early on: see p. 15 and the discussion of examples like *the child seems sleeping* and *read you a book on modern music?* These examples contrast with those above in *not* being examples of constructional homonymity. Rather they indicate that grammaticality cannot be reduced to meaningfulness. The indicated examples are fully comprehensible and so their unacceptability must be traced to something other than their semantic viability.

SS also proposes the model that until very recently was at the core of every GG account. Gs contained a PSG component that was instrumental in generating kernel sentences (which effectively specified thematic dependencies) and a T component that created further structures from these inputs.[7] Minimalism has partially stuck to this conception. Though it has (or some versions have) collapsed PSG kinds of rules and T rules treating both as instances of Merge, minimalist theories have largely retained the distinction between operations that build thematic structure and those that do everything else. So, even though Ts and PSG rules are formally the same, thematic information (roughly the info carried by kernel sentences in SS) is the province of E(xternal)-merge applications and everything else the province of I(nternal)-merge applications. The divide between thematic information and all other kinds of semantic information (aka the duality of interpretation) has thus been preserved in most modern accounts.[8]

Last, SS identifies two different but related linguistic problems: finding a G for a particular L and finding a theory of Gs for arbitrary L. This can also be seen as explicating the notions "grammatical in L" for a given language L vs the notion of "grammatical" tout court. This important distinction survives to the present as the difference between Gs and FL/UG. SS emphasizes that the study of the notion grammatical in L is interesting to the degree that it serves to illuminate the more general notion grammatical for arbitrary L (i.e. Gs are interesting to the degree that they illuminate the structure of FL/UG). As a practical matter, the best route into the more general notion proceeds (at least initially) via the study of the properties of individual Gs. However, SS warns against thinking that a proper study of the more general notion must await the development of fully adequate accounts of the more specific.

Indeed, we would go further. The idea that investigations of the more general notion (e.g. of FL/UG) are parasitic on (and secondary to) establishing solid language particular Gs is to treat the more general notion (UG) as the summary (or generalization of) of properties of individual Gs. In other words, it is to treat UG as if it were a kind of Structuralist level, reducible to the properties of individual Gs. But if one rejects this conception, as the SS discussion of levels and discovery procedures suggests we should, then prioritizing G facts and investigation over UG considerations is a bad way to go.

---

[7] This puts some words into SS's mouth. Kernel sentences were products of the PS rules *and* obligatory transformations. Kernel sentences are the closer analogue to later Deep Structures, and they serve to specify what we would now call theta roles, but they are not formally quite identical.

[8] One of the editors, NH, would be remiss if he did not point out that this is precisely the assumption that the movement theory of control rejects.

We suspect that the above conclusion is widely appreciated in the GG community with only those committed to a Greenbergian conception of Universals dissenting. However, the logic carries over to modern minimalist investigation as well. The animus against minimalist theorizing can be understood as reflecting the view that such airy speculation must play second fiddle to real linguistic (i.e. G based) investigations. SS reminds us that the hard problem is the abstract one and that this is the prize we need to focus on, and that it will not just solve itself if we just do concentrate on the "lower" level issues. This would hold true if the world were fundamentally Structuralist, with higher levels of analysis just being generalizations of lower levels. But SS argues repeatedly that this is not right. It is a message that we should continue to rehearse.

The papers gathered here as companions to the re-issued edition of SS discuss these issues and many others. They make a powerful case that SS should still be on most reading lists of graduate level courses in linguistics.

Noam Chomsky
Syntactic Structures. Some retrospective comments

The monograph *Syntactic Structures* was not initially written for publication. It is based on notes for an undergraduate course that I was teaching at MIT. Cornelis van Schooneveld, a Dutch colleague and acquaintance, visited MIT, saw the notes on my desk, and suggested that Mouton, where he was an editor, might be interested in publishing them if I wrote them up, as I did.

The lectures drew from the much more extensive study *Logical Structure of Linguistic Theory*.[1] This was also not intended for publication. It was for my own personal use; a few copies were distributed to friends. Interest in such topics at the time was slight. A draft of *LSLT* submitted to MIT press at Roman Jakobson's suggestion was rejected with the rather sensible comment by reviewers that it did not fall within any recognizable field. That began to change soon after, particularly with the publication of an important review-article by Robert Lees (1957) in *Language*.

SS differed somewhat in orientation from *LSLT* because of the audience. Students in the class were mostly engineers and mathematicians, so the course began with systems and ideas with which they were familiar and that were very much in the air at the time, topics ignored in *LSLT*. The course then moved on to material discussed much more extensively in *LSLT*: phrase structure grammar and its inadequacies, and finally transformational grammar, the framework that seemed to me more appropriate to human language. Technical papers of mine at the same time had basically the same structure and intent.[2]

In the 1950s it was generally assumed in the emerging behavioral and information sciences that human languages fell within a narrow subclass of Markov sources (MS). The grammatical status of an expression, insofar as it was discussed at all, was attributed generally to order of statistical approximation to texts, motivated by Claude Shannon's very significant work; alternatively to substitutability within frames or a semantic property of "meaningfulness" (for example, the influential discussion in Quine (1953)). The early part of the course was therefore devoted to examining these ideas and showing that they cannot be sustained. Showing furthermore that even the much broader class of finite automata (FA)

---

[1] Most of a revised 1956 version was published in 1975: Plenum, Chicago.
[2] Particularly Chomsky (1956).

cannot capture elementary properties of human language; that probabilistic models, while doubtless appropriate for study of acquisition and use of language, do not play the assumed role in determining the grammars of language[3]; and that the substitution-semantic proposals also collapse on investigation.

The course then went on to develop a different model, Phrase Structure Grammar PSG, which overcomes the specific difficulties of MS/FAs, but are still, so I sought to show, inadequate for human language.

The monograph keeps to this structure.

MS/FA and PSG models are flawed in different ways. In the former case, it is easy to show that even *weak generative capacity* cannot be attained by these systems: that is, even the set of strings without structure lies beyond their reach. The argument against PSG, in contrast, relies on deficiencies of *strong generative capacity* (generating the right structures). And more broadly, on what later came to be called *explanatory adequacy*, accounting for the properties of language in ways that meet the norms of the sciences, which seek deeper principles that explain what is observed.

The failure of strong generative capacity of PSG goes beyond what is discussed in *SS* and *TMDL*. It is a failure of principle, as shown by unstructured coordination: e.g., "the man was old, tired, tall, ... , but friendly".[4] Even unrestricted rewriting systems fail to provide such structures, which would require an infinite number of rules.[5] The more serious failure, however, is in terms of explanatory adequacy.

A more fundamental deficiency of then-prevailing approaches, with a long history,[6] is the failure to distinguish between capability and behavior—between competence and performance, in terms later used. MS approaches, for example, are (flawed) models of performance, but they do not seek to elucidate the underlying capacity that enters into the use of language in production and perception. A related deficiency is the failure to distinguish grammaticality from acceptability, the latter involving many factors beyond underlying competence.

These distinctions are crucial. For example, in studying the shared arithmetical capacity of humans, we do not restrict ourselves to investigation of how people multiply numbers in their heads. Rather, we seek to determine the underlying arithmetical knowledge that is only one factor in such performance, along with

---

[3] Though they might play some role. In *LSLT* it is suggested that word boundaries are determined by analysis of transitional probabilities, adapting a proposal of Zellig Harris's for identification of morphemes (which however, unlike words, do not have the required linearity property).
[4] Chomsky (1961, 1963).
[5] Chomsky and Miller (1963) propose a solution in terms of generalized transformations, but it fails, as observed by Lasnik (2011). See Chomsky (2013) for an account in terms of pair-Merge.
[6] For some comment, see Chomsky (2017).

many others: for example, memory limitations, which are not part of arithmetical knowledge.

The study of language envisioned in *LSLT* and *SS* is in this regard analogous to study of arithmetical knowledge. It seeks to determine the internal system of linguistic capacity, shared among humans—"universal grammar" (UG), the term that came to be used, modifying a traditional notion. And concurrently, it studies how this capacity is instantiated in the particular languages (I-languages in current terminology) that are acquired and put to use, interacting with other factors such as, again, memory limitations, another topic that began to be investigated as soon as the crucial concepts and distinctions were clarified: competence-performance, grammaticality-acceptability, and related notions.[7]

These conceptual changes of course relied on the work of the great 20th century mathematicians who established the theory of computability on a firm basis: Gödel, Turing, Post and others, providing tools that could be adapted easily to the purpose at hand.

There has been a good deal of misunderstanding of *SS*, from the outset, perhaps a result of the exposition as class notes. Thus the monograph opens (p. 13) by defining a *language* as a set of sentences, including both natural and formal languages. Hence a fundamental goal of grammar is to distinguish grammatical from ungrammatical sentences. It is, however, immediately pointed out (p. 16) that for natural language this sharp distinction should be modified in favor of levels of "grammaticalness,"[8] a matter discussed later and in considerable detail in *LSLT*. The qualification, irrelevant to the study of formal languages, has often been ignored though it is essential for natural language and is a familiar and important feature of technical work: the distinction between ECP and subjacency violations, for example.

The considerations developed in *LSLT* imply that every expression, even word salad, can be assigned some interpretation, including deviant expressions. Deviant expressions play a significant role in inquiry into the nature of language, as in the ECP-subjacency case. They appear as intermediate stages of perfectly legitimate derivations, as in successive-cyclic movement. They are, furthermore, often used quite appropriately as in many cases that I and others have discussed over the years. There is no problem of "overgeneration," where the term is understood to mean generation of deviant expressions when rules apply freely (as they must, for many reasons). There are problems of truth: the grammar should assign the

---

[7] Miller and Chomsky (1963)
[8] The non-English term "grammaticalness" was selected to make it clear that it is a new technical concept, perhaps a mistake. I will keep here to the familiar "grammaticality".

correct interpretations throughout, including deviant expressions. The proposals of *LSLT* are surely inadequate, later efforts as well. But that is a separate matter.

Related misunderstandings have arisen, from the outset, concerning an illustration that has, for some reason, achieved notoriety:

(1)   colorless green ideas sleep furiously

This is one of a series of examples presented to illustrate the inadequacy of the approaches to grammaticality that were then standard, those mentioned above. This example does suffice to show that all are inadequate, hence its utility as an illustration.

Of course, an interpretation can be assigned to the sentence; rather easily thanks to the fact that it is an instance of the category sequence AANVD (D = adverb), a sequence with many grammatical instantiations. In this as in other respects described, (1) differs from the same string read backwards. In contrast, no interpretation need be constructed to interpret (2), an instance of the same category sequence:

(2)   revolutionary new ideas occur infrequently

The sentence (2) has a literal meaning. It requires no act of the imagination to assign an interpretation (a standard device of poetry, as often discussed in literary theory). That is one reason why the sentence was selected as an illustration.

At once, and often since, alleged refutations have been presented with poems and other imaginative constructions to show that interpretations can be assigned—exactly the point of the example.

Even stranger, perhaps, are efforts to show that if we consider assignment to categories, then it is possible to develop elaborate statistical models that show that the sentence (1) is more "probable" than its inverse—reflecting the reason for the choice of the example as an instance of a grammatical category sequence. These topics are discussed in much more detail in *LSLT*, which suggests a method with an information-theoretic flavor to determine categories (at varying levels of grammaticality). The complex statistical models yield a more confused and arguably worse result than the approach they are presented to refute.[9]

A related misunderstanding is a frequent claim that *SS* rejects statistical/probabilistic approaches to the study of language. The source of this misunderstanding appears to be the statement (p. 16) that "the notion 'grammatical in English' cannot be identified in any way with the notion 'high order of statistical approxi-

---

9 For discussion, see Berwick (2017)

mation to English'." The statement is accurate, and implies no rejection of statistical/probabilistic approaches (see note 3). Similarly, the (accurate) observation that such distinctions as (1) versus (2) cannot be reduced to the semantic distinction ± meaningful has been misinterpreted to imply that semantic considerations are irrelevant to the study of language.

Commonly overlooked are the comments a few paragraphs later on "the undeniable interest and importance of semantic and statistical studies of language," with some illustrations, and the further comment that "One might seek to develop a more elaborate relation between statistical and syntactic structure than the simple order of approximation model" that was standard at the time.

Much more significant than misinterpretations such as these is the common conclusion that the basic problem with the simple models rejected in *SS* is failure of weak generative capacity—or for that matter even strong generative capacity, though that has been much less discussed. Again, the basic thrust of *SS*, *TMDL*, and other work of mine and others, then and since, is the problem of explanatory adequacy: to what extent can we provide real explanations of why languages have the specific properties they do: the properties of displacement and structure-dependency, to take two examples discussed early on that have been a central research topic since, yielding (in my opinion) considerable understanding, particularly in recent years.[10]

In the 1950s, what is now called "biolinguistics" was just beginning to take shape, and by the time *SS* appeared there were a few publications in the works suggesting how the framework might be pursued; and soon after, publications of Eric Lenneberg began to appear, leading to his classic work founding modern biology of language.[11] As this perspective developed, new issues began to take center stage, specifically learnability and evolvability. These developments provide a broader framework for the kind of work outlined in *SS* and *LSLT*, with many important results since and exciting prospects for the future of the disciplines in which language plays a central role, much as a long and rich tradition anticipates.

---

10 For some recent reviews, see Chomsky (2016), Berwick and Chomsky (2016).
11 Chomsky 1959; Lees 1957; Lenneberg 1964, 1967. Much of this work grew out of the interests of a small group of Harvard graduate students in the early 1950s who were dissatisfied with the prevailing behavioral science doctrines (Lenneberg, Chomsky, Morris Halle, a few friends).

Bibliography

Berwick, Robert. 2017. Revolutionary new ideas appear infrequently. In *Syntactic Structures after 60 Years: The Impact of the Chomyskan Revolution in Linguistics*, ed. Norbert Hornstein, Howard Lasnik, Pritty Grosz-Patel, and Charles Yang. Berlin: De Gruyter.
Berwick, Robert, and Noam Chomsky. 2016. *Why Only Us*. Cambridge, MA: MIT Press.
Chomsky, Noam. 1956. Three models for the description of language. *IRE Transactions on Information Theory* 2:113–124.
Chomsky, Noam. 1959. A review of B.F. Skinner's *Verbal Behavior. Language* 35:26–58.
Chomsky, Noam. 1961. On the notion 'rule of grammar'. In *Structure of Language and its Mathematical Aspects*, ed. Roman Jakobson. Providence, RI: American Mathematical Society.
Chomsky, Noam. 1963. Formal properties of grammars. In *Handbook of Mathematical Psychology 2*, ed. R.D. Luce, R.R. Bush, and E. Galanter. New York, NY: Wiley.
Chomsky, Noam. 2013. Problems of projection. *Lingua* 130:33–49.
Chomsky, Noam. 2016. *What Kinds of Creatures are We?*. New York, NY: Columbia University Press.
Chomsky, Noam. 2017. The Galilean Challenge. *Inference* 3.
Chomsky, Noam, and George Miller. 1963. Introduction to the Formal Analysis of Natural Languages. In *Handbook of Mathematical Psychology 2*, ed. R.D. Luce, R.R. Bush, and E. Galanter. New York, NY: Wiley.
Lasnik, Howard. 2011. What Kind of Computing Device is the Human Language Faculty? In *The Biolinguistic Enterprise: New Perspectives on the Evolution and Nature of the Language Faculty*, ed. A. M. di Sciullo and C. Boeckx. Oxford, UK: Oxford University Press.
Lees, Robert B. 1957. Review of *Syntactic Structures. Language* 33:375–408.
Lenneberg, Eric. 1964. Language disorders in childhood. *Harvard Educational Review* 34:152–177.
Lenneberg, Eric. 1967. *Biological Foundations of Language*. New York, NY: Wiley.
Miller, George, and Noam Chomsky. 1963. Finitary models of language users. In *Handbook of Mathematical Psychology 2*, ed. R.D. Luce, R.R. Bush, and E. Galanter. New York, NY: Wiley.
Quine, Willard Van Orman. 1953. *From a Logical Point of View*. Cambridge, MA: Harvard University Press.

Howard Lasnik
Syntactic Structures: Formal Foundations

Chomsky's 1955 *The Logical Structure of Linguistic Theory* (henceforth LSLT) laid out in great detail the formal foundations for a new way of looking at language scientifically. This awesome accomplishment was announced to the world in *Syntactic Structures* (henceforth SS; Chomsky 1957). The core formal syntactic theory of SS is essentially that of LSLT, since the former was based on his teaching notes for the latter. Many of the differences that do arise do so just because SS is simplified, sometimes substantially, to fit the material into a small book (or, indeed, into a one semester course at MIT).

The initial formal discussion in SS, centered on finite state Markov processes, is actually totally independent of LSLT. There is no discussion at all of such devices in LSLT. They are discussed in SS as they are the most limited computational machine capable of capturing one of the most fundamental properties of human languages—infinity. Markov processes with 'loops' can generate infinite languages. In SS, Chomsky shows the inadequacy of Markov processes, even with loops added, for languages with certain kinds of recursion, in particular those with dependencies nested within dependencies of essentially the same type. I note in passing that Markov processes can characterize certain dependencies with an unbounded amount of material between the dependents. For example, the following language is trivially finite state:

(1) This woman really is a good student
    This woman really really is a good student
    etc.

(2) The women really are good students
    The women really really are good students
    etc.

The subject agreement dependency here can be Markov-captured even though there is no limit on the number of *really*s between the agreeing elements. But when dependencies are nested within dependencies, we move beyond the bounds of finite state description. Chomsky gives some formal languages on the alphabet { a,b } as representative examples:

(3) ab, aabb, aaabbb, etc.

(4) aa, bb, abba, baab, aaaa, bbbb, aabbaa, abbbba, and, in general, all and only sentences consisting of a string X of as and bs followed by the 'mirror image' of X.

Both of these languages are beyond the bounds of finite state description. Chomsky then gives some templates for fragments of English that he suggests illustrate this kind of situation:

(5) If S_1, then S_2

(6) Either S_3 or S_4

(7) The man who said that S_5, is arriving today

Here the dependencies are between *if* and *then*, *either* and *or*, and *man* and *is* (cf. *men ... are*). Crucially, as Chomsky notes, each of S_1 to S_5 can contain another dependency of these types, and so on. This renders these constructions non-finite state derivable.

A certain irony arises in Chomsky's discussion at this point in SS, in fact two ironies. Chomsky observes that descriptive inadequacies of this sort do not arise with (more powerful) description in terms of systems of phrase structure rewrite rules (called by Chomsky Σ, F grammars). While (3) and (4) are, indeed, straightforwardly characterizable with Σ, F grammars, it is rather unlikely that (5–7) are. The way classic context-free nested dependencies like those in (3) and (4) are generated is by having each *a* or *b* in the first half of the sentence introduced along with the corresponding one in the second half by exactly the same occurrence of the same rewrite rule. For instance, language (3) is generated by the following grammar:

(8)   Σ: Z
        F: Z → ab
        F: Z → aZb

In any given sentence of the language, the first *a* is introduced simultaneously with the last *b*, then the second *a* with the penultimate *b*, and so on. This yields phrase structures such as:

(9)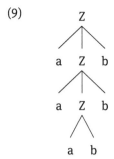

However, it is difficult to imagine linguistically plausible structures for (5–7) that have the mutually dependent items as siblings, that is, simultaneously introduced by the same operation of the same rewrite rule. To the extent that this is true, these phenomena are not just beyond the bounds of finite state description, they are also beyond the bounds of Σ, F description. This specific inadequacy lies in the realm of what Chomsky (1965) called 'strong generative capacity.'

The second irony involves a somewhat arbitrary limitation that LSLT imposes on Σ, F modules of human language grammars. The theory of human language grammar that Chomsky assumes in SS, following the one articulated in great detail in LSLT, restricts the power of the Σ, F module in precisely such a way that it cannot handle the phenomena discussed just above. In particular, the theory explicitly and completely disallows recursion in this module (pp. 517–519). In this model, the infinitude of human languages is the responsibility of generalized transformations—operations melding separate phrase markers together into one phrase marker. Though LSLT had indicated that the restriction constituted a simplification, Chomsky didn't actually offer any arguments to that effect. One might actually argue that removing this restriction is a simplification. After all, it seems to be a stipulation. Further, while trivial, it is not always simple to determine whether there is recursion in the base. Certainly, the determination is simple if there is a rule like (10):

(10) A → BA

But recursion might involve a pair of rules rather than any one rule:

(11) A → BC
      C → DA

Or a trio:

(12) A → BC
      C → DE
      E → FA

In fact, there is no limit on how large the minimal group of rules might be that yields recursion.

Chomsky (1965) claimed, contrary to his position in LSLT, that the theory of transformational grammar is simplified by *allowing* recursion in the Σ, F component, the simplification being that the notion 'generalized transformation' is eliminated entirely, at no apparent cost. Thus, in place of three kinds of syntactic operations—Σ, F rules, singular transformations (those operating on a single tree), and generalized transformations—we have just the first two. Further, the construct 'Transformation-marker' (a history of the transformational derivation) is eliminated, as its major work was to show exactly how the separate trees combine into one, but now that is transparently represented in the initial phrase marker, the 'deep structure.' Of course in Minimalism, generalized transformations (instances of 'external merge') are back with a vengeance. They are now responsible for *all* structure building, not just the combination of sentential phrase markers. The reply to the Chomsky (1965) simplicity argument is that we still just have two kinds of syntactic operations: generalized transformations (external merge) and singular transformations ('internal merge'). Σ, F rules are gone. In fact, the situation might be better still. Chomsky (1995) suggested in his footnote 13 that the two kinds of operations are both instances of the same basic operation, Merge. This has become a standard view, so we are down from three syntactic operations to one.

The SS presentation of formal limitations of finite state description included, in addition to (3) and (4) above (classic context free languages), a language that is not Σ, F generable, i.e., is not context free:

(13) aa, bb, abab, baba, bbbb, aabaab, abbabb, ..., and in general, all sentences consisting of a string X of *as* and *bs* followed by the identical string *X*, and only these.

Here, in place of the unbounded nested dependencies we saw above, we have unbounded cross-serial dependencies, exactly what context free rewriting systems cannot handle. The fact that some cross-serial dependencies do arise in English provides part of the motivation in SS for adding transformations to the theory of syntax, where a transformation relates one phrase structure representation to another. It is interesting to observe a striking difference in the SS treatments of Markov process limitations and Σ, F limitations. In the latter instance, the response was to add onto the insufficient device another device, transformations, so the resulting theory has both devices. Not so for the former, in which case the insufficient device is simply banished, possibly not the correct move, as discussed in Lasnik and Uriagereka (2012).

What is an initial phrase structure representation? Though this aspect of the formal machinery of LSLT is not stated explicitly in SS, the model is set theoretic (rather than, say, graph theoretic). The initial phrase structure representation of a sentence U (its 'phrase marker') given a particular Σ, F grammar G is constructed as follows. The Σ, F grammar comprises a designated initial symbol, or set thereof, (Σ), and a set of rewrite rules (F), which consist of one symbol on the left, followed by an arrow, followed by at least one symbol. Symbols that appear on the left side of arrows are non-terminal symbols. Those that appear only on the right are terminal symbols. A *derivation* consists of a series of lines such that the first line is one of the designated initial symbols, and the procedure for moving from one line to the next is to replace exactly one symbol by the sequence of symbols it can be rewritten as. For all but the most trivial grammars, there will be multiple *equivalent* derivations for any particular string, where two derivations are equivalent if and only if they involve the same rewrite rules the same number of times, but not necessarily in the same order. The phrase marker of the produced terminal string is the set of all strings occurring in any of the equivalent derivations. For illustrative purposes, I give a toy example:

(14) Σ: S
F: S → NP VP   NP → Mary   VP → V   V → laughs

This grammar generates one sentence:

(15) Mary laughs

The equivalent derivations of (15) are in (16)

(16) S   S   S
      NP VP   NP VP   NP VP
      Mary VP   NP V   NP V
      Mary V   NP laughs   Mary V
      Mary laughs Mary laughs   Mary laughs

The phrase marker (PM) is in (17)

(17)   { S, NP VP, Mary VP, Mary V, NP V, NP laughs, Mary laughs }

This suffices to capture what LSLT and SS took to be the essence of phrase structure, the 'is a' relations between portions of the terminal string and single non-terminal symbols. *Mary* is an NP, *laughs* is a V and a VP, *Mary laughs* is an S. A familiar graphic representation of this PM is the phrase structure tree in (18).

(18)
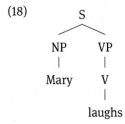

It is worth noting that a set theoretic representation of the sort in (17) has strictly less information than a graph like (18). For instance, the set is neutral between several graphs, including (18) and (19).

(19)
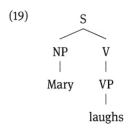

I will return to this difference between the two kinds of representations. But first, another difference. Consider a slightly augmented grammar and a slightly more complicated sentence:

(20)   Σ: S
       F: S → NP VP   NP → Mary   NP → John   VP → V
          VP → V NP   V → laughs   V → likes

(21)   Mary likes John

In familiar tree form, we have:

(22)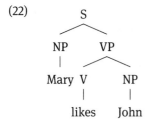

Notice that a constituent, e.g. VP here, is a sub-structure of the whole structure, a sub-tree of the tree. Consider now the LSLT/SS type set theoretic PM for (21) given grammar (20):

(23) { S, NP VP, Mary VP, NP V NP, Mary V NP, NP V John, Mary V John, NP likes NP, Mary likes NP, NP likes John, Mary likes John }

A set representing the phrase structure of the VP would be (24):

(24) { VP, V NP, V John, likes NP, likes John }

But there is no subset of (23) even remotely resembling (24). This case is completely representative. Thus, as discussed by Lasnik and Stone (2016) and by Stone (2017), the notion 'sub-structure' is surprisingly difficult to capture in a set-theoretic model like that in LSLT/SS, or the somewhat revised one in Lasnik and Kupin (1977).

The presentation of transformations in SS is rather informal. Especially with respect to 'structural change' (what the transformation does), it is just shorthand, not actually specifying, as the fuller presentation in LSLT does, the particular operation being performed, but rather just the revised sequence of terms. For expository purposes, I present here a slightly simplified version of the SS analysis of English verbal inflectional morphology (for my money, the single best syntactic analysis of anything ever), beginning with a fragment of the Σ, F module, then proceeding to the transformational module, where the terms are set off by hyphens. It is important to note, by the way, that in this model all the symbols are atomic. NP looks like it is complex, containing N, similarly for VP, etc. But this is illusion. NP, and all the other phrasal nodes, are single unanalyzable symbols, not decomposable into finer categories, and certainly not into distinctive features. This made many generalizations (such as VPs always contain Vs) difficult or impossible to state. This began to be rectified in Chomsky (1965), and the program was carried much further in Chomsky (1970) with the development of $\overline{\text{X}}$-theory. Note also that the rules introducing terminal symbols like *hire* are of exactly the same type as those introducing phrasal symbols like VP. Given that the Σ, F component was stipulated to be context free, this made the statements of lexical differences (transitive vs. intransitive, etc) extremely cumbersome to state. This too changed in Chomsky (1965) with the introduction of a lexicon and a separate component of lexical insertion transformations.

(25) Σ: Sentence
F:
Sentence → NP VP
NP → John   [Simplifying, to keep the set theoretic phrase marker (PM) from getting too unwieldy]
NP → Mary
VP → Verb NP
Verb → Aux V
Aux → C(Modal)(have en)(be ing)
C → past   [Simplifying again, for the same reason]
V → hire

(26)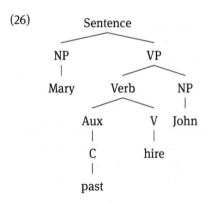

(27) { S, NP VP, NP Verb NP, NP Aux V NP , NP C V NP, NP past V NP, John VP, etc., etc., etc. }

(28) T_{not} — optional
Structural analysis:
$$\left\{\begin{array}{l} NP - C - V \ldots \\ NP - C + M - \ldots \\ NP - C + have - \ldots \\ NP - C + be - \ldots \end{array}\right\}$$
Structural change: $X_1 - X_2 - X_3 \rightarrow X_1 - X_2+n't - X_3$ [This is intended to be right adjunction of *n't* to the 2nd term of the SA.]

(29) T_q — optional [Interrogation "Subject Aux Inversion"]
Structural analysis: same as T_{not}
Structural change: $X_1 - X_2 - X_3 \rightarrow X_2 - X_1 - X_3$ [This is intended to be permutation of the 1st and 2nd terms of the SA.]

The SA of (28) and (29) (and a third related T as well) is interestingly different from that of the large majority of the transformations in SS and LSLT. Overwhelmingly, the transformations display a property later called 'structure dependence'. In particular, it is *constituents*, units of structure, that are manipulated. This is why SS claims that "... the behavior of a sentence under transformation provides valuable, even compelling evidence as to its constituent structure." (p.81) A fundamental way of enforcing structure dependence is to require that the terms in the SA of a transformation are single symbols. And generally they are, but this set of transformations do not conform. For the second, third, and fourth disjuncts, the second term is a *sequence* of two symbols (which, in general, do not even form a constituent). Beginning in the mid 1960's, a variety of proposals appeared that had the effect of combining the first auxiliary verb with the tense node into a single constituent. That single constituent could then be the target of transformations in a structure dependent way.

Continuing with the transformations in this fragment, we have:

(30) Auxiliary Transformation ("Affix Hopping") — obligatory
Structural analysis: $X - Af - v - Y$ (where Af is any *C* or is *en* or *ing*; v is any *M* or *V*, or *have* or *be*.) [This is a family of 20 SAs; the 2nd term is a disjunction of 5 items (past, S, ∅, *en*, *ing*), and the 3rd a disjunction of (M, V, *have*, *be*).]
Structural change: $X_1 - X_2 - X_3 - X_4 \rightarrow X_1 - X_3 - X_2\# - X_4$ [This is intended as right adjunction of the 2nd term to the 3rd, and insertion of # (word boundary).]

(31) Word Boundary Transformation — obligatory
Structural analysis: X — Y (where X≠v or Y≠Af)
Structural change: $X_1 - X_2 \rightarrow X_1 - \#X_2$

(32) do-Transformation — obligatory
Structural analysis: # — Af
Structural change: $X_1 - X_2 \rightarrow X_1 - do+X_2$

(31) and (32) together are trying to say that *do* gets left adjoined to an affix that has failed to hop.[1]

To determine applicability of T (30) to PM (27), find a member of the latter that satisfies the SA of the former, where satisfaction is identity for a constant and where any string, including the null string, satisfies a variable. For example, 'NP past V NP' satisfies the SA of the T, so it can apply (and being obligatory, it must). The past morpheme will then right adjoin to V.

Suppose, though, we had first applied (29) to (27), giving a derived PM that can be graphically represented as:

(33)
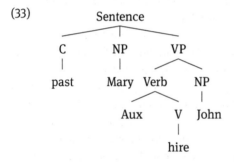

There is no member of the new derived PM that satisfies (30). Any string in the set that contains *past* followed by V has intervening symbols. But (30) crucially has no variable between its 3rd and 4th terms, so adjacency is required. Failure of (30) to apply sets the stage for (31) and (32), ultimately deriving:

(34) Did Mary hire John

Similarly, with WH-questions, SAI blocks Affix Hopping and triggers the supportive *do* complex. (The wh-movement transformation essentially takes a wh-

---

[1] They don't quite say it, even apart from the issue of the operation not being specified. See Lasnik (1981), Lasnik (1995) and Lasnik (2000) for discussion

expression anywhere in the PM and permutes it with the preceding string, whatever that string might be.)

(35) Who did Mary hire

(36)
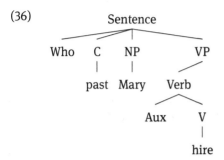

Chomsky in SS raises the interesting question of why supportive *do* isn't triggered when it is a subject that is questioned:

(37) Who hired John

He presents a very clever analysis where SAI takes place, in this case as usual separating past from *hire*, seen in (38). But then wh-movement effectively undoes what SAI did, making the affix and verb adjacent once again, possibly as seen in (39).

(38)
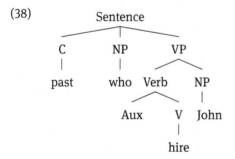

(39)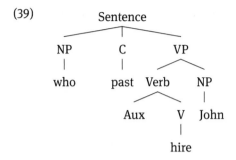

But there is a problem in taking the set graphically represented as (39) as input to (30). The SA of that T is not satisfied; there is no member of the set graphically represented in (39) that has *past* immediately followed by V. Any string with *past* and V will have Aux intervening. I used to think that Chomsky might have tacitly intended one of the 'pruning' conventions of the type later suggested by Ross (1967), in particular, the one eliminating any non-terminal symbol that ceases to dominate any terminal symbols, so Aux in (39). And, in fact, Chomsky (personal communication) indicated that he might have had that in mind, though he can't remember for sure. However, Max Papillon (personal communication) points out that that is not necessary. First, note that there is a general principle of transformational operation in LSLT that when a symbol is mentioned in a T, anything affecting that symbol will affect everything it dominates. This is generally so obvious that it hardly bears mentioning. For example, when a rule moves NP, it takes along the contents of that NP as well, or when SAI applies, affecting C in a case like (33) or (38), of course it doesn't move just C. Rather, it moves C and what C dominates, here *past*. But, as hinted at above, and discussed by Lasnik and Kupin (1977), in set-theoretic models like that in LSLT or Lasnik and Kupin (1977), non-branching domination is *symmetric*. There is no way to define 'dominates' so that C dominates *past* but *past* does not dominate C. Similarly, Papillon observes, in a structure like that graphically represented in (33), C also dominates Aux. Hence, the familiar trees above, arising from ones with Aux not branching, are all incorrect. (38) should, instead, be (40) (or, of course, any of the five other possibilities with Aux, C, and past in domination relation with each other).

(40)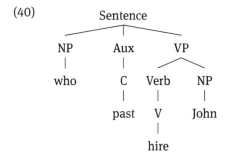

But then, we exactly obtain Chomsky's desired result. Wh-movement has, in fact, restored string adjacency between *past* and V, allowing Affix Hopping to take place. In some instances, this results in structurally surprising derived PMs, such as (41), or any of the five other equivalent ones, from Affix Hopping (but, of course, only when there is no branching),

(41)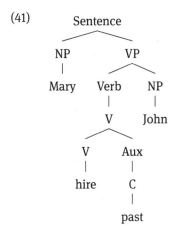

This looks peculiar, but I don't know of any wrong results that it predicts.

Since all the examples we have been considering involve the application of multiple transformations, it is important to indicate how this can be possible. This question arises because transformations are defined to apply to phrase markers, and phrase markers emerge from Σ, F derivations. Thus, once a transformation has applied, we no longer have a phrase marker. If we are ever to be able to construct a non-trivial transformational derivation, the result of applying a transformation must then be of just the same formal character as a phrase marker. There are principles of derived constituent structure in LSLT (presupposed in SS) that guarantee this.

The derivations in LSLT/SS generally have a strongly Markovian character, in that the applicability of a given transformation depends only on the current (derived) phrase marker. The set of transformations constitute a strict linear ordering, successively altering the phrase marker. But there is occasional 'globality'. For instance, T_W, which is responsible for WH-interrogatives, is flagged as "conditional on T_q". This means that even if the current PM satisfies the SA of the T, the T can only apply if earlier in the derivation T_q had applied. This is needed to rule out (42).

(42)   * Who Mary will hire   [c.f. Who will Mary hire]

The T-marker can provide this kind of information, but it is very seldom called upon. Interestingly, six decades later, I'm not sure there is a really satisfying analysis of (42).

The transformational component in SS seems somewhat ancient in consisting of many specific strictly ordered transformations, each stipulated as optional or obligatory, rather than the modern one or two very general ones (optional in GB, obligatory, in essence, under Minimalism). On the other hand, the modular character of the transformations has a bit of a current feel. For example, the interrogative and negation transformations given above are in part, but only in part, responsible for sentences like *Did Mary hire John* and *Mary didn't hire John*. This is so because those Ts set the stage for the insertion of supportive *do*, but don't in themselves effect it. There is a separate transformation for that. This means that all of the mentioned Ts can be kept relatively simple. Further, a huge generalization is captured: Whenever Affix Hopping is blocked, supportive *do* appears. Additional cases are the elliptical *Susan didn't hire John but Mary did hire John* and the WH-interrogative *Who did Mary hire*. Another instance of this kind of simplifying modularity is negative questions like *Didn't Mary hire John*. There is no negative question transformation, because we get such sentences for free by the interaction of the independently necessary interrogative, negation, and *do* transformations. All of these interestingly contrast with the strongly non-modular treatment of passive sentences. There are three clusters of properties distinguishing simple English passives from actives: passive morphology on the main verb, thematic object appearing in subject position, and displacement of subject into a PP headed by *by*. The Passive T in SS performs all these operations. Chomsky (1965) took steps towards modularizing passives, and Chomsky (1970) went much further. Chomsky (1981) completed the process.

The theoretical edifice built on the LSLT/SS foundation has undergone extensive revision over the years. Some of that edifice is hardly recognizable anymore. But much of it remains. All of the following are as important to transformational grammar as they were at their introduction sixty years ago: structure; abstract underlying structure; singular and generalized transformations; derivations. Any transformational grammarian (even any syntactician) has much to gain from investigating that foundation.

Bibliography

Chomsky, Noam. 1955. The Logical Structure of Linguistic Theory. MS, MIT.
Chomsky, Noam. 1957. *Syntactic Structures*. The Hague, The Netherlands: Mouton de Gruyter.
Chomsky, Noam. 1965. *Aspects of the Theory of Syntax*. Cambridge, MA: MIT Press.
Chomsky, Noam. 1970. Remarks on nominalization. In *Readings in English Transformational Grammar*, ed. R.A. Jacobs and P.S. Rosenbaum, 184–221. Waltham, MA: Ginn-Blaisdell.
Chomsky, Noam. 1981. *Lectures on Government and Binding*. Dordrecht, The Netherlands: Foris.
Chomsky, Noam. 1995. Bare phrase structure. In *Government and Binding Theory and the Minimalist Program*, ed. Gert Webelhuth, 383–439. Oxford, UK: Wiley-Blackwell. [Also in Evolution and revolution in linguistic theory: Essays in honor of Carlos Otero, eds. Hector Campos and Paula Kempchinsky. Washington D. C. : Georgetown University Press].
Lasnik, Howard. 1981. Restricting the theory of transformations: A case study. In *Explanation in Linguistics*, ed. Norbert Hornstein and David Lightfood, 152–173. London, UK: Longmans. [Reprinted in *Essays on restrictiveness and learnablity*, Howard Lasnik, 125-145. Dordrecht: Kluwer, 1990].
Lasnik, Howard. 1995. Verbal morphology: *Syntactic structures* meets the Minimalist Program. In *Evolution and revolution in linguistic theory: Essays in honor of Carlos Otero*, ed. Héctor Campos and Paula Kempchinsky, 251–275. Washington, DC: Georgetown University Press. [Reprinted in Howard Lasnik, *Minimalist analysis*, 97-119. Oxford: Blackwell, 1999].
Lasnik, Howard. 2000. *Syntactic Structures revisited: Contemporary lectures on classic transformational theory*. Cambridge, MA: MIT Press.
Lasnik, Howard, and Joseph J. Kupin. 1977. A restrictive theory of transformational grammar. *Theoretical Linguistics* 4:173–196. [Reprinted in Essays on restrictiveness and learnablity, Howard Lasnik, 17-41. Dordrecht: Kluwer, 1990].
Lasnik, Howard, and Zach Stone. 2016. Rethinking phrase structure. MS, University of Maryland, College Park.
Lasnik, Howard, and Juan Uriagereka. 2012. Structure. In *Handbook of Philosophy of Science Volume 14: Philosophy of Linguistics*, ed. Ruth Kempson, Tim Fernando, and Nicholas Asher, 33–61. Amsterdam, The Netherlands: Elsevier.
Ross, John Robert. 1967. Constraints on variables in syntax. Doctoral Dissertation, MIT, Cambridge, MA. Published as *Infinite Syntax!* Norwood, N.J.: Ablex (1986).
Stone, Zach. 2017. The spatial structure of minimalist syntax. MS, University of Maryland, College Park.

David Adger
The Autonomy of Syntax

1 Introduction

Chomsky's 1957 *Syntactic Structures* is, more or less throughout, an argument for the existence of syntax as both necessary for a full account of language, and as independent of other aspects of language. The book begins with arguments that the phenomenon of grammaticality cannot be explained by appeal to either probabilistic or semantic factors, and it ends with an argument that a theory of grammaticality can nonetheless provide a serious foundation for understanding questions of meaning.

This idea of the autonomy of syntax is fundamental to the generative perspective on language, but is often misunderstood. It does not entail that grammaticality is cut off from either probability or meaning. Rather it says that syntax cannot be reduced to either of these.

I think it's fair to say that the agenda laid out in *Syntactic Structures* has proved robust in both of these domains. There is no current theory of linguistics that takes human syntactic capacities to be reducible to general probabilistic relations between elements of unanalysed data, and the various research efforts into the nature of syntax have borne fruit in terms of a rich understanding of many questions of semantics that were unaskable beforehand (Portner and Partee, 2002).

Beyond the claims about autonomy of syntax from statistics and semantics in the initial and final chapters, a further argument is given in the central analytical section of *Syntactic Structures*, Chapters 3 through 7, for a different but equally important notion of autonomy.

This argument is based on analytical success. It says: here is a theory of some important and complicated facts about a human language (English). This language has certain properties that are best captured by a fundamentally computational model that defines an unbounded collection of hierarchically organized structures for English sentences at a number of different levels. It is therefore profitable to think of English as involving a system of that sort. Systems of this sort (finite devices that specify an infinite structured output) are generative grammars. Therefore the best theory of English incorporates a generative grammar. Further, the generative grammar given in *Syntactic Structures* for English is a more empirically successful theory than its competitors, and so the basic notion of an autonomous system of rules should be taken seriously. This is the notion of autonomy that Chomsky later explicitly sketched in 1982 (Chomsky et al., 1982): syntax as a computational system that interfaces with both semantics and phonology but whose functioning (that is the computations that are allowed by the system) is not affected by factors external to it.

In this paper I reprise the arguments for an autonomous syntactic component given over 60 years ago in the context of more recent research, and I evaluate whether current conceptions of syntax in the Minimalist Program are consistent with the position laid out then.

2 Grammaticality and probability

Chapter 2 of *Syntactic Structures*, titled "The Independence of Grammar", asks the question of how to go about separating grammatical sequences of elements from ungrammatical ones. The fundamental task the book engages with here is an explication, in theoretical terms, of an intuitive notion of grammaticality. Of course there is an existential presupposition buried in this task: that there is something in human language that the intuitive notion of grammaticality corresponds to—that is, that grammaticality is a real phenomenon. The chapter argues that there is indeed a notion of grammaticality because sentences of a language like English have properties that cannot be reduced to what is observed, and cannot be explained by what what is meaningful, or by what has a high order of statistical approximation to a language.

Chomsky very briefly first makes the point that the notion of grammatical sentence cannot be identified with a particular finite collection of utterances, as any grammar has to go beyond what has been observed to new utterances that are not in a specified finite corpus. This brief comment is actually fundamental to the argument made in Chapters 3 through 7 of *Syntactic Structures*, as it makes generativity a central desideratum for a theory of grammaticality. If a grammar has to go beyond a corpus, then it is not a list, so the question arises as to what sort of a thing it is. An obvious candidate is that a grammar specifies the legitimacy of sequences of linguistic elements. But then we need some notion of 'legitimate'. Chomsky identifies two candidates—that the sequence is some level of statistical approximation to the corpus, or that the legitimacy of the sequence is defined in terms of a notion of significance. He shows that both are inadequate, and suggests a solution that takes the grammar not to determine legitimate sequences, but rather legitimate structures. But this requires a generative grammar, defined in terms that are not reducible to statistical approximation to a language or in terms of meaningfulness.

Chomsky's argument against defining grammaticality in terms of statistical approximations to English is fundamentally an argument against an approach to language that stems from Shannon's work. Shannon (1948) provided a series of texts whose $(k+1)^{th}$ symbol was determined by a probability appropriate to the preceding k symbols. If the symbols are words, then the higher order approximations begin to look more and more like English. For example, Miller and Chomsky (1963) give the following 5th order approximation (that is with quintuples of words where the frequency of the transition between one word and the next in the sequence are representative of an extant corpus of English):

(1)   road in the country was insane especially in dreary rooms where they have some books to buy for studying Greek

Chomsky argues, however, that a Shannon-style notion of statistical approximation to English for a given sequence cannot be identified with the notion of grammaticality. Using the (now) famous pair of sentences in (2), he pointed out that both would be ruled out as being equally far from a statistical approximation to English. An approach along such lines would collapse impossible sentences and sentences with extremely low probability into a single class.

(2)   a.   Colorless green ideas sleep furiously.
        b.   Furiously sleep ideas green colorless.

Later work, however, (for example Pereira 2000), has shown that one can in fact treat both sequences of words as having calculable probabilities. Pereirra uses a statistical bigram model, where the probabilities are calculated by a method that includes a hidden variable encoding the class that the first word falls into, which conditions the likelihood of the second word. This allows the model to assign probabilities to pairs of words that don't exist in the training corpus. This, Pereira argues, sidesteps Chomsky's concern. Using this method, Pereira shows that the grammatical sequence in (2a) has a much higher total probability than the ungrammatical sequence in (2b) (setting aside, of course, cases where they are used in discussions of linguistics). Lappin and Shieber (2007) argue that Pereira's work indicates that "information theoretical approaches to modeling grammar are not vulnerable to the simple arguments for rich innate structure" widely accepted since *Syntactic Structures*.

However, no one (and I include Pereira, and Lappin and Shieber here) thinks that a bigram model smoothed in this way could serve as as a statistical model for grammaticality. Further, Chomsky's argument here is not for "rich innate structure".

His argument is simply that the two sentences will be treated as having the same *kind* of status by a statistical model, though they behave quite differently phenomenologically. As *Syntactic Structures* points out, native speakers read the examples with different intonation and have different capacity to recall them. Miller and Isard (1963) showed that humans can more easily pick out examples like (2a) from examples like (2b) in noisy environments. More recent work (Pallier et al. 2011) has shown that different neural structures are recruited when sequences like (2a) are encountered from those that are activated by ungrammatical sequences like (2b).

Further, recent work in Artificial Language Learning provides a new argument against the idea that our knowledge of grammar is stored via knowledge of the likelihood relations between words. Culbertson and Adger (2014) presented subjects with an online task of learning an artificial language, where the word order was distinct from English, but the lexical items were identical. Subjects were presented with a noun followed by one modifier (a demonstrative, or an adjective, or a numeral). Once subjects had learned this, they were asked to translate phrases with two modifiers into this language, requiring them to extend their knowledge beyond what they had evidence for. If they were storing their knowledge of order by transitional probabilities sensitive to syntactic class, then the prediction would be that they should preserve as much of the word order of English as possible. So they should favor examples like *boxes three big* or *balls those four*, since that would preserve the transitional probabilities between numerals and adjectives and between demonstratives and numerals. If they stored their knowledge structurally, in terms of what categories are closer to the noun, irrespective of sequence, then they should favor *boxes big three* and *balls four those*, as these preserve the closeness of the categories to the noun that we see in English. Culbertson and Adger showed that their subjects overwhelmingly preferred the latter kind of response, making the storage of ordering information as transitional probabilities between words or classes very unlikely. The online experiments have since been replicated in the lab, and are currently being extended to speakers whose first languages have other orders.

The crucial point made in *Syntactic Structures*, which remains true to this day, is that, as far as a statistical model is concerned, grammatical strings and ungrammatical strings are treated as phenomenologically the same, differing only in likelihood; as far as human interpreters and producers of language are concerned, however, they behave as though they are different kinds of thing. In order to capture this difference, a statistical model would have to somehow be mapped to a model of something which, in the end, amounts to grammaticality.

Syntactic Structures also provides a second argument against probabilistic models. This argument turns on the long distance nature of linguistic dependencies. If we examine a sentence with a relative clause attached to the subject, the question is how to capture the relationship between the grammatical number of that subject and a following auxiliary verb. Chomsky gives

(3)   The man who ... are here.

Chomsky points out that examples like (3) raise a logical problem. There is no limit to the size of the relative clause that can be inserted where ... appears in (3), yet the sentence will remain ungrammatical nevertheless. A bigram, trigram, *n*-gram model, no matter how extended, is unable to capture this true fact about the grammar of English, as any value of *n* will be finite. Chomsky's conclusion is, again, that we need an independent model of syntactic structure to capture dependencies that are, in linear terms, unbounded.

Recent work using Recurrent Neural Networks (RNNs) which have a Long Short-Term Memory (LSTM) architecture (of the sort recently released by Google) have proved impressive in their capacity to capture long-distance statistical regularities in texts. RNNs can extract statistical regularities across vast datasets; unlike *n*-gram models, they do not impose any specific limit on the distance between elements in the dependency, which means that they don't suffer the same logical problem that Chomsky pointed out. With the LSTM architecture, RNNs remember information that has already been encountered. Can these address the worry laid out 60 years ago in a footnote in *Syntactic Structures*, using only statistical properties of sequences to explicate the notion of grammaticality?

Linzen et al. (2016) tested such a model on exactly the type of phenomenon Chomsky raised: number agreement. They found that a LSTM neural net could succeed on a number of cases where NPs of a different number intervened between the head of the subject NP and the agreeing verb.

(4)   a.   The only championship **banners** that are currently displayed within the *building* **are** for national or NCAA Championships.
      b.   Yet the **ratio** of *men* who survive to the *women* and *children* who survive **is** not clear in this story.

Intuitively, and somewhat simplifying, these networks are tracking the likely statistical regularities between particular nouns and verbs (basically how likely it is that the noun is a subject of the verb—what linguists would think of as semantic selection) and then that information is used to key the likelihood of matching for number.

The model succeeds pretty well on most examples that Linzen et al. tested it on that involved simple subject verb agreement, but, of course, for the purposes of Chomsky's argument, the crucial cases are where there is an unbounded dependency between the head noun and the verb. When the network was tested on relative clauses without complementizers, in examples like (5), it failed on a quarter of the cases.

(5) The **landmarks** this *article* lists here **are** also run-of-the-mill and not notable.

Moreover, for cases where there were intervening NPs between the head noun of the subject and the agreeing verb, as in (4) and (5), the model only achieved any measure of success when it was explicitly trained on the relevant data. The training of the network effectively provided explicit information as to where the verb would be (hence what the likely syntactic boundaries were) and that the important property of the verb was its grammatical number. Because grammatical information was explicitly fed into the network, it is an unlikely model for human language acquisition. When Linzen et al. used weaker supervision methods, for example, just training the network on whether a sentence was grammatical or ungrammatical, error rates rose substantially.

More relevant to the arguments made in *Syntactic Structures* is how the model behaved when it was unsupervised. In a pure language modeling task, with no grammatical information fed into the network, the network failed miserably, doing worse than chance. This suggests that it was actively tracking the properties of the irrelevant intervening NPs as opposed to learning anything about what the subject of the sentence is and its role in triggering agreement on the main verb. Of course, it is such a pure language modeling task that would identify the notion of grammatical sentence with probable sentence, and even with sophisticated neural net models, it seems that Chomsky's point from six decades ago still holds strong. Human beings don't seem to work in the way that statistical models do.

It is true that humans do, in production and in comprehension tasks, make errors somewhat like those made by Linzen et al.'s network. Bock and Miller (1991), and substantial follow-up research (Bock et al., 2001), demonstrate that people make "agreement attraction" errors, where the main verb agrees with the number of a linearly preceding noun which is not the head of the subject:

(6) The key to the cabinets are on the table

However, there are quite substantial differences between the behavior of human subjects and the RNN models tested by Linzen et al. Whereas the RNN models show a substantial effect of whether the intervening noun is in a PP or a relative clause, humans show no such effect (Linzen et al., 2017). Wagers et al. (2009) further argue that the attraction effect can be detected in sentence comprehension in ungrammatical, but not in grammatical sentences. This, they argue, suggests that it is a real-time processing effect, as opposed to being baked into the representation of linguistic information.

Further, the existence of agreement attraction errors actually strengthens Chomsky's argument for distinguishing grammaticality from probability. Agreement morphology is particularly fragile in language change (Ferguson, 1996). If there is no independent notion of grammaticality, then the combination of the fragility of agreement in historical change, the existence in the input of agreement attraction errors like (6), and the putative probabilistic nature of the grammar, should lead us to expect the historical development of systems of agreement in natural languages that are organized via a principle of contiguity: always agree with the immediately preceding NP. This is clearly the default behavior for the RNN network. But human languages just don't work like that. There are special cases where verbs agree with an adjacent NP, such as in first conjunct agreement (Aoun et al., 1999; Munn, 1999), but no language known organizes its agreement system in the way that would make things easy for an RNN.

This is essentially the flip side of Chomsky's argument in *Syntactic Structures*, but it also makes the case for autonomy. We now have a Goldilocks argument: probabilistic models are at once too powerful and not powerful enough. On the one hand, even RNNs augmented with the LSTM architecture are incapable of learning that grammatical agreement obtains between the head of a subject and the verb, irrespective of intervening material. On the other, many statistical models can easily learn all sorts of dependencies that we simply don't find in human languages. Ergo, grammatical capacity is a distinct system from statistical capacities.

However, one should not therefore dismiss the importance of work on probabilistic models. Chomsky's arguments are fundamentally that grammaticality cannot be identified with the probability of a sequence, so something more than that is needed. The crucial point is really about the inadequacy of sequences as a fundamental data structure for grammaticality; even when augmented with probabilistic information, they are still the wrong kind of basis for a theory language. Rather than sequences, Chomsky argues that the grammar must generate structures. Without doubt humans are sensitive to probabilities of words in contexts, and probabilistic models can provide insight into our use of language, in acquisition, in processing (Bod et al., 2003) and in broader contexts, such as sociolinguistic aspects of language (Labov, 2001). However, the usefulness of probabilistic information is orthogonal to whether sequences augmented with such information are a basis for grammaticality. It transpires that they are not.

3 Grammaticality and meaning

Chapter 2 of *Syntactic Structures* also provides two brief arguments that the notion "grammatical" cannot be identified with "meaningful" or "significant". Chomsky was reacting here to Quine's claim that linguists need to solve the "problem of defining the general notion of significant sequence." (Quine, 1953, page 53). Of course, Quine is in some sense correct—it is important for linguists to develop a theory of linguistic meaning—but Chomsky's point was that in order to address Quine's problem, we cannot assume some notion of "significance" in advance. Rather, the way to proceed is to work out a notion of grammaticality, and from there determine a theory of meaningfulness.

The first argument Chomsky gives is again on the basis of *Colorless green ideas sleep furiously* and its reversal. While neither is "significant" in any sense that Quine would accede to, they are clearly distinct in nature. We can see this even with a more minor modification of Chomsky's examples:

(7) a. Colorless green ideas sleep furiously.
     b. *Colorless green ideas sleeps furiously.

The difference in acceptability between the two examples here cannot be tied down to "significance" or meaningfulness in any obvious sense. It follows that we cannot identify the notion of grammatical sentence with that of significant sequence.

The other side of this argument is the contrast between cases where the meaning of a sequence of words is obvious by analogy with closely related sequences, but, irrespective of our ability to assign meaning, we still want to say that a sequence of words is ungrammatical.

(8) a. The book seems interesting.
     b. *The child seems sleeping.

Since (8b) is intuitively unacceptable as an English sentence, but perfectly interpretable on analogy with (8a), again there is a need to appeal to grammaticality as something distinct from meaningfulness.

The conclusions of these arguments have been broadly accepted in linguistics. Newmeyer, in a series of publications (e.g. Newmeyer 1983, Newmeyer 1998), has provided a huge range of examples which bolster both lines of argument. For example, the close paraphrase relation between (9a) and (9b) is irrelevant to the passivizability of one and not the other:

(9) a. Anson likes Lilly.
   b. Anson is fond of Lilly.

(10) a. Anson is liked by Lilly.
   b. *Anson is fonded (of) by Lilly.

What would a theory that denies the autonomy of syntax from semantics look like and how could it tackle the kinds of problems raised by examples like these? Cognitive Grammar (Langacker, 1987), and the closely related Cognitive Construction Grammar (Goldberg, 2003), approach this problem by combining statistical learning methods with rich semantic representations which, though innate, are not language specific, rather they are derivative of cognition general mechanisms and representations. The approach these theories take to Chomsky's arguments are that, while grammaticality cannot be reduced to either statistical pattern matching methods or to semantics, the combination of the two is sufficient to provide an explication of grammaticality.

For example, Langacker (2008) addresses (7) by arguing that the various words in the sequence are the phonological 'poles' of symbolic units whose semantic 'poles' are interwoven via learned associations. Langacker calls these learned relationships "constructional schemas", and argues that they are abstracted from encounters of occurring expressions through a cognition general process. The reason that the (b) example in (7) is ungrammatical is because the patterns in the sequence do not conform to any constructional schemas. In contrast, the (a) example in (7) does conform to the relevant constructional schemas. However, inconsistencies at the semantic level lead to a difficulty in assigning a coherent meaning to the whole.

We've already seen the challenges that non-adjacency in agreement raises for general pattern matching schemes: they do not learn the correct information to capture grammatical dependencies in even something as simple as subject-verb agreement. However, Langacker's system (and Goldberg's) adds semantic information to statistical processing. This semantic information is derived from the innate cognitive structure of the human mind interacting with experience, so the innate structure can be used to constrain the hypotheses that the probabilistic learning mechanism can use. Following Quine, these theories are "knowingly and cheerfully up to [their] neck[s] in innate mechanisms of learning readiness" (Quine 1969). One such innate mechanism is the undoubtedly important Figure

Ground relation (Talmy 1975), which underpins the difference between subjects and objects in these theories. The Figure (which Langacker calls the Trajector) corresponds to what traditional grammar would identify as the subject, and subject-verb agreement springboards off of this non-linguistic cognitive representation. This allows such theories to take the head noun in the subject to be the element which is involved in the agreement relationship—which is then just a conventionalization of the relationship between the cognitive semantic representations and the morphophonological form, with no autonomous syntactic level between them.

However, I think it's clear that Chomsky's judgment about the impossibility of building a theory of syntax on semantic grounds still holds. Indeed, work in generative grammar over the decades since has revealed many reasons to understand certain semantic phenomena as supervening on syntactic structure. Without an independent syntactic representation, no amount of rich innate semantic structure is sufficient to explain how language works.

Let us take, for example, the case of the relationship between quantified NPs and pronouns that they are semantically construed with, such as classical cases of bound variable anaphora (Reinhart, 1976). Adger and Svenonius (2015) use these to argue for the superiority of a structural over a semantic account.

(11) No woman denies that she has written a best selling novel.

Here the pronoun *she* can be construed as being bound by the quantifier phrase *no woman*. Certain kinds of relationship between the quantifier and the pronoun make this reading impossible.

(12) A man who no woman likes denies that she has written a best selling novel.

Here the quantified NP is embedded inside a relative clause. In such circumstances, the meaning where the quantifier binds the pronoun vanishes. This effect is cross-linguistically widespread (Déchaine and Wiltschko, 2014) and experimentally robust (Kush et al., 2015). The current consensus in syntactic theory is that this phenomenon is best explained by specifying a relationship between semantic scope and binding along the following lines (Barker, 2012; Safir, 2004):

(13) The Scope Generalization: For a quantifier to bind a pronoun it must scope over that pronoun.

Scope, in such theories, is constrained by syntax. In many languages, including English, a quantifier cannot scope outside of a finite clause. Since *no woman* is in a finite embedded relative clause in (13), it cannot scope at the matrix clause level and hence cannot take scope over the pronoun *she*. (13) therefore accounts for (12), when combined with a specification of what scopal freedom a language allows its quantifiers.

There is good evidence going beyond languages like English that a quantifier's ability to bind a pronoun tracks its ability to scope over the pronoun, and that scopal freedom is fixed differently in different languages, depending on the syntactic mechanisms of the language.

In Chinese, for example, the particle *dou* appears in the clause where an associated quantifier takes its scope. In (14), *dou* appears inside a relative clause, together with its associated quantifier phrase *meige ren*, 'every man'. Since *dou* marks the scope of that quantifier phrase as falling inside the relative clause, the Chinese example works just like English. The quantifier cannot scope outside of the relative clause, and a bound variable interpretation of the pronoun *ta* is impossible (Huang, 1982).

(14) meige ren dou shoudao de xin shangmian you ta taitai
 every man DOU receive DE letter top have he wife
 de mingzi
 DE name

 'The top of the letter that every man received has his wife's name (on it).'

However, the syntax of Chinese allows more freedom in how quantifiers scope than the syntax of English does. While in English a quantifier cannot scope outside of a relative clause, in Chinese a quantifier scopes just where *dou* tells it to. That is, *dou* marks the scope of its associated quantifier phrase, even when *dou* appears in the main sentence, rather than in the relative clause. This may be because finiteness is the crucial factor and finiteness differs in Chinese and English or it may be that the quantifier in Chinese is really *dou*, and that the apparent quantifier phrase just functions as a modifier of *dou* (extending the proposals in Shimoyama 2006). In any event, when *dou* appears in the main sentence, it marks the scope of the quantifier phrase embedded inside the relative clause as being the whole sentence, rather than just that relative clause. As predicted, the pronoun *ta* can now receive a bound variable meaning:

(15) meige ren shoudao de xin shangmian dou you ta taitai
    every man receieve DE letter top   DOU have he wife
    de mingzi
    DE mingzi

    'For each person, the tops of the letters he received have his wife's name on them'

The Chinese facts strongly support the Scope Condition, as the pronoun in (14) and (15) can only receive a bound variable interpretation when the quantifier scopes over it, as marked by the grammatical position of *dou*. They also strongly support the notion that scope is (morpho)-syntactically determined.

The Scope Condition is empirically solid across languages where the bound variable anaphora phenomenon is detectable and it is a condition that connects semantics to syntactic structure, and ultimately, phonological form. To the extent that it is correct, it would have to be learned, in a system like Langacker's, as a constructional schema. However, this strains credulity, as an identical abstract principle would have to be learned across a whole range of unrelated languages with quite different word order properties. The scopal behavior of quantifiers is also not obviously detectable from surface word order properties, so it is unclear how the phonological poles of the relevant constructional schemas could ever be learned.

An alternative is to provide a solution to the phenomenon that denies the relevance of the Scope Condition and builds an explanation of the facts on purely semantic grounds. This tack is taken by van Hoek (1996), who argues that whether a pronoun can be bound is dependent on the salience or prominence of the quantifier. Van Hoek defines salience in terms of a Figure Ground relationship, where the Figure is always more salient and can act as the "binder." Adger and Svenonius (2015) argue, however, that this approach does not fare well empirically. Talmy (2000) defines Figure Ground in the following way:

(16) a. The Figure is a moving or conceptually movable entity whose path, site, or orientation is conceived as a variable, the particular value of which is the relevant issue
    b. The Ground is a reference entity, one that has a stationary setting relative to a reference frame, with respect to which the Figure's path, site, or orientation is characterized

Adger and Svenonius give numerous cases where the subject of a sentence is the Ground, rather than the Figure but, counter to the expectations of a theory like van Hoek's, this does not impact on the distribution of bound variable anaphora.

For example, the verb *contain*, by definition, has a Figure as object and Ground as subject. If the Figure is always salient, van Hoek's system incorrectly predicts the wrong binding possibilities:

(17) a. Each book contains its author's biography as an initial chapter.
b. *Its initial chapter contains a synopsis of each book.

Examples of this kind, with the verb *contain*, also raise problems for approaches like that of MacWhinney (1977), where the notion of 'perspective' is used as a constraint on how various kinds of dependencies are learned. MacWhinney uses perspective to provide a non-syntactic, cognitive grounding to effects that are handled in generative grammar through structural command. For MacWhinney, linear and semantic factors intertwine with processing effects to determine which NP is prominent in the sentence for various apparently grammatical effects. Typically, the perspective holder is an initial NP. However, to handle cases like (17), some special statement about English needs to be made (essentially that the structural subject always ends up being the holder of the perspective irrespective of semantic considerations), which obviously recreates a space for autonomous structure. Languages like Palauan are also problematic for such an approach, which favors a semantic and linear explanation over a structural one. Palauan has VOS order, but disallows binding from the initial object, even when it is human, to the following subject (Georgopoulos, 1989, p202):[1]

(18) *temengull   er   a   rebek el 'ad   a   retonari   er   tir
     3pl.respect   P   every person   neighbors   P   their
for 'Their$_i$ neighbors respect everyone$_i$'

In (18), the universal quantifier *rebek el 'ad* is the object of the verb, but, in MacWhinney's approach it is an Initial NP (as it is processed first) and it is human, and so should serve as a perspectival centre. However, (18) shows that it still cannot bind the pronoun in the subject. This is straightforward to capture in a structural account, which constrains the scope of the quantifier to its c-command domain. Since the object is inside the VP, it cannot c-command the subject. Such an analysis makes the further prediction that if we can move the object to a higher

---

[1] The particle *a* marks NPs and is unglossed, P glosses a preposition-like element that, roughly, appears with human/specific object and possessive NPs.

position, it will be able to c-command the subject. This prediction is borne out, but is difficult to handle in a perspective based account, as no perspective changes[2].

(19)   rebek el 'ad   a   longull   er   tir   a   retonari   er   tir
       every person   3.respect   P   them   neighbors   P   their
       for 'Their$_i$ neighbors respect everyone$_i$'

When the object is placed to the left of the verb as a topic, leaving behind a resumptive pronoun, it can now bind into the subject, so that the reading is 'For every person, their neighbours respect them.' In MacWhinney's system, topics cannot act as binders, as they are semantic scene setters, as opposed to perspectival centres.

I have chosen here to look at two of the best developed accounts I know of which attempt to tackle binding effects in frameworks that do not have an autonomous syntactic component. These are serious attempts to address phenomena that have been discovered in generative grammar, and neither, I think, is successful. The need for an independent notion of grammaticality, and hence a theory of that phenomenon, stands firm.

4 (Some) semantics supervenes on syntax

Chomsky returns to the question of the independence of grammar in Chapters 8 and 9, which argue for an architecture where certain types of meaning supervene on grammar as opposed to underpinning it. Chapter 8 on "The explanatory power of linguistic theory" is about how a grammar which makes no reference to meaning in the rules it uses to define the grammaticality of sentences can nonetheless provide explanations of certain apparently semantic facts: why certain sentences are ambiguous while other similar ones are not, why certain collections of sentences whose members are quite distinct nevertheless share a core of meaning. Theories which capture such facts should, Chomsky suggests, be highly valued:

---

[2] For completeness sake, I should note that a subject cannot bind into the object in Palauan either, unless it is moved rightwards. Georgopoulous takes this to show that both structural and linear factors are relevant to the explanation. Of course, this still implies that one needs a structural account.

> ... we should like the syntactic framework of the language that is isolated and exhibited by the grammar to be able to support semantic description, and we shall naturally rate more highly a theory of formal structure that leads to grammars that meet this requirement more fully.
> *Syntactic Structures*, p102.

Chapter 9 "Syntax and Semantics" uses these results to argue that the fundamental question about the relationship between syntax and semantics is not whether semantic properties enter into syntax, but rather how the independently motivated syntactic devices are put to use for semantic purposes. As Chomsky puts it in the concluding summary chapter:

> More generally, it appears that the notion of "understanding a sentence" must be partially analyzed in grammatical terms. To understand a sentence it is necessary (though not, of course, sufficient) to reconstruct its representation on each level, including the transformational level where the kernel sentences underlying a given sentence can be thought of, in a sense, as the 'elementary content elements' out of which this sentence is constructed. In other words, one result of the formal study of grammatical structure is that a syntactic framework is brought to light which can support semantic analysis. Description of meaning can profitably refer to this underlying syntactic framework, although systematic semantic considerations are apparently not helpful in determining it in the first place.
> *Syntactic Structures*, p102.

We have come a long way in providing a grammatical basis for meaning. Much of the last half century in formal linguistics has been focussed on how syntactic form feeds meaning, and a great deal is now known about this. In addition to providing a basis for understanding ambiguity, synonymy and entailment, which were the notions under the spotlight in *Syntactic Structures*, work in formal semantics following on from Montague's work (Montague, 1974), with its focus on truth conditions, brought to light new methods for connecting syntax and certain parts of the theory of meaning. Emmon Bach, in his *Informal Lectures on Formal Semantics*, frames the relationship between generative syntax and formal semantics elegantly: while Chomsky put forward the hypothesis that natural languages could be described as formal systems, Montague proposed that they could be described as compositionally interpreted formal systems (Bach, 1989). The interaction between these two theses led to an explosion of research that showed how seemingly intractable puzzles in the meaning of languages could be addressed. For example, *Syntactic Structures* had proposed that the kernel sentences could be thought of as 'elementary content elements', but this conception raised some serious puzzles about how to calculate the meanings of combinations of these elements. Many of these puzzles could be given elegant solutions by using techniques from formal semantics that amounted to treating these elementary elements as having variables in them that could then be connected with other structures in more complex sentences (Hall Partee, 1975). The "striking correspondences between the structures and elements that are discovered in formal, grammatical analysis and specific semantic functions" (*Syntactic Structures, p101*), have, over the decades, become more striking and more compelling.

The success in building a theory of meaning that supervenes on a generative syntactic system might seem, at first blush, to raise the question of the autonomy of this system. In *Syntactic Structures* various grammatical elements were argued to lack meaning, including the infinitival marker *to* and the dummy support verb *do*. However, Stowell (1982) showed that *to* does carry some meaning (a kind of modal interpretation), while most current theories of *do*-support take it to involve an extra-syntactic morphological rule (Embick and Noyer, 1999). Indeed, if, as Berwick and Chomsky (2016) propose, the computational system of human language (the autonomous syntactic system) is a perfect solution to interfacing with the semantic systems of thought, one might expect a kind of isomorphism in this area.

Something along these lines is, if not a consensus, at least a major research area in the field today. There is wide, though not universal, acceptance of Borer's arguments that syntactic information should be taken out of lexical items and that a great deal of meaning should be stated in terms of the structure, as opposed to the content of lexical items (the exoskeletal mode of explanation—Borer 2003). Papers in theoretical syntax proposing various functional categories with syntactic effects typically (though not always) also provide a way of compositionally calculating their semantic effects. Chomsky's notion of Full Interpretation, its implementation via interpretable vs uninterpretable features, and the idea that syntactic dependencies have the consequence of eliminating the latter, lead to syntactic representations which are isomorphic with certain aspects of meaning (Chomsky, 1995). In what sense, then, is the system autonomous?

One area of autonomy in such a system might be that the organization of functional categories with respect to each other in an extended projection (Grimshaw, 2005) must be given as an independent syntactic stipulation, disconnected from semantics (Cinque, 2013). I think that this is a currently a minority perspective. Though little is known about how the categories in an extended projection are motivated by conceptual factors, there have been significant proposals. For example, following, ultimately, the lead of Ernst (1998), Ramchand and Svenonius (2014) propose that the reason that C contains T, which in turn contains v, is due to a kind of semantically based mereology of propositions, situations and events. Particular categories in the clause function to transition between these aspects of the semantics of a proposition. In such a proposal the building up of syntactic structure is simultaneously the building up of some aspects of semantic structure.

There are also other ways of conceiving of the reasons for why elements in an extended projection appear where they do, however, that sustain the notion of an autonomous structure building system interacting intimately with systems of thought and meaning, while being quite distinct from them. Take an example like the following:

(20) a. Those three green balls
b. *Those green three balls

As is well known, the order of the demonstrative, numeral and descriptive adjective in a noun phrase follows quite specific typological patterns arguing for a hierarchy where the adjective occurs closest to the noun, the numeral occurs further away and the demonstrative is most distant (Cinque, 2005; Greenberg, 1963). Why should this be? It seems implausible, for this phenomenon, to appeal to a mereological semantic structure. I'd like to propose a different way of thinking about this that relies on the way that a purely autonomous syntax interfaces with the systems of thought.

Imagine we have a bowl which has red and green ping pong balls in it. Assume a task (a non-linguistic task) which is to identify a particular group of three green balls. Two computations will allow success in this task:

(21) a. select all the green balls
b. take all subsets of three of the output of (a)
c. identify one such subset

(22) a. take all subsets of three balls
b. for each subset, select only those that have green balls in them
c. identify one such subset

Both of these computations achieve the desired result. However, there is clearly a difference in the complexity of each. The second computation requires holding in memory a multidimensional array of all the subsets of three balls, and then computing which of these subsets involve only green balls. The first simply separates out all the green balls, and then takes a much smaller partitioning of these into subsets involving three. So applying the semantic function of color before that of counting is a less resource intensive computation. Of course, this kind of computation is not specific to color—the same argument can be made for many of the kinds of properties of items that are encoded by intersective and subsective adjectives.

If such an approach can be generalized, then there is no need to fix the order of adjectival vs. numeral modifiers in the noun phrase as part of an autonomous system. It is the interface between a computational system that delivers a hierarchy, and the use to which that system is put in an independent computational task of identifying referents, plus a principle that favors systems that minimize computation, that leads to the final organization. The syntax reifies the simpler computation via a hierarchy of categories. This means that one need not stipulate the order in UG, nor, in fact, derive the order from the input. The content and hierarchical sequence of the elements in the syntax is delivered by the interface between two distinct systems. This can take place over developmental timescales, and is, of course, likely to be reinforced by the linguistic input, though not determined by it. Orders that are not isomorphic to the easiest computations are allowed by UG, but are pruned away during development because the system ossifies the simpler computation. Such an explanation relies on a generative system that provides the structure which the semantic systems fill with content.

The full ordering of the content of elements in a syntactic hierarchy presumably involves a multiplicity of sub ordering effects, some due to differences in what variable is being elaborated as in Ramchand and Svenonius's proposal, others, if my sketch of an approach to the noun phrase is correct, due to an overall minimizing of the computation of the use of the structure in referring, describing, presenting etc. In this approach, the job of the core syntactic principles is to create structures which have an unbounded hierarchical depth and which are composed of discrete elements combined in particular ways. But the job of populating these structures with content is delegated to how they interface with other systems.

How does this impact on the autonomy thesis? If all of the content of the categories that syntax works with are co-opted from other systems of thought, to what extent is syntax autonomous?

The answer to this involves recognizing two distinct areas where autonomy is relevant. One is related to the point made in the body of *Syntactic Structures*, that a generative system is required for a good explanation of syntactic phenomena, and that that system operates in a particular way, manipulating categories via their form, and not their meaning. This is autonomy of structure building.

In *Syntactic Structures* the structure building system is intimately tied to the system of categories, but that is clearly not necessary. Chomsky (1970) largely separates off the categories from the component of the grammar that licenses structure (X-bar theory), and recent approaches to bare phrase structure do this even more radically, by taking Merge to build uncategorized structures, with a distinct labelling algorithm doing the job of providing the categories (Chomsky, 2013). Adger (2013) goes further, labelling structures exocentrically via independently specified extended projection information (assumed to be derivable in the ways just discussed). This theoretical bifurcation opens up the second area of autonomy: autonomy of content. To what extent are the categories involved in labelling autonomously generated syntactic structures themselves specialized to syntax.

It is certainly the case that not every conceptual category is used in grammar. Cross-linguistic work in typological linguistics as well as in generative grammar identifies, over and over again, the same set of grammatically active categories. This is recognized by functional theorists as well as generative ones. For example Talmy (1985) remarks:

> There are many characteristics of an event's participants that are not marked anywhere in the verb complex, even though they seem as reasonable (from an a priori perspective) as the qualities that are marked. Thus, while an argument's numerosity and distribution can be marked, there will be no marking for its color or whether it has a symmetrical arrangement, even though these very qualities are important in other cognitive systems, such as visual perception. (p.134).

Similarly, many languages have miratives, where a verbal form grammatically expresses that the speaker's attitude to the proposition they are making is one of surprise, but no language has a 'solicitative', marking that the speaker is worried about the situation. Cinque (2013) provides a range of similar examples and asks the crucial question: "To say that the external and internal temporal constituency of an event (tense and aspect) or the attitude of the speaker toward the truth of the proposition (mood) are cognitively salient is beside the point. The question remains why these and only these cognitive distinctions are encoded grammatically in natural languages out of the many other salient ones." His conclusion is that UG determines what conceptual categories are grammatically encoded.

On similar lines, Hale (1986) argues that it it possible to have complete control of the grammar and phonology of a language without knowing the smallest thing about the worldview of the speakers of the language. Cultural concepts that may strongly influence how speakers of a language live their lives every day are not coopted into grammar. The way that a culture dissects the world can be embedded in the words of a language, in the myths told in the language, in idioms and turns of phrase, but grammar, and phonology, are disconnected from worldview. Hale discusses the philosophy of the Warlpiri aboriginal people of the central western parts of Australia's Northern Territory and identifies a theme, which he terms 'the logic of eternity'. This is a worldview that sees time in cyclical, rather than linear, terms and appears in many ways in how the Warlpiri conceive of objects in the world. For example, entities are thought of as persisting, even when they are transformed: an entity is just the current incarnation of something that is eternal. When someone makes something, they are not creating it new, but rather simply altering the stuff of the world to create a manifestation of an eternal object.

Hale argues that this world view can be seen in the ritual and totemic practices of the Warlpiri, in how they organize their kinship system, and in the vocabulary for words that loosely correspond to English "make". The meanings of these words treat the act of making as the act of transforming: *ngurrju-ma-ni*, means to 'perfect or fix', *yirra-rni*, meaning to 'put something in place', and various verbs of impact, such as *paka-rni*, to 'chop', *panti-rni* to 'pierce or gouge' and *jarnti-rni* to 'trim or sculpt'. Manufacture, or making, in Warlpiri vocabulary is coded not as creation, but as change. Hale points out that these aspects of Warlpiri culture that express the world view of the logic of eternity never seem to be at the level of grammar. He contrasts this with the kinds of concepts that often do appear in the grammar of the world's languages: cause, tense, evidence, and so on. This makes the same point as Talmy and Cinque: of all the possible concepts that humans have, only a restricted set of these appear in grammar. Something restricts which concepts human grammar co-opts from human thought. Whatever that is, it's another instance of grammatical autonomy.

This second autonomy thesis opens up a new research program: what are the co-optable concepts? Why are these the co-optable ones? What principles organize these into syntactic hierarchy? How are they 'digitized' by the syntactic system so as to enter into syntactic computations?

Rather than threatening the autonomy of syntax, grammar focussed investigations of questions of meaning have strengthened and clarified the issue of the autonomy of syntax, as well as opening up new research questions, showing just how fertile the core ideas, laid down in *Syntactic Structures* 60 years ago, remain.

Acknowledgements Many thanks to Norbert Hornstein and Tal Linzen for comments on an earlier draft.

Bibliography

Adger, David. 2013. *A syntax of substance*. Cambridge, MA: MIT Press.
Adger, David, and Peter Svenonius. 2015. Linguistic explanation and domain specialization: a case study in bound variable anaphora. *Frontiers in Psychology* 6.
Aoun, Joseph, Elabbas Benmamoun, and Dominique Sportiche. 1999. Further remarks on first conjunct agreement. *Linguistic Inquiry* 30:669–681.
Bach, Emmon W. 1989. *Informal lectures on formal semantics*. Albany, NY: State University of New York Press.
Barker, Chris. 2012. Quantificational binding does not require c-command. *Linguistic Inquiry* 43:614–633.
Berwick, Robert C., and Noam Chomsky. 2016. *Why Only Us?* Cambridge MA: MIT Press.

Bock, Kathryn, Kathleen M. Eberhard, J. Cooper Cutting, Antje A. Meyer, and Herbert Schriefers. 2001. Some attractions of verb agreement. *Cognitive Psychology* 43:83–128.
Bock, Kathryn, and Carol A. Miller. 1991. Broken agreement. *Cognitive Psychology* 23:45–93.
Bod, Rens, Jennifer Hay, and Stefanie Jannedy. 2003. *Probabilistic Linguistics*. Cambridge, MA: MIT Press.
Borer, Hagit. 2003. Exo-skeletal vs. endo-skeletal explanations: Syntactic projections and the lexicon. In *The Nature of Explanation in Linguistic Theory*, ed. John Moore and Maria Polinsky, 31–67. Standford, CA: CSLI Publications.
Chomsky, Noam. 1957. *Syntactic Structures*. The Hague, Netherlands: Mouton de Gruyter.
Chomsky, Noam. 1970. Remarks on nominalization. In *Readings in English Transformational Grammar*, ed. R.A. Jacobs and P.S. Rosenbaum, 184–221. Waltham, MA: Ginn-Blaisdell.
Chomsky, Noam. 1995. *The Minimalist Program*. Cambridge, MA: MIT Press.
Chomsky, Noam. 2013. Problems of projection. *Lingua* 130:33–49.
Chomsky, Noam, Riny Huybregts, and Henk C. van Riemsdijk. 1982. *Noam Chomsky on the generative enterprise: A discussion with Riny Huybregts and Henk van Riemsdijk*. Dordrecht, Netherlands: Foris.
Cinque, Guglielmo. 2005. Deriving Greenberg's Universal 20 and its exceptions. *Linguistic Inquiry* 36:315–332.
Cinque, Guglielmo. 2013. Cognition, universal grammar, and typological generalizations. *Lingua* 130:50–65.
Culbertson, Jennifer, and David Adger. 2014. Language learners privilege structured meaning over surface frequency. *Proceedings of the National Academy of Sciences* 111:5842–5847.
Déchaine, Rose-Marie, and Martina Wiltschko. 2014. Bound variable anaphora. Lingbuzz.
Embick, David, and Rolf Noyer. 1999. Locality in post-syntactic operations. In *Papers in Morphology and Syntax: Cycle Two*, volume 34, 265–317. MIT Working Papers in Linguistics.
Ernst, Thomas. 1998. The scopal basis of adverb licensing. In *Proceedings of the North East Linguistic Society*, ed. Pius N. Tamanji and Kiyomi Kusumoto, 127–142. University of Toronto: Graduate Linguistic Student Association.
Ferguson, Charles. 1996. Variation and drift: Loss of agreement in Germanic. In *Towards a Social Science of Language: Papers in honor of William Labov. Volume I, Variation and Change in Language and Society*, ed. Gregory Guy, Crawford Feagin, Deborah Schiffrin, and John Baugh, 173–198. Amsterdam: John Benhamins.
Georgopoulos, Carol. 1989. Syntactic variables: Resumptive pronouns and A'-binding in Palauan. Doctoral Dissertation, University of Utah.
Goldberg, Adele E. 2003. Contructions: a new theoretical approach to language. *Trends in Cognitive Sciences* 7:219–224.
Greenberg, Joseph H. 1963. Some universals of grammar with particular reference to the order of meaningful elements. In *Universals of Language*, ed. Joseph H. Greenberg, 73–113. Cambridge, MA: MIT Press.
Grimshaw, Jane. 2005. *Words and Structure*. Stanford, CA: CSLI Publications.
Hale, Kenneth. 1986. Notes on world view and semantic categories: Some Warlpiri examples. *Features and projections* 25:233–254.
Hall Partee, Barbara. 1975. Deletion and variable binding. In *Formal Semantics of Natural Language*, ed. E.L. Keenan, 16–34. Cambridge, UK: Cambridge University Press.
van Hoek, Karen. 1996. A cognitive grammar account of bound anaphora. In *Cognitive Linguistics in the Redwoods: The Expansion of a New Paradigm in Linguistics*, ed. Eugene Casad, 753–792. Berlin, Germany: De Gruyter.

Huang, James. 1982. Logical relations in Chinese and the theory of grammar. Doctoral Dissertation, MIT, Cambridge, MA.
Kush, Dave, Jeffrey Lidz, and Colin Phillips. 2015. Relation-sensitive retrieval: Evidence from bound variable pronouns. *Journal of Memory and Language* 82:18–40.
Labov, William. 2001. *Principles of Linguistic Change. Volume 2: Social Factors.* Oxford, UK: Blackwell.
Langacker, Ronald W. 1987. *Foundations of Cognitive Grammar: Theoretical prerequisites, Volume 1.* Standford, CA: Stanford University Press.
Langacker, Ronald W. 2008. *Cognitive grammar: A basic introduction.* Oxford, UK: Oxford University Press.
Lappin, Shalom, and Stuart M. Shieber. 2007. Machine learning theory and practice as a source of insight into universal grammar. *Journal of Linguistics* 43:393–427.
Linzen, Tal, Emmanuel Dupoux, and Yoav Goldberg. 2016. Assessing the ability of LSTMs to learn syntax-sensitive dependencies. *Transactions of the Association for Computational Linguistics* 4:521–535.
Linzen, Tal, Yoav Goldberg, and Emmanuel Dupoux. 2017. Agreement attraction errors in neural networks. In *Poster presented at CUNY Conference on Human Sentence Processing.*
MacWhinney, Brian. 1977. Starting Points. *Language* 152–168.
Miller, George A., and Noam Chomsky. 1963. Finitary models of language users. In *Handbook of Mathematical Psychology*, ed. D. Luce, 419–492. New York, NY: John Wiley & Sons.
Miller, George A., and Stephen Isard. 1963. Some perceptual consequences of linguistic rules. *Journal of Verbal Learning and Verbal Behavior* 2:217–228.
Montague, Richard. 1974. *Formal Philosophy: Selected Papers of Richard Montague.* New York: Yale University Press.
Munn, Alan. 1999. First conjunct agreement: Against a clausal analysis. *Linguistic Inquiry* 30:643–668.
Newmeyer, Frederick J. 1983. *Grammatical theory: Its limits and its possibilities.* Chicago, IL: University of Chicago Press.
Newmeyer, Frederick J. 1998. *Language Form and Language Function.* Cambridge, MA: MIT Press.
Pallier, Christophe, Anne-Dominique Devauchelle, and Stanislas Dehaene. 2011. Cortical representation of the constituent structure of sentences. *Proceedings of the National Academy of Sciences* 108:2522–2527.
Pereira, Fernando. 2000. Formal grammar and information theory: together again? *Philosophical Transactions of the Royal Society of London A: Mathematical Physical and Engineering Sciences* 358:1239–1253.
Portner, Paul, and Barbara Partee. 2002. *Formal Semantics: The Essential Readings.* Oxford, UK: Wiley-Blackwell.
Quine, Willard Van Orman. 1953. *From a logical point of view: 9 Logico-philosophical essays.* Cambridge, MA: Harvard University Press.
Quine, Willard Van Orman. 1969. Linguistics and philosophy. In *Language and philosophy*, ed. Sidney Hook, 95–96. New York, NY: New York University Press.
Ramchand, Gillian, and Peter Svenonius. 2014. Deriving the functional hierarchy. *Language Sciences* 46:152–174.
Reinhart, Tanya. 1976. The syntactic domain of anaphora. Doctoral Dissertation, MIT, Cambridge, MA.
Safir, Ken. 2004. *The Syntax of Anaphora.* Oxford, UK: Oxford University Press.

Shannon, Claude E. 1948. A mathematical theory of communication. *The Bell System Technical Journal* 27:379–423,623–656.

Shimoyama, Junko. 2006. Indeterminate phrase quantification in Japanese. *Natural Language Semantics* 14:139–173.

Stowell, Tim. 1982. The tense of infinitives. *Linguistic Inquiry* 13:561–570.

Talmy, Leonard. 1975. Figure and ground in complex sentences. *Proceedings of the First Annual Meeting of the Berkely Linguistics Society* 1:419–430.

Talmy, Leonard. 1985. Lexicalization patterns: semantic structure in lexical forms. In *Language Typology and Syntactic Description III: Grammatical Categories and the Lexicon*, ed. T. Shopen. Cambridge, UK: Cambridge University Press.

Talmy, Leonard. 2000. *Towards a Cognitive Semantics*. Cambridge, MA: MIT Press.

Wagers, Matthew, Ellen F. Lau, and Colin Phillips. 2009. Agreement attraction in comprehension: Representations and processes. *Journal of Memory and Language* 61:206–237.

Robert C. Berwick
Revolutionary New Ideas Appear Infrequently

1 Introduction

Some of the most memorable novels spring to mind with a single sentence: Tolstoy's "Every happy family is alike; every unhappy family is unhappy in its own way"; Proust's "Longtemps, je me suis couché de bonne heure." When it comes to linguistics though, most would agree that top honors could easily be awarded to Syntactic Structure's "colorless green ideas sleep furiously." And therein lies the rub. While possibly the most memorable sentence in modern linguistics, it's also perhaps become one of the most misunderstood. As we will find out, there's a whole lot more to this colorless story than you might think, even though you may have read this sentence a thousand times. You'll be surprised.

To understand why, it's helpful to recall the role "colorless green ideas sleep furiously" (CGI) plays in SS and modern generative grammar generally. CGI stands front and center literally as Example #1 in SS's first bona-fide chapter, "The Independence of Grammar," with no less a goal than to establish exactly what the chapter's title claims. Why "Independence of Grammar"? As pointed out in Robert B. Lees' famous review of SS in *Language* that appeared the same year, SS aimed to place linguistics on an equal footing with the other physical sciences, with SS "one of the first serious attempts on the part of a linguist to construct within the tradition of scientific theory-construction a comprehensive theory of language which may be understood in the same sense that a chemical, biological theory is ordinarily understood" (1957:376). As with other physical sciences, SS sets out a primary object of inquiry, the Fundamental Question preoccupying generative grammar ever since: to demarcate and explain the shape of the space of possible human grammars, "since we are interested not only in particular languages, but also in the general nature of Language"—here deliberately with a capital "L", p. 14.

With the Fundamental Question in hand, SS next confronts us with two big "Fundamental Facts." First, a speaker/signer can produce and understand an indefinite number of distinct sentences with different meanings—Humboldt's famous gift, the infinite use of finite means. No other animal comes close. And second, a related empirical fact, all normal speakers manage to project from a finite, limited corpus to an infinite one, "the behavior of the speaker who, on the basis of a finite and accidental experience with language, can produce or understand an indefinite number of new sentences" (SS:15)—the problem of induction. Though Chomsky doesn't explicitly say so, this sort of induction encompasses the child's situation as well—as he wrote elsewhere the same year SS was published, in his critique of Skinner's *Verbal Behavior*. Taken together, the Fundamental Question and explanations for the two corresponding "big facts" make up the scientific Big Game that transformational generative grammar hunts to this day, just like physics' search for a theory that will account for why we see *this* particular array of fundamental particles and not some other, "the actual nature of the system, not just its external manifestations" (Chomsky 2015:92). Compare Feynman who says that the aim of physics is to "see complete nature as different aspects of one set of phenomena" (Feynman 1989:26).

From such beginnings, modern transformational generative grammar has continued to parallel Richard Feynman's quest to "understand this multitude of aspects, perhaps in resulting from the action of a relatively small number of elemental things and forces acting in an infinite variety of combinations" (1989:53)—one couldn't ask for a neater definition of what's now called the Minimalist Program. Here Feynman invokes scientific method: "observation, reason, and experiment" (1989:54). But what's the linguistic counterpart of an observation? We need some probe that assesses *grammar*, i.e., syntax, while holding everything else constant.

And that finally brings us back around to SS's chapter title, "The Independence of Grammar," the notions of grammaticality and acceptability, and examples (1), CGI and (2), CGI's mirror image, *furiously sleep ideas green colorless* (call this CGI-rev). If grammar (syntactic structure) is *not* independent of "everything else," then, just as in any other science, it might become well-nigh impossible to cleanly tease apart the factors that make (1) sound OK for English speakers and (2) not so great. Informally we say that (1) is "acceptable" and (2), not so much, but the question is how to unpack "acceptability," which clearly intertwines both knowledge of language and many other behavioral factors as to how people process or produce sentences. Note, crucially, that here SS contrasts a *sentence pair*. That's key to the whole approach, which follows standard experimental design, as we describe in more detail below.

Chomsky observes that CGI has Mary Poppins syntax—"practically perfect in every way"—but it's semantic gibberish—in complete contrast to CGI-rev, which is just as much semantic gibberish as CGI, but, crucially, is also *syntactic* gibberish. Consequently, there seem to be at least two dimensions that vary independently: ±syntax-ok, and ±semantics-ok. CGI is +syntax-ok, −semantics-ok, and CGI-rev is −syntax-ok, −semantics-ok. The contrast thus lets us factor apart syntax from semantics. This is what SS means when it says that "in any statistical model for *grammaticalness*, these sentences will be ruled out on identical grounds as being equally 'remote' from English" (p. 16, my emphasis). The keyword here is *grammaticalness*—not the same at all as whether the sentences are "acceptable" or not, an important point that has apparently misled others and that we address in Section 2 below. Perhaps SS should have stuck to the ±syntax/semantics contrast in the two sentences that Chomsky originally had in his *The Logical Structure of Linguistic Theory* (LSLT, 1955/1975): "this is a round square" vs. "this are a round square". Both are nonsensical, but only the first is syntactically well-formed—another example pair that illustrate a dissociation between syntax and semantics.

Importantly, there's a lot more to the story than this. Chomsky provides crucial additional *empirical* evidence that in fact native English speakers have truly grasped the syntactic differences between sentences (1) and (2): CGI is pronounced with "normal sentence intonation" (p. 16), so evidently have chunked it into constituents of the expected sort; while CGI-rev is "read with falling intonation on each word," that is, as though it were just a laundry list of unrelated words without any assigned structure (*Ibid*, p. 16). Nor is the CGI-rev sentence as easily recalled as CGI. (You can test out this psycholinguistic experiment yourself in the comfort of your own home, without human subject approval; I find that I have to first think of CGI and then mentally invert the word order.)

So how do native speakers recognize the difference between CGI and CGI-rev? It can't be by literally memorizing sentences, since these sequences don't appear. SS doesn't say much more, but a glance at the much longer work from which SS is drawn, *The Logical Structure of Linguistic Theory*, chapter 4, does provides a good answer. We return to Chomsky's solution in Section 2 below, since it turns out to actually be a better solution than a particular statistical approach advanced sixty years later, ironically as a claimed dismissal of SS. In any event, as Chomsky says, the notion "grammatical" can't be the same as "meaningful" because we can factor these two notions apart.

This two-way contrast amounts to very basic experimental logic—essentially like an analysis of variance. Typically, we have two examples that vary on a dimension of interest, here, syntax/"meaningfulness", while attempting to hold all other conditions constant (sentence length, word token frequencies, etc.). We compare whether speakers get the same contrast—and they do. Given this, we are therefore licensed to conclude that syntax can be factored apart from "meaningfulness"—the independence of grammar. This logic has provided the basic data fodder for much of generative grammar over the past sixty years. (Of course, there are other sorts of evidence available besides these contrasts, such as brain imaging, psycholinguistic tasks; and the like, but we're sticking to the SS sort here.) The unstarred/starred sentence contrast and the corresponding speaker judgments are thus observations set within the context of particular theories. Crucially, as Chomsky and others have stressed many times over the intervening years, *the observations themselves are not the central object of inquiry*. The Fundamental Question tells us that our main job is not in itself to figure out which linguistic objects are good and which are bad, some categorization problem regarding acceptability of these sentences, or even the gradience as to which sentences are more acceptable than others, because such observations aren't in and of themselves grammars. Rather, such sentences serve as data fodder into the shape of human grammar space—and apparently a good one, if we believe in the results of transformational generative grammar over the past sixty years.

Finally, Chomsky remarks that it seems difficult to use any simple notion of statistical analysis as a proxy for this kind of analysis of variance and insight into grammar space, because the contrasts do not seem to line up "with the notion 'high order of statistical approximation to English.'" (*Ibid.*, p. 16). CGI and CGI-rev are "equally 'remote' from English" (p. 16). By "order" here Chomsky is referring to the familiar structure of so-called Markov models, the most well-known approach to statistically predicting English word sequences at the time when SS was published. Informally, the *order* of such a model refers to how many words (tokens) of "memory" states can be consulted in order to determine the next word output. For example, if we have estimates of word probabilities conditioned on the immediately previous words in a sequence, e.g., an estimate of the probability of *green* given that we have just seen *colorless*, then this is an order 1 Markov model, or *bigram*. If we extend this to an estimate of the probability that ideas follows the sequence colorless green, then this is an order 2 Markov model, a *trigram*. In general, by conditioning the probability of word n on the preceding $n - 1$ words in a sequence, we have an order-$n - 1$ Markov model. The higher the order, the more closely a Markov model's sequences tend to resemble actual English word sequences—trigrams work better than bigrams, and Google's 5-grams predict actually occurring word sequences better still. However, as SS notes, no matter how high the order, there will be some sequences that cannot be captured by this sort of model.[1]

---

[1] SS hedges its bets here, and in footnote 4 explicitly says that its argument that statistical modeling won't help applies only to this simple kind of Markov process: "One might seek to develop a more elaborate relation between statistical and syntactic structure than the simple order of approximation model we have rejected. I would certainly not care to argue that any such relation is unthinkable but I know of no suggestion to this effect that does not have obvious flaws" *Ibid.* p. 17. We will see that one can introduce "more sophisticated" statistical models—this is what Lau et al. do—but the most sophisticated ones we have, recurrent neural networks, still don't capture the bulk of the variance in human acceptability judgements; see Sprouse et al. 2016.

What of SS's statement that "Grammaticality cannot be identified in any way with the notion "high order of statistical approximation to English"? At least for the CGI type sentences, statistical models like trigrams or recursive neural networks (RNNs) seem to capture only about 10 % of the variation in speakers' *acceptability* judgments—even putting to one side the point that acceptability isn't the same as grammaticality. If we extend this to a more linguistically relevant collection of sentences from *Linguistic Inquiry* (Sprouse et al., 2013), then Sprouse et al. (forthcoming) we don't do that much better. As a result, from this rather modest ability to predict the likelihood of word sequences one cannot really get at an answer to the Fundamental Question. Neither does such an approach explain the "two big facts." Rather, such sequence modeling asks about something else, because *n*-gram values (and more sophisticated statistical sequence prediction models like recurrent neural networks) work better not by *unraveling* the manifold interactions between syntax and semantics, and much else about language use, but by *folding* together all these factors and vigorously stirring the probabilistic pot. But, predicting the next word that one might say isn't the same goal at all as explaining the faculty of language—it confuses language *capacity* with language *use*. We may get much better word sequence predictions by such blends, but we can too easily lose sight of the component parts—Feynman's combination of elemental things—that constitute them. If it turned out to be true that one can just dump observations of external events—all the sentences on the web—into a statistical hopper, turn a Bayesian wheel, and then, via extracted mixtures of "latent" variables get a prediction machine that beats doing experiments in the traditional way, that would indeed be a news story of the first order. Yet, we would still be missing the Galilean/Feynman notion of "explanation."

In any event, the two-way ±syntax/semantics distinction leads to the conclusion that "grammar" can be dissociated from "meaning," and we are then free to use starred/unstarred sentence pairs as probes into syntactic theory. Let the scientific games begin!

2 Objections

Or then again, maybe we jumped the gun. Apparently, not everyone buys the CGI story and neither do all agree about what's the Fundamental Question for linguistics to answer. In the remainder of this chapter we consider two recent examples that push back against SS and the entire framework of modern generative grammar: Pereira (2000), henceforth P; and Lau, Clark, and Lappin (2017), henceforth LCL. For these researchers, the goals of linguistic research appear rather different from the basic SS contrastive logic and an account of *grammar*: rather, they seek in part to best predict native speakers' linguistic *behavior* on individual sentences, using statistical methods. LCL have even bigger game in their sights: their general claim is that the categorical representation of knowledge of language presented in SS is simply incorrect, and should be replaced with different theories entirely, whose representations are inherently probabilistic—the motivation being the clear gradience in acceptability judgments. For them, the acceptability contrast between CGI and CGI-rev arises because the former is *more likely*—it's assigned a higher probability than the latter under a statistical model. However, nobody really disputes that human judgments are probabilistic or gradient in nature, or that human linguistic performance is to some extent stochastic. That does not pose a problem for conventional grammatical approaches because it is relatively straightforward to *add* a probabilistic component to conventional linguistic grammars to yield gradient behavior, as is done, for example, in Keller (2000), among others. One can even place probability distributions on the derivations in modern minimalist grammars, as shown by Hunter and Dyer (2013), Hale (2006), and Adger (2006), among several others. In short, there's no *conceptual* barrier to accommodating stochastic language behavior by wedding probabilistic distributions with conventional linguistic representations. We will put aside remaining discussion of this important point in what follows, leaving this discussion for Sprouse et al. (forthcoming).

In any case, it seems that on the LCL view, we don't need or want a generative grammar developed in the traditional way to achieve the goal of predicting sentence acceptability measures. Rather, we can use the tools of statistical language analysis applied to externally observed sentences—for example, *n*-grams or recurrent neural networks (RNNs). Further, the "big fact" of language induction, as least for P, can also be readily explained statistically—via statistical learning theory.[2] In this context, the "abstract categories" of conventional generative grammar (e.g., features, phrases like NP or VP, or abstract internal "states" generally)

---

[2] Pereira here points to general, well-known results about language learnability as solutions to the "big fact" about child/human language induction, but this is not so clear. For example, P cites the work by Horning (1969) demonstrating that probabilistic (unambiguous) context-free grammars are learnable from positive-only examples. But whether these methods *actually* work given cognitive constraints is not apparent. (Like most commentators, P does not note Horning's explicit restriction to unambiguous grammars which presumably rules out natural language grammars.) A general discussion of formal learnability results in the context of cognitively feasible constraints on language learners is well beyond the scope of this article; in general, even given somewhat positive results like Horning's, it is fair to say that this problem of sample size complexity given positive-only examples has yet to be solved; see Clark and Lappin (2011) for additional discussion that agrees with this point about sample size.

reappear as latent variables uncovered by statistical means, just as in principle components analysis, where some complex linear combination of input variables yields predictors of observed outcomes. (The latent variable approach generalizes this to nonlinear combinations, as in recurrent neural networks.)

There is, however, a potent critique of this position that turns on precisely this shift in the explanatory target. Explicitly, positions like P's have one goal: better prediction of word sequences—and so what has sometimes been called "E-language" ("E" for external and extensional, a collection of sentences "out there in the world," Bloomfield's (1926) "totality of utterances made in a speech community" putting aside whether this is even a coherent concept). Predicting word sequences has turned out to be *very* valuable for many engineering and business purposes—like placing ads in the right places on web pages—winning billions for Google.

In the speech recognition research community, the value of accurate sequence prediction has led to the definition of a "language model" as a probability distribution over a set of utterances. It's worthwhile examining this definition more closely in the context of SS. A "language model" *must* be a quintessentially *external* and *behavioral* target. But this diverges from "Language" (with a capital L) in the SS sense. Rather than being an explanation of the essential nature of language, "language models" are, rather, accounts of sets of *particular* utterance sequences, language with a lowercase "l." Literally anything at all that helps boost sequence predictive power, like knowing the age of the speaker or their socioeconomic status, is grist for the data prediction mill. To be sure, learning theory typically introduces regularization terms—penalties terms for over-parameterization—but this does not deflect the argument that sequence prediction might not after all be the sought-after objective function for linguistics.

A possibly apt comparison in this regard is that of Ptolemaic earth-centered epicyclic analysis as compared to the (factually correct) Copernican heliocentrism. Ptolemaic epicycles, as a super-positioned sum of different-sized epicycles and so in effect function approximation by a series expansion, can predict with arbitrary precision *any* periodic motion set against the fixed stars—by analogy to a method that can perfectly match *any* distribution of utterances, including nonhuman language sequences. In contrast, Copernican heliocentrism is more explanatory because it must obey Kepler's empirically observed laws of motion for the sun and planets—Feynman's "complete nature" again. Not just any periodic motion will do. That's what makes heliocentrism a part of *natural* science rather than just some glass bead game. Ultimately, of course, those solar and planetary motions themselves were seen by Newton to be the result of yet simpler laws, yielding an even stronger explanatory account. In precisely the same way, the predictive statistical summaries of sentences powered by "big data" and enormous computing power yield impressive predictive accuracy—at the price of models that are many gigabytes in size with opaque, uninterpretable latent combinations. (The recurrent neural network models developed below are larger than 4 or 5 gigabytes in size, after training on about 5 million sentences.) Consequently, one is left with no explanation of why Language looks the way it does rather than some other way—in part because this isn't the goal of such methodology. The statistical machinery is equally content to produce the same size models for *unnatural* languages, like those described by Moro (2016), e.g., where negation does not follow any human language syntactic rules.

We begin with Pereira's critique of SS and CGI. P's main point is to argue that one can use statistical modeling to demonstrate that CGI is far more likely than CGI-rev, by a factor of about 200,000. At first blush this indeed seems to refute Chomsky's statement that "in any statistical model for grammaticalness, these sentences (CGI and CGI-rev) will be ruled out on identical grounds"—e.g., if the probability of CGI is just the product of its individual bigram probabilities— (*beginning-of-sentence*)-*colorless, colorless-green, green-ideas, ideas-sleep, sleep-furiously*, and *furiously-*(*end of sentence marker*)—then if any of these bigram estimates are zero because we've never encountered any such two-word combinations, the entire product is zero. Of course, n-gram modelers know how to handle zero counts, as we describe below. Before jumping ahead though, it's interesting to recall that since SS goes on to show explicitly that speakers both *know* and *behave* as though CGI is well-formed (i.e., grammatical), and CGI-rev is not, that SS *also* implies—and then later on directly says that speakers know how to get around this zero frequency problem, and further that "grammatical" can't possibly amount to the same thing as "likely." (That's the position that LCL also hold, as it turns out.) The confusion is a conflation between "grammatical" and "acceptable."

However, P skips right over this contradictory bit of evidence explicitly in SS, and focuses instead on the apparent stumble with the "in any statistical model" part, countering SS by developing a statistical model that indeed points to CGI as more likely than CGI-rev by a factor of about 200,000. However, there's one problem with this solution: it turns out to be a less linguistically informed variant of precisely the same solution that Chomsky already offered a few years before in *LSLT*. Moreover, Chomsky's solution—and P's—both rely on the approach of induction from a finite corpus, inferring the unseen from the seen, with Chomsky's account having the added value of empirical backing

What then is P's approach to statistically modeling a contrast in likelihood between CGI and CGI-rev? He proposes to lump words into classes, and then use the resulting class-based frequencies to replace any zero count word sequences. Here's the relevant excerpt: "we may approximate the conditional probability $p(x, y)$ of occurrence of two words x and y in a given configuration as, $p(x, y) = p(x) \sum_c p(y|c)p(c|x)$ ... In particular, when (x, y) [are two words] we have an *aggregate* bigram model (Saul and Pereira, 1997), which is useful for modeling word sequences that include unseen bigrams." (Pereira 2000:7). Roughly then, instead of estimating the probability that word y follows the word x based on actual word counts, we use the likelihood that word x belongs to some word class c, and then use the likelihood that word y follows word class c. For instance, if *colorless green* never occurs, a literal count of 0, we instead record that *colorless* is in the same word class as *revolutionary*—i.e., an Adjective—and calculate the likelihood that *green* follows an Adjective. In turn, if we have a zero count for the pair *green ideas*, then we replace that with an estimate of the likelihood Adjective-*ideas*... and so on down the line. And where do these word classes come from? As Saul and Pereira note, when trained on newspaper text, these aggregate classes often correspond to meaningful word classes. For example, in Saul and Pereira's Table 3, with 32 classes, class 8 consists of the words *can, could, may, should, to, will, would* (so, roughly, a cluster of modal verbs). P then continues: "Using this estimate for the probability of a string and an aggregate model with $C = 16$ [that is, *a priori* assuming 16 different word classes, rcb] trained on newspaper text ... we find that ... p(colorless green ideas ...)/p(furiously sleep ideas ...) $\approx 2 \times 10^5$" (i.e., about 200,000 times greater). In other words, roughly speaking, the part of speech sequence Adjective-Adjective-Noun-Verb-Adverb is that much more likely than the sequence Adverb-Verb-Noun-Adjective-Adjective.

What about Chomsky's solution to this puzzle? Since in actual fact no English speaker has *actually* encountered either CGI or CGI-rev before, how do they *know* the two are different, and so assign CGI a normal intonation contour, with "normal" syntactic structure, while pronouncing CGI-rev as though it had no syntactic structure at all? P fails to discuss this crucial point. Clearly then, even according to SS, English speakers must be using some other information than simply their *literal count* of occurrences in order to infer that *colorless green...* seems OK, but *furiously sleeps...* is not. In short, it *must* be the case that, just as Chomsky says in SS, speakers are drawing some inference about a sentence that has not been seen from English sentences they have already seen. This indicates that Chomsky was well aware that the zero frequency count statistical problem could be overcome by some kind of induction, another point apparently missed. What are people doing with these sentences?

Chomsky offered the following answer to this question in his *Logical Structure of Linguistic Theory*. "This distinction can be made by demonstrating that (1) [CGI] is an instance of the sentence form *Adjective-Adjective-Noun-Verb-Adverb*, which is grammatical by virtue of such sentences as revolutionary new ideas appear infrequently that might well occur in normal English" (1955, IV-146; 1975:146). That is, when the observed frequency of a particular word string is zero, Chomsky proposed that people surmount the problem of inferring the "unseen from the seen" by lumping together word sequences like "colorless green" together with "revolutionary new"—that is by *aggregating* these individual words into *classes* rather than literal word sequence counts, so that *colorless* falls together with *revolutionary*; *green* with *new*; and so forth. People then assign an aggregated word-class analysis to CGI, sentence (1), so that *colorless green ideas sleep furiously* is analyzed as a string of word classes associated with *revolutionary new ideas appear infrequently*... In short, this is precisely the same idea as P's—just sixty years earlier and without any of the newer statistical shiny bits.[3]

Summarizing so far, SS's solution to the zero frequency count problem rests on Big Fact #2: after exposure to a finite corpus, all children (adults) project to an infinity of sentences—they do induction. In the statistical literature, shaving bits of probability mass from what's already seen and distributing that to what's unseen so far is sometimes called *smoothing*.[4] It is easy to see, as P observes, that smoothing is really just a particular form of induction—in this case, the projection from a finite corpus to an infinite one. As we have just seen, SS is well aware of all of this, though not the formal statistical approach.

In the n-gram analysis of the CGI-type sentences that we'll turn to while examining LCL's analysis, when there are zero examples of *colorless-green* and the like (a so-called *bigram* frequency count from a corpus, an *estimate* of a bigram probability), then one typical smoothing approach might be to "back off" and use the frequency of the single word *colorless* seen in the corpus—a *unigram* estimate. (If there are no examples of *colorless*, then this might in turn be estimated as the relative frequency of an "out of vocabulary" or OOV "word" that has never been seen in the corpus at all.) We'll see that that a trigram analysis in fact pitches up a likelihood difference between CGI and CGI-rev of only about 38 times, rather than 200,000. By contrast, the trigram likelihood for "revolutionary new ideas occur infrequently" is estimated at 17 million times greater than that for CGI—a much larger difference than that between CGI and CGI-rev. In fact, the "revolutionary new ideas" sentence is the only one of these three sentences that has any non-smoothed trigram—all the others contain just a few non-smoothed bigram

---

[3] In the Appendix to *LSLT* Chapter IV, 1955, again contrary to P's assertion that 1955/1957 marked a "split" between Chomsky's "algebraic" linguistic theory and Harris' "information theoretic" account—Chomsky even provided an information-theoretic clustering algorithm to automatically construct such categories, with a worked example, done jointly with Peter Elias.

[4] Perhaps the most well-known and earliest smoothing approach this is Laplace's "add-1" method used to estimate the likelihood that the sun will rise tomorrow, given that it's risen on n previous days. More recently, much more sophisticated methods have been developed.

values, with the rest of the sequence based on unigrams. This vividly illustrates how "sparse" the space of sentences really can be.

3 Acceptability and grammaticality, the modern way

This brief look at n-gram analysis above leads directly to Lau, Clark, and Lappin's approach to modeling speakers' acceptability judgments. LCL's goal is to argue for an inherently *probabilistic* cast to speakers' linguistic knowledge, rather than the categorical representations that linguists have conventionally used. They model the apparent gradience in sentence *acceptability*—which they properly distinguish from grammaticality—via a range of statistical models—everything from n-grams to Hidden Markov Models, to recurrent neural networks. (Here they seem to have been inspired by an initial take on the same problem by Sandiway Fong, the late Partha Niyogi, Michael Coen, and myself, that was presented in 2007 at a Cognitive Science workshop where Clark was a participant.) Here we will focus on just one of these models, a trigram analysis, and systematically investigate the CGI sentences, leaving further analysis to Sprouse et al. (forthcoming). (The results from more sophisticated models like recurrent neural networks are about the same.) LCL correctly note that one cannot ascribe probabilities to sentences directly, because by general consensus, there are a countably infinite number of sentences and so dividing up the probability mass so that above or equal to a certain threshold epsilon, sentences are "grammatical" and otherwise, ungrammatical, simply doesn't work (again as noted in SS).

As far as we know, this is the first time that the acceptability of the CGI sentences has been systematically analyzed at all; here, we have used the tools for sentence judgments developed by Sprouse et al. (2013). Our basic findings, displayed in Figure 1, are that: (1) if we plot human acceptability ratings vs. trigram probabilities, there is some positive correlation between human-judged acceptability and likelihood; but (2) the correlation is not that strong, with the statistical models accounting for only about 10 % of the variation in speaker's acceptability ratings—perhaps because all the CGI examples are somewhat odd. (As a result, the range in probabilities is fairly narrow.) There are some surprises. While CGI is more likely than CGI-rev, CGI is not the "most likely" sentence out of the 120 permutations even though it has almost the highest acceptability rating—it is actually about 20 down from the top; nor is CGI-rev the "least likely"—though CGI-rev is the fourth least likely sentence. In any case, these results, along the more systematically developed examination of linguistically relevant examples in Sprouse et al.

(forthcoming) point to real difficulties in using probability proxies of a proxy for acceptability judgments, and insight into knowledge of grammar, a conclusion at odds with LCL and with the "statistical" approach to language modeling generally.

To carry out this analysis, we constructed all 120 permutations of the CGI sentence, with CGI becoming sentence #1, and CGI-rev sentence #120.[5] Following the methodology of LCL, we then trained a trigram model by using the written portion of the British National Corpus, with a training set consisting of an 80 % random selection of the approximately 5 million sentence forms (87 million words, 3144 texts). The SRI language modeling toolkit was used to do the actual trigram calculations, including the smoothing method used.[6]

Figure 1 displays the findings as a scattergram of the Elo ratings for each sentence re-scaled between approximately −1 and +1 on the y-axis, vs. negative base 10 log probability of the trigram calculated values for sentences on the x-axis. (Recall that a negative log probability scale will run from −infinity for probability 0 to +1 for probability 1.) A best-fit linear regression line is drawn on the scattergram, with an r^2 value of 0.102. The regression line has a slight positive slope of 0.32, which is as expected: lower probability sentences have lower Elo scores. The logprob range is, as anticipated, fairly narrow. However, as the low r^2 value indicates, there is a great deal of scatter remaining in the plot, indicating that the log probability score captures only a small amount of the variance in the data. (Various variants of this score that attempt to normalize for sentence length as explored by LCL, aren't needed here because all the CGI sentences have the same length.)

The two circled points denote CGI (in the upper right portion of the scattergram) and CGI-rev (in the lower left part of the scattergram). They both have logprob values a bit removed from where one might expect a "perfect fit" (the red line) to be: CGI has a logprob value that is too low, given its high Elo rank, while CGI-rev, closer to the regression line, should have a slightly higher Elo score. The most likely sentence is in fact "furiously colorless green ideas sleep" (Elo score near 0, logprob −26.7837); the least likely are "colorless sleep ideas green furiously," and "colorless ideas green sleep furiously", and "colorless green sleep ideas furiously" (logprob −30.412). These might come as a bit of a surprise—especially since the human Elo acceptability ranking on the last sentence is not exceptionally low.

---

[5] As is conventional, we "padded" the sentences with "beginning of sentence" (BOS) and "end of sentence" (EOS) tags to ease the trigram calculation.

[6] Interpolated Knesser-Ney smoothing was used—if a trigram value is missing, it is "backed off" to a bigram, and then to a unigram.

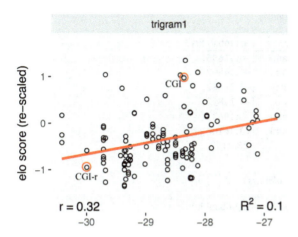

Fig. 1: Scattergram of Elo acceptability forced-choice decision task values, scaled, vs. predicted trigram −log probability measures, for the 120 permuted CGI sentences. A best-fit linear regression line is shown. The circled points denote CGI and CGI-rev, as indicated.

Note that "Revolutionary new ideas appear infrequently" would not fit onto the scale of the Figure 1 scattergram, with its logprob value of −21.

Finally, it is of some interest to carefully examine the individual word-to-word trigram analysis, for the three sentences CGI, CGI-rev, and "revolutionary new ideas", as shown below, which indicates how rare trigram and even bigram sequences actually are even in a large corpus. Note that none of the sentences except "revolutionary new ideas" even has a non-zero count trigram. "Revolutionary new ideas" has one: "<s> revolutionary new" (where "<s>" is the padded-out start of the sentence marker; </s> is the padded end of sentence marker). "Revolutionary new ideas" also has 4 non-zero bigrams (<s>-*revolutionary*; *revolutionary-new*; and *appear-infrequently*). CGI has only 2 non-zero bigrams (*green-ideas*; and *sleep-furiously*)—note that these are different from those in from "revolutionary new ideas." CGI-rev has no non-zero bigrams at all internal to the sentences, and just a single one overall: <s>-*furiously*. The point is that in all these cases, smoothing is essential—sometimes smoothing all the way back to counts of the single words (unigrams or "1-grams").

i. CGI: *colorless green ideas sleep furiously*

Conditional probability	Type	log probability
$p(\text{colorless}| <s>) =$	[1gram]	[−8.37655]
$p(\text{green}|\text{colorless}) =$	[1gram]	[−3.94502]
$p(\text{ideas}|\text{green}) =$	[2gram]	[−3.38882]
$p(\text{sleep}|\text{ideas}) =$	[2gram]	[−4.15892]
$p(\text{furiously}|\text{sleep}) =$	[1gram]	[−5.18633]
$p(</s> |\text{furiously}) =$	[1gram]	[−3.36108]
Overall log probability =		**−28.4167**

ii. CGI-r: *furiously sleep ideas green colorless*

Conditional probability	Type	log probability
$p(\text{furiously}| <s>) =$	[2gram]	[−5.52461]
$p(\text{sleep}|\text{furiously}) =$	[1gram]	[−5.18682]
$p(\text{ideas}|\text{sleep}) =$	[1gram]	[−4.55034]
$p(\text{green}|\text{ideas}) =$	[1gram]	[−4.60936]
$p(\text{colorless}|\text{green}) =$	[1gram]	[−7.17263]
$p(</s> |\text{colorless}) =$	[1gram]	[−2.95282]
Overall log probability =		**−29.9966**

iii. Rev: *revolutionary new ideas appear infrequently*

Conditional probability	Type	log probability
$p(\text{revolutionary}| <s>) =$	[2gram]	[−5.16126]
$p(\text{new}|\text{revolutionary}) =$	[3gram]	[−1.14879]
$p(\text{ideas}|\text{new}) =$	[2gram]	[−2.5155]
$p(\text{appear}|\text{ideas}) =$	[1gram]	[−5.16899]
$p(\text{infrequently}|\text{appear}) =$	[2gram]	[−4.10388]
$p(</s> |\text{infrequently}) =$	[1gram]	[−3.08977]
Overall log probability =		**−21.1882**

4 Conclusions

Summarizing, what hath statistics wrought? Two numbers for CGI and CGI-rev, and one for "revolutionary new ideas." But an actual revolutionary new idea? Not so much. All the numbers say is that I'm 200,000 times more likely to say *colorless green ideas sleep furiously* (if I embrace P's model) than *furiously sleep ideas green colorless*—a statistical summary of my external behavior. But that's it, and it's not nearly enough. As we have seen, it's a statistically polished rehash of the same part-of-speech based smoothing analysis from 60 years ago. And it actually doesn't really explain why people bore full-steam ahead on CGI and assign it right-as-rain constituent syntactic structure, pronounced just like *revolutionary new ideas* and just as memorable, with CGI-rev left hanging as a limp laundry list of words. The likelihood gap doesn't—can't—match the grammaticality gap. But that's not a problem, because it's simply not the game we're playing after all.

The rejection of the idea that linguistic competence is just (a possibly fancy statistical) summary of behaviors should be recognized as the linguistic version of rejecting the general Rationalist endorsement of the distinction between powers/natures/capacities and their behavioral/phenomenal effects—that is to say, an endorsement of Empiricism. But for SS, grammars describe the space of possible linguistic objects and Universal Grammar (UG) the space of possible grammars. That's what generative grammar hunts—the algebraic structure of grammar space. From this perspective, LCL and P seem to be confused about the object of inquiry, because probabilities can be attached to algebraic spaces but cannot substitute for them. Recall that (e.g., Kolmogorov's) axioms for probability theory first of all *presume* what's typically called a sigma algebra. No algebra, no probabilities. The enterprise of figuring out the algebraic structure of grammars and the space of grammars is thus central. More generally, that's so because probability presupposes possibility, but not the reverse. The confusion between these two is characteristic of Empiricism, which tries to reduce possibility to actual correlation. But the former is a modal notion and so cannot reduce to the actual tracking of correlations.

In short, Universal Grammar's not a theory about statistically driven language regularities but about *capacities*. Nobody doubts that statistics have some role to play in the (complex but still murky) way that grammar and knowledge of language and who knows what else interact, so that the chance of my uttering *carminative fulvose aglets murate ascarpatically* works out to near zero, while for David Foster Wallace, that chance jumps by leaps and bounds. That's in fact a near-consensus view that every sensible card-carrying linguist, computational or otherwise, accepts.

Certainly, this role for statistics in human language *behavior* is not pushed aside in *Syntactic Structures*—articles and Internet memes to the contrary. Quite the reverse in fact, since in the course of describing *colorless green ideas*, *Syntactic Structures* explicitly *endorses* statistical methods as a way to model human linguistic behavior. But though this is a perfectly worthy goal for many, including those like Google engineers who *do* need to predict exactly what people actually say, I at least don't give an apatropaic penny about modeling the *actual* words coming out of my mouth. Rather, I would like to explain what underlies my linguistic *capacity*, and for that one does need a revolutionary new idea. Evidently, truly revolutionary new ideas *do* appear infrequently. Fortunately, however, one appeared in SS as generative grammar, and linguistics really never has looked back.

Acknowledgements Special thanks to Jon Sprouse for setting up the experimental work with CGI, and Sandiway Fong and the late Partha Niyogi for initial inspiration that CGI might be fun to look at and Norbert Hornstein for his urging to write up a much simpler version of this analysis on his blog. Beracah Yankama and Sagar Indurkya provided essential and detailed statistical analysis and implementation runs of the recursive neural networks. Audiences at *NELS* and *GLOW* helped improve the contents and presentation.

Bibliography

Adger, David. 2006. Combinatorial variability. *Journal of Linguistics* 42:503–530.
Bloomfield, Leonard. 1926. A set of postulates for the study of language. *Language* 2:153–164.
Chomsky, Noam. 1955/1975. *The Logical Structure of Linguistic Theory*. Chicago, IL: University of Chicago Press.
Chomsky, Noam. 1957. *Syntactic Structures*. The Hague, The Netherlands: Mouton de Gruyter.
Chomsky, Noam. 2015. Some core contested concepts. *Journal of Psycholinguistic Research* 44:91–104.
Clark, Alexander, and Shalom Lappin. 2011. *Linguistic Nativism and the Poverty of the Stimulus*. New York, NY: Wiley-Blackwell.
Feynman, Richard P. 1989. *Six Easy Pieces*. New York, NY: Perseus Books.
Hale, John. 2006. Uncertainty about the rest of the sentence. *Cognitive Science* 30:609–642.
Horning, Jay. 1969. A Study of Grammatical Inference. Doctoral Dissertation, Stanford University.
Hunter, Tim, and Chris Dyer. 2013. Distributions on minimalist grammar derivations. Proceedings EMNLP.
Keller, Frank. 2000. Gradience in grammar: Experimental and computational aspects of degrees of grammaticality. Doctoral Dissertation, University of Edinburgh.
Lau, Jey Han, Alexander Clark, and Shalom Lappin. 2017. Grammaticality, acceptability, and probability: a probabilistic view of linguistic knowledge. *Cognitive science* 41:1202–1241.
Moro, Andrea, ed. 2016. *The Boundaries of Babel: The brain and the enigma of Impossible Languages*. MIT Press.
Pereira, Fernando. 2000. Formal grammar and information theory: together again? *Philosophical Transactions of the Royal Society of London A: Mathematical Physical and Engineering Sciences* 358:1239–1253.
Sprouse, Jon, T. Schütze Carson, and Almeida Diogo. 2013. A comparison of informal and formal acceptability judgements using a random sample from *Linguistic Inquiry*, 2000-2010. *Lingua* 134.
Sprouse, Jon, Beracah Yankama, Sagar Indurkya, Sandiway Fong, and Robert C. Berwick. 2016. Colorless green ideas do sleep furiously – the necessity of grammar. GLOW 36, Göttingen, Germany.

Sprouse, Jon, Beracah Yankama, Sagar Indurkya, Sandiway Fong, and Robert C. Berwick. forthcoming. Two challenges for Lau, Clark and Lappin's (2016) probabilistic grammatical models.

Jon Sprouse
Acceptability judgments and grammaticality, prospects and challenges

1 Acceptability judgements in *Syntactic Structures*

Acceptability judgments constitute a substantial portion of the empirical foundation of generative syntax. Acceptability judgments are first proposed as a proxy for grammaticalness in generative syntax in *Syntactic Structures* (Chomsky, 1957) in the first paragraph of chapter 2:

> The grammar of L will thus be a device that generates all of the grammatical sequences of L and none of the ungrammatical ones. One way to test the adequacy of a grammar proposed for L is to determine whether or not the sequences that it generates are actually grammatical, i.e., acceptable to a native speaker, etc. We can take certain steps towards providing a behavioral criterion for grammaticalness so that this test of adequacy can be carried out. For the purposes of this discussion, however, suppose that we assume intuitive knowledge of the grammatical sentences of English and ask what sort of grammar will be able to do the job of producing these in some effective and illuminating way. (Chomsky 1957: 13)

In this quote, the precise method of collecting and interpreting acceptability judgments is left as a promissory note, so that Chomsky can get down to the core business of generative syntax, i.e., constructing a theory of grammar. My goal in this chapter is to provide a brief discussion of the prospects and challenges of using acceptability as a proxy for grammaticality, 60 years later.

This chapter is organized around two themes in current research on acceptability judgments: the methodology of acceptability judgments, and the theory of acceptability judgments. Research on judgment methodology is concerned with the act of collecting and analyzing acceptability judgments. Because methodological questions are relatively straightforward to investigate empirically (e.g., Does property X affect acceptability judgments?), it is perhaps unsurprising that generative syntacticians have made quite a bit of progress on this front over the past 60 years. Section 2 will discuss several fundamental questions about judgment methodology that have been investigated over the past 60 years. The theory of acceptability judgments is concerned with Chomsky's question of how to interpret acceptability judgments as evidence of "grammaticalness", and therefore as evidence for specific grammatical theories. Theoretical questions linking observable evidence to unobservable cognitive constructs are less straightforwardly empirical, as they involve exploring different linking hypotheses the observable and unobservable (in this case, acceptability and grammaticality). Linking hypotheses are rarely amenable to direct investigation, so progress can only be measured by the success of the theory that results from the linking hypothesis plus the empirically collected data. It goes without saying that the fundamental component of the linking hypothesis for acceptability judgments—that acceptability judgments are (relatively directly) influenced by grammaticality—has been well established by the success of the grammatical theories that have been constructed from acceptability judgments. But the answers to higher-level questions about the grammar, such as whether the grammar distinguishes two or more than two levels of grammaticality, have remained elusive. Section 3 will discuss several higher-level questions about the theory of acceptability that are currently the focus of much research on acceptability judgments. Section 4 attempts to tie these two strands together: the past 60 years have demonstrated that acceptability judgments are a robust, replicable, and reliable data type that appears to reveal deep information about the theory of grammar; but there is still much work to be done when it comes to using acceptability judgments (and any other relevant data types from psycholinguistics) to answer higher-level questions about the theory of grammar.

2 The methodology of acceptability judgements

Methodological research on acceptability judgments only requires two assumptions to get off the ground. The first assumption is that acceptability judgments are a behavioral task just like any other behavioral task in experimental psychology. In this case, it is a task that involves explicitly asking speakers to judge whether a string of words is a possible sentence of their language (either relative to the participants' best guess at the intended meaning, or relative to an explicitly given intended meaning). The second assumption is that this particular behavioral task is influenced by the theory of grammar (though, likely not exclusively). With these two assumptions in hand, we can ask any number of questions about the impact of various methodological choices on the properties of acceptability judgment data. Here I will discuss some of the most contentious questions, and therefore some of the most interesting findings, over the past several decades of methodological work on judgments.

2.1 Differences between acceptability judgment tasks

There are any number of tasks one can use to ask participants to report acceptability judgments. To ground this first part of the discussion, I will focus on four relatively common task types in the generative syntax literature:

(i) **n-point (Likert-esque) rating scales (LS)**: participants are presented with one sentence at a time, and asked to rate the acceptability of the sentence along a scale with a finite number of ordered points (e.g., 1–7), with endpoints labeled to indicate the direction of increasing acceptability.

(ii) **two-alternative forced-choice with nominal categories (YN)**: participants are presented with one sentence at a time, and asked to categorize the sentence into one of two categories, typically labeled grammatical/ungrammatical or yes/no.

(iii) **two-alternative forced-choice comparing the sentences (FC)**: participants are presented with two sentences, and asked to indicate which of the two sentences is more (or less) acceptable.

(iv) **(iv) magnitude estimation (ME)**: participants are presented with a reference sentence (called the standard), which is assigned a numerical acceptability level (called the modulus). They are then asked to rate target sentences (one at a time) as multiples of the acceptability of a reference sentence. For example, if the reference sentence is assigned an acceptability value of 100, participants might rate a target sentence that is twice as acceptable as 200.

The first question one can ask about these tasks is what kind of information each yields. The LS and ME tasks yield information about the location of a sentence along the continuum of acceptability, and therefore also yield information about the size of the difference in acceptability between two (or more) sentence types. As such, LS and ME are particularly well-suited to questions about relative acceptability. The YN task yields category information, which roughly correlates with the location of sentences along the continuum of acceptability. It is therefore particularly well-suited for questions about categorical acceptability, but ill-suited for questions about relative acceptability between sentence types that are both in the same category. It is also less well-suited for questions about effect sizes than LS and ME, because the only information it yields about the size of the difference between two sentences is the relative difference between the two category counts (number of yes's and number of no's), which is likely to be coarser-grained than scale-based information. The FC task yields information about a direct comparison between two sentences. It is therefore particularly well-suited to questions about differences between conditions. It does not yield any information about the location of the two sentences along the continuum of acceptability. And like YN, it is less well-suited to effect size questions, because the effect size information is mediated by counts. It almost goes without saying that the first criterion for choosing a task should be that it provides the type of information that will help to answer the theoretical question of interest. If the question is about relative acceptability, effect sizes, or location information, then LS and ME will likely be the best choice. If the question is about categorical information, then YN will be the best choice. If the question is about the presence of a difference between conditions, then FC will be the best choice.

The second question one can ask is how sensitive each task is to differences in acceptability between two (or more) conditions. Sprouse and Almeida (2017) investigated the sensitivity of these four tasks for 50 two-condition phenomena that span the range of effect sizes in the generative syntax literature, and for sample sizes from 5 participants up to 100 participants. They first collected ratings from 144 participants for each task, then used this real-world data to run re-sampling simulations (sampling with replacement) to estimate the proportion of (simulated) experiments that would successfully detect the difference between the two conditions in each phenomenon at each possible sample size from 5 participants to 100 participants. Figure 1 below shows the results of those re-sampling simulations. The y-axis reports the proportion of simulations that yielded a significant difference (an estimate of the statistical power of the experiment at that sample size). The x-axis reports the sample size from 5 to 100 participants. To make the plot more manageable, the phenomena were grouped into small, medium, large, and extra-large effect sizes, which are arranged by column. The colored lines report the change in the statistical power for each task as the sample size is increased. There are three very clear patterns in these results. First, the FC task is by far the most sensitive (i.e., shows the highest statistical power at smaller sample sizes and smaller effect sizes). This is not surprising given that the FC task is particularly well-suited to detecting differences between two conditions, which was exactly the definition of success in these experiments. Second, the YN task is often the least sensitive. Again, this is not surprising given how ill-suited the YN task is to detecting differences between conditions, especially in the cases where the two conditions are both in the same category (e.g., both yes or both no). Finally, the LS and ME tasks tend to track each other fairly closely for medium, large, and extra large effect sizes (but not small effect sizes). This parallelism is potentially interesting, but in order to understand it fully, we should take a closer look at the methodological studies that led to the adoption of ME in the generative syntax literature.

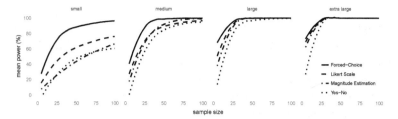

Fig. 1: Statistical power for four acceptability judgment tasks (adapted from Sprouse and Almeida 2017) displaying the relationship between sample size and estimated power, organized by effect size category (columns), with all four tasks plotted together. For clarity, only the (loess) fitted lines are plotted (no data points).

To understand the ME task it is important to first note that the LS task has two potential limitations, first discussed by Stevens (1957): (i) LS has a finite number of response options, which might lead to participants failing to report a distinction that they can nonetheless perceive; and (ii) LS assumes that participants treat the intervals between the response points as equal, but provides no mechanism to guarantee that. In an attempt to overcome these potential limitations, Stevens (1957) developed the ME task, which employs (i) a potentially infinite number of response options (any positive real number, though in practice responses are likely to be positive integers), and (ii) a reference stimulus that participants are instructed to use as a perceptual interval (thus guaranteeing that the intervals will be equal across trials within a single participant, though not necessarily between participants). Bard et al. (1996) and Cowart (1997) both observed that the LS task for acceptability judgments could potentially suffer from general LS limitations, and proposed adapting the ME task for acceptability. They both showed promising results with the ME task (as did Featherston (2005)). This raised the interesting question of whether the ME task should replace the LS task as the standard rating task for acceptability judgments. Featherston (2008) was perhaps the first to question the practical reality of the theoretical superiority of the ME task, reporting that, in his experience with the task, he did not believe that participants could truly perform the ratio judgments that the ME task requires (e.g., determine that one sentence is twice as acceptable as a reference sentence). Sprouse (2011) tested this issue directly by investigating whether participants' judgments in ME were commutative (i.e., the order of two successive judgments does not matter), which is one of the fundamental mathematical assumptions of the ratio judgments in ME (Luce, 2002; Narens, 1996). Sprouse (2011) found that participants' judgments were not commutative, confirming Featherston's 2008 observation that participants could not make the ratio judgments that ME requires. As both Featherston (2008) and Sprouse (2011) observe, this is not unexpected given that (i) ratio judgments require a meaningful zero point, and (ii) it is not clear that acceptability has a meaningful zero point (i.e., it is not clear what it would mean to say that a sentence has zero acceptability). Weskott and Fanselow (2011) also found that ME judgments showed higher variability than LS judgments, further undermining any claims that ME is superior to LS. It is possible that it is this increased variability that leads to ME having less statistical power than LS for small effect sizes in the Sprouse and Almeida 2017 study.

Despite the inability of participants to perform ratio judgments, it is still the case that ME judgments are robust, replicable, and reliable (as demonstrated by Bard et al. 1996, Cowart 1997, Featherston 2005, and all of the studies directly investigating the ME task). Though I know of no direct investigation of the source of ME judgments, it seems plausible that, when participants are faced with the impossible task of performing magnitude estimation of acceptability, they default to a type of LS task with an implicit scale defined by the number assigned to the reference sentence. There are at least two pieces of evidence indirectly supporting this possibility. The first is the nearly identical statistical power of the LS and ME tasks in the Sprouse and Almeida 2017 study for medium, large, and extra-large effect sizes (Figure 1 above). The second is the nearly perfect correlation between LS and ME judgments for the 300 distinct sentence types tested by Sprouse et al. (2013), both in the ratings of individual sentences, and in experimentally-defined effect sizes (the difference between a violation condition and a minimally different grammatical control condition). Though Sprouse et al. (2013) do not report that correlation in their paper, it is easily demonstrated using their data set, as in Figure 2. Under the assumption that ME becomes an LS task when used for acceptability judgments, several researchers have suggested exploring alternative tasks that preserve some of the potentially superior features of ME. Two promising tasks are Featherston's (2008) thermometer task, and rating tasks the employ a visual slider.

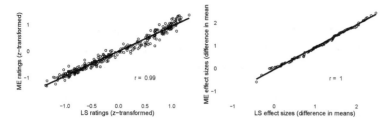

Fig. 2: A comparison of LS and ME for individual sentence type ratings (left panel) and experimentally defined effect sizes (the difference between a violation condition and a control condition; right panel). The Pearson correlation (rounded to two decimal places) is reported in each panel. Data is from Sprouse et al. (2013).

2.2 The validity of existing acceptability judgment data

A second major topic in the methodology of judgments has focused on the potential impact of the relatively informal judgment collection methods that typify generative syntax. The fundamental concern is that informal data collection methods might lead to spurious results (e.g., false positives), either because small sample sizes and lack of statistical significance testing might lead syntacticians to mistakenly see a signal in what is in fact noise, or because the practice of asking professional linguists for judgments might lead to effects driven by the cognitive bias of the professional linguists. This concern has arisen in one form or another since the earliest days of generative grammar (e.g., Hill 1961; Spencer 1973), it has played a central role in the two books that began the trend of employing more formal acceptability judgment experiments in the 1990s (Cowart, 1997; Schütze, 1996), and it has led to several high-profile discussions in the literature over the past decade and a half (see Featherston 2007; Ferreira 2005; Gibson and Fedorenko 2013; Wasow and Arnold 2005 for some criticisms of informal methods, and Marantz 2005 and Phillips 2009 for some rebuttals). To be clear, there is a straightforward method for determining whether this lack of confidence in informal methods is justified: compare the results of informal methods with the results of formal experimental methods. The results that converge between the two methods will benefit from the increase in confidence. The results that diverge can then be further investigated to determine which method is more likely giving the valid result (i.e., by manipulating the factors that give rise to concern in each method, such as the linguistic knowledge of the participants). Unfortunately, until the advent of crowdsourcing platforms like Amazon Mechanical Turk, it was nearly impossible to test the large number of phenomena that would be required to truly evaluate these concerns. The studies mentioned above do present a number of phenomena as examples of (purportedly) spurious judgments in the literature; however, in every case the phenomena were chosen with bias—the authors chose the phenomena because they suspected them to be spurious for one reason or another. It is impossible to estimate properties of a population from a biased sample. We simply do not know whether the dozen or so examples given in the studies mentioned above represent a small portion of the (purportedly) spurious results in the literature, or a large portion. The only way to truly address this issue is with non-biased sampling, either through the exhaustive testing of every phenomenon in a given population of phenomena, or through random sampling (which allows us to estimate a convergence rate for the population with a margin of error based on the sample and population sizes).

Two non-biased sampling studies have been conducted in English: Sprouse and Almeida 2012 tested every English data point in a recent generative syntax textbook (Adger, 2003), and Sprouse et al. (2013) randomly sampled 150 two-condition phenomena from a ten-year span of a leading generative syntax journal (*Linguistic Inquiry* 2001–2010). These studies used the best practices of experimental syntax (8 items per condition, latin square designs, sample sizes over 100 participants), tested these data points using several judgment tasks (LS, ME, FC, and YN), and analyzed the results using multiple statistical methods (standard frequentist tests like t-tests and sign-tests, Bayes Factors, and mixed-effects models). Because these studies used multiple tasks and multiple types of statistical tests, the results suggest a range of convergence rates depending on the precise properties of the experiment and the precise definition of the presence of an effect: Sprouse and Almeida (2012) found that 98–100 % of the data points from Adger's 2003 textbook replicated with formal experiments, and Sprouse et al. (2013) found that 86–99 % of the phenomena that they randomly sampled from Linguistic Inquiry 2001–2010 replicated with formal experiments, suggesting an estimate of 86–99 % ±5 for the complete set of data points published in the journal during that ten-year span. To be absolutely clear, these results do not reveal which method yields the better results. These results simply quantify the difference between the two methods. We would need targeted follow-up studies that manipulate specific mechanisms that could give rise to the divergent phenomena in order to establish which method provides the more accurate results. But what we can say with these results is that the divergence between the two methods is between 0 % and 14 %, depending on the population of phenomena, the judgment task (because they vary in statistical power), and the statistical test employed.

We can also use these studies to test the specific claim that the judgments of professional linguists may be impacted by theory-driven cognitive bias. An unambiguous signal of cognitive bias would be a sign reversal between the results of the formal experiments with naïve participants and the results of the informal experiments with professional linguists. Sprouse and Almeida (2012) found no sign reversals for Adger's textbook data. Sprouse et al. (2013) report a 1–3 % sign-reversal rate for the *Linguistic Inquiry* data with a margin of error of ± 5 on the estimate for the population. Mahowald et al. (2016) and Häussler et al. (2016) have replicated the Sprouse et al. (2013) results without reporting an increased sign reversal rate (0–6 %). Furthermore Culbertson and Gross (2009) performed direct comparisons of naïve and expert populations, and reported high inter- and intra-group correlations on 73 sentence types. Similarly, Dąbrowska (2010) found that while experts gave less variable ratings than naïve participants on several sentence types, the experts rated certain theoretically interesting syntactic violations as more acceptable than naïve participants, in apparent conflict with their theoretical commitments.

Taken together, these results suggest very little difference between informally collected and formally collected acceptability judgments, and very little evidence of cognitive bias influencing the judgments of (English-speaking) professional linguists. Of course, these studies all focused on one language, English, and all focused on one specific type of acceptability judgment (the type that can be given to a single written sentence, out of context, with no specific training on the intended interpretation). It is therefore logically possible that larger differences could obtain for other languages or other acceptability judgment types. But for now, the current state of evidence suggests that generative syntactic theories are built on robust, reliable, and replicable acceptability judgments, regardless of the specific method of collection.

2.3 The effect of factors other than grammaticality

A third major topic in methodology of judgments is to what extent factors other than grammaticality affect acceptability judgments. Because acceptability judgments are provided during or after the act of sentence processing, it is widely assumed that acceptability judgments will be impacted by all of the factors that influence sentence processing (complexity, ambiguity, frequency, plausibility, the disruption caused by a violation, etc.), as well as the various effects that might be caused by the judgment task itself (fatigue, repetition effects, comparison effects, etc). In other words, acceptability is assumed to be a multi-dimensional percept that is reported as a scalar value. As such, it is possible that any given acceptability effect might ultimately be due to extra-grammatical factors rather than grammaticality itself. The canonical example of this are doubly center-embedded sentences, as in (1) below. Miller and Chomsky (1963) argued that sentences like (1), which contain two relative clauses in the subject position, are unacceptable due to an inability to process the sentence, not due to a constraint in the grammar. Their primary argument was logical. They argued that grammars should not include constraints that count the number of operations that are deployed: if one relative clause can be constructed by the grammar, then two (or more) should also be able to be constructed. This analysis receives some empirical support from the fact that two (or more) relative clauses can be constructed in sequence if the relative clauses always appear in object positions (i.e., right-branching instead of center-embedded relative clauses) as in (2), and from the fact that the acceptability of doubly center-embedded relative clauses can be increased by manipulating factors known to decrease the processing complexity of sentences as in (3).

(1) The reporter who the senator that the president insulted contacted filed the story.

(2) The president insulted the senator who contacted the reporter that filed the story.

(3) Every reporter that the senator you voted for sent a press release to managed to file a story.

Though it is logically possible that sentence processing factors could be driving the effects that generative syntacticians build into their grammars, to my knowledge, doubly center-embedded relative clauses are still the only uncontroversial example of this phenomenon. There are controversial candidates. For example, it has been proposed several times in the literature that island effects—the unacceptability that arises when the tail of a long-distance dependency is inside certain structures, such as the embedded polar question in (4)—may arise due to sentence processing complications (Deane, 1991; Hofmeister and Sag, 2010; Kluender and Kutas, 1993).

(4) * What do you wonder whether Mary wrote ___ ?

However, unlike doubly center-embedded relatives, the preponderance of evidence currently suggests that sentence processing theories cannot account for the full range of facts surrounding island effects. First, there are several properties of island effects that make any simple sentence processing based account unlikely, such as the fact that there is cross-linguistic variation in island effects (Engdahl, 1982; Rizzi, 1982), the fact that wh-in-situ languages like Chinese and Japanese still show a subset of island effects despite the wh-word sitting in its interpreted position (Huang, 1982; Lasnik and Saito, 1982), and the fact that dependencies with tails inside of island structures are grammatical (in some languages) when there is an additional gap outside of the island structure (these are called parasitic gap constructions, Engdahl 1982). Second, direct investigations of sentence processing based theories of island effects have tended to yield results that run contrary to the plausible predictions of those theories. For example, one prominent theory proposed by Kluender and Kutas (1993) is that island effects arise from limitations in working memory that prevent the parser from completing long-distance dependencies inside of island structures. One potential prediction of this theory is that the parser will not be able to complete dependencies inside of island structures. However, Phillips (2006) found that the parser could in fact complete dependencies inside of certain island structures—namely those that can host parasitic gaps—despite the fact that participants rate those sentences as unacceptable. This suggests that the unacceptability is not driven by a failure of the parser, but rather by something else, such as a constraint in the grammar. Another potential prediction is that the unacceptability of island effects will vary as a function of the working memory capacity of individual speakers. However, Sprouse et al. (2012) found that there is no correlation between working memory capacity and island effects for two types of working memory tasks and four types of island effects (a result that was replicated by Michel 2014 for additional working memory tasks). One final potential prediction is that island effects should arise for all dependencies that involve the same sentence processing mechanisms as wh-dependencies. However, Yoshida et al. (2014) demonstrated that certain (backward) binding dependencies do not respect island structures, despite the fact that those binding dependencies appear to be processed using mechanisms that are behaviorally similar to wh-dependencies (Kazanina et al., 2007; Sturt, 2003; Van Gompel and Liversedge, 2003), and despite the fact that the processing of those binding dependencies involve the same cortical areas as the processing of wh-dependencies (Matchin et al., 2014). In the end, though it is logically possible that sentence processing effects could be the cause of the unacceptability for each of the sentence types that syntacticians label as ungrammatical, uncontroversial examples of sentence processing effects causing (substantial) unacceptability appear to be few and far between (with doubly center-embedded relative clauses perhaps being the only one).

In contrast to doubly center-embedded relative clauses, which suggest that sentence processing effects can substantially lower acceptability, there are also constructions that suggest that sentence processing effects can substantially increase acceptability (at least temporarily). These constructions are sometimes called *grammatical illusions*: sentences that are (widely assumed to be) ungrammatical, but are nonetheless rated as acceptable by native speakers (or at least more acceptable than one might expect). These constructions are potentially interesting as they potentially reveal the complex relationship between grammatical theories and sentence processing theories (Lewis and Phillips, 2015; Phillips and Lewis, 2013). However, from the point of view of detailing the effects of processing on acceptability, grammatical illusions are similar to doubly center-embedded relative clauses in that there are relatively few constructions that show this behavior. Lewis and Phillips (2015) find just three examples:

(5)   More people have been to Russia than I have.

(6)   The key to the cabinets are missing.

(7)   The bills that no senators voted for will ever become law.

The first is the comparative illusion, first noted by Montalbetti (1984), and further explored by Townsend and Bever (2001). The comparative illusion has no meaning, and is therefore assumed to be ungrammatical (under the assumption that grammaticality entails a meaning). Yet it is nonetheless reported to be acceptable by native speakers (e.g., Wellwood et al. 2014). The second example is a phenomenon called agreement attraction. The sentence in (6) is ungrammatical: the subject of the sentence (key) is singular, while the verb shows plural agreement (are). Nonetheless, agreement attraction illusions arise in both production tasks (Bock and Miller, 1991), and comprehension tasks (Staub, 2010; Wagers et al., 2009). The third example is illusory negative polarity item (NPI) licensing. It is widely assumed that NPIs such as ever must be c-commanded by a downward entailing operator such as negation. By this assumption, the sentence in (7) should be ungrammatical: no is within a relative clause, and therefore does not c-command ever, leaving ever unlicensed. Nonetheless, some portion of speakers rate (7) as if it were acceptable, at least for a short while (Parker and Phillips, 2016; Xiang et al., 2009). Each of these phenomena have given rise to a rich literature that goes far beyond the scope of this chapter (but see the citations above for a good starting point in each of these literatures). For our purposes, the take-home message of each of these phenomena is that sentence processing mechanisms can increase acceptability, but only in very limited cases where the implementation of grammatical constraints in an online processor creates the opportunity for errors.

The other major strand of research in the literature on extra-grammatical factors has focused on the effects of the acceptability judgment task itself. To date, there have been at least three major questions in this strand. Two of these we have covered in previous sections: the statistical power of different tasks and the consequences of naïve versus expert participant populations. The third is the effect of repetitions on acceptability judgments. Repetition effects are a potential issue for any data type—as participants are repeatedly exposed to a stimulus, their responses to that stimulus could change (at both the behavioral and neurophysiological levels). For acceptability judgments, it has been reported that some violation types are rated higher after repeated exposures (e.g., Nagata 1988, 1989; Snyder 2000). However, instead of simply viewing repetition effects as a potential confound to be avoided in judgment experiments, repetition effects have become a special topic of interest within the acceptability judgment literature because of some initial results that suggest that repetition effects could be used as a tool to differentiate different types of phenomena, either based on categorical repetition (those that show effects and those that do not), or based on the rate of repetition effects. This is a potentially interesting tool for syntacticians to leverage; however, the empirical results of repetition studies are mixed. Whereas some studies report results that suggest potentially theoretically interesting patterns of repetition effects (e.g., Snyder 2000), attempts to replicate those results have met with mixed success (Braze, 2002; Hiramatsu, 2000; Sprouse, 2009). The current state of evidence suggests that, to the extent that repetition effects exist, they are relatively small, and may be influenced by factors that are not relevant to grammatical theories (see, e.g., Francom 2009 for evidence that interpretability of violations may be a critical factor).

3 The theory of acceptability judgements

The primary goal of research on the theory of acceptability judgments is to determine exactly what we can (and cannot) learn about the grammar from acceptability judgments. As briefly mentioned in section 1, this requires an explicit formulation of the linking hypothesis between acceptability judgments and the theory of grammar. There is likely a lot of variation among syntacticians when it comes to beliefs about the linking hypothesis of acceptability judgments, so much so that it is impossible to do justice to all of the possible positions in a chapter of this size. Therefore my strategy in this section is to first lay out (in sections 3.1 and 3.2) a subset of the components of a linking hypothesis that I think are fairly widely assumed in the generative syntax literature (though perhaps not universally assumed), and then to use the remainder of this section to explore some of the major questions that arise in the use of acceptability judgments to make inferences about the grammar (sections 3.3 and 3.4).

3.1 Common, though perhaps not universal, assumptions about acceptability judgments

The first common assumption, and one that was implicit in the preceding sections, is that there is a percept called *acceptability* that arises for native speakers of a language during the comprehension of sentence-like word strings. Exactly how this percept arises is a matter of debate. For many, it is assumed to be an error signal of some sort. The precise mechanisms that give rise to the error signal are often left unspecified, presumably because the details of the error detection mechanisms do not (yet) impact the interpretation of acceptability judgments. Similarly, this error signal is often commonly assumed to be an automatic process (as opposed to a controlled process); though again, it is not clear how much impact the automatic/controlled distinction has on the interpretation of acceptability judgments. The second common assumption, and one that was central to the discussion in the preceding sections, is that acceptability is a scalar percept that is derived from multiple sources. This fits well with the error-signal assumption: there are multiple types of errors that can be detected, some of which can co-occur in the same sentence; these errors are then combined to form a single percept. It is also common to assume that the combination of factors is linear, both because linear models are the simplest starting point, and because there is currently little evidence that *distinct* factors combine non-linearly. To be clear, there is some evidence that *similar* factors combine non-linearly: see Hofmeister et al. (2014) for some evidence of non-linear combination of processing factors, and Keller (2003) for evidence of non-linear combination of grammatical factors. But these could be explained as interactions of similar components, rather than a fundamental non-linearity of the system. The final assumption, which again, has figured prominently in the preceding discussions, is that the multiple sources contributing to acceptability include both grammatical factors and sentence processing factors. Though this is easy enough to state (and to encode in a general linear model), from a cognitive point of view, the fact that both grammatical and sentence processing factors influence acceptability raises difficult (but interesting) questions about what the relationship is between grammatical theories, sentence processing theories, and the cognitive systems in the human mind—a question that we turn to next in our exploration of the relationship between acceptability and grammaticality.

3.2 What is syntactic theory a theory of?

This question is obviously much larger than the question of building a theory of acceptability judgments, but it is a critical component of building such a theory because acceptability appears to be affected by both grammatical factors and sentence processing factors. Therefore the relationship that one assumes between the theory of grammar and the theory of sentence processing will directly impact the formulation of a complete linking hypothesis for acceptability judgments, and concomitantly constrain the types of inferences one can make about the grammar from acceptability judgments. There have been a number of discussions of this question in the literature recently, such as Lewis and Phillips (2015); Neeleman and van de Koot (2010); Phillips and Lewis (2013). The discussion here will largely mirror those discussions, albeit with much less detail. The first question one can ask is whether syntactic theories are theories of a cognitive system in the human mind (mentalistic) or theories of an object outside of the human mind (non-mentalistic). Though there is a rich tradition of non-mentalistic approaches to linguistics, I am going to focus exclusively on mentalistic syntactic theories here, partly because the theory in Syntactic Structures is mentalistic, and partly because it is not clear what the linking hypothesis for acceptability judgments would be for non-mentalistic theories of syntax.

The second question we can ask is what is the cognitive system that syntactic theories describe. Is there a "grammar system" in the mind that is distinct from other cognitive systems that subserve language, such as the sentence processing system (what Lewis and Phillips 2015 call the "two-system" approach)? Or is it the case that syntactic theories and sentence processing theories are two different descriptions of a single cognitive system (what Lewis and Phillips 2015 call a "one-system" approach)? The answer to this question will determine the relationship between the grammar and sentence processing terms in the specification of a model of acceptability judgments. If there are two systems, then the terms will be separate: a complete grammatical model plus a complete sentence processing model, plus a theory of how the two interact. If there is only one cognitive system, then the theory of acceptability judgments is really a theory of error signals from sentence processing, with syntacticians attempting to partial out the component of the error signal that corresponds to the component of sentence processing that syntactic theories characterize. Though the two-system approach is reminiscent of some sentence processing models (e.g., Ferreira and Patson 2007; Townsend and Bever 2001) that posit two stages of processing, and though the two-system view does arise from time to time in conversations among syntacticians, I know of no detailed defense of the two-system view in the generative syntax literature (except, possibly, Seely and Epstein 2006. Therefore here I will primarily entertain the one-system view, and ask the natural follow-up question: If syntactic theory is a description of the sentence processing system at some level of abstraction, which component of sentence processing is it a theory of?

One popular approach to levels of description is Marr's (1982) famous three-level typology: the computational level describes the problem that needs to be solved, the algorithmic level describes the algorithm for solving that problem, and the implementation level describes the physical machine that instantiates the algorithm. There are a number of criticisms of Marr's levels as applied to cognition, so I will not argue that this is the correct (or only) way of thinking about theories of languages here. Instead, what I want to demonstrate is that once one uses a typology of levels (Marr's, or any other), it rapidly becomes clear that syntactic theory is not an abstraction of the complete sentence processing system; it is only an abstraction of a subcomponent of the sentence processing system. For example, it is not uncommon for syntacticians to describe syntactic theory as a computational level description (following Marr himself), i.e., a description of the problem that needs to be solved. But syntactic theory does not have components to encode many of the problems that are central to sentence processing, such as ambiguity resolution, dependency processing, memory processes, and many others. In fact, if one were to attempt to extrapolate from syntactic theories (assumed to be a computational level description) up to the algorithmic and implementation levels, the resulting machine would likely be one that could generate all and only the sentences of a given language, but with no components that could successfully parse or produce sentences incrementally. This suggests that, under the one-system approach, syntactic theories are a (computational-level) description of a subset of the sentence processing system, specifically the structure-building component, abstracting away from the precise algorithms of structure-building. This is exactly the conclusion reached by a number of syntacticians (e.g.,Neeleman and van de Koot 2010; Phillips and Lewis 2013), and I suspect the most common view in generative syntax. What this means for the theory of acceptability is that the "grammar" component of the theory of acceptability will be something like an error signal from the structure-building component of the sentence processor. This in turn means that the "sentence processing" component of the theory of acceptability judgments will be everything that isn't structure-building: parsing strategies for various types of ambiguity resolution, the complexity that arises from ambiguity resolution (e.g., surprisal, Hale 2001; Levy 2008), the complexity that arises from dependency processing (Gibson, 1998), the complexity that arises from working memory operations more generally (Lewis and Vasishth, 2005; McElree et al., 2003), and many others components.

3.3 Gradience in acceptability judgments

Once we've settled on the relationship between grammatical theories and sentence processing theories, we can begin to investigate how it is that acceptability can be used to make inferences about the grammar. One major question in current research on acceptability judgments is what consequence, if any, does the fact that acceptability judgments are gradient have for inferences about the grammar. Acceptability judgments are gradient in at least two ways. The first is that the acceptability ratings of individual sentence types appear to form a continuum (no categorical clumping) when a large number of distinct sentence types are plotted simultaneously. The left panel of Figure 3 demonstrates this for the 300 distinct sentence types tested by Sprouse et al. (2013) in their study of data points from *Linguistic Inquiry* by plotting the mean ratings for each sentence type (ordered by increasing acceptability). The second way that acceptability judgments are gradient is that the effect sizes of experimentally-defined phenomena also appear to form a continuum (with no categorical clumping). The middle panel of Figure 3 demonstrates this for the 150 two-condition phenomena that Sprouse et al. (2013) tested from *Linguistic Inquiry* by plotting the means of the two conditions of each phenomena (thus highlighting the difference between means as an effect size), and the right panel of Figure 3 demonstrates this by plotting a standardized effect size measure (Cohen's d, which is the difference between means scaled by the standard deviations of the conditions). Crucially, these two-condition phenomena were specifically designed to isolate a putative grammatical manipulation while holding other potential sources of acceptability judgment variability constant.

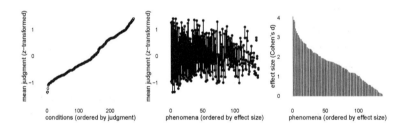

Fig. 3: Three demonstrations of gradience. The left panel plots the mean ratings for 300 sentence types from *Linguistic Inquiry*, arranged by increasing acceptability. Although the line looks solid, it is 300 empty circles. The middle panel plots the means of the two conditions in each of 136 phenomena that replicated under a strict statistical criterion of replication in Sprouse et al. 2013. This highlights their effect sizes in natural units (z-scored ratings), arranged by decreasing effect size. The right panel plots standardized effect sizes (Cohen's d) for the same 136 phenomena, again arranged by decreasing effect size.

The question, then, is what is driving this gradience. Is the grammar itself gradient (i.e., is the structure-building component of sentence processing gradient)? Or is the grammar categorical, with the gradience of acceptability deriving from the other aspects of the sentence processing system?

This question is impossible to answer from acceptability judgments alone. Both categorical and gradient grammars can explain gradient acceptability judgments; they simply do so with different mechanisms. For categorical grammars, the structure-builder itself is limited to contributing a finite number of levels of acceptability (typically two, but in principle any finite number is possible). The apparent continuum that we see in the acceptability of individual sentences (left panel of Figure 3) must therefore come from some combination of the following:

(i) the effects of typical sentence processing over the portion of the sentence that can be processed typically, such as dependency complexity, ambiguity resolution complexity (e.g., surprisal), working memory, etc,
(ii) the effects of atypical sentence processing over any structure-building violations, such as processes that are designed to construct an interpretable structure out of word strings.
(iii) plausibility and real-world knowledge effects,
(iv) task effects, and
(v) any number of other components of sentence processing and acceptability judgments that we may not have explored yet.

That said, we can minimize the impact of the effects of typical processing, plausibility and real-world knowledge, task effects, and possibly even unexplored factors by using experimentally-defined phenomena (as in the right panel of Figure 3), and focusing on the effect size of the difference between them. This effect size is primarily a combination of the structure-builder error signal, the effect of atypical processing, plus whatever factors weren't perfectly controlled in the design itself. Therefore, under a binary categorical grammar the gradience we see in the right panel of Figure 3 is primarily the effect of atypical processing and any uncontrolled factors (because each phenomenon contains one grammatical and one ungrammatical sentence, so the contribution of the structure-builder error signal is the same for each phenomenon).

Gradient grammatical theories differ in their explanation of gradience in two ways. The first is obvious: instead of the structure-building component contributing only a finite number of values, truly gradient grammatical theories posit that the structure-building component can contribute a potentially infinite number of values. This means that a major component of the gradience of acceptability for individual sentences would simply be the gradient value returned by the structure-builder when it is asked to construct the target structure, and the gradience for experimentally-defined effects would be the difference in those values. In many gradient grammars the value returned by the structure-builder is grounded in some primitive of the theory, such as harmony values in harmonic grammars (with OT being a special case of harmonic grammars; Keller 2000; Smolensky and Legendre 2006) or probabilities in various probabilistic grammars (e.g. Lau et al. 2017). The second way that gradient grammatical theories could, at least in principle, differ is in the contribution of atypical processing (item (ii) above). Whereas atypical processing is logical option for categorical grammars when the structure-builder encounters a violation, it is not clear to what extent atypical processing would occur for gradient grammars; and indeed, it is not clear what would constitute "atypical" for a truly gradient structure-builder. It is therefore possible that atypical processing, whatever that might mean for a gradient grammar, would have a decreased role, if any, in determining acceptability in gradient grammars. This means that for many gradient grammars, the gradience in acceptability we see in Figure 3 is potentially a fairly direct reflection of the values of the gradient grammar (modulo any uncontrolled factors in the design).

As a quick aside, it is important to note that the components listed above are not intended to exhaust the space of possible factors influencing acceptability judgments (as indicated by item (v) above). For example, one potentially relevant idea that is sometimes discussed in the field is that minimum (linguistic) edit distances may be relevant for gradient acceptability. The idea is that, during an acceptability judgment task, participants might be implicitly comparing violation sentences to the minimally different grammatical sentences that have the same meanings. If so, it could be the case that acceptability judgments are impacted by the similarity/dissimilarity between the violation sentence and the grammatical counterpart. Similarity/dissimilarity can be quantified using a multidimensional distance measure, such as the number of (linguistic) edits necessary to convert from the ungrammatical sentence to the grammatical sentence. Crucially, distance effects are very likely to correlate with atypical processing costs: as dissimilarity between an ungrammatical sentence and its grammatical counterpart increases, the distance between them increases, as does the need to do atypical processing to derive an interpretable sentence. This means that if such an implicit comparison is part of the theory of acceptability judgments, the cost that arises for minimum (linguistic) edit distance could either be an additional factor influencing acceptability, or a factor that partially (or completely) overlaps with atypical processing.

The debate between categorical and gradient grammars will only be settled by constructing large chunks of theories, spanning dozens or hundreds of phenomena. With large chunks of theories, one could probe both external predictions of the theory, such as predictions about language acquisition, and internal predictions, such as predictions about gradient acceptability. For example, for categorical grammatical theories, one way to probe internal predictions about gradient acceptability would be to evaluate how well independently-motivated aspects of sentences processing can be combined with categorical grammars to yield empirically attested patterns of gradient acceptability. Though the logic of this is straightforward enough, there are two major challenges to constructing a complete theory of acceptability judgments using categorical grammars. The first is that theories of typical sentence processing are an active area of research. It is true that there are candidate theories for calculating dependency costs (Gibson, 1998), memory costs (Lewis and Vasishth, 2005; McElree et al., 2003), and even complexity for the different continuations of ambiguous strings (e.g., surprisal as in Hale 2001 and Levy 2008, perhaps combined with the Hunter and Dyer 2013 method for creating probabilistic minimalist grammars); however, these theories have not yet been applied to the full range of sentence types that appear in the large acceptability judgment corpora that one would like to test (and indeed, doing so would be a monumental undertaking, as it would require creating both formal grammars with coherent coverage of the sentences types, and sentence processing models with coherent coverage of the sentence types). The second major challenge is that there is little to no research on the atypical sentence processing that arises for ungrammatical sentences. Most of the syntax and sentence processing literatures has focused on the categorical detection of errors, not the costs or processes associated with those errors. Aside from the research on doubly center-embedded sentences and grammatical illusions, it is not clear that this kind of atypical processing is a priority for either field at the moment.

Similarly, for gradient grammatical theories, one way to probe internal predictions about gradient acceptability would be to calculate the (cognitively grounded) values of the gradient grammar independently of acceptability judgments, and then ask how well those values correlate with acceptability. The major challenges with this approach will be unique to each type of gradient grammatical theory, because those challenges will be driven by the type of value that the gradient grammar is built upon. For example, for harmonic grammars, the value in question is harmony, which is a value grounded in the activation of a neural network. Since we cannot independently measure network activation in human minds, the challenge would be to empirically build harmonic grammars using the acceptability judgments of a set of phenomena that involve the same constraints as a distinct, second set of phenomena, and then see how well the grammar can predict acceptability of the second set of phenomena. As a second example, for probabilistic grammars, the value in question is a probability, likely derived from the production probabilities of sentences in natural language corpora. The challenge with this is that both classes of theories, categorical and gradient, predict a relationship between acceptability and production probabilities. For the gradient grammars, the probabilities in the grammar give rise to the production probabilities and give rise to the acceptability judgments. For categorical grammars, the grammar plus the sentence processing system give rise to the production probabilities, and the grammar plus the sentence processing system give rise to the acceptability judgments. The difference between gradient and categorical theories would therefore be in the degree of correlation between production probabilities and acceptability judgments. One relatively simple prediction would be that the correlation would be lower for categorical grammars because the sentence processing system might cause different effects in acceptability (where the primary issue is atypical processing) and production (where the primary issue is typical processing). But without specific theories to work with, it is difficult to quantify exactly what the difference would be. In the end, this means that for many types of gradient grammatical theories, the best we can say is how well acceptability correlates with the value of interest, without being able to quantify if the correlation is exceptionally high, mediocre, or low for the space of possible grammars.

Despite these challenges, the gradience of acceptability is one of the more fruitful research questions in the acceptability judgment literature today. For one, the stakes are high: this question directly bears on the architecture of the grammar. For two, the only way to make progress on this question is to investigate corners of language that are often overlooked in generative syntax, such as atypical processing, formalizing full grammars, and directly evaluating the cognitively grounded values of gradient grammars. Finally, this question requires large-scale research projects spanning dozens, or hundreds, of sentence types. Given these properties, it is almost impossible for well-designed projects to fail to reveal something new about syntactic theory.

3.4 Absolute acceptability, experimentally-defined effects, and effect sizes

Another major question in current research on acceptability judgments is how to use the different aspects of acceptability judgments as evidence for (un)grammaticality. There are at least three aspects of acceptability that are used as evidence in syntactic theories: (i) the acceptability of individual sentence types, (ii) the presence or absence of a difference in acceptability between two (or more) minimally different sentence types (what I have called an experimentally-defined effect), and (iii) the size of the difference in acceptability between two (or more) sentence types (the size of the experimentally defined effect). The first, and most obvious, approach is to focus exclusively on the acceptability of individual sentence types. In Syntactic Structures, Chomsky assumes a transparent mapping between grammaticality and the acceptability of individual sentence types (modulo well-known counter-examples like doubly center-embedded sentences), such that sentence types at the low end of the spectrum are assumed to be ungrammatical, and sentences at the high end are assumed to be grammatical. As Chomsky anticipates, sentences near the middle of the spectrum will be problematic for this transparent mapping. In *Syntactic Structures*, Chomsky argues that a suitably well-defined grammar will simply predict the grammaticality of intermediate sentences, so that we do not need to rely on acceptability judgments at all: "In many intermediate cases we shall be prepared to let the grammar itself decide, when the grammar is set up in the simplest way so that it includes the clear sentences and excludes the clear non-sentences (p.14)". In other words, a grammar that is well-specified for the clear cases should predict (some number of) the unclear cases. Based on the previous discussion, we can also add that a well-specified theory of the extra-grammatical factors that influence acceptability could also help to predict some number of the unclear cases. But in the absence of those two well-specified theories, we must rely on syntacticians' best scientific judgment about what might be driving the acceptability of the unclear cases. Because scientific opinions differ, this can lead to syntacticians interpreting unclear cases in opposing ways (see Schütze 1996 for some examples, and see Hoji 2015 for a strict criterion for separating clear from unclear cases).

Given the potential difficulty of interpreting the acceptability of individual sentences in the middle of the spectrum, one might wonder whether focusing on experimentally-defined effects (differences between two or more conditions) might help to solve the problem. The simplest way to do this would be to look for the presence or absence of a difference between two (or more) sentence types that have been constructed to control for as many extra-grammatical properties as possible, such that any resulting difference is likely to be driven by grammatical differences. The problem with using the presence/absence of effects as a discovery procedure for grammatical effects is the phrase "likely to be drive by grammatical differences". We can never control for every possible extra-grammatical effect on acceptability in the design. This means that there is always going to be some difference between the conditions in our experiment, albeit potentially very small (meaning that to detect it with standard statistical tests, we may need relatively large sample sizes). Because there is always some difference between our conditions, this means that the interpretation of the presence/absence of an effect is in fact an interpretation of the size of the effect. Is the size of the effect the size we would expect from a grammatical effect (given the design of the experiment, and what we know about grammatical effects), or is it the size we would expect from an extra-grammatical effect (given the design of the experiment, and what we know about extra-grammatical effects). This is the same issue that we have seen throughout this section: even the experimentally-defined effects require a theory of acceptability judgments to be interpreted. What we have at the moment is a partial (and ever-growing) theory, so some amount of interpretation must be filled in by the scientific judgment of individual researchers. (To be fair, this issue is not unique to syntax. I know of no complete theory of any data type in language science, from reading times, to event-related potentials, to BOLD signals. In each case, there are partial theories that are augmented by the best scientific judgment of researchers and reviewers.)

Given the issues that arise when individual acceptability and experimentally-defined effects are used in isolation, another option is to interpret both individual acceptability and experimentally-defined effects in combination with one another. Though I know of no studies counting the different approaches to acceptability-grammaticality mappings, my impression is that this combination approach is the one most frequently adopted by syntacticians. The underlying idea is that a clear grammatical effect should yield a relatively large experimentally-defined effect, with the individual rating of the ungrammatical sentence near the low end of the spectrum of acceptability. To be clear, this approach does not eliminate the problems of intermediate individual acceptability and small effect sizes. But it does make it a bit easier to draw attention to these issues. In fact, this combination approach has uncovered some potentially interesting mismatches between individual acceptability and the presence of experimentally-defined effects, where there is a statistically significant effect, but all of the sentences in the design would still be labeled as "acceptable" in a categorical task. For example, Featherston (2005) famously observed a pattern of acceptability judgments that indicated a Superiority effect in German, despite the fact that many German native speakers label the critical sentences as "acceptable". Similarly, Almeida (2014) found a pattern of acceptability that is indicative of a wh-island effect in Brazilian Portuguese, despite the critical sentences being marginally or fully acceptable. Kush et al. (submitted) found a similar pattern for wh-islands in Norwegian. These results raise interesting questions for syntactic theories. Are these effects driven by a grammatical violation or an extra-grammatical factor (that is specific to the critical condition)? Is it possible for the violation of a grammatical constraint to result in marginal, or even fully acceptable, sentences? Must there be a mitigating factor in these cases (e.g., a sentence processing effect that raises acceptability)? Or are these effects simply evidence that a gradient approach to syntactic theory is more likely to be correct? There are no easy answers to these questions; but the ability to quantify both aspects of acceptability has brought these questions into sharper focus, potentially yielding new evidence about the nature of syntactic theories.

Though it goes beyond the scope of this chapter, for completeness it is important to note that another method for dealing with indeterminate acceptability facts (beyond building a complete theory of acceptability, and beyond relying on syntacticians' scientific judgments) is to look for converging evidence from other sentence-processing data types, such as reading times, eye-movements, and electrophysiological measures such as event-related potentials. This literature is far too large to review in any detail here, but it is worth noting that there is an impressive literature demonstrating (i) that many grammatical constraints are respected by real-time sentence processing mechanisms, and (ii) that grammatical violations are often detected within a few hundred milliseconds of the violating word in real-time sentence processing (see Lewis and Phillips 2015 for some review; see also Sprouse and Lau 2013 for an extensive bibliography of ERP studies that detect syntactic violations relatively rapidly). Given the sheer number of grammatical effects that have been catalogued in the sentence-processing literature, it seems likely that indeterminate acceptability effects that are based on true grammatical violations would also show some sort of real-time processing consequence; however, as always, the exact nature of that consequence will depend upon developing a theory of sentence processing, and, of course, a theory of the data type in question.

4 Acceptability and grammaticality, prospects and challenges

At a methodological level, I take the current state of evidence to suggest: (i) judgment tasks are fairly sensitive, especially for the relatively large effects that characterize syntactic theory, (ii) judgments are robust, reliable, and replicable, regardless of the method used to collect them (at least for English), (iii) judgments are only affected by sentence processing effects in relatively limited circumstances (that may be revealing of the architecture of sentence processing more than the architecture of the grammar), and (iv) judgments are relatively unaffected by task effects such as repetition (at least within the scope of typical judgment experiments). With the caveat that future research could potentially overturn one or more of these trends, I find the current state of affairs incredibly encouraging for the use of acceptability judgments as a data type in generative syntax. Acceptability judgments are a well-described data type that yields surprisingly robust data. That said, the methodological landscape is as fertile as ever. There are literally dozens of topics left to explore when it comes to judgment methodology, such as the effect of the composition of the experiment, the effect of instructions (see Cowart 1997 for a first study), the effect of word and construction frequency (see Featherston 2009 for some comments on this), the effect of the size of rating scales, the comparison of informal and formal methods for other languages and data types, and many others.

At a theoretical level, many of the same challenges that the field faced in 1957 are still present today. We are still far from constructing a complete theory of typical and atypical sentence processing, or developing a complete theory of the (cognitive) values that ground gradient grammars. Nonetheless, there are reasons to be optimistic. Though we don't have complete theories of these systems, we do have partial theories, and an ever-growing array of tools to make progress on those theories. Furthermore, the field is cognizant as ever of the challenges facing the use of acceptability judgments as evidence for grammar, and is meeting those challenges head-on by focusing on difficult topics, such as gradience in acceptability and the role of effect sizes, that will necessarily spur advances in the theory of acceptability. Some challenges still remain for the daily work of syntacticians, such as indeterminate acceptability effects and clashes between individual acceptability ratings and experimentally-defined effects, but this challenge too may spur advances, as syntacticians increasingly seek converging evidence from multiple data types. All in all, I believe it has been a productive 60 years, and can hardly wait for the next 60.

Bibliography

Adger, David. 2003. *Core syntax: A minimalist approach*, volume 33. Oxford University Press Oxford.
Almeida, Diogo. 2014. Subliminal wh-islands in brazilian Portuguese and the consequences for Syntactic theory. *Revista da ABRALIN* 13.
Bard, Ellen Gurman, Dan Robertson, and Antonella Sorace. 1996. Magnitude estimation of linguistic acceptability. *Language* 32–68.
Bock, Kathryn, and Carol A Miller. 1991. Broken agreement. *Cognitive psychology* 23:45–93.
Braze, David. 2002. Grammaticality, Acceptability and Sentence Processing: A psycholinguistics study. Doctoral Dissertation, University of Connecticut.
Chomsky, Noam. 1957. *Syntactic Structures*. The Hague, The Netherlands: Mouton de Gruyter.
Cowart, Wayne. 1997. *Experimental Syntax: Applying objective methods to sentence judgments.*. Thousand Oaks, CA: Sage.
Culbertson, Jennifer, and Steven Gross. 2009. Are linguists better subjects? *The British journal for the philosophy of science* 60:721–736.

Dąbrowska, Ewa. 2010. Naïve v. expert intuitions: An empirical study of acceptability judgments. *The linguistic review* 27:1–23.
Deane, Paul. 1991. Limits to attention: A cognitive theory of island phenomena. *Cognitive Linguistics (includes Cognitive Linguistic Bibliography)* 2:1–64.
Engdahl, Elisabet. 1982. Restrictions on unbounded dependencies in Swedish. In *Readings on unbounded dependencies in Scandinavian languages*, ed. E. Engdahl and E. Ejerhd, 151–174. Stockholm, Sweeden: Almqvist & Wiksell.
Featherston, Sam. 2005. Magnitude estimation and what it can do for your syntax: Some wh-constraints in German. *Lingua* 115:1525–1550.
Featherston, Sam. 2007. Data in generative grammar: The stick and the carrot. *Theoretical linguistics* 33:269–318.
Featherston, Sam. 2008. Thermometer judgements as linguistic evidence. In *Was ist linguistische evidenz*, ed. C. M. Riehl and A. Rothe. Aachen, Germany: Shaker Verlag.
Featherston, Sam. 2009. Relax, lean back, and be a linguist. *Zeitschrift für Sprachwissenschaft* 28:127–132.
Ferreira, Fernanda. 2005. Psycholinguistics, formal grammars, and cognitive science. *The Linguistic Review* 22:365–380.
Ferreira, Fernanda, and Nikole D Patson. 2007. The 'good enough' approach to language comprehension. *Language and Linguistics Compass* 1:71–83.
Francom, Jerid. 2009. Experimental syntax: Exploring the effect of repeated exposure to anomalous syntactic structure — evidence from rating and reading tasks. Doctoral Dissertation, University of Arizona.
Gibson, Edward. 1998. Linguistic complexity: Locality of syntactic dependencies. *Cognition* 68:1–76.
Gibson, Edward, and Evelina Fedorenko. 2013. The need for quantitative methods in syntax and semantics research. *Language and Cognitive Processes* 28:88–124.
Hale, John. 2001. A probabilistic Earley parser as a psycholinguistic model. In *Proceedings of the second meeting of the North American Chapter of the Association for Computational Linguistics on Language technologies*, 1–8. Association for Computational Linguistics.
Häussler, Jana, Tom Juzek, and Thomas Wasow. 2016. To be grammatical or not to be grammatical — Is that the question? Poster presented at the Annual Meeting of the Linguistic Society of America.
Hill, Archibald A. 1961. Grammaticality. *Word* 17:1–10.
Hiramatsu, Kazuko. 2000. Accessing linguistic competence: Evidence from children's and adults' acceptability judgements. Doctoral Dissertation, University of Connecticut.
Hofmeister, Philip, Laura Staum Casasanto, and Ivan A Sag. 2014. Processing effects in linguistic judgment data:(super-) additivity and reading span scores. *Language and Cognition* 6:111–145.
Hofmeister, Philip, and Ivan A Sag. 2010. Cognitive constraints and island effects. *Language* 86:366.
Hoji, Hajime. 2015. *Language Faculty Science*. Cambridge, UK: Cambridge University Press.
Huang, CT James. 1982. Move WH in a language without WH movement. *The linguistic review* 1:369–416.
Hunter, Tim, and Chris Dyer. 2013. Distributions on minimalist grammar derivations. In *The 13th Meeting on the Mathematics of Language*, 1.

Kazanina, Nina, Ellen F Lau, Moti Lieberman, Masaya Yoshida, and Colin Phillips. 2007. The effect of syntactic constraints on the processing of backwards anaphora. *Journal of Memory and Language* 56:384–409.

Keller, Frank. 2000. Gradience in grammar: Experimental and computational aspects of degrees of grammaticality. Doctoral Dissertation, University of Edinburgh.

Keller, Frank. 2003. A psychophysical law for linguistic judgments. In *Proceedings of the 25th annual conference of the Cognitive Science Society*, 652–657.

Kluender, Robert, and Marta Kutas. 1993. Subjacency as a processing phenomenon. *Language and cognitive processes* 8:573–633.

Kush, Dave, Terje Lohndal, and Jon Sprouse. submitted. Investigating Variation in Island Effects: A Case Study of Norwegian. *Natural Language and Linguistic Theory*. .

Lasnik, Howard, and Mamoru Saito. 1982. On the nature of proper government. *Linguistic Inquiry* 15:235–289.

Lau, Jey Han, Alexander Clark, and Shalom Lappin. 2017. Grammaticality, acceptability, and probability: a probabilistic view of linguistic knowledge. *Cognitive science* 41:1202–1241.

Levy, Roger. 2008. Expectation-based syntactic comprehension. *Cognition* 106:1126–1177.

Lewis, Richard L, and Shravan Vasishth. 2005. An activation-based model of sentence processing as skilled memory retrieval. *Cognitive science* 29:375–419.

Lewis, Shevaun, and Colin Phillips. 2015. Aligning grammatical theories and language processing models. *Journal of Psycholinguistic Research* 44:27–46.

Luce, R Duncan. 2002. A psychophysical theory of intensity proportions, joint presentations, and matches. *Psychological Review* 109:520.

Mahowald, Kyle, Peter Graff, Jeremy Hartman, and Edward Gibson. 2016. SNAP judgments: A small N acceptability paradigm (SNAP) for linguistic acceptability judgments. *Language* 92:619–635.

Marantz, Alec. 2005. Generative linguistics within the cognitive neuroscience of language. *The Linguistic Review* 22:429–445.

Marr, David. 1982. *Vision: A Computational Investigation into the Human Representation and Processing of Visual Information*. Cambridge, MA: MIT Press.

Matchin, William, Jon Sprouse, and Gregory Hickok. 2014. A structural distance effect for backward anaphora in Broca's area: An fMRI study. *Brain and language* 138:1–11.

McElree, Brian, Stephani Foraker, and Lisbeth Dyer. 2003. Memory structures that subserve sentence comprehension. *Journal of Memory and Language* 48:67–91.

Michel, Daniel. 2014. Individual cognitive measures and working memory accounts of syntactic island phenomena. Doctoral Dissertation, University of California San Diego.

Miller, George A., and Noam Chomsky. 1963. Finitary models of language users. In *Handbook of Mathematical Psychology*, ed. D. Luce, 419–492. New York, NY: John Wiley & Sons.

Montalbetti, Mario. 1984. After binding. On the interpretation of pronouns. Doctoral Dissertation, MIT, Cambridge, MA.

Nagata, Hiroshi. 1988. The relativity of linguistic intuition: The effect of repetition on grammaticality judgments. *Journal of Psycholinguistic Research* 17:1–17.

Nagata, Hiroshi. 1989. Effect of repetition on grammaticality judgments under objective and subjective self-awareness conditions. *Journal of Psycholinguistic Research* 18:255–269.

Narens, Louis. 1996. A theory of ratio magnitude estimation. *Journal of Mathematical Psychology* 40:109–129.

Neeleman, Ad, and Hans van de Koot. 2010. Theoretical validity and psychological reality of the grammatical code. In *The linguistics enterprise: From knowledge of language to knowl-*

edge in linguistics, ed. H. De Mulder, M. Everaert, O. Nilsen, T. Lentz, and A. Zondervan, volume 150, 183. Amsterdam, Netherlands: John Benjamins.

Parker, Dan, and Colin Phillips. 2016. Negative polarity illusions and the format of hierarchical encodings in memory. *Cognition* 157:321–339.

Phillips, Colin. 2006. The real-time status of island phenomena. *Language* 82:795–823.

Phillips, Colin. 2009. Should we impeach armchair linguists. *Japanese/Korean Linguistics* 17:49–64.

Phillips, Colin, and Shevaun Lewis. 2013. Derivational order in syntax: Evidence and architectural consequences. *Studies in Linguistics* 6:11–47.

Rizzi, Luigi. 1982. Violations of the wh-island constraint and the subjacency condition. In *Issues in Italian syntax*, ed. Luigi Rizzi, 49–76. Dordrecht: Foris.

Schütze, Carson T. 1996. *The empirical base of linguistics: Grammaticality judgments and linguistic methodology*. Chicago, IL: Chicago University Press.

Seely, T Daniel, and Samuel David Epstein. 2006. *Derivations in minimalism*. Cambridge, UK: Cambridge University Pbrress.

Smolensky, Paul, and Géraldine Legendre. 2006. *The harmonic mind: From neural computation to optimality-theoretic grammar (Cognitive architecture), Vol. 1*. Cambridge, MA: MIT press.

Snyder, William. 2000. An experimental investigation of syntactic satiation effects. *Linguistic Inquiry* 31:575–582.

Spencer, Nancy Jane. 1973. Differences between linguists and nonlinguists in intuitions of grammaticality-acceptability. *Journal of psycholinguistic research* 2:83–98.

Sprouse, Jon. 2009. Revisiting satiation: Evidence for an equalization response strategy. *Linguistic Inquiry* 40:329–341.

Sprouse, Jon. 2011. A test of the cognitive assumptions of magnitude estimation: Commutativity does not hold for acceptability judgments. *Language* 87:274–288.

Sprouse, Jon, and Diogo Almeida. 2012. Assessing the reliability of textbook data in syntax: Adger's Core Syntax1. *Journal of Linguistics* 48:609–652.

Sprouse, Jon, and Diogo Almeida. 2017. Design sensitivity and statistical power in acceptability judgment experiments. *Glossa* 2:1.

Sprouse, Jon, and Ellen F Lau. 2013. Syntax and the brain. In *The Cambridge handbook of generative syntax*, ed. Marcel den Dikken. Cambridge, UK: Cambridge University Press.

Sprouse, Jon, Carson T Schütze, and Diogo Almeida. 2013. A comparison of informal and formal acceptability judgments using a random sample from Linguistic Inquiry 2001–2010. *Lingua* 134:219–248.

Sprouse, Jon, Matt Wagers, and Colin Phillips. 2012. A test of the relation between working-memory capacity and syntactic island effects. *Language* 88:82–123.

Staub, Adrian. 2010. Response time distributional evidence for distinct varieties of number attraction. *Cognition* 114:447–454.

Stevens, Stanley S. 1957. On the psychophysical law. *Psychological Review* 64:153.

Sturt, Patrick. 2003. The time-course of the application of binding constraints in reference resolution. *Journal of Memory and Language* 48:542–562.

Townsend, David J, and Thomas G Bever. 2001. *Sentence comprehension: The integration of habits and rules*. Cambridge, MA: MIT Press.

Van Gompel, Roger PG, and Simon P Liversedge. 2003. The influence of morphological information on cataphoric pronoun assignment. *Journal of Experimental Psychology: Learning, Memory, and Cognition* 29:128.

Wagers, Matthew W, Ellen F Lau, and Colin Phillips. 2009. Agreement attraction in comprehension: Representations and processes. *Journal of Memory and Language* 61:206–237.

Wasow, Thomas, and Jennifer Arnold. 2005. Intuitions in linguistic argumentation. *Lingua* 115:1481–1496.

Wellwood, Alexis, Roumyana Pancheva, Valentine Hacquard, and Colin Phillips. 2014. Deconstructing a comparative illusion. Ms., Northwestern University, University of Southern California, and University of Maryland.

Weskott, Thomas, and Gisbert Fanselow. 2011. On the informativity of different measures of linguistic acceptability. *Language* 87:249–273.

Xiang, Ming, Brian Dillon, and Colin Phillips. 2009. Illusory licensing effects across dependency types: ERP evidence. *Brain and Language* 108:40–55.

Yoshida, Masaya, Nina Kazanina, Leticia Pablos, and Patrick Sturt. 2014. On the origin of islands. *Language, Cognition and Neuroscience* 29:761–770.

Jeffrey Lidz
The explanatory power of linguistic theory

1 Introduction

Chapter 8 of *Syntactic Structures* (Chomsky, 1957) elucidates the idea of levels of representation in linguistic theory, introduced in earlier chapters, using the phenomenon of *constructional homonymity* as a probe. Chomsky observes that a single string may have two interpretations, supporting the idea that that string has distinct derivations. In some cases, the analysis is both independently supported and obvious. The phonetic string [əneym] can be interpreted as two words, either with the word boundary before or after the [n], *a name* vs. *an aim*. Thus, there must be more to a linguistic representation than just a string of phones. Instead, we have an additional morphological level of representation, where each of these possibilities is independently justified (for example, by *a football, an elephant, his name* and *her aim*), and hence provides an automatic explanation for the ambiguity. Similarly, a string consisting of one analysis at the phonological and morphological levels can nonetheless have two syntactic analyses, giving rise to familiar ambiguities at the level of phrase structure. The two analyses of I saw the man with the telescope are independently justified by sentences such as [[*The man* [*with the telescope*]] *is tall*] or [*I* [*hiked* [*with the snowshoes*]]]. Chomsky goes on to argue for levels of representation determined by different transformational analyses, based on the ambiguity of *the shooting of the hunters*, where *the hunters* may be interpreted as shooter or shot, analogous to *the growling of lions* or *the raising of flowers*, respectively. Here, there is a single analysis at the phonological, morphological and phrase structural levels, but still there is an ambiguity. The analytic idea was that the NP is derived via transformation from a kernel sentence, either *The hunters shot something* or *Someone shot the hunters*. The argument was that this ambiguity is predicted by a theory containing transformations, but not one whose only level of syntactic analysis was phrase structure. The transformational theory was thus to be preferred due to the transparency of the explanation, given that the relevant ambiguity follows automatically from independently justified pieces of analysis.

This notion of explanation, of capturing generalizations in a way that explains more than just the facts they were crafted to describe, remains a central part of linguistic theory today. Chomsky states "any scientific theory is based on a finite number of observations, and it seeks to relate the observed phenomena and to predict new phenomena by constructing general laws in terms of hypothetical constructs such as (in physics, for example) mass and electron." (Chomsky 1957, p. 49). At the time, the new phenomena to be explained were facts about the particular language under investigation, what Chomsky called "external conditions of adequacy." And the hope was that conditions of generality would allow for a theory of grammar in which basic terms such as phoneme or phrase could be justified independently of any particular language.

Moreover, in Chapter 6, Chomsky explores the relation between the general theory of grammar and the language particular grammars that follow from it, suggesting that the strongest requirement we could put on such a relation would be that the theory "provide a practical and mechanical method for actually constructing the grammar, given a corpus of utterances." It is worth noticing that this formulation is stated from the perspective of the scientist. How would a scientist take a corpus of sentences in a language and, using the theoretical vocabulary of the general theory, discover the grammar behind the corpus?

But in the years immediately following *Syntactic Structures*, these ideas about justifying grammars were ported over wholesale as a theory of the cognitive mechanisms that lay the foundation for language acquisition (Chomsky, 1959, 1965). Although *Syntactic Structures* never mentioned human cognition or children's language acquisition, it put into place the pieces required for expanding the reach of linguistic theory quite broadly. Indeed, that such an expansion was already in the air in 1957 can be seen in Lees' review of the book. Lees notes that if it were possible to expand the reach of linguistic theory to include language acquisition, "then the mechanism which we must attribute to human beings to account for their speech behavior has all the characteristics of a sophisticated scientific theory," (Lees 1957, p. 406) by which he means that the general principles of grammar, discovered on the basis of linguistic analysis, would contribute to an explanation of language acquisition, despite not being designed for that purpose. Lees spells these ramifications out slightly more when he says, "If we are to account adequately for the indubitable fact that a child by the age of five or six has somehow reconstructed for himself the theory of his language, it would seem that our notions of human learning are due for some considerable sophistication." (Lees 1957, p. 408).

Indeed, it is this notion of generality and sophistication to which we now turn, connecting the transformational structures revealed by constructional homonymity to explanations of how the relevant grammatical principles contribute to children's ultimate attainment of a grammar for their language.

2 Constructional homonymity and the poverty of the stimulus

2.1 Movement and reflexives: a puzzle

Consider the sentences in (1–2) (Barss, 1986).

(1) a. Norbert remembered that Ellen painted a picture of herself
    b. * Norbert remembered that Ellen painted a picture of himself

(2) a. Norbert remembered which picture of herself Ellen painted
    b. Norbert remembered which picture of himself Ellen painted

The facts in (1) illustrate a very simple generalization: a reflexive pronoun must take its antecedent in the domain of the closest subject (Chomsky, 1973, 1981). Only *Ellen* can be the antecedent of the reflexive.

In (2), however, there are two possible antecedents for the reflexive (depending on gender). Either *Norbert* or *Ellen* will do. Here it would seem that we have a constructional homonymity. The sentences in (2) have one phonological, morphological and phrase structural analysis and yet we have two interpretations. Given an independently motivated theory of wh-movement, through which the phrase *which picture of himself* simultaneously satisfies the requirement that *paint* take a direct object and the requirement that wh-phrases occur in the left-periphery of the clause, we can explain the ambiguity. Specifically, there exists a representation in which the wh-phrase is in the position of the object of *paint*. In this position, the local domain of the reflexive is the clause that has *Ellen* as its subject, and in this structure, only *Ellen* can be the antecedent. There exists another representation in which the wh-phrase is in the peripheral position of the embedded clause. In this position, the local domain of the reflexive is the matrix sentence and only *Norbert* is in a position to bind the reflexive in that domain.

In (3) we represent the wh-phrase in two positions and strike through the one not considered for the interpretation of the reflexive. There are many roughly equivalent formal treatments that can capture the basic insight.

(3) a. Norbert remembered [[which picture of himself] Ellen painted [which picture of himself]]
b. * Norbert remembered [[which picture of herself] Ellen painted [which picture of herself]]
c. * Norbert remembered [[which picture of himself] Ellen painted [which picture of himself]]
d. Norbert remembered [[which picture of herself] Ellen painted [which picture of herself]]

So, given a theory of movement, either the base position or the surface position of the moved expression can be considered for defining the locality domain for reflexive pronouns contained in the moved expression. The ambiguity highlights the necessity of two representations, despite only one surface syntactic structure, exactly along the lines suggested by Chomsky (1957).

These facts are immediately complicated by the paradigm in (4–5).

(4) a. Norbert remembered that Ellen was very proud of herself
b. * Norbert remembered that Ellen was very proud of himself

(5) a. Norbert remembered how proud of herself Ellen was
b. * Norbert remembered how proud of himself Ellen was

The facts in (4) are consistent with our generalization about reflexives. Only the local subject can be the antecedent. However, when we move the wh-phrase [*how proud of herself*], still only the embedded subject can serve as antecedent for the reflexive, unlike in (2). What distinguishes (2) from (5)? Given the premises that (a) wh-phrases occur in the left-periphery and maintain their relation to their base positions and (b) reflexives must be locally bound, we would expect (5) to be ambiguous in exactly the same way as (2). The difference seems to be that the wh-phrase in (2) is an argument, but the wh-phrase in (5) is a predicate.

Before we pursue a solution based on the predicate-argument distinction, let us first turn to the learnability problem that the constructional homonymity of (2) reveals.

2.2 From Constructional Homonymity to the Poverty of the Stimulus

As we have noted, the analytic problem of identifying a grammar from a corpus that the linguist faces is analogous to the learning problem that children face in identifying a grammar from the sentences they are exposed to. To the extent that grammars have levels of representation that are not signaled in the surface forms, children must somehow figure out that these levels of representation exist.

In the case of the interaction between wh-movement and reflexives, a child who learned each of these phenomena separately would have an analytic choice to make in representing them in a way that covered their interaction. In principle, there are three options: (a) only the surface position is relevant, (b) only the base position is relevant, or (c) either position is relevant. If (a) were true, then (2) would allow only *Norbert* as antecedent. If (b) were true, (2) would allow only *Ellen* as antecedent, and if (c) were true, either could be the antecedent. We have seen that (c) is true. We can determine that the grammar is constructed that way by creating sentences like (2) and seeing what interpretations they have. Do children learning English hear sentences that reveal the correct analysis? If not, then what they know is a projection beyond their experience, based either on other observations or on prior beliefs/constraints concerning how grammars can be built.

Leddon and Lidz (2006) looked at children's input in order to assess whether the correct generalization in supported in their experience. They found that in 10,000 wh-questions addressed to children there were no wh-phrases that contained a reflexive pronoun, non-reflexive pronoun or a name.[1] So, children must generalize to the rule that either position can be treated as relevant for binding without *any* direct experience of the relevant form-meaning pairs. And, of course, if there is no evidence at all, then there is no straightforward inductive solution to the learning problem.

We might say that the solution children arrive at is the simplest one in some intuitive sense of simple. Given that the grammar produces two positions, both of which are relevant to some aspect of interpretation (i.e., the upper one determining the scope of the wh-phrase and the lower one satisfying the argument structure of the verb), the simplest solution would be that either position could be relevant for interpreting reflexive pronouns inside the moved wh-phrase. On this view, children would choose the system that would add the least additional structure to the grammar, perhaps reflecting a domain-general constraint on mental computation.

However, such a solution immediately runs into trouble when we consider the facts in (5) concerning moved predicate wh-phrases. Given a different kind of wh-

---

[1] One might complain, fairly, that 10,000 wh-questions is not that many and that if we had looked at a bigger corpus we might have found some with the relevant properties. We did search Google for strings containing wh-phrases like those in (2) and the only hits we got were example sentences from linguistics papers. This gives us some confidence that our estimate of the experience of children is accurate.

phrase, children evidently generalize differently, treating only the base position as relevant for interpretation. With only the facts of (5) in mind, one might be led to the conclusion that there is some domain general notion of simplicity from which the facts in (5) could follow. For example, suppose that the antecedent for the reflexive must be found at the earliest possible point in the derivation. This would yield the correct facts in (5), but not for those in (2). This discussion illustrates a deep fact about learning, sometimes referred to as the no-free-lunch theorem (Wolpert and Macready, 1997), that there is no single inductive bias that will yield the correct generalization for all learning problems. One can form an intuitive basis for generalizing in a diverse set of ways, and each of these may be appropriate for different learning problems, but none of them will be appropriate for all.

Now, given that reflexives contained in fronted wh-arguments behave differently from reflexives contained in fronted wh-predicates, we have a puzzle about how to account for this asymmetry. The existence of the constructional homonymity for (2) could lead us to expect a similar constructional homonymity for (5), contrary to facts. Thus, our task is to discover the grammatical principles from which the asymmetry between (2) and (5) follows. And, as noted, the analytic problem is paired with a corresponding learning problem. Given the general lack of evidence about reflexives contained in fronted wh-phrases, what forces learners to generalize in a way that leads to the appropriate asymmetry? In principle, there are 9 possible combinations of judgments, varying in whether the reflexive is contained in an argument or predicate wh-phrase, and for each of these, whether it takes as its antecedent the matrix subject, the embedded subject or both. Out of these 9 possibilities, learners all seem to converge on only 1, namely the one where the reflexive inside an argument wh-phrase can take either antecedent but the reflexive inside a predicate wh-phrase can only take the embedded antecedent.

This kind of puzzle concerning the factors that force children to generalize in one very specific way out of a wide array of possible generalizations has come to be known as the poverty of the stimulus (Chomsky, 1971).

3 The Predicate Internal Subject Hypothesis

Let us now consider a solution to the analytic problem, due to Huang (1993). The first part of the solution is that we maintain our generalization about reflexives: reflexives must find their antecedent in the domain of the nearest subject. The second part capitalizes on the difference between (2), in which the wh-phrase is an argument of the lower verb, and (5), in which the wh-phrase is the lower predicate itself. In (2), the domain of the nearest subject is underspecified. If we calculate it in terms of the "base position" of the wh-phrase, then the embedded subject is the nearest subject and so only *Ellen* can be the antecedent. If we calculate it in terms of the "surface position" of the wh-phrase, then the matrix subject is the nearest subject and so only *Norbert* can be the antecedent. For (5), however, the closest subject is the same, independent of whether we interpret the wh-phrase in its "base" or "surface" position.

This calculation of closest subject follows from the Predicate Internal Subject Hypothesis (PISH): The predicate carries information about its subject wherever it goes. Because of PISH, the wh-phrase [how proud of himself/herself] contains an unpronounced residue of the embedded subject and so is really represented as [how ~~Ellen~~ proud of himself/herself].

The derivation for the sentence is given in (6).

(6) a. Build predicate
      [proud of herself]
  b. Add subject
      [Ellen [proud of herself]]
  c. Modify
      [how [Ellen [proud of herself]]]
  d. Insert aux
      [is [how [Ellen proud of herself]]]
  e. Raise subject
      [Ellen [is [how [~~Ellen~~ proud of herself]]]]
  f. wh-movement
      [[how [~~Ellen~~ proud of herself]] [Ellen [is ~~[how [Ellen proud of herself]]~~]]]
  g. Embed
      [Norbert [remembers [[how [~~Ellen~~ proud of herself]] [Ellen [is ~~[how [Ellen proud of herself]]~~]]]]]

Because the phrase *how proud of herself* contains a silent residue of *Ellen*, the nearest subject to the reflexive is *Ellen*, independent of whether this is calculated in the base position or in the derived position. The reflexive must be bound within that domain and so *Ellen* is the only possible antecedent for that reflexive. This analysis explains the asymmetry straightforwardly. We maintain the general rule through which the binding domain for the reflexive can be identified based on any of its positions in the derivation, but with the complication that in predicate questions both positions yield the same binding relations.

Now we have two related questions. First, is there independent evidence for PISH? If there is, then the binding facts follow deductively from PISH plus the theory that any occurrence of the reflexive can be treated as relevant for the calculation of binding domains. Second, if the binding asymmetry is not exhibited in speech to children and if PISH offers an explanation of the binding asymmetry, is PISH exhibited in speech to children? That is, if children can't learn the binding asymmetries by observation, then could they learn PISH? If they can, then we would see the deductive character of the learning theory. If they cannot, then we would both see the deductive character of the learning theory, and isolate a piece of the general theory of grammar that licenses those deductions. In other words, if PISH cannot be learned, then it must be innate (or follow deductively from something else, either learned or innate) so that we can explain how children come to generalize in just the right way.

Let us repeat the conclusion. As long as the learner knows the PISH, then the predicate-argument asymmetry follows deductively. The learner requires no experience with wh-phrases containing reflexives in order to reach the correct generalization.

This argument says only that learners must know PISH prior to encountering sentences like (2). It doesn't yet require that knowledge to be innate. So, the poverty of the stimulus problem posed by (2) shifts to the problem of determining whether subjects are generated predicate internally.

4 Independent evidence of PISH and its acquisition

Our next question is whether we have independent support for PISH and whether the data that supports PISH can also lead to its acquisition. Several important patterns of facts argue in favor of PISH.

4.1 Scope ambiguities

The first concerns the relative scope of negation and a universal quantifier in subject position (Ladusaw, 1988; McCloskey, 1997). Consider the following sentences:

(7)   a.   Every horse didn't jump over the fence
        b.   A Fiat is not necessarily a reliable car
        c.   A Fiat is necessarily not a reliable car

The important thing to notice about these sentences is that (7a) is ambiguous, providing yet another constructional homonymity, but that neither (7b) nor (7c) is. (7a) can be interpreted as making a strong claim that none of the horses jumped over the fence or a weaker claim that not all of them jumped. This ambiguity concerns the scope of negation. Does the negation apply to something that includes the universal or not? If it does, then we get the weak reading that not all horses jumped. If it does not, then we get the strong reading that none of them did.

How does this scope ambiguity arise? The case where the subject takes scope over negation is straightforward if we assume (uncontroversially) that scope can be read directly off of the hierarchical structure of the sentence. But what about the reading where negation takes wide scope? We can consider two possibilities. First, it might be that the negation can take the whole sentence in its scope even if it does not occur at the left edge of the sentence. But this possibility is shown to be false by the lack of ambiguity in (7c). If negation could simply take wide scope over the entire sentence independent of its syntactic position, then we would expect (7c) to be ambiguous, contrary to fact. (7c) just can't mean what (7b) does. The second possibility is PISH: the structure of (7a) is really (8), with the struck-out copy of every horse representing the unpronounced residue of the subject-predicate relation:

(8)   every horse didn't [~~every horse~~] jump over the fence

Given that there are two positions for *every horse* in the representation, we can interpret negation as either taking scope relative to either the higher one or the lower one.

Is there evidence in speech to children concerning the ambiguity of (7a)? If there is, then that might count as evidence that they could use to learn PISH and hence solve the poverty of the stimulus problem associated with the predicate-argument asymmetry. Here we run into two difficulties. First, Gennari and Mac-Donald (2006) show that these sentences do not occur in speech to children (and are pretty rare in speech between adults). Second, when we present such sentences to preschoolers, they appear to be relatively deaf to their ambiguity.

Several studies on the acquisition of quantification have shown that when given a Truth Value Judgment Task (TVJT), preschoolers, unlike adults, display a strong preference for the isomorphic interpretation of sentences like (19–20) (Musolino (1998), Musolino et al. (2000), Lidz and Musolino (2002), Musolino and Gualmini (2004), Noveck et al. (2007), among others). This isomorphism is not strictly grammatical, however (Gualmini et al., 2008; Musolino and Lidz, 2006; Viau et al., 2010). Rather, under certain discourse conditions, children's ability to detect the nonisomorphic structure may appear. Conroy (2008) and Viau et al.

(2010) argue that the isomorphic interpretation is children's first interpretation and that children's well known difficulty with revising structure (Trueswell et al., 1999) makes it difficult for them to access the nonisomorphic interpretation.

So, even if such sentences did occur in speech to children, their dominant interpretation from the children's perspective is the one where the subject scopes over negation (even when that interpretation is not consistent with the context or the intentions of the speaker) and so this potential evidence is unlikely to be perceived as evidence of PISH. And if PISH is not learned from that, then we are left with a mystery of how it comes to be responsible for the pattern of facts in (2).

4.2 Bare plurals

A second argument in favor of PISH concerns the interpretation of bare plural subjects (Diesing, 1992), like in (9)

(9)   Linguists are available (to argue with)

This sentence is ambiguous between a generic and an existential reading of the bare plural subject (Carlson, 1977). Under the generic reading, it is a general property of linguists (as a whole) that they are available. Under the existential reading, there are some linguists who are available at the moment.

Diesing observes that these two interpretations are associated with different syntactic positions in German, as illustrated in (10).

(10)   a.   ... weil   ja   doch Linguisten Kammermusik   spielen
              since PRT   PRT   linguists   chamber music play
       '... since there are linguists playing chamber music.'

       b.   ... weil   Linguisten ja   doch Kammermusik   spielen
              since linguists   PRT   PRT   chamber music play
       '... since (in general) linguists play chamber music.'

The existential interpretation arises when the subject occurs inside the VP (i.e., to the right of the VP-level adverb *ja doch*), providing evidence for the availability of a VP-internal subject position crosslinguistically. The generic interpretation arises when the subject occurs outside of VP (i.e., to the left of *ja doch*).

Diesing argues that we can capture a cross-linguistic generalization about the interpretations of bare plural subjects by positing that the same mapping between position and interpretation occurs in English. The difference is that in English, the existential interpretation is associated with the unpronounced residue of the subject inside the predicate. PISH allows us to link the German and English facts together in a way that PISH-less theory would not. So we can take it as evidence for PISH.

Let us turn now to acquisition. Should learners take evidence of existential interpretations of bare plural subjects to be evidence of PISH? Maybe, if they already know something about how positions relate to interpretations. But in the end, the issue is moot because (Sneed, 2009) showed that in speech to children, bare plural subjects are uniformly used with the generic interpretation. How children come to know about the existential readings is itself a poverty of the stimulus problem (and one that could also be solved by antecedent knowledge of PISH and the rules for mapping from syntactic position to semantic interpretation). So, if we think that the predicate-argument asymmetry whose acquisition we are trying to explain follows from PISH, then we still need a source for PISH in speech to children.

4.3 Active-passive coordination

A final argument in favor of PISH comes from Burton and Grimshaw (1992). These authors show that it is possible to coordinate an active and a passive verb phrase:

(11)   Norbert insulted some psychologists and was censured

The argument takes advantage of three independent generalizations. First, passives involve a relation between the surface subject and the object position of the passive verb, represented here by the invisible residue of *Norbert*:

(12)   Norbert was censured [Norbert]

Second, extraction from one conjunct in a coordinated structure is ungrammatical (Ross (1967)'s Coordinate Structure Constraint):

(13)   * Who did [Norbert criticize the book] and [Jeff insult who]

Third, extraction from a conjunct is possible as long as the extracted phrase is associated with both conjuncts (Across The Board extraction, Ross 1967):

(14)   Who did [Norbert criticize who] and [Jeff insult who]

So, if there were no predicate internal subject position in (11), then we would have the representation in (15):

(15)   Norbert [$_{T'}$ insulted some psychologists and [$_{T'}$ was censured ~~[Norbert]~~]]

This representation violates the coordinate structure constraint and so the sentence is predicted to be ungrammatical, contrary to fact. However, if there is a predicate internal subject position, then the sentence can be represented as an across the board extraction:

(16)   Norbert [$_{T'}$ [$_{VP}$ ~~[Norbert]~~ insulted some psychologists] and [$_{T'}$ was censured ~~[Norbert]~~]]

So, we can understand the grammaticality of (11) straightforwardly if it has the representation in (15), as required by PISH.

Do sentences like (11) occur in speech to children? I don't know of any evidence about this, but I also don't think it matters. It doesn't matter because if the learner encountered (11), that datum would support either PISH or the conclusion that movement out of one conjunct in a coordinate structure is grammatical (i.e, that the coordinate structure constraint does not hold). If there is a way of determining that the learner should draw the PISH conclusion and not the other one, I don't know what it is.

5 Putting it all together

We began with the observation that a reflexive pronoun contained in a fronted argument wh-phrase shows different binding possibilities than one contained in a fronted predicate wh-phrase. We argued that this presented an analytic problem and an acquisition problem. The analytic problem is simply to explain the asymmetry. The acquisition problem is that children encounter no direct evidence about these interpretations, and hence however they come to acquire the asymmetry must involve significant projection beyond their experience.

We then argued that the analytic problem dissolves if PISH is adopted. On this view, we maintain the general theory that the binding domain of a reflexive may be established with respect to any of its positions in a derivational structure. This explains why reflexives contained inside argument wh-phrases can be bound either in the base or surface position of the wh-phrase. In the case of predicate wh-phrases, the predicate-internal subject position (containing an unpronounced copy of the subject) is carried along with the wh-phrase. Consequently, a reflexive contained in that wh-phrase will always find its binding domain defined as the wh-phrase itself, and hence must be bound by the predicate internal subject. This explains the lack of ambiguity of sentences like (5).

Further, we argued that antecedent knowledge of PISH would explain how children acquired the predicate-argument asymmetry. If children know that the surface subject is a derived position, then the predicate-argument asymmetry would follow deductively, as described above. We then asked whether this asymmetry could be acquired from experience. We considered three phenomena that provide independent support for PISH and showed that none of these provide a likely database from which children could discover PISH. In each case, the relevant data that would force the child to reach that conclusion is lacking from children's experience. Thus, we are led to the conclusion that PISH is innate.[2] Given that everyone seems to acquire grammars containing PISH, but that children do not encounter experiences that would provide evidence for PISH, it must be that PISH-less grammars are impossible for children to construct.

6 Final thoughts

The central ideas of *Syntactic Structures* continue to resonate 60 years after its publication. Perhaps the most important analytic proposal in *Syntactic Structures* is the introduction of transformations, the idea that a phrase structural analysis of a sentence does not exhaust its syntactic structure. Instead, a sentence can be viewed as a sequence of phrase structure analyses, which together define the syntax of that sentence. On top of the analytic proposals, *Syntactic Structures* also took steps towards identifying considerations of explanation in linguistics, noting that we should aim to justify a grammatical proposal not simply with respect to coverage in that language, but also with respect to a more general grammatical vocabulary in which all analyses are couched. This move towards identifying the criteria of explanation in linguistics set the stage for placing grammatical theory in the domain of human psychology. The problem that linguists face in justifying grammatical analyses are equally faced by children learning their language. If we view a grammar as a kind of knowledge, then children must construct this knowledge based on evidence that is only a shadowy reflection of the grammar that

---

[2] Logically, another possibility remains, namely that the predicate internal subject hypothesis is not itself innate, but derives from a more general feature of grammars (either learned or innate). Since I know of no arguments deriving this hypothesis from other features of grammar, we leave the discovery of such a feature for others to pursue.

generated it. Viewed this way, *Syntactic Structures*, despite never mentioning human psychology, was the first step towards a rationalist computational theory of mind. It set up the hypothesis that children's grammatical knowledge is severely constrained by a Universal Grammar that defines the space of possible grammars (Chomsky, 1965), which illustrated what a computationally explicit and innately structured theory of the human mind could look like in one domain. This illustration opened the possibility that such immanent structure could be found in many domains of the mind, an idea whose consequences we are continuing to grapple with today both within linguistics and across the cognitive sciences.

Bibliography

Barss, Andrew. 1986. Chains and Anaphoric Dependence: On Reconstruction and its Implications. Doctoral dissertation, MIT, Cambridge, MA.

Burton, Strang, and Jane Grimshaw. 1992. Coordination and VP-internal subjects. *Linguistic Inquiry* 305–313.

Carlson, Greg N. 1977. A unified analysis of the English bare plural. *Linguistics and philosophy* 1:413–457.

Chomsky, Noam. 1957. *Syntactic Structures*. The Hague, The Netherlands: Mouton de Gruyter.

Chomsky, Noam. 1959. Review of B.F. Skinner's *verbal behavior*. *Language* 35:26–58.

Chomsky, Noam. 1965. *Aspects of the Theory of Syntax*. Cambridge, MA: MIT Press.

Chomsky, Noam. 1971. Some Empirical Issues in the Theory of Transformational Grammar. In *Goals of Linguistic Theory*, ed. P. Stanley Peters, 63–130. Englewood Cliffs, NJ: Prentice-Hall, Inc.

Chomsky, Noam. 1973. Conditions on Transformations. In *A Festschrift for Morris Halle*, ed. Stephen R. Anderson and Paul Kiparsky, 232–286. New York, NY: Academic Press.

Chomsky, Noam. 1981. *Lectures on Government and Binding*. Dordrecht, The Netherlands: Foris.

Conroy, Anastasia Marie. 2008. The role of verification strategies in semantic ambiguity resolution in children and adults. Doctoral Dissertation, University of Maryland, College Park.

Diesing, Molly. 1992. *Indefinites*. Cambridge, MA: MIT Press.

Gennari, Silvia P, and Maryellen C MacDonald. 2006. Acquisition of negation and quantification: Insights from adult production and comprehension. *Language Acquisition* 13:125–168.

Gualmini, Andrea, Sarah Hulsey, Valentine Hacquard, and Danny Fox. 2008. The question–answer requirement for scope assignment. *Natural language semantics* 16:205.

Huang, C-T James. 1993. Reconstruction and the structure of VP: Some theoretical consequences. *Linguistic Inquiry* 103–138.

Ladusaw, William. 1988. Adverbs, negation, and QR. *Linguistics in the morning calm* 2:481–488.

Leddon, Erin, and Jeffrey Lidz. 2006. Reconstruction Effects in Child Language. In *Proceedings of Boston University Conference on Child Language Development*. Cambridge, MA: Cascadilla Press.

Lidz, Jeffrey, and Julien Musolino. 2002. Children's command of quantification. *Cognition* 84:113–154.

McCloskey, Jim. 1997. Subjecthood and subject positions. In *Elements of grammar*, 197–235. Springer.

Musolino, Julien. 1998. Universal Grammar and the Acquisition of Semantic Knowledge: An Experimental Investigation of Quantifier-Negation Interactions in English. Doctoral Dissertation, University of Maryland, College Park.

Musolino, Julien, Stephen Crain, and Rosalind Thornton. 2000. Navigating negative quantificational space. *Linguistics* 38:1–32.

Musolino, Julien, and Andrea Gualmini. 2004. The role of partitivity in child language. *Language Acquisition* 12:97–107.

Musolino, Julien, and Jeffrey Lidz. 2006. Why children aren't universally successful with quantification. *Linguistics* 44:817–852.

Noveck, Ira A, Raphaele Guelminger, Nicolas Georgieff, and Nelly Labruyere. 2007. What autism can reveal about every...not sentences. *Journal of Semantics* 24:73–90.

Ross, John R. 1967. Constraints on variables in syntax. Doctoral dissertation, MIT, Cambridge, MA.

Sneed, Elisa German. 2009. Availability of generic NP interpretations in 4-year olds. In *Paper presented at Genericity: Interpretation and Uses*.

Trueswell, John C, Irina Sekerina, Nicole M Hill, and Marian L Logrip. 1999. The kindergarten-path effect: Studying on-line sentence processing in young children. *Cognition* 73:89–134.

Viau, Joshua, Jeffrey Lidz, and Julien Musolino. 2010. Priming of abstract logical representations in 4-year-olds. *Language Acquisition* 17:26–50.

Wolpert, David H., and William Macready. 1997. No Free Lunch Theorems for Optimization. In *IEEE Transactions of Evolutionary Computation*, volume 1, 67.

Heidi Harley
Kernel sentences, phrase structure grammars, and theta roles

I first describe and discuss features of the *Syntactic Structures* model (Chomsky, 1957) that bear on selection, argument structure and grammatical relations, noting consequences that the architecture of the model has for analyses related to these issues. In particular, I highlight two distinct selectional issues in verb phrases that the SS model does not formalize: a verb's subcategorization constraints, i.e. whether it's transitive or intransitive, and a verb's interpretive constraints, i.e. the kinds of features that its argument has to have to yield a felicitous utterance—objects of *drink* have to be liquid, objects of *worry* have to be intentional beings, etc. I then relate the SS proposals to debates and positions in the modern literature, half a century later, and suggest that the SS model was correct in not incorporating such constraints into the grammatical model.

All page and example numbers are from Syntactic Structures unless otherwise noted.

1 Phrase structure grammar, selection and transformations.

In chapter 5 of SS, Chomsky first motivates the introduction of a transformational component, arguing that transformations permit a more revealing analysis of certain grammatical features of English than a PSG is able to. Two of the cases, which motivate the introduction of the Affix Hopping and Passivization transformations, share an underlying feature, despite their apparent dissimilarity. Both cases turn on the same problematic property of context-free PSGs: the impossibility of implementing selectional restrictions.

In the case of the English auxiliary system, the problem arises because of the inviolable connection between the form of the tense, auxiliary or modal element and the form of the following verb. The problem is compounded because there is no evidence that the identity of the following verb[1] matters in the least; the

---

[1] Really the following 'verb-like thing' (Lasnik, 2000), which Chomsky abbreviates as 'v' in the Affix-hopping transformation.

identity of the Aux tells you everything you need to know, including what affix should attach to the following verb.

Chomsky's solution is to propose that the affix is really part of Aux's terminal string, not part of the verb's. In the PSG, Aux is rewritten into a branching terminal string like C+*have*+*-en*, or C+*be*+*-ing*.[2] The Affix-hopping transformation then disguises the locus of origin of the affix. Chomsky writes (p 41):

> By allowing ourselves the freedom of [the Affix hopping transformation], we have been able to state the constituency of the auxiliary phrase... without regard to the interdependence of its elements, and it is always easier to describe a sequence of independent elements than a sequence of mutually dependent ones. To put the same thing differently, in the auxiliary verb phrase we really have discontinuous elements ... But discontinuities cannot be handled within [context-free phrase-structure] grammars.

That is, we can't encode the selectional relationship between an auxiliary and a particular verb form in any straightforward way in a context-free PSG—and this is a feature, not a bug! The introduction of Aux to a verb phrase *should*, intuitively, be 'context-free' in the relevant sense. That is, there's something right about the idea that the insensitivity of Aux to the content of the verb arises from the formal properties of the system: the very context-freeness of the PSG *guarantees* that Aux can't be sensitive to the identity of the following verb, and it isn't. Once Aux is developed by the PS rule that rewrites it, everything else should follow; the Affix-hopping transformation captures this.

The passivization transformation is initially motivated in a remarkably similar way, although in addition to a dependence in form between the passive Aux and its following verb, the passive also involves two other dependencies. First, it exhibits a selectional dependence in phrase structure, forbidding the presence of a direct object following the verb, and permitting the presence of a *by*-phrase—passive verbs are necessarily intransitive. Second, there are constraints on identity, or maybe even content, imposed by an active verb on its following object, and by a passive verb on its preceding subject. Chomsky writes (p. 43):

> Finally, note that ... we will have to place many restrictions on the choice of V in terms of subject and object in order to permit such sentences as "John admires sincerity," "sincerity frightens John," "John plays golf," "John drinks wine," while excluding the inverse, non-sentences, "sincerity admires John," "John frightens sincerity," "golf plays John," "wine drinks John." But this whole network of restrictions fails completely when we choose be+en as part of the auxiliary verb. In fact, in this case the same selectional dependencies hold but in the inverse order ... If we try to include passives directly in the [PS] grammar, we shall

---

[2] C is the abstract symbol for the obligatory finite tense specification, and is itself developed into one of -S, -ø or *past*, which undergo affix hopping as well.

have to restate all of these restrictions in the opposite order for the case in which be+en is chosen as part of the auxiliary verb. This inelegant duplication ... can only be avoided if we deliberately exclude passives from the grammar of phrase structure, and reintroduce them by a [transformational] rule

Although in this case Chomsky couldn't avoid some statement of selectional constraints completely by introducing a transformation, as was possible in the case of Affix-hopping, he pointed out that we can achieve a more parsimonious grammar if the active/passive relationship is in the transformational component rather than in the phrase structure grammar. The structural constraint on passive verbs—especially the mandatory absence of a direct object—follows from the transformational approach, since the object is moved to subject position by the transformation. Furthermore, the fact that the identical restrictions are placed on the subject of the passive form of a verb and the object of the active form is also predicted by the transformational approach. The verb-object constraints are imposed in the phrase structure that generates the kernel sentence, and as a consequence will naturally continue to hold in the transformed structure derived from it.[3]

The argument is clear. However it raises a deep and troublesome question, which still actuates debate around these issues in the field today: Should the unacceptability of a sentence like "Sincerity admires John" or "Wine drinks John" be modeled as ungrammaticality *per se*, or treated in some other way? Chomsky himself (fn. 7 p 42) writes that "we might make use of a notion of levels of grammaticalness ... Thus 'sincerity admires John,' though clearly less grammatical than 'John admires sincerity,' is certainly more grammatical than 'of admires John'."

It should be clear that whether the source of the infelicity of "Sincerity admires John", and "John was admired by sincerity" is grammatical or not, the theory should impose it only once and yet yield the same result with the subject of passives and the object of actives. That is, even if the restriction is extragrammatical, it motivates a transformational approach to the passive. But whether to locate the restriction in the grammar itself is deeply unclear. Indeed, the first and best reason to doubt that these types of infelicities count as 'ungrammaticality' in the usual sense comes from Chomsky's most famous example pair, (1) and (2) in SS: *Colorless green ideas sleep furiously* vs. *Furiously sleep ideas green colorless*. Of these, he writes, "... any speaker of English will recognize that only the former is grammatical," and thence follows, ultimately, the autonomy of grammar. But the problems with ideas sleeping, or being furious, green or colorless, seem to be *of the same kind* as the problems with sincerity admiring. If one is a grammatical

---

[3] In §7.5 he suggests that the relevant information could be stated in terms of grammatical classes of noun ('abstract', 'proper' etc.); such a system of noun classes (in concert with PSGs)

violation, then so is the other, and if one isn't then neither is the other. Taking the moral of *colorless green ideas* seriously, it thus seems reasonable to ascribe this type of infelicity to some other source than the grammar.

Luckily, the notion of passive as a transformation is supported by other purely formal criteria as well, as discussed in Chapter 7—the ill-formedness of **They were considered a fool by him*, for example, demonstrates that the grammatical number of the subject of the passive form is relevant to the number of the nominal predicate *a fool*, in the same way that the number of the object of the active form is (**He considered them a fool*), which again follows from the transformational treatment of passive. However, once raised, the set of issues introduced by *Sincerity admires John* did not disappear.

2 Transitivity, argument structure and kernel sentences

The *Sincerity admires John* issue is related to another, more clearly grammatical one: In SS, there is no rule in the base for generating an intransitive VP. Lasnik (2000:125) notes that the SS model is unable to guarantee that transitive verbs are generated only in transitive VPs and intransitive verbs in intransitive VPs, potentially yielding sentences like *John solves* and *John slept the problem*. Although a system of verb sub-types (V_i, V_t) is set up in LSLT to model the existence of intransitives, the question is not addressed in SS. Yet optional (in)transitivity is important in SS in another argument that motivates the existence of the transformational level.

This argument is based on the concept of 'kernel sentences', or, more precisely, the phrase structures that underlie them. Derivations generated by the base PSG and subjected to all obligatory transformations and morphophonemic rules, but no optional transformations, have a special status. They yield a (finite) class of sentences called 'kernel sentences', roughly, all grammatical active declarative monoclausal sentences. The phrase structure representations that underlie kernel sentences are the foundation upon which all other sentences are built, via the application of transformations.

Chomsky notes (p. 88) that the nominalized phrase *the shooting of the hunters* admits of two interpretations, one in which *the hunters* corresponds to the subject of *shoot*, and one in which it corresponds to the object. In this regard, *the shooting of the hunters* contrasts with *the growling of lions* (subject-only) and *the raising of flowers* (object-only). Phrase-structurally, the two different interpretations are not differentiated, both being represented as *the* — V+*ing* — *of* — NP. However if such *ing-of* nominalizations are introduced by transformation, then a formal source for the ambiguity emerges. The verb *shoot* occurs in both transitive and intransitive kernel sentences (*the hunters shoot* and *the soldiers shoot the hunters*), but *growl* can only occur in intransitive ones (*lions growl*, **lions growl cheetahs*) and *raise* in transitive ones (**gardeners raise*, *gardeners raise flowers*). Given that there are two possible kernel sentences involving *shoot*, one transitive and one intransitive, if the *of-ing* nominalization is a transformation and thus predicted to be able to apply to either kernel, the ambiguity of *the shooting of the hunters* is derived from the existence of two distinct kernels involving *shoot*. Similarly the non-ambiguity of *the raising of the flowers* and *the growling of the lions* is expected given that there is only one kernel phrase structure to which the *of-ing* nominalization could apply for each of these verbs.

It is important to note that here Chomsky is not ascribing the variable interpretations of *the hunters* directly to the ambiguity of *shoot* as an optionally transitive verb. In fn. 3 (p. 88) he makes clear that he is making a claim about the *grammatical relations* borne by the NP *the hunters* in the nominalization: 'subject' in one case and 'object' in the other. Recall that he has already suggested (p. 30) that grammatical relations are not primitives of the grammar, instead they are defined in terms of phrase structure diagrams. If that is the case, there must be two different phrase structure representations underlying the different interpretations of the nominalization, corresponding to two different kernel sentences, in which *the hunters* occupies different positions and hence bears different grammatical relations in each. (In the nominalization, *the hunters* only occupies a single position no matter the interpretation, so the ambiguity does not arise from the constituent structure of the nominalization.) A transformational theory of *of-ing* nominalizations predicts that the different kernel sentences will yield different roles for *the hunters* based entirely on their formal, structural properties, not because *shoot* has two different interpretations.

More generally, the difference between the phrase-structural 'core', yielding all and only representations that become kernel sentences, and the optional transformations which can apply to them, is supported by the observation (90–91) that certain groups of sentences with significantly distinct surface forms and phrase structures are nonetheless "understood in a similar manner", as in this paradigm:

(1) [(115)]

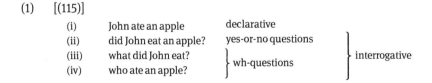

The 'felt-relatedness' between these formally distinct structures has a natural explanation within the *Syntactic Structures* model, namely, the fact that they are all surface developments of the same kernel phrase structure, differing only in the transformations applied in the course of their derivation.

Kernel sentences, or, more precisely, the phrase structures that underlie them, thus play the role in the SS model that Deep Structure played in the Aspects model, and that the vP does in the Minimalist architecture, establishing the core argument-structural relations which are exploited in the interpretation of the final sentence.

3 Complex predicates: Verb-particle constructions, small clauses, verbal adjuncts

The formal system developed in SS for passivization, and for identifying grammatical relations via structural relations, directly leads to very specific proposals for the analysis of sentences containing verb-particle constructions and small clauses. In particular, Chomsky considers pairs like the following:

(2) [(82)]
 (i) The police brought in the criminal.

(3) [(87)]
 (i) The criminal was brought in by the police.

(4) [(88)] Everyone in the lab considers John incompetent.

(5) [(89)] John is considered incompetent by everyone in the lab.

(6) [(103)]
 (ii) John found the boy studying in the library.

(7) [(104)]
 (iii) The boy was found studying in the library (by John).

In the verb-particle example in (82), (87), the phrase-marker must be able to undergo the passivization transformation, which means that at some level it must meet the structural analysis for the passivization transformation. The structural analysis for passivization requires the string *NP — Aux — V — NP*, which the surface string of (82) does not obviously meet, since it's *NP — Aux — V — Prt — NP*.

However, if *bring in, drive away, call up* etc. are introduced by a phrase structure rule which rewrites V as V+Prt, then there *is* a string in the description of (82) that meets the SA for passive. Consequently Chomsky adds a rule of the type V →V Prt to the PSG.

Famously, the verb-particle construction permits string variants inverting the particle and the object, as in *The police brought the criminal in*. This is a natural candidate for another transformation, later known as 'particle shift'. However, there are cases where particle shift is obligatory, and the V-Prt string never surfaces in the final sentence. This occurs when the object NP is a pronoun (**They brought in him*). Nonetheless, the fact that pronominal objects of particle verbs can also passivize freely (*He was brought in*) shows that the V+Prt sequence must exist as a development of V at some point in the phrase structure, even when the object is pronominal. As long as the passivization transformation can apply before obligatory particle shift, passive of a particle verb with a pronominal object is correctly predicted to occur (and to bleed the particle shift transformation) (p. 76).

With the pronominal verb-particle paradigm in mind, Chomsky then proposes a parallel analysis for constructions in which verb and its co-conspirator never surface as a string. This is exemplified by *consider* small clauses as in (88), but is clearly intended also to cover resultatives like *hammer the metal flat* as well. The VP in (88), *consider John incompetent*, is base-generated as *consider incompetent John*, via a PS rule V →V+Comp, and (in the active) undergoes mandatory Complement Shift. The V source of *consider incompetent*, however, guarantees that this phrase undergoes passivization like any other normal NP — Aux — V — NP construction.

This then leads to the claim that the gerundive complement interpretation of *John found the boy studying in the library* (103ii) also involves a V+Comp string, *found+studying in the library*, permitting the object *John* to undergo passivization independently of the depictive string *studying in the library*. The analysis is not developed further, but even the sketch is extremely intriguing. Presumably most such verbal modifiers would then be analyzed as instantiations of V →V+Comp. Presumably, also, the rule rewriting V as V+Comp would have to be moved into the (generalized) transformational component, since *studying in the library* would be derived from the PS of its own kernel sentence, *the boy studies in the library*.

In SS, then, many constructions that could roughly be called complex predicates, many involving arguments 'shared' between the matrix verb and a modifying phrase, are analyzed as internally complex Verbs. Such structures have figured heavily in modern theories of argument structure and syntax, and the SS treatment prefigures one prevalent line of analysis that developed in subsequent years.

4 Grammar as a tool: No semantics

One final important note about the SS model. Despite the fact that phrase structural ambiguity is clearly related to interpretive ambiguity, and the fact that interpretive ambiguity is often taken as a suggestive clue triggering a search for formal ambiguity, in SS the correlation between phrase structure and interpretation is ascribed to the fact that grammar is a formal tool that is *used* by speakers in a systematic way (p 108). That is, the semantic interpretation of a sentence does not supervene on its structural properties. Chomsky expresses great skepticism about whether phrase structural representations have a semantics: "It is questionable that the grammatical devices available in language are used consistently enough so that meaning can be assigned to them directly." In the SS model, then, there is no interpretive semantics. Semantics is independent, having points of connection with phrase structure that enable language use. Semantics does not arise from phrase-structural representations.

Furthermore, Chomsky rejects, with examples, the notion of constructional meaning, another idea which has seen a resurgence in multiple guises over the years. He writes (p. 100):

> Such sentences as "John received a letter" or "the fighting stopped" show clearly the untenability of the assertion that the grammatical relation subject-verb has the 'structural meaning' actor-action, if meaning is taken seriously as a concept independent of grammar. Similarly, the assignment of any such structural meaning as action-goal to the verb-object relation as such is precluded by such sentences as "I will disregard his incompetence" or "I missed the train."

Which these ideas and observations have modern resonance? All of them, is the short answer.

5 Theta roles, selection, and constructional meaning, oh my!

In Syntactic Structures, the projection and selection of arguments is largely left as a free-for-all, with a few notes here and there suggesting that this is not ideal. Lexical insertion is subsumed in the phrase structure grammar, and crucially so; the rewriting of nonterminals as lexical items—i.e. as terminals—is what enables the derivation to complete. Selectional relationships between verbs and their objects and/or subjects are not incorporated into the grammar in any formal way.

Sentences like *John slept the problem* are grammatical in this system (as would be *Gardeners raise*, if there was an intransitive VP rule in the PSG component). Further, there is no formal mechanism to account for the infelicity of *Sincerity admires John*, or, for that matter, *colorless green ideas sleep furiously*.

In the model subsequently developed in *Aspects* (Chomsky, 1965), a separate lexicon with idiosyncratic subcategorization information is added to the base, and lexical-insertion transformations put lexical items into the phrase-structural representation. Lexical items are annotated with subcategorization information, which constrains which phrase-markers the transformation can insert them into. The derivation of a phrase structure plus relevant lexical insertion operations constitutes the 'deep structure' of a sentence, prior to the application of any other transformations. As noted above, deep structure plays the role that kernel sentences did in SS, and constraints having to do with argument structure—subcategorization frames, and, later, the theta criterion—apply at this level. In the *Aspects model*, and subsequent developments of it, the grammar proper rules out **John slept the problem* and **Gardeners raise*, and provides tools (in the form of theta roles) to talk about what might be peculiar about *Sincerity admires John*.

Both types of system have modern descendants. In most modern syntactic theories, the role of kernel sentences, or deep structure representations, is now played by the vP constituent, the domain of first merge of arguments—First Phase Syntax, in Ramchand's (2008) felicitous phrase. Argument structural relations are established in this domain, and have been shown to be typically rigidly hierarchical in character. The syntactic vP argument hierarchy lines up with the hierarchy typically found in active, declarative, monoclausal sentences quite well in fact, modulo a few now well-known exceptions like unaccusative and psych-verbs. Subsequent movement may permute the hierarchy, but its effects are felt throughout the derivation, and can be diagnosed with a multitude of syntactic and morphological tests. Most modern theories agree on the role of the vP and its general internal syntactic structure (see, e.g. Harley 2011 for a review). They differ sharply, however, on whether and how overgeneration of argument structures and selectional clashes should be constrained.

The exoskeletal model put forward in (Borer, 2003, 2005), for example, hews closely to the model presented in SS. Roots, the core of a lexical item, can be inserted in any syntactically appropriate location; it's wugs all the way down. Extragrammatical factors—Encyclopedic Information—comes into play only afterwards, in the generation of interpretations for a structure. The strong position Borer takes is that 'grammatical' or 'ungrammatical' is relevant to the functional vocabulary and feature checking operations only. Sentences like *Gardeners raise*, *John slept the problem*, or *Sincerity admires John* are syntactically grammatical, but hard to interpret given the encyclopedic information associated with the roots in each lexical item, just as for *colorless green ideas sleep furiously*.[4]

The First Phase Syntax framework of Ramchand (2008), in contrast, is more similar to the *Aspects* grammar. Verbal lexical items have syntactic features which determine where in the vP syntax they can be inserted, which corresponds closely to their interpretive and event-structural properties. The phrase structure is built according to an event structure template. Arguments are associated with particular subevents introduced by different pieces of the event-structure template, and verbs compatible with the particular template may be inserted and interpreted in particular places. Sentences like **Gardeners raise* or **John slept the problem* are ungrammatical in the model.

The development of our understanding of the internal structure of the vP owes a great deal to the morphosyntactic proposals of Ken Hale and S. Jay Keyser (1993; 2002, among others). Their theoretical goal was to explain why there seemed to be an upper bound on the number of arguments possible for any verb—three being the observed fairly rigid limit. In a formal logical system, there is no reason to limit the argument-taking abilities of a predicate, so Hale and Keyser went searching for an explanation in the formal properties of syntactic structure. In this way, the Hale and Keyser model is a clear example of a line of investigation prompted by the SS idea that the grammatical system is fully autonomous, with intrinsic formal properties that can be exploited as a tool for representing semantic information, but which themselves are not semantic in character. For Hale and Keyser, the limitation on the number of verbal arguments arises because X-bar theoretic representations, constrained by a theory of category structure, are limited in their combinatory possibilities (Specifier and Complement, and no more).

Interestingly, and somewhat ironically, Hale and Keyser framed their discussion in terms of theta roles. That is, rather than ask Why so few arguments (or, in addition to that question), they asked, Why so few theta roles? Since their answer was purely structural in character, the way it ultimately came to be interpreted was that theta role information was itself structural in character, and that

---

[4] Encyclopedic information is clearly relevant to syntactic structure, but its specific effects are challenging to formalize. One famous example—the failure of an agentive nominalization for causative grow, **John's growth of tomatoes*, demonstrated in (Chomsky, 1970)—has been variously treated. Levin and Rappaport-Hovav (1995) demonstrated that this effect is dependent on the kind of causation involved; an internally-caused event like *grow* or *amuse* does not license agentive nominalization while an externally-caused event like destroy does (*John's destruction of the hotel room*). Harley and Noyer (2000) further demonstrated that the internal/external causation distinction can be compositionally determined, contrasting #*John's accumulation of dust* with *John's accumulation of wealth*, arguing against a syntactic approach to this pattern.

one could read constructional meaning off of vP structure (Spec-vP=Agent, Spec-PP=Theme, Comp-PP=Goal) in the same way that one can read grammatical relations off of phrase structure. This interpretation, related to Baker's (1988) Universal Theta Alignment Hypothesis, comes very close to the 'constructional meaning' which Chomsky cautioned against in SS, in the quote above. It is *possible* that the introduction of the distinction between thematic relations and grammatical relations allows us to maintain a version of 'constructional meaning' even in the face of counterexamples like the ones Chomsky raised, but, as discussed below, there are still reasons to be very cautious.

The very notion that autonomous syntactic structures can come to be associated with particular meanings is foundational to frameworks like Construction Grammar and others.[5] Eschewing an interpretive semantics that supervenes on phrase structure, as Chomsky does in SS, seems to me to lead quite naturally to constructional meaning, despite Chomsky's words of warning. Construction Grammar and related architectures are concrete proposals about the 'points of contact' between an autonomous semantic representation and the grammar.

However, almost all generative syntactic theorizing has now internalized the message from natural language philosophy that semantics is interpretive, compositional, and supervenes on phrase structure. That is, there is a syntactic level of Logical Form that is the direct basis for semantic interpretation. Ample evidence for the existence of such a level has by now accumulated. It is important to note that compositionality is only guaranteed in such an interpretive model. In a noninterpretive semantics, the possibility of arbitrary, Construction Grammar-style constructional meanings opens the door to noncompositionality. In such frameworks, the meaning of a sentence is not only derived from the meanings of its parts and how they're put together, but is also the result of any Saussurean, arbitrary meanings that the structure itself might introduce. A commitment to compositionality leads naturally to a commitment to interpretive semantics, despite the conclusions about the independence of semantics and syntax at the end of SS.

The details of how such an interpretive semantic theory develops a semantic representation from a logical form have been quite thoroughly worked out in several variations; I will take Heim and Kratzer (1998) as a representative widely-used approach.[6] Lexical items are interpreted as functions relating elements from various ontological classes (entities, events, worlds, truth-values) to each other

---

5 Bever and Townsend (2001) implement an actor-action, action-goal association with NP – V – NP structures directly in their two-stage model of sentence processing, despite counterexamples like those Chomsky raised in SS.
6 Lasnik (2000: 132–3) writes, "The slight problem with this is that we have a way of formalizing selectional restrictions ... but we have no clear idea of how to formalize lexical meaning, we just

via various composition operations, imposing truth conditions on the output of each compositional step. The final output of a successful interpretation is a set of truth conditions which allow a determination of the truth value of a sentence in a model. In a simplified form, we can think of an intransitive verb as a function from an entity to a truth value, <e,t>—e.g. sleep(J)=T iff John sleeps, F otherwise. A transitive verb V is a function from an entity to a VP predicate, which is itself a function from an entity to a truth value (<e,<e,t>)—e.g. raise(flowers)(J)=T iff John raises flowers, F otherwise.

This kind of view of predicate meaning can obviate the need for, or (more accurately) replace, the subcategorization and theta-theoretic machinery that has been used since *Aspects* to constrain the lexicon/syntax interface. Heim and Kratzer (1998: 49–53) note that structures in which the Theta Criterion would be violated are structures where normal compositional interpretation will fail due to type mismatch: Functions without arguments and arguments without predicates will not produce a convergent LF interpretation. Similarly, if a function's truth conditions require an argument of a certain type (e.g. animate cognitive being, as the subject argument of *admire* must be) to be evaluated, and if they are provided with an argument that does not meet those requirements, presupposition failure will occur; the truth of the (syntactically grammatical) utterance will not be evaluable.[7]

The two cases—argument saturation failure, and presupposition failure— even have different formal properties, which correlates well with the intuitive feeling that the unacceptability of #*Gardeners raise* is of a qualitatively different type than #*Sincerity admires John*, and that both are of a qualitatively different type than the syntactically ill-formed **What John admires?* or **Furiously green sleep ideas colorless* or similar. We do not need to constrain the insertion of lexical items into phrase-structure representations at all, in fact. A *Syntactic Structures*-style free-for-all, respecting only syntactic well-formedness conditions, is a perfectly reasonable approach. Until you get past LF, it really is wugs all the way down.

---

know it's there. We'll have to leave this task to the semanticists." I can confirm that they're on the case.

7 The problem of argument mapping (Agent in Spec-vP, Theme in Spec-VP, etc.), which principles like UTAH or Tenny's (1992) Aspectual Interface Hypothesis described, then comes down to the particular identity of the predicates which head the projections in the vP: arguments merged in Spec-vP are interpreted as Agents because of the content of v; arguments introduced by an Applicative will be subject to the syntactic and interpretive constraints imposed by the Appl head. The stipulated hierarchy of thematic roles becomes instead a cartographic or selectional hierarchy of the heads in the vP constituent, for which a principled explanation is still waiting.

Bibliography

Baker, Mark. 1988. *Incorporation*. Cambridge, MA: MIT Press.

Bever, Thomas G, and David J Townsend. 2001. *Sentence comprehension: The integration of habits and rules*, volume 1950. Cambridge, MA: MIT Press.

Borer, Hagit. 2003. Exo-skeletal vs. endo-skeletal explanations: Syntactic projections and the lexicon. In *The Nature of Explanation in Linguistic Theory*, ed. John Moore and Maria Polinsky, 31–67. Standford, CA: CSLI Publications.

Borer, Hagit. 2005. *Structuring sense, vol. II: The normal course of events*. Oxford, UK: Oxford University Press.

Chomsky, Noam. 1957. *Syntactic Structures*. The Hague, The Netherlands: Mouton de Gruyter.

Chomsky, Noam. 1965. *Aspects of the Theory of Syntax*. Cambridge, MA: MIT Press.

Chomsky, Noam. 1970. Remarks on nominalization. In *Readings in English Transformational Grammar*, ed. R.A. Jacobs and P.S. Rosenbaum, 184–221. Waltham, MA: Ginn-Blaisdell.

Hale, Ken, and Samuel J. Keyser. 1993. On argument structure and the lexical expression of syntactic relations. In *A view from building 20*, ed. Ken Hale and Samuel J. Keyser. Cambridge, MA: MIT Press.

Hale, Ken, and Samuel J. Keyser. 2002. *Prolegomenon to a theory of argument structure*. Cambridge, MA: MIT Press.

Harley, Heidi. 2011. A minimalist approach to argument structure. In *The Oxford handbook of linguistic minimalism*, ed. Cedric Boeckx. Oxford, UK: Oxford University Press.

Harley, Heidi, and Rolf Noyer. 2000. Licensing in the non-lexicalist lexicon. In *The lexicon/encyclopedia interface*, ed. Bert Peeters, 349–374. Amsterdam, Netherlands: Elsevier.

Heim, Irene, and Angelika Kratzer. 1998. *Semantics in generative grammar*. New York, NY: Wiley.

Lasnik, Howard. 2000. *Syntactic Structures revisited*. Cambridge, MA: MIT Press.

Levin, Beth, and Malka Rappaport-Hovav. 1995. *Unaccusativity*. Cambridge, MA: MIT Press.

Ramchand, Gillian. 2008. *Verb meaning and the lexicon*. Cambridge, UK: Cambridge University Press.

Tenny, Carol L. 1992. The aspectual interface hypothesis. In *Lexical matters*, ed. Ivan Sag and Anna Szabolsci, 1–27. Stanford, CA: CSLI Publications.

Mamoru Saito
Transformations in the Quest for a Simpler, more Elegant Theory

1 Introduction

Syntactic Structures is the work that made transformational grammar widely known, and, to borrow David Lightfoot's expression in the Introduction to the 2002 edition, was "the snowball which began the avalanche of the modern 'cognitive revolution'." The purpose of this chapter is to discuss how transformational rules are motivated in this work and how the relevant discussion and proposals led to the remarkable development of syntactic theory in the subsequent 60 years.

Simply put, the motivation for the transformational rules is that its incorporation makes a grammar much simpler and enables us to capture deeper generalizations. It is however instructive to go over what kinds of simplicity Chomsky had in mind and how the same quest for simplicity and elegance led to later developments in syntactic theory. In order to do this, I discuss the famous analysis of the English auxiliary system in the following section and the passive transformation in Section 3. The proposal of transformations in *Syntactic Structures* started intense investigations on their properties, which in turn made it possible to raise the fundamental question why Language has transformations. In Section 4, I consider the recent developments on this question in the Minimalist framework.

Before I start the discussion of transformations, let me briefly comment on 'simplicity of the overall system' as a motivation because this itself marked a sharp departure from the dominant view on linguistic theory at the time. In Chapter 6, titled "On the Goals of Linguistic Theory," Chomsky lays out the methodological foundation for linguistic research. He first argues against the position widely held in American structuralism that it is among the goals of linguistic theory to provide a discovery procedure for grammars, a manual of mechanical method to construct a grammar on the basis of a given corpus. His alternative is stated as follows:

> The point of view adopted here is that it is unreasonable to demand of linguistic theory that it provide anything more than a practical evaluation procedure for grammars. (p.52)

An evaluation procedure is a way to choose among proposed grammars. And the criterion for the evaluation, aside from adequacy in description, is nothing but simplicity. This, Chomsky states, necessitates investigation into the notion of simplicity itself. At the same time, he proceeds with syntactic analysis with the following statement:

> Nevertheless, it should be fairly clear that under any reasonable definition of "simplicity of grammar," most of the decisions about relative complexity that we reach below will stand. (p.55)

Transformations, then, are motivated because they yield simpler, or more elegant, grammars.

Chomsky emphasizes here that the simplicity at issue is not simplicity at a particular level or within a particular component of grammar but is overall simplicity. In this context, he also argues against another idea that is closely associated with a discovery procedure, that is, that linguistic research should proceed in a bottom-up fashion, from phonemic analysis to morphology and then to syntax. Chomsky notes that "the higher levels of linguistic description depend on results obtained at the lower levels" but "the converse is true" as well. (p.59) This is amply demonstrated throughout the discussion in *Syntactic Structures*. Then, we simply try to formulate the general theory of syntax and the grammars of particular languages as precisely and as elegantly as possible, and continue to develop them on the basis of empirical and conceptual considerations. This is taken for granted in the current research in generative grammar, which makes no methodological distinction between linguistics and (other) natural sciences. But it is worth noting that it is this approach to linguistics that led to the proposal of transformational rules over 60 years ago.

2 Inadequacy of Phrase Structure Rules for Discontinuous Elements

In this section, I briefly go over the analysis of the English Auxiliary system in *Syntactic Structures* and discuss the model of syntax it leads to.

2.1 English Auxiliary System

After Chomsky introduces phrase structure rules of the following kind in Chapter 4 to capture constituent analysis, he points out their inadequacies in Chapter 5:

(1) a. Sentence → NP + VP
    b. VP → Verb + (NP)
    c. NP → (Art) + NP
    d. Art → the
    e. N → man, ball, book, etc.
    f. Verb → hit, took, etc.

One case concerns the auxiliary system. (2) illustrates the point.

(2) The man had been reading the book.

Here, the perfect is expressed by *have* and the affix *en* on the following element, and the progressive by *be* and the affix *ing* on the following verb. In other words, the perfect and the progressive are expressed by discontinuous elements. Phrase structure rules fail to capture elements of this kind.

Chomsky then goes on to propose the celebrated transformational analysis. He first adds the phrase structure rules in (3) to (1a–f).

(3) a. Verb → Aux + V
    b. Aux → Tense + (Modal) + (have + en) + (be + ing)[1]
    c. V → hit, take, walk, read, etc.
    d. Tense → past, present
    e. Modal → will, can, may, shall, must

Note that *have* and *be* are contiguous with their associated affixes in (3b). Then, he introduces the rules in (4) to derive the surface form.

(4) a. Let *Af* stand for any of the affixes *past, present, en, ing*. Let *v* stand for any *Modal* or *V*, or *have* or *be* (i.e., for any non-affix in the phrase *Verb*.) Then:
    $Af + v \rightarrow v + Af \#$, where # is interpreted as word boundary.
    b. Replace + by # except in the context $v - Af$. Insert # initially and finally.

(4a), which later came to be called 'affix hopping' and more recently 'phonological merger', moves affixes to the end of the following elements. (4b) specifies the word boundaries.

---

[1] In *Syntactic Structures*, C is employed instead of *Tense* and it expands to *past, s* (for singular subject) or ø (for plural subject). I use the more familiar *Tense* here and accordingly in (3d).

(5) illustrates how (2) is derived by the rules in (1), (3) and (4).

(5) a. the + man + past + have + en + be + ing + read + the + book
 b. the + man + have + past # be + en # read + ing # the + book
 c. # the # man # have + past # be + en # read + ing # the # book #

The phrase structure rules generate the string in (5a). (4b) applies to this string and places *past* after *have*, *en* after *be*, and *ing* after *read* as in (5b). (4c) inserts word boundaries except before the suffixes to yield (5c). Finally, it is assumed that morphophonemic rules of the following form apply to (5c):

(6) *walk* → /wɔk/, *take* + *past* → /tʊk/, *have* + *past* → /həd/, *be* + *en* → /bɪn/,...

What matters here is the simplicity and the elegance of this analysis. Chomsky never claimed that phrase structure rules cannot accommodate the English auxiliary system. The rules in (7), for example, can be employed instead of (3b) and (4a) to generate the grammatical patterns.

(7) a. Verb → V + Tense
 b. Verb → Modal + Tense + V
 c. Verb → have + Tense + V + en
 d. Verb → be + Tense + V + ing
 e. Verb → Modal + Tense + have + V + en
 f. Verb → Modal + Tense + be + V + ing
 g. Verb → have + Tense + be + en + V + ing
 h. Verb → Modal + Tense + have + be + en + V + ing

But this is clearly more complex than the analysis that emplys (4a), and misses the generalization that the perfect is expressed by two discontinuous elements *have* and *en* and the progressive by *be* and *ing*.

The analysis outlined above leads to the model of grammar quoted in (8) from p.46 of *Syntactic Structures*.

(8)   Σ: Sentences:

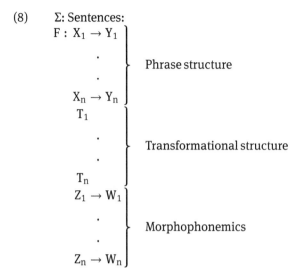

Phrase structure rules generate strings with structures that constitute inputs to transformational rules. Then, transformations yield strings that morphophonemic rules apply to. This raises the question whether the outputs of phrase structure rules and transformations encode specific information and if they do, what sorts of information they express. The pursuit of this question led to the postulation of D-structure, S-structure and PF in the Standard Theory of the 1960's and the Extended Standard Theory (EST) later.

2.2 The Generality of the Affix Hopping Analysis

The beauty of the affix hopping rule in (4a) is that it applies quite generally to any structure regardless of how the structure is created, and further, leads to an explanation of an otherwise mysterious phenomenon, namely, the appearance of the "dummy verb" *do* in some contexts. Let us consider a few cases from *Syntactic Structures*.

Chomsky observes that a sentence can be analyzed as having three parts, $1-2-3$, as in (9), and elements of negation, *not* and *n't*, occur after the second.

(9) a. *NP — Tense — V ...*
    b. *NP — Tense+Modal — ...*
    c. *NP — Tense+have — ...*
    d. *NP — Tense+be — ...*

Thus, *not* appears after *have* and *be* in (10a) and (10b) respectively.

(10) a. The man had not taken the book.
     b. The man was not taking the book.

The derivation of (10a) is illustrated in (11).

(11) a. *the + man + past + have + en + take + the + book*
     b. *the + man + past + have + not + en + take + the + book*
     c. *the + man + have + past # not + take + en # the + book*
     d. *# the # man # have + past # not # take + en # the # book #*

The phrase structure rules generate the string in (11a), and then, *not* is inserted after *have* in (11b).[2] The affix hopping transformation in (4a) applies as in (11c), placing *past* after *have* and *en* after *take*. The example shows that (4a) serves to generate negative sentences as well as affirmative ones.

The interesting case is (9a), instantiated by (12).

(12) The man did not take the book.

The derivation of this example is as in (13).

(13) a. *the + man + past + take + the + book*
     b. *the + man + past + not + take + the + book*
     c. *# the # man # past # not # take # the # book #*
     d. *# the # man # do + past # not # take # the # book #*

The insertion of *not* after *Tense* blocks the application of (4a) to *Tense + V* as (13b) shows. Hence, *take* does not appear in past tense and *past* as an affix is stranded after the insertion of word boundaries in (13c). Chomsky, then, proposes the rule in (14), now known as '*do*-support', in order to save the stranded tense affix.

---

2 It is thus proposed in *Syntactic Structures* that negative elements are inserted into the structure by a transformation. But this is not important for the point to be made here, that is, the generality of the application of the affix hopping rule in (4a).

(14) # Af → # do + Af

This rule inserts *do* before a stranded affix as in (13d) and yields (12) correctly. Note that this analysis is possible because the phrase structure rule (3b) treats *Tense* and *V* as independent elements and (4a) serves to combine them when they are adjacent. If *V + Tense* enters the structure as a single element, there is no straightforward way to account for the appearance of *do* in (12).

Chomsky goes on to show that basically the same analysis applies to other independent constructions. One of them is *yes/no* questions, exemplified in (15).

(15) a. Had the man taken the book?
      b. Was the man taking the book?
      c. Did the man take the book?

Yes/no questions are formed by the question transformation that fronts the second element in (9) to the sentence-initial position. And interestingly, *do* appears in (15c) just as in (12). The derivation of the example is shown in (16).

(16) a. the + man + past + take + the + book
      b. past + the + man + take + the + book
      c. # past # the # man # take # the # book #
      d. # do + past # the # man # take # the # book #

The fronting of *past* by the question transformation in (16b) blocks the application of (4a) and produces a stranded *Tense* as in (16c). This triggers the *do*-support rule in (14) and yields the form in (15c). Thus, the forms of questions are explained by exactly the same set of rules as negative sentences.[3]

It is mentioned in *Syntactic Structures* that the apparent asymmetry in (17) follows as a consequence of the analysis.

(18) a. What did the man take?
      b. Who took the book?

---

[3] Chomsky points out that the same set of rules accounts for examples of conjunction with *so* as in (i).

(17) [(i)]
      a. John has arrived and so have I.
      b. John arrives and so do I.

It extends to examples of VP-ellipsis and VP-preposing as well, as it is now standardly taught in introductory syntax courses.

As (17a) indicates, a wh-question is generated with further fronting of a wh-word (or phrase).[4] However, *do* does not show up and there is apparently no word-order change in (17b) with a wh-word in the subject position. It seems then that neither the question rule nor the wh-fronting rule applies in this case. Are wh-questions generated in two distinct ways depending on the location of the wh-word? Chomsky's answer is negative. The derivation of (17b) with the question transformation and wh-fronting is shown in (18).

(20) a. *who + past + take + the + book*
    b. *past + who + take + the + book*
    c. *who + past + take + the + book*
    d. *who + take + past # the + book*
    e. *# who # take + past # the # book #*

The question transformation fronts *past* to the sentence-initial position as in (18b). At this point, the subject intervenes between *past* and *take*. However, the wh-fronting rule fronts the wh subject as in (18c), making *past* and *take* adjacent again. Then, the affix hopping rule (4a) can apply and form *take + past*. Thus, the question transformation and the wh-question rule apply uniformly regardless of the location of the wh-word. The analysis is clearly simpler than having two sets of distinct phrase structure rules for subject and non-subject wh-questions.

In the discussion above on the affix hopping rule (4a), I introduced a few more transformations from *Syntactic Structure*. Each of them can be motivated on the basis of simplicity. For example, one may assume the phrase structure rules in (19) and (20) in place of the question transformation.

(21) a. Sentence → *Do + Tense + NP + VP$_1$*
    b. Sentence → *Modal + Tense + NP + VP$_2$*
    c. Sentence → *have + Tense + NP + VP$_3$*
    d. Sentence → *be + Tense + NP + VP$_4$*

---

4 More precisely, the transformation is defined in Footnote 2 on p.69 as a rule that adds *wh* to pronouns and fronts *wh + pronoun*. Then, morphophonemic rules of the following form apply:

(19)   [(i)] *wh + he/she* → /huw/, *wh + it* → /wat/

I assume for the sake of simplicity that phrase structure rules directly generate strings with wh-words.

(22) a. $VP_1 \rightarrow Verb_1 + (NP)$
 b. $Verb_1 \rightarrow V$
 c. $VP_2 \rightarrow Verb_2 + (NP)$
 d. $Verb_2 \rightarrow have + be + en + V + ing$
 e. $Verb_2 \rightarrow have + V + en$
 f. $Verb_2 \rightarrow be + V + ing$
 g. $Verb_2 \rightarrow V$
 h. $VP_3 \rightarrow Verb_3 + (NP)$
 i. $Verb_3 \rightarrow be + en + V + ing$
 j. $Verb_3 \rightarrow V + en$
 k. $VP_4 \rightarrow Verb_4 + (NP)$
 l. $Verb_4 \rightarrow V + ing$

It should be obvious that this is far more complex than the question transformation and that it misses generalizations on the formation of questions and the placement of affixes. According to the analysis in *Syntactic Structures*, questions are formed by fronting the second element in (9) and the rest of the derivation is automatically taken care of by the independently motivated affix hopping rule and *do*-support. On the other hand, it is not clear that the complex set of rules in (19) and (20) expresses any generalization. For example, given these rules, it is simply an accident that what appears before the subject NP in (19) is missing from the VP in the same rule. One can in fact easily restate the rules so that this generalization does not obtain.

2.3 Refinements of the Analysis

As argued and demonstrated in Lasnik (1995), the essential part of the analysis introduced in this section still remains a viable possibility even today, 60 years after it was proposed. It was in fact refined in the details over the years.[5]

Recall that the formulations of negative placement and question transformations are based on the tri-part analysis of sentences as in (9), repeated below in (21).

(23) a. NP — Tense — V ...
 b. NP — Tense+Modal — ...
 c. NP — Tense+have — ...
 d. NP — Tense+be — ...

---

[5] See, in particular, Lasnik (1981) and the references cited there.

This indicates that *Tense* forms a unit with the following *Modal, have* or *be*, but not with a main verb *V*. This is captured by the generation of *Modal* under *Tense* and the head-movement of *have* and *be* to *Tense*. Then, the elements of negation, *not* and *n't*, occur right after *Tense*, and it is *Tense* that is fronted in question formation. The derivation of (15b), repeated in (22), in more modern terms is shown in (23).

(24) Was the man taking the book?

(25)

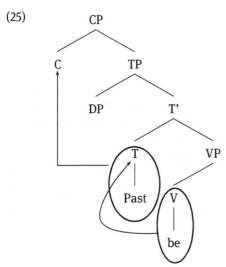

Then, *Tense* combines with *have* and *be* by head movement, and with the main verb by affix hopping.

There is a remark in *Syntactic Structures* on why the forms in (24) are both attested in dialects whereas (25b) is excluded.

(26) a. Have you the book?
 b. Do you have the book?

(27) x. Are you comfortable?
 x. *Do you be comfortable?

It is stated that (24a) and (24b) are both permissible because the main verb *have* can be analyzed as *have* in (21c) or as *V* in (21a). The proposal for (25) is that the main verb *be* does not belong to the class of verbs and hence can only be analyzed as *be* in (21d).

The head movement analysis captures the facts more straightforwardly. *Be*, whether it is an auxiliary verb or a main verb undergoes head movement to *Tense* when it is the first element among auxiliaries and verbs. Whether the main verb *have* moves to *Tense* depends on the dialect. Emonds (1978) extends the analysis to French where all main verbs are raised to *Tense* in appropriate contexts. Thus, contrasts such as that in (26) obtain between French and English.

(28) a. Jean (n') aime pas Marie
         (ne) love Neg
    b. John does not love Mary.

The main verb precedes *pas* in (26a) as it raises to *Tense* whereas it follows *not* in (26b).

3 Phrasal Movements and Selection

There are very important discussions on passive in *Syntactic Structures*, which pave the way to the postulation of D-structure in later works. In this section, I go over the presented arguments for the passive transformation and discuss their consequences.

3.1 The Passive Transformation

The passive transformation is proposed in the following form in Chapter 4:

(29) If S_1 is a grammatical sentence of the form $NP1 - Aux - V - NP_2$, then the corresponding string of the form $NP_2 - Aux+be+en - V - by+NP_1$ is also a grammatical sentence.

This rule derives (28b) as in (29).

(30) a. Sincerity frightens John.
    b. John is frightened by sincerity.

(31) a. *sincerity + present + frighten + John*
    b. *John + present + be + en + frighten + by + sincerity*
    c. *John + be + present # frighten + en # by + sincerity*
    d. *# John # be + present # frighten + en # by # sincerity #*

The phrase structure rules generate (29a), which underlies the active sentence (28a). The passive transformation applies to this string, yielding (29b). The rule exchanges the positions of the subject and the object, adds *by* before the postposed subject, and adds *be* + *en* after *Aux*. The affix hopping rule applies to the output of the passive rule as in (29c), and finally (29d) is produced as the input to morphophonemics.

Chomsky considers the possibility to introduce *be* + *en* as part of *Aux* in the phrase structure rule as in (30).

(32)   *Aux* → *Tense* + (*Modal*) + (*have* + *en*) + (*be* + *ing*) + (*be* + *en*)   (cf. (3b))

However, he rejects the possibility as heavy restriction must be placed on the selection of *be* + *en*. The following *V* must be transitive and at the same time the *V* cannot be followed by *NP*. The statement of these complicates the grammar.

It is worth noting here that the now standard argument on the basis of selectional relations is already presented in *Syntactic Structures* for the passive rule. The comparison of (28a) and (31a) shows that *frighten* selects an animate object.

(33)   a.   # John frightens sincerity.
       b.   # Sincerity is frightened by John.

And the ungrammaticality of (31b), as opposed to (28b), indicates that the same selectional requirement is imposed on the subject instead of the object in the passive counterpart. In short, the selectional requirements on the object and the subject are reversed in passives. If passive sentences are directly generated by phrase structure rules, the selectional requirements must be stated separately for active and passive sentences, which would be an inelegant reduplication. With the passive transformation, the same requirements can be imposed on the output of phrase structure rules uniformly for both active and passive sentences.

It is sometimes stated that the passive transformation is motivated because an active-passive pair are synonymous. It is also often assumed that the active sentence is the "basic form" because it directly represents the predicate-argument structure. Neither of these is assumed in *Syntactic Structures*. In Chapter 7, Chomsky considers the possibility that the passive rule only introduces *be* + *en* and *by*, and does not exchange the positions of the subject and the object (or more precisely the NP that immediately follows *V*). He notes first that this would complicate the statement of selectional requirements because the rule derives (31b) from what underlies (28a). Then, he goes on to present another similar argument against this option on the basis of the contrast between (32) and (33).

(34) a. All the people in the lab consider John a fool.
 b. John is considered a fool by all the people in the lab.

(35) a. *John considers all the people in the lab a fool.
 b. *All the people in the lab are considered a fool by John.

Chomsky analyzes *consider + a fool* in (32a) as a complex *V* that selects a singular object. The object *John* is then placed before *a fool* by a transformation. If the passive transformation is formulated as in (27) and makes NP_2 the new subject, (32b) is correctly predicted to be grammatical. The selectional requirement of *consider + a fool* is met by the singular NP, *John*, before the transformation applies. The rule also correctly predicts (33b) to be ungrammatical. *All the people in the lab* originates in the object position and it contradicts the selectional requirement of the complex *V* in that position. Thus, (33b) is ruled out in exactly the same way as (33a).

On the other hand, if the passive rule preserves the positions of the subject and the object, (33b) would be derived from (32a). A stipulation would then be required to exclude the example. Similarly, it would have to be explained why (32b) is grammatical despite the fact that it is derived from a string that underlies the ungrammatical (33a). Then, the overall simplicity is attained with the formulation of passive that exchanges the positions of NP_1 and NP_2 as in (27). Note that this argument stands independently of the complex *V* analysis of *consider + a fool*. Suppose that *John + a fool* in (32a) constitutes a small clause with the predicate *a fool* and the subject *John* as proposed by Stowell (1981). Then, the predicate *a fool* selects a singular subject. The NP, *John*, satisfies this requirement in the example. With the passive transformation in (27), exactly the same analysis can be given to (32b). The example is grammatical because the subject, *John*, originates as the subject of the small clause. (33b), on the other hand, is not because the subject, *all the people in the lab*, fails to satisfy the selectional requirement of the predicate, *a fool*, in its initial position.

Chomsky also argues on the basis of simplicity that a passive sentence should be derived from what underlies its active counterpart and not vice versa. The specific argument given in this context is based on the examples in (34).

(36) a. The wine was drunk by the guests.
 b. John was drunk by midnight.

(34a) is a passive sentence whereas *drunk* in (34b) is an adjective, as the following contrast attests:

(37) a. *The wine was very drunk by the guests.
  b. John was very drunk by midnight.

If the "active transformation" applies to what underlies (34a) to generate (36a), then it would incorrectly generate (36b) as well.

(38) a. The guests drank wine.
  b. *Midnight drank John.

Stronger arguments can be built also on the basis of simplicity and elegance. For example, if active transitive sentences are produced only by "active transformations," then there should be two distinct ways to generate active sentences. When V is not immediately followed NP, the sentence is generated by phrase structure rules. On the other hand, a sentence with a $V + NP$ sequence is produced by the "active transformation." This clearly misses important generalizations that apply to all active sentences. Suppose instead that active transitive sentences can be generated either by phrase structure rules or by the "active transformation." Then, the transformation would just be redundant. In any case, what is noteworthy here is that Chomsky considers all possibilities without preconception, including the derivation of active from passive, and argues for a set of specific proposals on the basis of the simplicity of syntactic analysis and the overall system. And as will be discussed in the following subsection, the set of proposals in *Syntactic Structures* lays the foundation for research in syntactic theory for the next 40 years.

3.2 The Emergence of a Model for Syntax

Chomsky argued for transformations in pursuit of the simplest and most elegant theory, and arrived at the model of derivation in (8), which can be restated as in (37).

(39) phrase structure rules → transformations → morphophonemic rules

This is only a step away from the Standard theory of Chomsky (1965) with D-structure as the output of phrase structure rules (and lexical insertion) and S-structure as the output of the transformational component, and from the Extended Standard Theory pursued, for example, in Chomsky (1981), with the added level of representation, Logical Form. Particularly important in this context is the proposal that selectional relations are represented at the output of phrase structure rules before transformations apply. This leads to the postulation of D-structure as a pure representation of selectional or thematic relations. The pursuit of the simplest theory of constituent structure, described initially by phrase structure rules, culminated into X' principles applying at D-structure. Accordingly, the clause structure was reanalyzed as in (38).[6]

(40)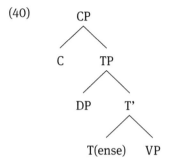

Syntactic Structures also suggests directions for later research on the transformational component and its output, S-structure. Relevant here is its discussions on rule ordering and optional vs. obligatory transformations. I briefly go over them in this subsection.

Rule ordering is first introduced with respect to the affixing hopping rule (4) and *do*-support in (14), repeated below as (39) and (40) respectively.

(41) a. Let *Af* stand for any of the affixes *past, present, en, ing*. Let *v* stand for any *Modal* or *V*, or *have* or *be* (i.e., for any non-affix in the phrase *Verb*.) Then:

$Af + v \rightarrow v + Af \#$, where # is interpreted as word boundary.

b. Replace + by # except in the context $v - Af$. Insert # initially and finally.

(42) $\# Af \rightarrow \# do + Af$

Let us consider (41a), which underlies (41b).

(43) a. the + man + past + take + the + book
 b. The man took the book.

---

[6] See, for example, Chomsky (1970, 1986a); Stowell (1981), and the references cited there for this development on clause structure.

If (39b) is applied first to (41a) as in (42a), then the context is set for the application of *do*-support as in (42b).

(44) a. # the # man # past # take # the # book #
b. # the # man # do + past # take # the # book #

This generates (43) incorrectly in non-emphatic context.

(45) * The man did take the book.

Then, (39a) must apply before (39b) and (40), and (40) must be construed as a "last resort" rule, an assumption that is maintained even today.

More serious cases of rule ordering arise when the interaction of (39)-(40) and the wh-fronting rule is considered. (44) is a relevant case.

(46) Who took the book?

(45a) is the input to the transformational component.

(47) a. who + past + take + the + book
b. past + who + take + the + book
c. # past # who # take # the # book #
d. # do + past # who # take # the # book #
e. # who # do + past # take # the # book #

The question rule fronts *past* as in (45b). The application of (39)-(40) to this string yields (45d). Finally, the wh-fronting rule places the wh-word in the sentence-initial position as in (45e). This results in (46), which is again illicit in non-emphatic context.

(48) * Who did take the book?

The problem here is that (39)–(40) apply before the wh-fronting rule. If wh-fronting is ordered before (39)–(40), only the grammatical form is generated as in (47).

(49) a. who + past + take + the + book
b. past + who + take + the + book
c. who + past + take + the + book
d. who + take + past # the + book
e. # who # take + past # the # book #

Then, (39)–(40) are ordered after the other transformations. This was taken later as evidence that these rules map the output of the transformational component to the morphophonemic or phonological component. The revised model of derivation in (48) obtains.

(50) phrase structure rules → D-structure → transformations → affix-hopping/do-support → phonological component

In addition to rule ordering, there is what appears to be an ordering paradox in the analysis in *Syntactic Structures*. Tense, which is called C in *Syntactic Structures*, is expanded by the following rule:

(51) $C \rightarrow \left\{ \begin{array}{l} S \text{ in the context of } NP_{sing\_} \\ \emptyset \text{ in the context of } NP_{pl\_} \\ past \end{array} \right\}$

This looks like a phrase structure rule although it is context-sensitive. However, as Chomsky points out, it must apply after the passive transformation as *present* agrees with the surface subject. Then, (49) is included among the transformational rules in *Syntactic Structures*. But, aside from the fact that it has a peculiar format as a transformation, it leads to further rule ordering. For example, it not only has to apply after passive but also has to apply before the question transformation in examples like (50).

(52) What do the men eat?

In this example, *present* agrees with *the men*, not with *what*.

The ordering of "agreement" with passive is avoided in later works such as Chomsky (1981) by making agreement apply or be checked after the transformational component, that is, at S-structure. The copy (or trace) theory of movement accommodates (50) as illustrated below.

(53)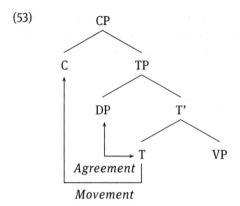

The movement of *T(ense)* to *C* leaves a copy behind, and the copy participates in agreement with the subject. The copy theory, in turn, suggests that the passive transformation does not involve rightward movement of the subject NP and simply moves the object NP to a "vacant" subject position. If the subject NP moves rightward, its copy should block the movement of the object NP. This simplification of passive is supported by the optionality of *by*-phrase as shown in (52).[7]

(54) The book was stolen (by a thief)

The considerations above have narrowed the range of transformations and have led to the following model:

(55)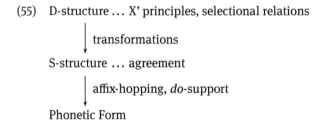

The phrase structure rules specified the possible constituent structures and raised the question why those structures and only those structures are possible. This led

---

[7] The treatment of *by*-phrase under this approach poses interesting questions and has been discussed over the years. See, for example, Jaeggli (1986) Baker et al. (1989); Collins (2005).

to the proposal of X' principles, which resulted in radical simplification of syntactic theory and particular grammars. Similarly, the transformational rules described how movement takes place and raised the question why movement applies in the way it does. This was a major research topic in the 1970's that led to the LGB theory of Chomsky (1981).

Important in this research topic was the distinction between obligatory and optional applications of transformations raised in *Syntactic Structures*. There, the passive transformation which derives a passive sentence from what underlies its active counterpart is mentioned as a typical optional transformation. If it applies, a passive sentence is generated, and if it does not, the derivation proceeds to generate an active sentence. On the other hand, the affix hopping rule was included among the obligatory transformations. The later research on transformations focused on NP movement to subject position as in passive and operator movement to Spec, CP as in wh-question movement, and the question on the obligatory vs. optional applications of transformations took a somewhat different shape. For example, movement to the subject position is apparently obligatory in the example of passive in (54) and the example of raising in (55).

(56) a. * (There) was stolen a book.
     b. A book was stolen ___ .

(57) a. * (It) is likely [John to succeed].
     b. John is likely [___ to succeed].

The question was why the movements in (54) and (55) are obligatory.

An answer was proposed in Chomsky and Lasnik (1977), which showed that independently of movement, the distribution of NPs in English is limited to the four positions in (56).

(58) a. the position following a transitive verb
     b. the position following a preposition
     c. the subject position of a tensed clause
     d. the subject position of a noun phrase

(54a) and (55a) are ungrammatical simply because *a book* and *John* appear in illicit positions in these examples. As is well known, this kind of analysis led to the unification of all movement transformations as *Move-α*, which states, "Move anything anywhere optionally." *Move-α* may but need not apply to *John* in (55a).

If it does not, the sentence is ruled out as *John* appears in an illicit position. If it applies to *John* and move it to the end of the sentence, the result is still ungrammatical because the NP ends up in a position that is not included in (56). Finally, if *Move-α* yields (55b), locating *John* in the matrix subject position, then the sentence is grammatical because the NP is in the subject position of a tensed clause, the position specified in (56c).

It was Jean-Roger Vergnaud's Case theory that provided an explanation for the distribution of NPs in (56). He proposed that nouns need to be specified for Case to assume proper phonetic forms, as can be witnessed in the paradigms of pronouns as in *he – him – his*, and (56) lists the positions where nouns can receive Case. For example, (56a) and (56c) are the positions for accusative and nominative respectively. Chomsky (1981) proposed the Case filter in (59) to formally accommodate the idea.

(59)   * NP if NP has phonetic content and no Case.

The Case filter applies at S-structure as indicated in the revised model in (60).

(60)   D-structure ... X' principles, selectional relations

$\quad\quad\quad\quad\Big\downarrow$ Move-α

S-structure ... agreement, Case filter

$\quad\quad\quad\quad\Big\downarrow$ affix-hopping, *do*-support

Phonetic Form

(60) shows only part of the model proposed in Chomsky (1981), but its significance should be clear. Syntactic theory consists of levels of representations, in particular, D-structure and S-structure, and the principles that define them. Transformations are now reduced to a single principle on the relation between the two levels, *Move-α*. As often noted, this revolutionalized syntactic theory as it conceives of grammar as a set of principles (and parameters) instead of a system of rules. Yet, it is a direct descendent of the model of *Syntactic Structures* in many ways. Notably, the very same quest for simplicity and elegance led to this model. The transformational component is radically simplified and the addition of the Case filter not only aids the simplification but broadens the empirical coverage of the overall theory. And the core part of the model retains its shape. First, the basic constituent structure is specified, reflecting the selectional relations. Then, trans-

formations apply to this structure and produce the input to morphophonemic (or morphophonological) operations.

4 A Minimalist Perspective on Transformations

It was seen in the preceding sections that the LGB theory of Chomsky (1981) can be viewed as a direct descendant of the model proposed in *Syntactic Structures*. In both, there is a sharp distinction between what generates the basic phrase structure, phrase structure rules in the case of *Syntactic Structures*, and transformations. They are distinct in form and the latter applies to the output of the former. An effort to eliminate this distinction was initiated in the Minimalist research, in particular, in Chomsky (1994). Although this led to departure from the conception of transformations in *Syntactic Structures*, I discuss it in this section because it addresses a fundamental question that originates in the work, namely, what transformations are, and brings us right to the current research. Section 4.1 concerns the last resort nature of phrasal movement transformations and Section 4.2 discusses the issue of movement of NPs into selected positions.

4.1 Merge and the Last Resort Nature of Phrasal Movement

The Minimalist model proposed in Chomsky (1993) eliminates D-structure and S-structure. Pursuing this model, Chomsky (1994) proposes that phrase structure is constructed by *Merge*, the minimal operation required for Language. It takes two objects α and β, and forms a constituent as in (61).

(61) γ = { α, β }

When α and β are independent objects as in (62a), the operation is called external Merge.

(62) a.   b.

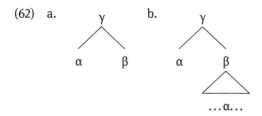

On other hand, when α is contained within β, and *Merge* applies α and α as in (60b), it is called internal Merge. Both are instances of the minimal operation *Merge*, and phrasal movement is nothing but internal Merge.

The derivation of the simple example in (61) is illustrated in (62).

(63) The man took the book.

(64)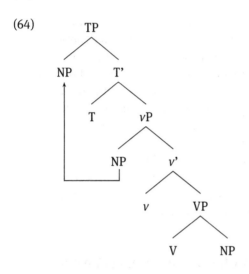

The structure assumes the predicate-internal subject hypothesis as formulated in Chomsky (1995), and consequently, the subject NP is initially merged at the specifier position of *v*P.[8] The structure is straightforwardly built with *Merge*, including internal Merge of the subject NP to the surface subject position.

The conception of phrasal movement as an instance of *Merge* eliminates its special status, and answers the question why phrasal movement exists. Language has phrasal movement just because it has the minimally required operation, *Merge*. However, a few more steps were required to make this hypothesis truly feasible. Recall that movement transformations were unified as a single principle, *Move-α*, which allows movement of anything anywhere. This overgenerates vastly as the examples in (65) and (66) show.

(65) a. The man ate nothing.
 b. *Nothing the man ate ___.
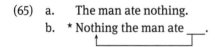

---

[8] See, for example, Koopman and Sportiche (1991) for arguments for the predicate-internal subject hypothesis.

(66) a. The man did not eat anything.
    b. * Anything, the man did not eat ___ .

The objects in (63a) and (64a) are merged with TP in (63b) and (64b) respectively, and the results are ungrammatical. A proposal to avoid this problem is made in Chomsky (1986b). He notes that the movement in (65), for example, applies with "a purpose."

(67) John is likely [___ to succeed].

If *John* stayed in the original position, it cannot receive Case. Hence, it must move to the matrix subject position for Case reasons. Chomsky then proposes that movement, or internal Merge, applies as a last resort, that is, only when it is necessary for the moved element. This is incorporated into the definition of movement in Chomsky (1995). But then, internal Merge is distinguished from external Merge as there is no such restriction on the latter.

A solution to this problem, as far as I know, was first provided in Chomsky (2013). There he proposes that *Merge* must accompany a labeling algorithm that specifies the nature of the newly formed object. When a verbal element and a nominal element are combined, for example, the interpretive component must be informed whether the formed object is verbal (VP) or nominal (NP). Chomsky first notes that the three cases of *Merge* in (66) must be considered in this respect.

(68) a. $\gamma = \{ H, \alpha P \}$
    b. $\gamma = \{ \alpha P, \beta P \}$
    c. $\gamma = \{ H_1, H_2 \}$

A head and a phrase are merged in (66a). Chomsky states that the head determines the label of γ in this case as search into γ immediately yields a unique head. On the other hand, (66b) and (66c), the mergers of two phrases and two heads respectively, are problematic because the labels cannot be determined straightforwardly in this way. Chomsky notes, however, that (66b) occurs in actual derivations and make two proposals for this case.

Let us consider the derivation of (61) again, repeated in a somewhat different form in (67).

(69)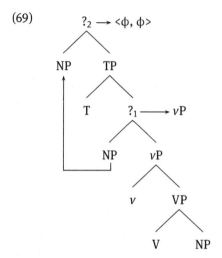

First, the verb *take* merges with the object *the book*. This is unproblematic as it instantiates (66a), the merger of a head and a phrase. Then, *v* merges with VP, which is also straightforward. But then, a problem arises when the subject NP *the man* merges with *v*P. Chomsky notes that the subject NP internally merges with TP after T is introduced into the structure. Then, $?_1$ only dominates a copy of this NP and does not contain it in full. He proposes that this disqualifies the NP as a label provider for $?_1$ and consequently *v*P does the work. When the subject internally merges with TP, another configuration of (66b) is created. In this case, T and NP share the same ϕ-features (person, number and gender features) because of agreement. Chomsky proposes that this enables $?_2$ to be labeled <ϕ, ϕ>. This captures the fact that movement always terminates with the internal merge of two phrases that share some features.

Chomsky extends the analysis to wh-question movement, as illustrated in (68).

(70) [$_{?2}$which book [$_{CP}$do you think [$_{?1}$which book [$_{CP}$John bought which book]]]]
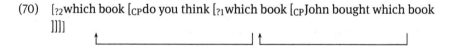

On the assumption that movement takes place cyclically, the wh-phrase *which book* moves as indicated by the arrows in (68). In this case, the movement cannot terminate at the edge of the embedded CP. This is predicted because the first internal merge creates $?_1$ = {NP, CP}, which fails to be labeled. A wh-phrase always ends up at the edge of a question sentence, and (68) is indeed fine when the wh-phrase moves on to the matrix-initial position. This is also expected. As the wh-phrase moves out of $?_1$, it can now be labeled by the CP it properly contains. The internal merge in the matrix clause creates $?_2$ = {NP, CP}. But in this case, NP is a wh-phrase and CP is a question. Then, they share the feature Q(uestion) and $?_2$ is labeled <Q, Q>.

The hypothesis on labeling in Chomsky (2013) provides an independent explanation for the last resort nature of internal Merge. Consider again (64b), repeated in (69).

(71)   * Anything the man did not eat ___ .

As the negative polarity item *anything* does not qualify as a topic, the example is not an instance of topicalization. It is then simply internally-merged with the matrix TP as in (69).

(72)

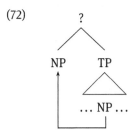

But in this case, there is no feature sharing between the NP and TP, and consequently, ? cannot be labeled. Thus, (69) is excluded because of failure in labeling.

If this analysis is correct, last resort is not a property of internal Merge *per se*. Phrasal movement always creates an {XP, YP} structure. And there are two ways to label this. One is to move XP out of the structure. This is effective, but one cannot keep using this strategy forever as the movement must terminate at some point. And movement can terminate when it creates a configuration of feature sharing, the other case in which {XP, YP} can be labeled. This is the reason why movement appears to take place as the last resort.

4.2 Transformations and the Selectional Relations

There is another issue that arises when phrasal movement transformation is analyzed simply as *Merge*. Recall that it is argued in *Syntactic Structures* that selectional relations are represented at the pre-transformation structure. Phrase structure rules build the basic phrase structure that reflects selectional (thematic) relations, and transformational rules modify this basic structure. If external Merge and internal Merge apply in the parallel manner, a hypothesis can be entertained that NPs enter the structure at their selected positions by external Merge and then may move to non-thematic positions by internal Merge. In (67), for example, the subject NP is initially merged with vP at its thematic position and moves to the specifier position of TP, a non-thematic position. But the hypothesis implies that there is after all a distinction between external Merge and internal Merge as only the former can create configurations of selection.

However, arguments against this distinction have been presented in Bošković (1997) and Hornstein (1999), among others. They both argue that movement into thematic positions takes place. Hornstein, for example, first argues that there is good reason to allow this type of movement on conceptual grounds. In the LGB theory of Chomsky (1981), it is assumed just as in *Syntactic Structures* that selectional relations are represented at the pre-transformation structure, namely, D-structure. Hornstein points out that it followed from this assumption that a movement transformation cannot create a new selectional relation between a predicate and an argument. If it does, this new selectional relation was not represented at D-structure in contradiction with the assumption. However, once D-structure is abandoned, nothing blocks movement into a thematic position unless it is prohibited by stipulation. Then, it would be conceptually desirable to allow this type of movement.

Then, Hornstein goes on to reanalyze examples of control, such as (71a), in terms of movement as in (71b).

(73) a. The man tried [PRO to buy the book].
 b. The man tried [___ to buy the book].

The man enters into selectional relation with the matrix verb *try* as the subject. Then, the LGB theory demands that it appears in the matrix subject position at D-structure. Since the embedded verb *buy* also selects for a subject, an independent element must appear in the position at D-structure. It was therefore assumed that a pronominal without phonetic content, PRO, appears in the position. However, Hornstein argues that given the elimination of D-structure, the example is best analyzed with movement as in (71b). *The man* is externally merged at the embedded subject position and receives the agent role there. Then, it internally merges at the matrix subject position, where it is interpreted as the agent of *try*.⁹ If this analysis is on the right track, the distinction between external Merge and internal Merge is eliminated completely. Both freely apply and can create configurations that satisfy selectional requirements.

The discussion above suggests that phrasal movement transformation, now called internal Merge, can be totally assimilated into *Merge*, a minimal operation that is required of Language. Then, it is clear why language has phrasal movement transformations. A language must have *Merge*, and phrasal movement comes with it.

5 Conclusion

Transformations were proposed in *Syntactic Structures* as they yield a simple, elegant theory. Further quest for simplicity and elegance led to the unification of phrasal movement transformations as a single principle *Move-α* on the relation between D-structure and S-structure. This, together with the elimination of D-structure and S-structure in the Minimalist program, made it possible to address deeper questions such as what transformations really are and why Language has them. Chomsky (1994) proposes that phrasal movement is an instance of the operation *Merge*, which forms a constituent of two elements. As discussed in the preceding section, efforts have been made to completely assimilate phrasal movements into *Merge*. If this project is successful, it identifies transformations, proposed on the basis of simplicity in *Syntactic Structures*, as instances of the minimal operation required of Language.

There was a great progress in the research on transformations in the last 60 years, and the Minimalist analysis entertained now is drastically simpler than its predecessors. And the progress undoubtedly will continue, as stated in the following passage from *Syntactic Structures*:

> Notice that neither the general theory nor the particular grammars are fixed for all time, in this view. Progress and revision may come from the discovery of new facts about particular languages, or from purely theoretical insights about organization of linguistic data—that is, new models for linguistic structure. ... At any given time we can attempt to formulate as precisely as possible both the general theory and the set of associated grammars that must meet the empirical, external conditions of adequacy. (p.50)

---

9 More precisely, the NP is merged at the specifier position of *v*P and receives a theta role there in both the embedded and the matrix clauses. Independent support for this movement analysis of control can be found, for example, in Hornstein and Polinsky (2010).

That is, *Syntactic Structures* initiated research on syntax as a science, and the quest for simplicity will continue as long as syntax continues to be pursued as a science.

Acknowledgements I would like to thank Norbert Hornstein for his helpful feedback on the initial version of this manuscript.

Bibliography

Baker, Mark, Kyle Johnson, and Ian Roberts. 1989. Passive arguments raised. *Linguistic Inquiry* 20:219–252.
Bošković, Željko. 1997. *The syntax of nonfinite complementation: An economy approach*. 32. MIT Press.
Chomsky, Noam. 1965. *Aspects of the Theory of Syntax*. Cambridge, MA: MIT Press.
Chomsky, Noam. 1970. Remarks on nominalization. In *Readings in English Transformational Grammar*, ed. R.A. Jacobs and P.S. Rosenbaum, 184–221. Waltham, MA: Ginn-Blaisdell.
Chomsky, Noam. 1981. *Lectures on Government and Binding*. Dordrecht, The Netherlands: Foris.
Chomsky, Noam. 1986a. *Barriers*. Cambridge, MA: MIT Press.
Chomsky, Noam. 1986b. *Knowledge of Language: Its Nature, Origin and use*. New York, NY: Praeger.
Chomsky, Noam. 1993. A minimalist program for linguistic theory. In *The view from Building 20: Essays in linguistics in honor of Sylvain Bromberger*, ed. Ken Hale and Samuel Jay Keyser, 1–52. Cambridge, MA: MIT Press.
Chomsky, Noam. 1994. Bare Phrase Structure. In *Government and Binding Theory and the Minimalist Program*, ed. Gert Webelhuth, 383–439. Oxford, UK: Blackwell.
Chomsky, Noam. 1995. *The Minimalist Program*. Cambridge, MA: MIT Press.
Chomsky, Noam. 2013. Problems of projection. *Lingua* 130:33–49.
Chomsky, Noam, and Howard Lasnik. 1977. Filters and control. *Linguistic inquiry* 8:425–504.
Collins, Chris. 2005. A smuggling approach to the passive in English. *Syntax* 8:81–120.
Emonds, Joseph. 1978. The verbal complex V'-V in French. *Linguistic inquiry* 151–175.
Hornstein, Norbert. 1999. Movement and control. *Linguistic inquiry* 30:69–96.
Hornstein, Norbert, and Maria Polinsky, ed. 2010. *Movement theory of control*, volume 154. John Benjamins Publishing.
Jaeggli, Osvaldo A. 1986. Passive. *Linguistic Inquiry* 17:587–622.
Koopman, Hilda, and Dominique Sportiche. 1991. The position of subjects. *Lingua* 85:211–258.
Lasnik, Howard. 1981. Restricting the Theory of Transformations: A Case Study. In *Explanation in Linguistics: The Logical Problem of Language Acquisition*, ed. Norbert Hornstein and David Lightfoot. London, UK: Longman.
Lasnik, Howard. 1995. Verbal Morphology: *Syntactic Structures* Meets the Minimalist Program. In *Evolution and Revolution in Linguistic Theory: Essays in Honor of Carlos Otero*, ed. Héctor Campos and Paula Kempchinsky, 251–275. Washington, DC: Georgetown University Press.
Stowell, Timothy. 1981. Origins of Phrase Structure. Doctoral Dissertation, MIT.

Gillian Ramchand
Grammatical vs. Lexical Formatives

1 Introduction

For a generative linguist, (re)reading *Syntactic Structures* is to be presented with a disorienting combination of ideas so clear and completely obvious as to be scarcely worth expending rhetorical energy on, together with others that seem bizarre, unintuitive or unwieldy to those who are not old enough to have read it in its time. The dissonance is unsurprising. *Syntactic Structures* inaugurated a field of inquiry that has progressed through many changes in its formal devices and theoretical constructs since 1957. But at the same time, it is impressive how much the enterprise has remained true to its origins in terms of methodological principles and the very nature of the questions being asked.

The modern stage-level generative linguist inhabiting her own moment in space and time, with her own articles of faith, and collections of open questions, might be surprised at how many of the most commonly accepted results of generative grammar were not at all obvious or conceived of in the same way at the very start of the enterprise.

As a case in point, the issue of the difference between lexical and grammatical formatives is a pervasive feature of much modern theorizing about syntax and its relation to the lexicon, and syntax in its relation to semantics. The distinction between the functional and the lexical is ingrained in the modern syntactic theoretical assumptions, and is almost never questioned, even across different architectures within the generative tradition. It is therefore surprising to (re)discover that these ideas are entirely absent from *Syntactic Structures*.

Chomsky's position on the inexistence of a distinguished class of 'grammatical formatives' is expressed directly and clearly in only one passage of the book, which I repeat here in full.

> Another common but dubious use of the notion 'structural meaning' is with reference to the meanings of so-called 'grammatically functioning' morphemes such as *-ing*, *-ly*, prepositions etc. The contention that the meanings of these morphemes are fundamentally different from the meanings of nouns, verbs, adjectives, and perhaps other large classes, is often supported by appeal to the fact that these morphemes can be distributed in a series of blanks or nonsense syllables so as to give the whole the appearance of a sentence, and in fact, so as to determine the grammatical category of the nonsense elements. For example, in the sequence "Pirots karulize elatically." we know that the three words are noun, verb and adverb by virtue of the *s*, *ize* and *ly*, respectively. But this property does not sharply

> distinguish 'grammatical' morphemes from others, since in such sequences as "the Pirots karul — yesterday" or "give him — water", the blanks are also determined as a variant of the past tense, in the first case, and as "the", "some" etc. but not "a" in the second. The fact that in these cases we were forced to give blanks rather than nonsense words is explained by the productivity or 'open-endedness' of the categories Noun, Verb, Adjective, etc., as opposed to the categories Article, Verbal Affix, etc. In general, when we distribute a sequence of morphemes in a sequence of blanks, we limit the choice of elements that can be placed in unfilled positions to form a grammatical sentence. Whatever differences there are among morphemes with respect to this property are apparently better explained in terms of such grammatical notions as productivity, freedom of combination, and size of substitution class, than in terms of any presumed feature of meaning.
> pg 104–105

To understand this position, it is necessary to understand Chomsky's position on the autonomy of syntax and on the relationship between syntax and semantics, both of which I would claim have been misunderstood in various ways, both by adherents and detractors (see also Adger, this volume, for a discussion). My purpose in this short article is to deconstruct the motivations behind the division largely assumed today between grammatical and lexical formatives, and explore the intuition about how they contribute differently to meaning. A clearer picture of what is at stake will lead to the conclusion that Chomsky's position in *Syntactic Structures*, far from being a temporary aberration on the road to the by now established position, is a serious candidate for actually being right.

2 Signs and Symbols

Ferdinand de Saussure in his seminal work on semiotics spent a good deal of time thinking about the phenomenon of the sign, and how an arbitrary, conventionally agreed external form comes to be associated with a conventionally agreed concept. In his discussion, he conceives of the 'signified' as some essentially arbitrary (though probably culturally motivated) partition of the flow of reality, or space of possible things that can be 'meant'. The 'signifier' is the arbitrary conventionalized sequence of sounds it is paired with (or indeed in principle any systematically externalizable form perceptible to others). In the *Cours* (de Saussure 1959), the sign is given a kind of primitive, mystical status, but for one often touted as the father of synchronic linguistics, Saussure is dramatically silent on the subject of syntax as we know it. Moreover, the sign, while interesting in its own right, is in no way unique to humans, even if we confine our attention to cases of conscious deployment. Many other species consciously deploy conventionalized signs to convey highly specific meanings (Pearce 2008), and pass them on to their offspring. Vervet monkey calls are the most famous primate examples (Demers 1988, but all see recent work by Philippe Schlenker and his Paris lab on monkey semantics Philippe Schlenker and Zuberbühler 2016).

But the syntax of human languages goes way beyond this, as *Syntactic Structures* is at pains to point out. The grammar of a language is a complex symbolic system, generating infinite forms from finite means, in a way that is not reducible to transitional probabilities between linearly adjacent 'signifiers', or to the nature of the 'signified' (again see Adger, this volume). Language is not just a bag of 'signifiers' (something the vervet monkeys have, albeit in reduced form), but a system of structurally combining 'signifiers' to make complex 'signifiers'. As Terence Deacon put it in his book, *The Symbolic Species* (Deacon 1997), the defining property of this kind of system is that in addition to the signifier-signified nexus explored by Saussure, human linguistic systems crucially employ *sign-to-sign relationships*.

2.1 Two kinds of Meaning?

So doesn't this mean that there are two kinds of 'meaning', then? I think so. There is one kind of meaning that involves a conventional association to some aspect of the world, or our cognitive reality, and there's another kind of meaning that is essentially relational that provides the interpretational glue between signs. Avoiding the contentious terms 'meaning' and 'semantics', and in keeping with the Saussurean theme, we could call the former 'external significance'[1], and the latter 'relational significance'. In other words, one needs to know of English that when one puts the word *red* together with *car* to form *red car*, the result is something that you could also describe as a kind of 'car' but with the additional property of being 'red'. It does not describe a particular shade of red, or refer to a person who 'owns a red car', it means 'a car that is red', and this knowledge does not need to be acquired on a collocation by collocation basis, but is part of the productivity of the system as understood by the native speaker. Illustrations of this sort could be multiplied, and underlie the creative semantic competence of human language users. I think therefore that there are two kinds of meaning in the most informal sense, that need to be importantly distinguished in understanding

---

1 I am intentionally staying away from words like reference, and truth conditions, since it is not clear to me that the external significance of signs needs to be explicated in terms of material conditions in the real world, but they do clearly need to reach out of the language module itself and signify independently studiable cognitive products of the mind/brain. It is for this reason I use the term 'external'.

the functioning of human languages. This very distinction lies at the heart of what distinguishes the linguistic symbolic system from collections of signs.

Another way to think of it is the following. Consider a language for describing big integers in terms of smaller integers. Both big integers and small integers have themselves external significance, in terms of the quantity of things they correspond to when counting. But we can build the number 101 from a system that adds $1 + 1 + 1 + \ldots$ one hundred and one times. Or from a system that builds it up as $(5 \times 20) + 1$. In these latter case, we also have the elements $+$ and $\times$ which have 'relational significance' and the round brackets which establish locality domains. Understanding the grammar of language is equivalent to knowing what the external significance of the primary formatives are, *and* what the relational signifiers are that compose them into larger units which also have external significance. But this analogy to the mathematical symbolic system is only suggestive because it already reifies an absolute difference between the elements with external significance and those with purely relational significance. The question is whether language is indeed like that, with a categorical distinction between formatives that have external significance ('lexical' under this conception) and those that are only functional.

2.2 Meaning and Autonomy of Syntax

I read Chomsky's position on 'meaning' in *Syntactic Structures* as a claim about external signification. External signification simply does not bear on the functioning of the grammar *qua* system. The system of grammar is remarkably independent from its external products (both in terms of the externally signified, and the external manifestations of signifying). Chomsky's position is that we can and must study these abstract properties if we want to understand nature of human language.

Chomsky is also sceptical about the extent to which external significance, in the sense of reference, is achieved purely by any lexical formative at all. Reference is achieved as a joint outcome of the grammatical deployment of linguistic formatives in an utterance context, with an attendant interpretational judgement. I quote here from Chomsky (1995), and there is every reason to believe that this has been his consistent position (my italics).

Neurologist Rodolfo Llinás (1987) puts the matter well when he describes perception as "a dream modulated by sensory input", the mind being a "computational state of the brain generated by the interaction between the external world and an internal set of reference than often assumed, *even at the level of the lexicon*, still more so when we turn to expressions formed by the computational processes.
Chomsky (1995), pg 23

So even though sensory input from the world is crucial to how we interpret it, language combines this with an internal set of reference frames and organizational principles which *impose* their own logic and interpretation on the world. These internal frames are 'intricate', 'even at the level of the lexicon', and the relational signification that comes along with being a symbolic system instead of a finite collection of signs, pervades the entire system.

From this point of view, we could conclude that even a 'lexical' item like *dog* carries relational significance in addition to its contribution to external signification, by virtue of the fact that it bears the syntactic feature N, which determines how it slots in to the grammatical system and combines with other formatives around it.

Thus, we come to the entirely coherent position expressed in *Syntactic Structures* that ... *Whatever differences there are among morphemes with respect to this property* (i.e. 'structural meaning', GR) *are apparently better explained in terms of such grammatical notions as productivity, freedom of combination, and size of substitution class, than in terms of any presumed feature of meaning.*

Having laid out what I take to be the position taken in *Syntactic Structures*, I turn next to a brief description of how the notion of lexical vs. grammatical (or functional) formatives is employed in current syntactic theory, with some discussion of the reasons that have led to the partition of the lexicon in this way.

3 Lexical vs. Functional Categories Today

3.1 Early Classical Period

The tendency to divide language formatives into two main classes can be found consistently in the modern GB era of transformational grammar as the distinction between 'functional' and 'lexical' categories (Stowell 1981, Abney 1987, Ouhalla 1991, Kayne 1994), roughly corresponding to the rise and increase of the former in phrase structural representations. It applies to bound morphemes as well as independent words and corresponds basically to a difference between formatives that are essentially contentive, or theta-assigning ('lexical'), versus those that are not ('functional'). In addition, functional elements are conceived of as the abstract, grammatical outer scaffolding of lexical elements, forming 'extended projections' of the latter (Grimshaw 1991). An early list of commonly assumed functional categories includes at least C(omplementizer), INFL (T and Agr) (Pollock 1989), Asp(ect) (Tenny 1987), Neg(ation) (Ouhalla 1991), Det(erminer) (Abney 1987), and K(ase) (Bittner and Hale 1996). Abney (1987) provides an important early discussion of the criteria by which one distinguishes the two classes of formative, as part of his argument in favor of Det as heading its own functional projection. These criteria include:

- Lexical formatives belong to 'open' classes of expressions, while functional or grammatical formatives are drawn from 'closed' classes.
- Functional formatives tend to be phonologically reduced compared to lexical formatives
- Functional formatives do not undergo derivational processes
- Functional formatives appear in more restricted syntactic contexts than lexical formatives
- Functional formatives have a 'grammatical' meaning, while lexical formatives have a substantive or 'contentful' meaning.

All of these criteria have problems and exceptions (see Section 4 for discussion), but they seem to converge roughly on their target. Moreover, a pleasing system seems to emerge from such a classification, whereby functional sequences are rooted in contentful lexical items in a low, theta-zone and are successively modulated by functional material in a hierarchical expansion. This further enforces the sense of a cutoff between the lexical and the functional. The only source of substantial disagreement appears to be with regard to the number and fine-grainedness of such functional projections in the functional sequences rooted in the lexical categories (assumed to be, at least, V, N and A).

The lexical-functional division is often invoked in the statement of the Borer-Chomsky conjecture concerning the locus of cross-linguistic variation. The following formulation comes from Baker (2008).

(1) **Borer-Chomsky Conjecture**
All parameters of variation are attributable to differences in features of particular items (e.g. the functional heads) in the lexicon.

In fact, variation of course applies to all aspects of the lexicon, it is just that *syntactic* variation can only arise from variation in a narrower subset of lexical items. The formulation in Chomsky (2001) is given in (2).

(2) Parametric variation is restricted to the lexicon, and insofar as syntactic computation is concerned, to a narrow category of morphological properties, primarily inflectional. (Chomsky, 2001, 2) (Derivation by Phase)

So Chomsky's own formulation does not invoke a distinct class of formatives, just a distinct subset of *properties* of lexical items.

3.2 Distributed Morphology

In Distributed Morphology (henceforth DM), the distinction between two classes of formatives is in some sense taken to its logical conclusion. The functional morphemes, the ones that are part of the generative system are in the syntax, while lexical morphemes, or roots, are syntactically completely inert and have only conceptual content (Halle and Marantz 1993, Harley and Noyer 1999, Harley 1995). For DM, this means that they do not even bear category features, because this is part of the relational significance of grammar and must therefore come from the syntax. Roots bear information of the 'external significance' type described above, and are only categorized once they are in a particular syntactic context.

The different so-called lexical categories are split between a single l-morpheme type, the root, in local syntactic relation with an f-morpheme which categorizes it. A verb is the name for a root in the context of the f-morphemes v, Asp and T, while noun is the name for a root in the context of Det.

The distinction between f-morphemes and l-morphemes (using the terms from Harley and Noyer (1999), also corresponds to a difference in how they interact with spell out processes, which originally in DM was a consistent 'late insertion' model. But there was a difference. F-morphemes had completely deterministic spell-out; they were not part of a paradigmatic family of forms but bore purely syntagmatic information. L-morphemes on the other hand, allowed a choice; they were an open class with a wide variety of paradigmatic options (e.g. *dog* vs. *cat* vs. *triceratops*).

The difference between f-morphemes and l-morphemes was given even more drastic architectural implications when Harley and Noyer (Harley and Noyer 2000, Harley and Noyer 1999) argued that the mutual exclusivity constraint on language acquisition prevents root suppletion. This conjecture was architecturally enforced when Embick (2000) proposed that roots were inserted early, while only functional items were inserted late. This had the consequence that suppletion should only apply to functional items, and there simply could never be such as thing as root suppletion in the system. This is because late insertion of vocabulary items is the only mechanism by which suppletive items can arise by allomorphic selection. Roots, being inserted early, could be subject to readjustment rules, but not suppletion.

Thus, the past 15 years of DM theorizing have involved a strict separation between conceptual content and functional information, operationalized in distinct zones of the syntactic derivation.

DM is also a theory which denies the existence of the Lexicon as a domain for rules or productive processes, or even implicit patterns and generalizations. The lexicon in DM is an inert repository of formless content, and generalizations across lexical formatives can be expressed only in terms of the functional vocabulary that they combine with.

However, the non-lexical aspect of DM is orthogonal to the decision to separate out structural or grammatical meaning from conceptual content. Within lexical theories like that of Levin and Rappaport-Hovav (Levin and Rappaport Hovav 1995, Levin and Rappaport 1998), lexical representations are structured pieces of information which can be separated into templates that express event structure and grammatically relevant meaning, in addition to loci of syntactically inert conceptual content, which they call 'constants'.

(3) *splash*: [x Cause [y TO COME TO BE AT z]/ SPLASH
The variables x, y and z get filled in by the the DPs 'the pigs', 'mud' and 'the walls' respectively in the syntax.
"*the pigs splashed mud on the walls*" (after Levin and Rappaport 1998)

So here, SPLASH provides the conceptual content to a structural semantic template consisting of event structure notions such as 'causing', and 'becoming'. These latter are the kinds of notions that are reified as functional heads within the syntax in a framework like DM.

Thus, in lexical theories these two kinds of information coexist in a structured lexical representation, while in DM they are radically separated. But both kinds of theory distinguish sharply between the different *types* of information—the structural vs. the conceptual.

3.3 Psycholinguistic and Neurolinguistic Evidence

The theoretical elegance of the architectures that enforce a radical and categorical distinction between functional and lexical is bolstered by the fact that there is psycholinguistic and neurological evidence for some such distinction as well. The evidence comes from three main sources: (i) processing, (ii) aphasias and language impairment and (iii) acquisition. I briefly summarize the three kinds of evidence in turn.

In production, switching errors occur between elements of like categories. What we find is that contentful categories can switch to create spoonerisms, but that contentful categories do not switch with functional ones in production disfluencies. This led Garrett (1976) and Garrett (1980) to propose a model in which the combination of lexical items precedes the insertion of functional elements. Lexical decision tasks are subject to frequency effects for contentful items, but this effect seems to be neutralized for functional items (D. Bradley and Zurif 1980). In word priming, contentful lexical items behave differently from functional items in that they prime homophones and semantically related items, while functional elements do not (Shillcock and Bard 1993).

In aphasia, the two classic types of aphasia, Broca's vs. Wernicke's, have been characterized by the fact that the former type of patient struggles with grammatical structure but has fairly intact comprehension of contentful lexical items, while the latter is a fluent producer of grammatical formatives but struggles with the production and understanding of contentful lexical elements (see Goodglass 1976).

In first language acquisition as well, it has been claimed that lexical items are acquired earliest, before functional elements (Bloom 1970, Bowerman 1973).

Despite this seeming consensus, I am going to argue in Section 4, that the prevailing view is not correct.

4 Against a Categorical Distinction Among Formatives

Although minimalist approaches to syntax seem to all (at least informally) endorse the distinction between lexical and grammatical formatives, and although the distinction seems to be supported at the cognitive and neurological level, there are serious empirical and technical problems with the idea of a categorical distinction among formatives.

The discussion of the 'sign' in Section 1 argued that what is unique about the human language symbolic system is that in addition to signs bearing *external significance*, they also needed to bear *relational significance*.[2] So there is no doubt in my mind that this distinction between two types of meaning is powerful and

---

[2] Once again, I am using this abstract distinction as the proxy for whatever it is that defines the different ways of meaning corresponding to lexical and grammatical morphemes. The distinction

important, particularly in comparing human linguistic signs ('formatives in the grammar') with the conscious or unconscious signing of other species, and with general semiotic devices employed by humans in non-linguistic domains.

I also find unassailable the facts and generalizations about linguistic patterning across human languages which robustly support certain ordering restrictions in the hierarchical phrase structural sequence corresponding to complex signifiers. To take just one example, tense always occurs outside of causational and participant selectional information in the hierarchical construction of the extended verbal projection (see Julien 2003 for discussion).

The substantive claim of the lexical vs. grammatical formatives idea is that there is some special kind of meaning that is located *all and only* at the bottom of the tree, and a qualitatively different kind of meaning that is located in the hierarchically higher domains. Further, the formatives, the building blocks of a language as stored in declarative memory, are specialized to one or the other of these different types of meaning.

As we have seen, DM, is one of the theories that makes an especially sharp distinction between the lexical and the functional in terms of the specific *formatives* involved. Now, however, that the most clear cut aspects of that architectural distinction even in DM are now being eroded in the face of empirical evidence. Over the past five years, it has now been convincingly argued that root suppletion is real (Haugen and Siddiqi 2013, Harley 2011), and late insertion of roots must be reinstated as part of the architecture. This has the desirable consequence that readjustment rules, a powerful and unconstrained mechanism required in the context of early root insertion, can plausibly be eliminated from the DM architecture altogether (see Haugen and Siddiqi 2013 for discussion). This means, among other things that the sharp distinction between l-morphemes and f-morphemes starts to erode. I quote from Haugen and Siddiqi (2013) here.

> ...nor does it require that we treat a subclass of the Vocabulary (i.e. Roots) as needing a special status with respect to the syntax (i.e. Early Insertion, or visibility). We suggest that the real issue for suppletive pairs in natural languages is not necessarily one of "functional" morphemes vs. "lexical" ones; rather, it is one of high word frequency for suppletive pairs. Haugen and Siddiqi (2013), pg 501

The reader does not need me to remind them of the quote from *Syntactic Structures* in Section 1.

---

has also been described in terms of 'logical' vs 'notional' or 'denotative' but there are problems with applying these terms in any consistent manner (see Cann 2000 for discussion).

Further, if a model like spanning (Svenonius 2012), or Siddiqi's version of DM (Siddiqi 2009) is correct in allowing 'roots' to fuse with the functional heads in their extended projection before spelling out as particular vocabulary items, then the formatives themselves seem to be morphemes that are featurally specified for syntactic functional information, as well as bearing lexical-conceptual content.

The view from morphology now would suggest, that actual 'formatives' must be allowed in principle at least, to have 'relational significations', at least with regard to syntactic contexts of insertion, and the possession of inflectional features, even when they also possess 'external signification'.

However, this still does not undermine the distinction between lexical and functional/grammatical at the level of syntactic structure and *abstract* formatives. We could recoup the distinction in terms of lower versus higher category labels in the functional sequence (i.e. V versus Asp and T), and state a weaker generalization about a certain class of grammatical formatives, that encode meaning in the functional domain, stating that they are concomitantly devoid of lexical conceptual meaning or 'external signification' in my sense. I will argue that even the weakest version of this idea is probably false.

4.1 Lack of Categoricality

Those who would take the extended projection view would argue that N, and V are lexical labels (abstract formatives) while everything that sits on top of N and V—the things that the syntactician has deemed necessary for the analysis of language above and beyond the simple word classes—are functional items. But once we go beyond the obvious example that *dog* is a lexical formative while *the* is functional, it is quite hard to find even abstract formatives that are categorical in this regard.

Take the lowly preposition. In Grimshaw's original paper on extended projections, this was taken to be an extension of the nominal extended projection, and therefore by this reasoning, a functional element. However, if we look at the class of prepositions in English, we see that in addition to possessing clear and abstract relational content, they also possess conceptual information that distinguishes one kind of spatial relationship from another. (In general, see Svenonius 2010 for a detailed decomposition of the extended projection of P, and for a careful discuss of the separation of conceptual content from structural semantic content).

		structural	conceptual
	on	FIGURE located with respect to GROUND	ON
(4)	in	FIGURE located with respect to GROUND	IN
	under	FIGURE located with respect to GROUND	UNDER
	opposite	FIGURE located with respect to GROUND	OPPOSITE

If we are to separate the functional formatives from the lexical, then what is the label for the lexical category that P is rooted in? LOCATION, perhaps? But then how do we integrate that with the denotation of the DP that the preposition combines with? In fact, it is the preposition that seems to be doing the explicitly relational job. But if these are relational meanings, and this should be encoded in a functional head, then where do the differences between the different spatial prepositions get represented, if not in the conceptual content/'external signification' part of the formative's meaning? One alternative might be to say that in fact there is a different functional subtype of P for each different relation. It is exactly this kind of reasoning in the verbal domain that leads certain analysts to the idea of 'flavors' of functional heads (flavors of little v handle phenomena that would otherwise be dealt with by abstract selectional facts about verbal lexical items, deprecated under the asyntactic roots idea of DM). Here, we would have to have flavors of locational heads. There is a fairly large class of relational spatial prepositions in English, much larger than the number of tense or aspect distinctions for example, so there would have to be as many of these flavors are there are distinct prepositional formatives.

The logical alternative is to preserve the simple structural description of FIGURE-GROUND as a universal and pervasive structuring principle in natural language expressions of space, and combine it in parallel with conceptual content that specifies the physical properties of that relation for different real life situations that English speakers feel the need to have a word for.

To repeat, the alternative idea is to see the prepositional formative as combining both 'relational' and 'external' signification. There is no motivation for decomposing all prepositions into a prepositional root and a little p head, which it *always* occurs with. Apart from everything else, it also causes problems for the combination of the decomposed P root with the compositionally built up DP that represents the GROUND in the relation, since by hypothesis roots are at the bottom of the functional sequence and should be completely syntactically inert.

The same sorts of problems arise with different types of modal verbs in English (*must* vs. *should*), or for languages where there are different 'flavors' of PAST (for example, Wikipedia tells me that "the six-tense language *Kalaw Lagaw Ya* of

Australia has the remote past, the recent past, the today past, the present, the today/near future and the remote future.").

Even the evidence from psycholinguistics does not show that lexical and grammatical information are cleanly separable from each other. It shows that they are different and that they are negotiated differently in the overall hardware of the brain, but nothing we currently know actually lines up this difference with formatives (or even labels) in a clean categorical way. Pathways that connect sensory and affective information communicate anatomically with those regions of the brain that deal with syntactic combination, and all of our actual data shows combined and distributed activation on all tasks, and graded, not categorical difficulties for different formatives.

To summarize, any detailed categorization of the formatives, or even abstract formatives of a particular language, will immediately expose cases (possibly the majority), where the grammatical MORPHEME in question bears both grammatical and conceptual content. See also the discussion in Svenonius (2014), which comes to the same general conclusions based on the noncategoricality of the distinction between the lexical and functional in practice. Even the seemingly unproblematic *dog* is only purely conceptual if we deprive it of its category label N (as DM does). If we reinstate N for *dog*, then it too carries some minimal sliver of 'relational' signification, grammatical information that shows how it is to be integrated into a system of symbolic representation.

4.2 Systematic Polysemies

Another argument for the integration of both grammatical meaning and conceptual meaning within *every* formative in grammar comes from cases of polysemy. It is well known that diachronically, formatives can be reanalyzed from more contentful lexical behavior into being grammatical morphemes (an intuition going back to Meillet 1912, Kurylowicz 1965). However, what is less often acknowledged is the large number of cases of systematic polysemy where the same formative coexists in the language in both lexical and more 'grammatical' incarnations. The recourse of the l-morpheme vs. f-morpheme person is to say that these simply have to be distinct, homophonous, formatives. This move belies the ubiquity of the phenomenon, and the deep generalizations that carry over between the different polysemous meanings. To take an example from my own work on light verbs (Ramchand 2014), the phenomenon of light verbs regularly conforms to what I have labelled *Butt's Generalization*, repeated here in (5):

(5) **Butt's Generalization** (Butt 2003, Butt and Lahiri 2013):
Unlike auxiliaries which may become grammaticalized over time to have a purely functional use, light verbs always have a diachronically stable corresponding full or 'heavy' version in all the languages in which they are found.

The significance of this generalization is that there is a stable polysemy here, where one member of the pair is fairly functional and abstract, and the other member of the pair has richer conceptual content. If the two versions (to put it neutrally) of the lexical item were merely related diachronically via some grammaticalization chain, then we would expect the members of the pair to be subject to semantic drift and reanalysis. We would also expect the two versions to potentially drift apart from each other over time, both phonologically and allomorphically, and to eventually count as distinct lexical items. The situation we do see however, points to systematic polysemy rather than diachronic relatedness, if Butt and Lahiri (2013) are right.

If light verbs were f-morphemes and their heavy counterparts were roots, as for example in the theory of Persian light verbs given in Folli et al. (2005), then there would be no ready explanation for their systematic relatedness. But in fact, as I show in Ramchand (2014), the polysemies are stable and show systematic generalizations. A theory that sees all formatives as combining both grammatical and conceptual information has a chance of capturing these generalizations in a constrained theory of polysemy.

4.3 The Meaning Integration Problem

The final argument comes from the technical problems of meaning integration. If the root, or lexical morpheme carries *only* conceptual information devoid of relational or syntactic content, then we are owed a theory of how these components of meaning compose systematically. How does the conceptual content integrate with the functional structure so as to deliver the interpretational facts for (6a) and (6b).

(6) a. The boy broke the glass.
    b. The boy hammered the metal.

In (6a), the conceptual content of *break* tells us something about the result state of the event, namely that the UNDERGOER becomes 'broken'. In (6b), the conceptual content of *hammer* tells us something about the manner in which a pounding event was effected. In a Levin and Rappaport style representation of the meaning of these verbs would combine both structural and relational facts with the conceptual, these are explicitly separate, but unified in the nature of the representation, with the conceptual content modifying the structurally introduced subevents.[3]

(7) *break*: [x Cause [CHANGE IN MATERIAL INTEGRITY OF Y] / BREAK
hammer: [x Do [MAKE CONTACT WITH y]/ HAMMER

However, nobody has ever shown me a compositional semantic treatment of how the root is integrated with the functional structure of the verb phrase to give the right results, if the root is uniformly at the bottom of the structure in each case. I could imagine a proposal for the functional structure of *break* which differs from the functional structure of *of hammer* in a diacritic way. The semantic structural effect of these heads would then need to be specified directly so that one can see whether it makes the right predictions. Alternatively, one could imagine a system in which differential positions of the root in different parts of the structure combine according to different mechanisms (as in recent proposals about 'manner' roots vs. 'result' roots in e.g. Mateu and Acedo-Matellán 2012), which will conspire to give the correct results. But these devices will have to be augmented with selectional information that ensures that the roots match up with the correct functional structures. A fully explicit implementation of how the structural and conceptual pieces of information combine, I suspect, will reduce to a notational variant of the positions advocated in Ramchand (2008) or Levin and Rappaport (1998) where verbal roots possess both conceptual and and structural information, with regulated points of integration.

5 Conclusion

There is a famous passage in Jonathan Swift's *Gullivers Travels* where he describes the denizens of Laputa who have a bizarre Academy involved in a number of experiments, one of which has to do with language, and a scheme for making communication 'easier'.

---

[3] Ramchand (2008) also expresses these facts directly using a decomposed event structure within a neo-Davidsonian style representation, based on the syntactic specification of the verbal item. The conceptual content of the root modifies/describes the different types of subevents introduced.

> ...since Words are only Names for Things, it would be more convenient for all Men to carry about them, such Things as were necessary to express the particular Business they are to discourse on ...I have often beheld two of those Sages almost sinking under the Weight of their Packs, like Pedlars among us; who when they met in the Streets would lay down their Loads, open up their Sacks, and hold Conversation for an Hour together; then put up their Implements, help each other to resume their Burthens, and take their Leave. (185–6)

It is intuitively obvious to most readers that Swift's example is an absurd one. Language simply doesn't work like that. Apart from the fact that not all words are physicalizable in this way, language isn't just a sequence of presentations of signs. I have argued that the 'relational signification' of language signs are central to what it takes to be a human language, because it is essentially a *syntactic* system. However, this does not mean that a Swiftian bag of 'signs' needs to be carried around on the Laputan backs of an autonomous syntax machine.

Chomsky does not seem to use the word 'meaning' to pick out 'relational signification' in my sense, but I agree with him that 'external signification' is irrelevant to the functioning of the syntactic system. Relational signification on the other hand is an inseparable part of the syntactic system that eventually allows it to provide the scaffolding for the productive construction of meaning, broadly construed.

Actual investigation of the formatives of natural language shows that relational signification and external signification do not seem to be separable from each other in practice, even at the level of the easiest cases *dog* vs. *the*. Each linguistic sign is a complex signifier, which seems to exist as a potent *combination* of the outward looking (external signification) and sideways-looking (relational signification). We have seen that attempting to separate these within the grammar leads to paradoxes, extra mechanisms, and loss of generalizations. All the effects of grammatical vs. lexical can be seen to be epiphenomenal of the differences in degree of sensory associations, and the size of the paradigmatic choices for each formative available within the system.

Bibliography

Abney, Steven. 1987. The English Noun Phrase in its Sentential Aspect. Doctoral Dissertation, MIT, Cambridge, Ma.

Baker, Mark. 2008. *The Syntax of Agreement and Concord.* Cambridge: Cambridge University Press.

Bittner, Maria, and Ken Hale. 1996. The Structural Determination of Case and Agreement. *Linguistic Inquiry* 27:1–68.

Bloom, L. 1970. *Language Development: Form and Function in Emerging Grammars*. Cambridge, MA: MIT Press.
Bowerman, Melissa. 1973. *Early Syntactic Development: A Cross-linguistic Study with Special Reference to Finnish*. Cambridge: Cambridge University Press.
Butt, Miriam. 2003. The Morpheme that Wouldn't Go Away. Handout, University of Manchester seminar series.
Butt, Miriam, and Aditi Lahiri. 2013. Diachronic Pertinacity of Light Verbs. *Lingua* http://dx.doi.org/10.1016/lingua.2012.11.006.
Cann, Ronnie. 2000. Functional versus lexical: A cognitive dichotomy. *Syntax and Semantics* 26:37–78.
Chomsky, Noam. 1995. Language and Nature. *Mind* 104:1–61.
Chomsky, Noam. 2001. Derivation by Phase. In *Ken Hale: A Life in Language*, ed. Michael Kenstowicz, 1–52. Cambridge, Ma.: MIT Press.
D. Bradley, M.F. Garrett, and E. B. Zurif. 1980. Syntactic Deficits in Broca's Aphasia. In *Biological Studies of Mental Processes*, ed. D. Caplan. Cambridge, MA: MIT Press.
Deacon, Terence. 1997. *The Symbolic Species*. Harmondsworth, UK: Penguin.
Demers, R. A. 1988. Linguistics and Animal Communication. In *Linguistics: the Cambridge survey*, ed. F. J. Newmeyer, volume 3. Language:Psychological and Biological Aspects, 314–335. Cambridge University Press.
Embick, David. 2000. Features, syntax and categories in the Latin perfect. *Linguistic Inquiry* 31:185–230.
Folli, Raffaella, Heidi Harley, and Simin Karimi. 2005. Determinants of event type in Persian complex predicates. *Lingua* 115:1365–1401.
Garrett, M. 1976. Syntactic processes in sentence production. In *New Approaches to Language Mechanisms*, ed. R. Wales and E. Walker. Amsterdam: North-Holland Publishing.
Garrett, M. 1980. Levels of processing in sentence production. In *Language Production*, ed. B. Butterworth. London: Academic Press.
Goodglass, H. 1976. Agrammatism. In *Studies in Neurolinguistics*, ed. H. Whittaker and H.A. Whittaker. New York: Academic Press.
Grimshaw, Jane. 1991. Extended projections.
Halle, Morris, and Alec Marantz. 1993. Distributed Morphology and the pieces of inflection. In *The View from Building 20: Essays in Linguistics in Honor of Sylvain Bromberger*, ed. Kenneth Hale and Samuel Jay Keyse, 111–176. Cambridge, Ma.: MIT Press.
Harley, Heidi. 1995. Subjects, Events, and Licensing. Doctoral Dissertation, Massachusetts Institute of Technology, Cambridge, MA.
Harley, Heidi. 2011. On the identity of roots. Ms., University of Arizona (Available at http://ling.auf.net/lingBuzz/001527.
Harley, Heidi, and Rolf Noyer. 1999. State of the Article: Distributed Morphology. *GLOT International* 4.4:3–9.
Harley, Heidi, and Rolf Noyer. 2000. Licensing in the non-lexicalist lexicon. In *The Lexicon/Encyclopaedia Interface*, ed. Bert Peeters. Amsterdam: Elsevier.
Haugen, Jason, and Daniel Siddiqi. 2013. Roots and the Derivation. *Linguistic Inquiry* 44:493–517.
Julien, Marit. 2003. On the negated past in Finnic and Saami. In *Generative approaches to Finnic and Saami linguistics*, ed. Diane Nelson and Satu Manninen, 419–446. CSLI Publications.
Kayne, Richard S. 1994. *The Antisymmetry of Syntax*. Cambridge, MA.: MIT Press.

Kurylowicz, Jerzy. 1965. L'évolution des catégories grammaticales. *Diogenes* 51:54–71.
Levin, Beth, and Malka Rappaport. 1998. Building Verb Meanings. In *The Projection of Arguments: Lexical and Compositional Factors*, ed. Miriam Butt and Wilhelm Geuder, 97–134. CSLI publications.
Levin, Beth, and Malka Rappaport Hovav. 1995. *Unaccusativity: At the Syntax-Lexical Semantics Interface*. Cambridge, Ma.: MIT Press.
Mateu, Jaume, and Victor Acedo-Matellán. 2012. The Manner/Result Complementarity Revisited: A Syntactic Approach. *The end of argument structure* 38:209–228.
Meillet, Antoine. 1912. L'évolution des formes grammaticals. *Scientia (Revista di scienza)* 12:384–400.
Ouhalla, Jamal. 1991. *Functional Categories and Parametric Variation*. London: Routledge.
Pearce, J. M. 2008. *Animal Learning and Cognition*. Hove, UK: Laurence Erlbaum.
Philippe Schlenker, Emmanuel Chemla, and Klaus Zuberbühler. 2016. What Do Monkey Calls Mean? *Trends in Cognitive Sciences* 20:894–904.
Pollock, Jean Yves. 1989. Verb movement, Universal Grammar, and the structure of IP. *Linguistic Inquiry* 20:365–424.
Ramchand, Gillian. 2008. *Verb Meaning and the Lexicon*. Cambridge University Press.
Ramchand, Gillian. 2014. Structural Meaning and Conceptual Meaning in Verb Semantics. *Linguistic Analysis* 39:211–247.
de Saussure, Ferdinand. 1959. *A Course in General Linguistics*. Fontana/Collins, translated from the French by Wade Baskin edition.
Shillcock, R. C., and E. G. Bard. 1993. Modularity and the processing of closed class words. In *Cognitive Models of Speech Processing*, ed. G. Altman and R. Shillcock, 163–185. Cambridge, MA: MIT Press.
Siddiqi, Daniel. 2009. *Syntax within the word: Economy, allomorphy, and argument selection in Distributed Morphology*. Amsterdam: Benjamins.
Stowell, Tim. 1981. Origins of Phrase Structure. Doctoral Dissertation, MIT, Cambridge, Ma.
Svenonius, Peter. 2010. Spatial P in English. In *The Cartography of Syntactic Structures*, ed. Guglielmo Cinque and Luigi Rizzi, volume 6, Mapping Spatial PPs. Oxford University Press.
Svenonius, Peter. 2012. Spanning. Ms., University of Tromsø, http://ling.auf.net/lingBuzz/001501.
Svenonius, Peter. 2014. Generalized Applicatives: Reassessing the Lexical-Functional Divide. *Theoretical Linguistics* 40:439–446.
Tenny, Carol. 1987. Grammaticalizing aspect and affectedness. Doctoral Dissertation, Massachusetts Institute of Technology, Cambridge, MA.

Bronwyn Moore Bjorkman
Syntactic Structures and Morphology

An ongoing debate in generative linguistics concerns the relationship between word formation, the domain of *morphology*, and sentence formation, the domain of *syntax*. Because both words and sentences are composed hierarchically, and the form of a word often depends on its position in a sentence, the question arises of how sharply syntax and morphology should be distinguished from one another, or indeed whether they should be distinguished as separate components at all.

Answers to these questions have varied widely. At one logical extreme is the view that word and sentence formation are totally distinct components of grammar, a position generally known as *lexicalism*, after the lexicalist hypothesis of Chomsky's (1970) *Remarks on Nominalization*. At the opposite extreme is to deny any separation between syntax and morphology, locating both sentence formation and word formation within a single component, usually syntax. Distributed Morphology (DM: Halle and Marantz 1993, 1994; Harley and Noyer 1999) and Nanosyntax (Starke 2010) are derivational generative approaches of this kind. These are often referred to as *realizational* approaches to morphology: they take the atoms manipulated by the syntax to be (abstract) morphemes or features, and to the extent that there is a derivationally distinct morphological component, it operates on the output of syntax.

Though both these extremes, and many intermediate positions, continue to be adopted in generative work, the last few decades have seen a steady transition from lexicalism as the default theoretical position towards an increasing assumption of realizational morphology. This trend might lead us to expect the same trajectory to extend further into the past, to the earliest days of modern generative linguistics and the seminal work of *Syntactic Structures*.

Instead, what we find in *Syntactic Structures* is an approach to morphology that more closely resembles contemporary realizational theories than it does lexicalism, in that phrase structure rules and transformations are responsible for both word and sentence formation. Moreover, this is not an incidental property of the framework, but is instead central to the description and analysis of some of the phenomena for which *Syntactic Structures* is best known, including Affix Hopping and *Do*-support, as well as its treatment of gerunds and present participles. In each case, the account of these phenomena relies on the ability of syntactic transformations to generate morphologically complex words—a view incompatible with the strong lexicalist hypothesis that would later be adopted in much generative work. Nonetheless, the way that *Syntactic Structures* understood and described these phenomena persisted, deeply influencing even lexicalist analyses. What is striking is not that the details of the *Syntactic Structures* analyses have been preserved unchanged—they haven't been—but that their insights sufficiently significant to be preserved despite other changes in generative theory.

1 Lexicalism, realization, and *Syntactic Structures*

To evaluate the extent to which *Syntactic Structures* differs from later lexicalist approaches, it is worthwhile to consider the latter in somewhat more detail. As noted above, lexicalism in modern generative syntax is often traced back to *Remarks on Nominalization*. But though *Remarks* introduced the idea that some derived words are not built syntactically, but instead generated in a separate lexical component, it nonetheless retained a role for some words to be built transformationally. This has come to be known as *weak* lexicalism: the view that some, but not all, word formation is non-syntactic.

By contrast, Halle (1973) can be seen as the origin of *strong* lexicalism: the view that *all* word formation is non-syntactic. Strong lexicalism holds that the atoms manipulated by syntax are full words, and that all affixation (or any other process of complex word formation) occurs in an autonomous morphological component. Syntax thus never creates words, even via operations such as head movement, and has no access to word-internal constituents.

Both strong and weak lexicalism are committed to the existence of a morphological component of grammar, distinct from syntax. Weak lexicalism must further identify a boundary between words created by syntax from those created by an independent morphology. The most common division has been to limit syntactic word formation to inflection only, with all derivation separated into the lexical component (as in, for example, Anderson 1982). Other divisions are possible as well, however: in *Remarks on Nominalization*, Chomsky draws a boundary between syntactic and morphological word formation instead on the basis of productivity and interpretive transparency, arguing that deverbal nominals like *growth* are lexical, while fully productive clausal gerunds in *-ing* are transformationally derived. A division even among instances of the same inflectional morphology is suggested by Lasnik (1995), who proposes for verbal inflection in English that though main verbs unite with inflection syntactically, auxiliary verbs enter syntax already inflected.

The lack of a clear boundary between syntactic and non-syntactic word formation has been the chief challenge facing weak lexicalism: not only has it proven difficult to identify a consistent and principled boundary between components, but both mechanisms of word formation also create outputs of the same type, i.e. morphophonological *words*, and so theoretical economy would seem to prefer that one or the other be eliminated.

Neither strong lexicalism nor realizational morphology face this issue, and perhaps for this reason they have been adopted more widely in work with a directly morphological focus. The strong lexicalist position can be found for example in Lapointe (1980) and Di Sciullo and Williams (1987), as well as in Lexical Phonology and Morphology, which located not only morphology but also much of phonology in the lexicon, as in Kiparsky (1985), Halle and Mohanan (1985), and Mohanan (1986). Strong lexicalism is also adopted in non-derivational theories such as Generalized Phrase Structure Grammar (GPSG, later Head-Driven Phrase Structure Grammar, HPSG: Pollard and Sag 1994) and Lexical Functional Grammar (LFG: Bresnan 1982), as well as in early Minimalist work, including Chomsky (1993, 1995).

Strong lexicalism is committed to the view that syntax has no access to word-internal structure—indeed, is unable to distinguish simplex from complex words—except indirectly, via the features and lexical properties that determine the contexts in which a word can occur. The atoms of syntax, on this view, are necessarily words, not individual morphemes.

Strong lexicalism is thus challenged in turn by any evidence of syntactic word formation. One such class of evidence, though by no means the only one, has come from polysynthetic languages, where single words can express often very complex propositions, and principles of argument licensing, phrase structure, and even movement appear to apply to sub-word "morphological" constituents. The syntactic nature of word formation in polysynthetic languages was raised in early work by Sadock (1980) on incorporation in Greenlandic, as well as in Baker's (1988) work on Mohawk, and Jelinek's (1984) Pronominal Argument Hypothesis. While these authors varied in the extent to which they argued against a lexicalist approach to morphosyntax, their work has highlighted the limits of lexicalism in accounting for polysynthesis. Such languages require either that syntactic principles and parameters be duplicated in morphology, duplication that would be uneconomical, and so conceptually undesirable, or else that languages vary in whether syntax can assemble complex words. The latter of these is a concession to weak lexicalism—and a concession that abandons any principled separation between syntax and morphology. If syntax can generate words in some languages, why not in all languages?

Against this backdrop, in what sense does *Syntactic Structures* develop a non-lexicalist and realizational model of morphology? In one sense the debate between lexicalism and realization is a debate about the derivational order in which morphology and syntax apply. In this sense, the debate does not apply directly to *Syntactic Structures*, which is agnostic between a derivational view of its model and a non-derivational constraint-based implementation. Conceptually, however, the "top down" model of syntax developed in *Syntactic Structures* has a realizational flavor: structures are derived by phrase structure rules that allow a single element to be rewritten as a string of one or more other elements, and so information about specific lexical items is not available until the point in the derivation after which they have been inserted.[1] Terminals are moreover not the final realization of syntactic structure, but are themselves subject to rewriting via the morphophonemic rules of a language, which differ from phrase structure rules in that they can rewrite more than a single element, and their output is never the input for subsequent morphophonemic rules (though it may be the input for phonological/phonetic rules). Morphophonemic rules parallel the post-syntactic realization rules of Distributed Morphology and Nanosyntax—though without the possibility of *underspecified* realization, which has played a key role in morphological theory since at least is not introduced in *Syntactic Structures*. So in this somewhat shallow sense, *Syntactic Structures* resembles modern realizational theories.

In a deeper sense, however, the debate between lexicalism and realization is not about derivational order, but instead about whether morphology and syntax belong to separate cognitive modules, in the sense of Fodor (1983).[2] *Syntactic Structures* identifies morphology as a separate *level*, in the use of levels of representation leading out of American Structuralism, but this is not the same as arguing that it constitutes a distinct component.[3] A linguistic level is a level of analysis, independent of any claim of cognitive modularity. A grammatical component in a cognitive sense, by contrast, is an operationally encapsulated domain. Phonology and syntax, for example, are treated in modern generative theory as components in this sense, as operate over different types of elements, and are governed by different principles.

The cognitive view of components is not present in *Syntactic Structures*, but can be applied retrospectively. To the extent that *Syntactic Structures* treats words and phrases as governed by the same principles or mechanisms, it resembles

---

[1] The phrase structure rules of *Syntactic Structures* are not directional, in that they could be reinterpreted as static requirements on syntactic representations. They are nonetheless "top down" (in scare quotes because the rules themselves are defined over strings rather than hierarchical structures) in the sense that the rules are deterministic only rewriting elements in terms of their subconstituents, and not in reverse.

[2] Fodor was in turn building on the modular approach to language introduced in generative lingusitics.

[3] Though *Syntactic Structures* does not directly discuss the status of morphology as a level, it references the elaboration in Chomsky's (1975) *The Logical Structure of Linguistic Theory*.

modern realizational approaches in gathering morphology and syntax within a single component. To the extent that it proposes distinct mechanisms for each, it resembles the two-component framework of lexicalism.

In *Syntactic Structures* the phrase structure and transformational rules that introduce and manipulate words are formally the same as those that introduce and manipulate bound affixes, and unite them with appropriate hosts. The fact that (a subpart) of morphology is interleaved with phrase structure is discussed in *The Logical Structure of Linguistic Theory* (Chomsky, 1975):

> [W]e can regard M [= morphology] as a level intermediate between the level W of words and the level P of phrase structure. This suggests that it might be useful to consider separately two classes of morphological elements, those that figure in the statement of phrase structure and those whose function is limited to the description of word structure. In the first (call it $\overline{M}$), we have what we can call "morphological heads" as well as those affixes that function syntactically (e.g. morphemic long components expressing agreement in gender and number, etc.). In the second class we have such elements as English -*ess* (*actress*, etc.) which do not themselves enter into the description of phrase structure but which enter into the formation of the minimal units that play some role in syntax. $\overline{M}$ can be pictured (for the time being) as embedded into the level P [=phrase structure]. Derivations in P thus lead from the representation *Sentence* to strings in $\overline{M}$ (Chomsky, 1975, §47: 168)

Because $\overline{M}$ is fully interleaved with the syntactic grammar, there is no bright line between the processes that assemble words and those that assemble sentences. It is in this respect that the interaction of morphology and syntax in early generative syntax closely resembles current realizational theories, and contrasts sharply with later (strong) lexicalist approaches. As we will see in the next several sections, this is particularly true of *Syntactic Structures*'s treatment of verbal inflection: its transformational analysis of Affix Hopping, *Do*-support, and gerunds has been carried forward in generative syntax.

2 Inflection as a syntactic transformation: Affix Hopping

Some of the transformations for which *Syntactic Structures* is most famous concern elements of $\overline{M}$. Chief among these is Affix Hopping, introduced in §5.3 though not referred to by that name. Affix Hopping implements the descriptive observation that each inflectional element in English (tense, modals, the perfect auxiliary *have*, the progressive auxiliary *be*, and the passive auxiliary *be*) determines the inflection of the element immediately following it. Affix hopping is the focus of the chapter by Aronoff (this volume), but it also plays a key role in defining the interaction between morphology and syntax envisioned in the *Syntactic Structures* system.

The intuition expressed by the Affix Hopping analysis is that inflection on verbs belongs systematically to other positions in the clause, an idea that underlies subsequent developments in syntactic theory expanding clausal syntax into a sequence of projections headed by inflectional categories such as tense, agreement, aspect, and mood. Chomsky implements this intuition by introducing each affix together with the auxiliary that determines it, as in (1a) with a subsequent transformation moving each affix onto the next verb in the sequence, as in (1b).

(1)   a.   the student (**-S**) (have **-en**) (be **-ing**) (read) the book
      b.   the student (have **-S**) (be **-en**) (read **-ing**) the book

Affix Hopping is very clearly an instance of word formation in the syntactic component: not only are inflectional affixes introduced via phrase structure and transformational rules (the passive auxiliary and affix being introduced via transformation), they are then united with their hosts via a further transformation which produces abstract sequences such as *read* + PAST, whose actual phonetic form is determined by subsequent morphophonemic rules (in this case: *read* + PAST → /rɛd/). Its elegant description of the facts considerably simplifies the description of inflection not only in English, but in auxiliary constructions cross-linguistically, and this description has been maintained in subsequent generative analyses even when it has been at odds with aspects of later syntactic theories.

A theoretical obstacle faced by this description in subsequent frameworks, however, has been that it requires rightwards movement of inflectional affixes (later understood as downwards movement), which is typical of morphological processes but not generally attested for phrasal movement (except perhaps in Right Node Raising and Heavy NP Shift). This has led to various treatments that are united by their goal of maintaining *Syntactic Structures*'s intuition that Affix Hopping is transformational in character, but that differ considerably in technical detail: Lowering followed by covert re-raising at LF, Lowering as a post-syntactic morphological operation, feature licensing via "Reverse" Agree, feature percolation. But preserving the transformational character of Affix Hopping is necessarily incompatible with a strong lexicalist view of morphosyntax, because it requires syntax to play a role in building finitely-inflected verbs.

The *description* underlying Affix Hopping is not in itself incompatible with lexicalist views of morphosyntax, however, but can be recast in terms of selection or checking (see, for example, Freidin 1992, 2004 for a selectional analysis of English inflection, or Chomsky 1993, 1995, Lasnik 1995, 2000, Pesetsky and Torrego 2007) for various checking-based proposals. On such an approach, verbs enter the derivation already inflected (whether with finite tense or agreement, as bare infinitives, or as present or past participles), and the role of syntax is not to unite a verb with inflection appropriate to the context in which it occurs, but instead to filter out any derivation that began with the wrong set of inflected verbs. The central insight of Affix Hopping, that the inflection with which a verb surfaces is determined by its syntactic context, is preserved, but indirectly: if a derivation happens to contain verbs bearing the correct inflection, in the correct order, all will be well, but if any verb is out of place licensing will be impossible and the derivation will fail to converge.[4]

The core insight of the Affix Hopping analysis is preserved more directly in realizational approaches, that it is the context in which verbs occur that determines their morphological form, not their morphological form that determines the contexts in which they occur. Realizational theories have nonetheless had to contend with many of the same theoretical issues noted above, in particular the issue of directionality: the movement necessitated by Affix Hopping is unlike other instances of syntactic movement. Reacting to this conflict, some realizational approaches have preserved the intuition from Affix Hopping that inflection unites with verbs transformationally, but have located the relevant transformation in a post-syntactic morphological component rather than in the syntax itself (Bobaljik, 1995; Embick and Noyer, 2001; Halle and Marantz, 1993). Others have set aside a strictly transformational view of inflection, instead adapting the insight of lexicalism that syntactic dependencies can be understood in terms of the valuation and licensing of formal morphosyntactic features (Bjorkman, 2011; Cowper, 2010; Wurmbrand, 2012).

---

[4] The precise licensing configuration has varied considerably. In GB, following Pollock (1989), the assumption was that affixes lowered onto their hosts and then subsequently covertly re-raised at LF. A lexicalist reinterpretation of this in Chomsky (1993, 1995) dispenses with lowering and assumes that the features of an inflected verb are checked as a result of (possibly covert) head movement. Subsequent to the introduction of Agree as a general mechanism of feature licensing in Chomsky (2000), efforts have been made to account for verbal inflection via Agree, though complications arise from the fact that the direction of the dependency is different for verbal inflection that it is taken to be for other instances of feature correspondence, notably ɸ-agreement. See Pesetsky and Torrego (2007), Cowper (2010), and Wurmbrand (2012) for various approaches to the directionality issue.

Though it is possible to restate the contextual dependency of inflection in lexicalist terms, many researchers who have focused on the interaction of inflection with auxiliaries have argued on empirical grounds that auxiliary verbs such as *have* and *be* must not enter the derivation fully inflected, but instead occur only as a means of realizing inflection that was not licensed on the main verb (Dechaine, 1995; Schütze, 2003; Cowper, 2010; Bjorkman, 2011). If correct, this line of research is incompatible with strong lexicalism, and a weak lexicalist implementation faces the conceptual challenges noted in the previous section.

The degree to which Affix Hopping is restated is of some significance, because its transformational character in *Syntactic Structures* is crucial to another morphosyntactic phenomenon described there that has been profoundly influential in subsequent generative syntax: *Do*-support.

3 Morphosyntax and inflectional repairs: *Do*-support

The interest of *Syntactic Structures* in the inflectional properties of English finite clauses continues in its treatment of *Do*-support in §7.1. Like Affix Hopping, *Do*-support provides an elegant description of some of the inflectional properties of English clauses, and has cast a long realizational shadow over subsequent generative treatments of the facts.

Chomsky's key observation is that periphrastic *do* in English occurs in exactly those environments where another transformation has disrupted the adjacency that would otherwise hold between tense and the main verb. Because Affix Hopping can only apply between an affix and an immediately following verb, disruption of adjacency leads to a stranded affix, rescued by an operation inserting a dummy verb *do* immediately before such stranded affixes (technically between an affix and a preceding word boundary) "as the 'bearer' of an unaffixed affix" (Chomsky, 1957: 62):

(2) # Af → # do + Af

This remains the generally accepted view of *Do*-support through to the present, 60 years later. But its central intuition—that *do* is inserted when other operations bleed the environment in which finite inflection unites with a main verb—is both realizational and strongly derivational, and proves difficult to reconcile with a strongly lexicalist view of morphosyntax: if verbs enter the syntax already affixed (or not), then it is not possible for syntactic operations to bleed that inflection, and so *do* cannot occur to provide a morphological host for a stranded affix.

The height of efforts to accommodate *Do*-support in a strong lexicalist framework can perhaps be found in Chomsky's (1995) *Minimalist Program*.[5] In order to

---

[5] The repair analysis of *Do*-support could more easily be maintained in the weak lexicalist framework assumed (sometimes implicitly) in syntactic work of the GB era; it was the conceptual considerations moving the field towards strong lexicalism, or else towards realization, that eventually required that the repair analysis be reconceptualized. Non-derivational and lexicalist ac-

preserve the intuition that *do* occurs as an inflectional repair of some kind, while also maintaining the view that verbs enter a derivation already inflected, Chomsky (1995) develops an economy-based analysis of *Do*-support. He suggests that certain functional heads (including, for example, interrogative Q) are "affixal", and so must be the target of head movement in overt syntax.[6] Because main verbs do not move in English, *do* is inserted as a dummy element in order to support such heads in clauses without any other auxiliary element.

Importantly, the "affixal" status of heads in this model is purely syntactic: this is not a morphological requirement that an affix have a host. This choice of terminology preserves the rhetorical description of *Do*-support as a repair for stranded affixes, while implementing the analysis in quite different terms. The sense in which *Do*-support remains a repair operation is similarly only rhetorical. Syntactic derivations in Minimalism involve operations over an initial set of elements, the numeration. Strong lexicalism requires that this numeration contain either a finitely inflected version of the main verb, or the bare form that will be compatible with *do*; *Do*-support can thus only apply in derivations that are set up from the beginning to require it, and so there is no sense in which *do* enters the derivation in response to subsequent inflectional difficulties.

This raises the question of why *Do*-support is not *always* possible in (non-emphatic) declaratives, in free variation with clauses with no *do* and a finite main verb. To answer this question, Chomsky invokes principles of transderivational economy. In short, *do* is indeed freely able to occur in any derivation, but when a derivation with *do* and one without *do* both converge on (potentially) grammatical outputs, they are compared, the derivation with *do* is ruled out on the grounds that it is more costly.

Transderivational comparisons of this kind, which require comparison between derivations built from different initial numerations, have been argued against elsewhere. Even setting that aside, however, what is remarkable is that the *Minimalist Program rhetorically* preserves the analysis of *Do*-support from *Syntactic Structures*, even when each component part of the earlier analysis is incompatible with the lexicalist perspective adopted in the later work. Realizational frameworks, by contrast, have been able to retain the repair analysis of *Do*-support more directly, with the slight adaptation that insertion of *do* is

---

counts in which *Do*-support is nonetheless a last-resort repair are possible in constraint-based systems such as OT syntax; see Grimshaw (1997) for one such treatment.

6 The technical details of this account differ considerably for *Do*-support in the case of negation and affirmative focus, where the issue is re-raising of an Agr after lowering to the main verb. These details are orthogonal to the point here, and so I abstract away from them.

moved from the syntactic component into the realizational rules of the postsyntax (Bobaljik, 1995; Embick and Noyer, 2001; Halle and Marantz, 1993).

The point to make here is not that a repair analysis of *Do*-support is necessarily correct.[7] The point is instead to observe the long shadow cast by the syntactic treatment of inflectional morphology in *Syntactic Structures*, and how deep an impact it has had on how the field understands morphosyntactic phenomena, even when its perspective has been incompatible with subsequent developments in syntactic theory.

4 Morphology and syntactic category: participles and gerunds

Both Affix Hopping and *Do*-support are transformations introduced to account for the distribution of verbal inflection in canonical clausal sequences of auxiliaries and verbs—what would now be referred to as the clausal spine. Sections 7.2 and 8.2 address another dimension of verbal morphology, the nonfinite participles and gerunds created by affixation of *-ing*. Though less widely influential than other topics discussed in *Syntactic Structures*, the analysis of these forms has been perhaps more directly implicated in debates concerning the morphology-syntax interface, and so is worth discussing here in some detail.

The analysis of participles and gerunds in *Syntactic Structures* is notable in at least two respects. First, both are derived via syntactic transformation, thus including category-changing morphology (i.e. derivational morphology) in the syntactic component. Second, the affix *-ing* is united with verbs via the same transformation in participles and gerunds as it is in progressive auxiliary constructions (i.e. via Affix Hopping), highlighting the important descriptive observation that the distribution of participial and gerundive *-ing* is subject to the same generalizations as canonical verbal inflection such as tense—relevant because in many analyses, participial *-ing* and gerundive *-ing* are homophonous but nonetheless distinct elements.

Syntactic Structures distinguishes two classes of transformationally derived *-ing* forms: adjectival participles as in (3),[8] and nominal gerunds as in (4):

---

[7] Indeed, much recent work suggests that it may not be, or at least that the problem that *do* occurs to repair is not one of stranded inflection: see, for example, Schütze (2004), Haddican (2007), Platzack (2008), and Thoms (2011).

[8] Chomsky assumes that the progressive use of the participle is also adjectival—indeed, that it is the transformational source of the participle in (4). Evidence against Chomsky's assumption,

(3) the **sleeping** child

(4) a. **proving** that theorem
     b. **being** cheated
     c. the **growling** of lions

Chomsky argues directly that participles as in (3) must be syntactically adjectival, because they have the external distribution of adjectives, but that they cannot be introduced as adjectives via phrase structure rules because they do not occur in all positions where adjectives can be introduced. This apparent conflict is resolved by introducing participial adjectives via the transformational rule that affixes verbs with -*ing*: the output of this rule can be further transformed by any rule with the category *Adj* in its structural description, but because participles are not listed as adjectives they will never be introduced by phrase structure rules. This transformation analysis of the adjectival character of participles derives a further contrast between the distribution of participles and true lexical adjectives, even those ending in -*ing*, visible in (5): lexical adjectives, but not participles, can occur as the complements of verbs like *seem* (introduced in §2.3, discussed further in §7.3).

(5) a. * The children seem sleeping.
     b. The books seem interesting.

The forms *sleeping* and *interesting* are not only transparently morphologically complex but also transparently deverbal: the significant innovation of *Syntactic Structures* is to nonetheless divide them into separate components of grammar. The separation between listed forms and forms that are generated by syntax has remained central to investigations in morphosyntax, as well as carrying over into psycholinguistics via the dual route *words and rules* model (cf. Prasada and Pinker 1993, Pinker 1998).

The same division between listed forms and those derived transformationally arises in the analysis of nominal gerunds as in (4). Like participles, gerunds are given a transformational analysis in *Syntactic Structures*, generated by a rule essentially identical to the rule forming *to*-infinitives, differing only in that -*ing* is

---

in favor of distinguishing adjectival and progressive participles, comes from the fact that stative verbs can occur as adjectival participles, but are ungrammatical in the progressive: e.g. *Any student **knowing** the answer should raise their hand.* but **Any student who is knowing the answer should raise their hand.*. The post-nominal position of phrasal adjectival participles presents further puzzles, which there is not space to discuss here.

inserted instead of *to* (subsequently reordered with respect to a following verb by the Affix Hopping transformation).

The analysis of gerunds has been a testing ground for subsequent generative treatments of the divide between lexical listedness and syntactic derivation, as well as of the nature of syntactic categorization, and its interaction with morphology. This begins with *Remarks on Nominalization*, whose primary focus is on the contrast between gerunds like (6a) and derived nominals like (6b), but which briefly discusses examples like (6c) as an intermediate case.⁹

(6) a. my criticizing the book
 b. my criticism of the book
 c. my criticizing of the book

Though the lexicalist hypothesis for which *Remarks* is famous is advanced for derived nominals as in (6b), and more tentatively for gerunds as in (6c), the transformational analysis of gerunds as in (6a) is maintained from *Syntactic Structures*. One type of evidence for this that has remained relevant in subsequent work is that gerunds of this type can be formed from maximally complex aspectual structures, as in (7)

(7) This book's having been read repeatedly can be seen from its cracked spine.

The gerund subject in (7) is clearly nominal: not only is its subject genitive, but it has itself undergone passive movement from the underlying object position of the verb *seen*. But just as clearly, the *internal* syntax of the gerund is clausal: it contains the perfect auxiliary *have*, as well as the passive *be*, and is modified by the adverb *repeatedly* (not adjectival *repeated*). The problem for a lexical analysis of gerunds is how the same word can act both as a noun and as a verb within a single derivation.

For these reasons, most work on gerunds has maintained the idea that they are derived syntactically: an element like *criticize* enters the derivation as a verb, and so can participate in verbal and clausal structure, but at some point the nominalizing *-ing* affix is applied, and from that point forward a complex form like *criticizing* behaves instead as a noun. See for example Stowell (1981), Abney (1987),

---

9 The number and type of gerund constructions in English has been the subject of considerable debate. Though *Remarks on Nominalization* distinguishes only two, most authors distinguish at least three types: ACC-ing (*me reading the book*), POSS-ing (*my reading the book*), and ing-of (*my reading of the book*). See Milsark (2006) for a useful overview of the literature in this field.

and Milsark (1988), as well as analyses in Distributed Morphology such as Marantz (1997) and Harley and Noyer (1998) (where derived nominals like *criticism* are also syntactically derived).

Such treatments are fundamentally at odds not only with the strong version of the lexicalist hypothesis, which bans syntactic affixation altogether, but also with the most common implementation of weak lexicalism as well, because gerundive affixes like *-ing* induce a change of lexical category and so are classically treated as derivational affixes. Gerunds, and their counterparts in other languages, have thus presented a challenge for lexicalism: if the category of an element cannot change in the course of a syntactic derivation, then gerunds must be *simultaneously* nominal and verbal. Lapointe (1993) proposes for example a lexicalist treatment in which gerunds project simultaneously as both nouns and verbs; this idea is adapted into non-derivational frameworks in work such as Malouf (1998) and Bresnan (1997).

Here again we find that the perspective taken in *Syntactic Structures* has persisted despite shifts between lexicalist and realizational models of morphology. In this case, though, it is not that the descriptive reach of the *Syntactic Structures* model has been particularly long, so much as that a derivational account of gerunds has proven more empirically successful than lexicalist alternatives in terms of biprojection.

5 Conclusions

The legacy of *Syntactic Structures* is felt throughout modern linguistics, across quite different theoretical frameworks. Given that morphological phenomena, particularly relating to verbal inflection, lie at the heart of much of *Syntactic Structures*' transformational theory, it is unsurprising that its influence is particularly felt in morphosyntax.

The goal here has been to illustrate that the interleaving of word and sentence formation that lies at the heart of the transformational framework developed in *Syntactic Structures* has been carried forward in the descriptive understanding of morphological phenomena in generative syntax. And so even as the theoretical gravitational centre of the field has shifted, first towards lexicalism and more recently back towards realization, the way phenomena were first described there has continued to define how they are perceived, and so how they are analyzed.

The fact that a particular description of facts has persisted is not an argument that that description is correct. But the fact that the descriptions of Affix Hopping, *Do*-support, and participle and gerund formation have remained influential, though a period where they were fundamentally at odds with the dominant understanding of how syntax and morphology interact, is a testament to the insight behind their original formulation.

Bibliography

Abney, Steven. 1987. The English noun phrase in its sentential aspect. Doctoral Dissertation, Massachusetts Institute of Technology.

Anderson, Stephen R. 1982. Where's morphology? *Linguistic inquiry* 13:571–612.

Baker, Mark C. 1988. *Incorporation: A theory of grammatical function changing*. University of Chicago Press.

Bjorkman, Bronwyn M. 2011. BE-ing Default: the Morphosyntax of Auxiliaries. Doctoral Dissertation, MIT.

Bobaljik, Jonathan. 1995. Morphosyntax: The syntax of verbal inflection. Doctoral Dissertation, MIT.

Bresnan, Joan. 1982. *The mental representation of grammatical relations*. MIT Press.

Bresnan, Joan. 1997. Mixed categories as head sharing constructions. In *Proceedings of the LFG97 Conference.*. CSLI Publications Online.

Chomsky, Noam. 1957. *Syntactic Structures*. The Hague: Mouton.

Chomsky, Noam. 1970. Remarks on Nominalization. In *Readings in English Transformational Grammar*, ed. R. Jacobs and P. Rosenbaum. Waltham, MA: Ginn.

Chomsky, Noam. 1975. *The logical structure of linguistic theory*. New York: Plenum Press.

Chomsky, Noam. 1993. A minimalist program for linguistic theory. In *The View from Building 20: Essays in Linguistics in Honor of Sylvain Bromberger*, ed. Ken Hale and Samuel J. Keyser, 1–52. MIT Press.

Chomsky, Noam. 1995. *The minimalist program*. Cambridge, MA: MIT Press.

Chomsky, Noam. 2000. Minimalist Inquiries: the framework. In *Step by step: Essays on minimalist syntax in honour of Howard Lasnik*, ed. Roger Martin, David Michaels, and Juan Uriagereka, 89–155. MIT Press.

Cowper, Elizabeth A. 2010. Where auxiliary verbs come from. In *Proceedings of the 2010 annual meeting of the Canadian Linguistic Association*, ed. Melinda Heijl. http://cla-acl.ca/actes-2010-proceedings/.

Dechaine, Rose-Marie. 1995. One *be*. *Linguistics in the Netherlands* 12:73–88.

Di Sciullo, Anna Maria, and Edwin Williams. 1987. *On the Definition of Word*. Cambridge, MA: MIT Press.

Embick, David, and Rolf Noyer. 2001. Movement Operations after Syntax. *Linguistic Inquiry* 32:555–595.

Fodor, Jerry A. 1983. *The modularity of mind*. Cambridge, MA: MIT press.

Freidin, Robert. 1992. *FFoundations of Generative Syntax*. MIT Press.

Freidin, Robert. 2004. Syntactic Structures redux. *Syntax* 7:101–127.

Grimshaw, Jane. 1997. Projection, heads, and optimality. *Linguistic Inquiry* 28:373–422.

Haddican, Bill. 2007. On *egin*: *do*-support and VP focus in Central and Western Basque. *Natural Language & Linguistic Theory* 25:735–764.

Halle, Morris. 1973. Prolegomena to a theory of word formation. *Linguistic inquiry* 4:3–16.

Halle, Morris, and Alec Marantz. 1993. Distributed Morphology and the pieces of inflection. In *The View from Building 20: Essays in Linguistics in Honor of Sylvain Bromberger*, ed. Ken Hale and Samuel J. Keyser. Cambridge, MA: MIT Press.

Halle, Morris, and Alec Marantz. 1994. Some key features of Distributed Morphology. *MIT Working Papers in Linguistics* 21:275–288.

Halle, Morris, and Karuvannur P Mohanan. 1985. Segmental phonology of modern English. *Linguistic inquiry* 16:57–116.

Harley, Heidi, and Rolf Noyer. 1998. Mixed nominalizations, short verb movement and object shift in English. In *Proceedings of NELS*, volume 28, 143–157. GLSA Amherst, MA.

Harley, Heidi, and Rolf Noyer. 1999. Distributed morphology. *Glot International* 4:3–9.

Jelinek, Eloise. 1984. Empty categories, case, and configurationality. *Natural Language & Linguistic Theory* 2:39–76.

Kiparsky, Paul. 1985. Some consequences of lexical phonology. *Phonology* 2:85–138.

Lapointe, Steven G. 1980. The Theory of Grammatical Agreement. Doctoral Dissertation, University of Massachusetts Amherst.

Lapointe, Steven G. 1993. Dual lexical categories and the syntax of mixed category phrases. In *Proceedings of the Eastern States Conference of Linguistics*, ed. A. Kathol and M. Bernstein, 199–210.

Lasnik, Howard. 1995. Verbal morphology: Syntactic structures meets the Minimalist Program. In *Evolution and revolution in linguistic theory: Essays in honor of Carlos Otero*, ed. Héctor Campos and Paula Kempchinsky, 251–275. Washington, D.C.: Georgetown University Press.

Lasnik, Howard. 2000. *Syntactic Structures Revisited: Contemporary Lectures on Classic Transformational Theory*. MIT Press.

Malouf, Robert P. 1998. Mixed categories in the hierarchical lexicon. Doctoral Dissertation, Stanford University.

Marantz, Alec. 1997. No escape from syntax: Don't try morphological analysis in the privacy of your own lexicon. In *Proceedings of the 21st annual Penn linguistics colloquium*, 201–225.

Milsark, Gary L. 1988. Singl-ing. *Linguistic Inquiry* 611–634.

Milsark, Gary L. 2006. Gerundive Nominalizations. In *The Blackwell Companion to Syntax, Volume I*, ed. Martin Everaert and Henk Van Riemsdijk. Blackwell.

Mohanan, Karuvannur Puthanveettil. 1986. *The theory of lexical phonology*. Dordrecht: Reidel.

Pesetsky, David, and Esther Torrego. 2007. The syntax of valuation and the interpretability of features. In *Phrasal and clausal architecture: Syntactic derivation and interpretation. In honor of Joseph E. Emonds*, ed. S. Karimi, V. Samiian, and W. Wilkins, 262–294. Amsterdam: Benjamins.

Pinker, Steven. 1998. Words and rules. *Lingua* 106:219–242.

Platzack, Christer. 2008. Cross Linguistic Variation in the Realm of Support Verbs. LingBuzz/000766.

Pollard, Carl, and Ivan A Sag. 1994. *Head-driven phrase structure grammar*. University of Chicago Press.

Pollock, Jean-Yves. 1989. Verb movement, universal grammar, and the structure of IP. *Linguistic Inquiry* 20:365–424.

Prasada, Sandeep, and Steven Pinker. 1993. Generalisation of regular and irregular morphological patterns. *Language and cognitive processes* 8:1–56.

Sadock, Jerrold M. 1980. Noun incorporation in Greenlandic: A case of syntactic word formation. *Language* 56:300–319.

Schütze, Carson T. 2003. When is a verb not a verb? *Nordlyd* 31:400–415.
Schütze, Carson T. 2004. Synchronic and diachronic microvariation in English *do*. *Lingua* 114:495–516.
Starke, Michal. 2010. Nanosyntax: A short primer to a new approach to language. *Nordlyd* 36.
Stowell, Timothy Angus. 1981. Origins of phrase structure. Doctoral Dissertation, Massachusetts Institute of Technology.
Thoms, Gary. 2011. From economy to locality: *Do*-support as head movement. Ms., Strathclyde University.
Wurmbrand, Susi. 2012. The syntax of valuation in auxiliary–participle constructions. In *Coyote Working Papers in Linguistics*, 29. WCCFL, Tuscon: University of Arizona.

Henk C. van Riemsdijk
Constructions

1 Preliminaries

The word 'construction' is used in a variety of ways in Chomsky's *Syntactic Structures* (1957).[1] The sense of 'construction' that we will discuss in this chapter is not frequently used however. In section 7.4 on pp75ff of *Syntactic Structures* we find some discussion of the 'verb+particle' construction and of the 'verb+complement' construction. Just limiting ourselves to the verb+particle construction, Chomsky notes that while the verb and the particle 'belong together', that is, are generated together by the phrase structure rules, the particle can also be separated from the verb by a direct object, as in (1)[2]

(1)   a.   the police brought in the criminal
        b.   the police brought the criminal in

Assuming that (1b) is essentially like (1a) except that the verb and the particle are discontinuous, Chomsky notes that "discontinuous elements cannot be handled readily within the phrase structure grammar." He goes on to suggest a transformational solution for this construction.

On the whole, Chomsky does not seem to be using a uniform terminology to refer to what we now call constructions.[3] He does speak of conjunction, of the active-passive relation, yes-no-questions, nominalizations and, indeed, the particle construction. The reason why Chomsky calls this a construction is, presumably, that it constitutes a prime example of the type of phenomena in language that constitute strong empirical evidence in favor of a transformational treatment. Extrapolating from the verb+particle construction, then, we can search for similar configurations in the data that will yield comparable evidence for transformations. And it is easy to see that the properties of the verb+particle construction, when considered at a certain level of abstraction, will help identify similar phenomena in other natural languages, thereby strengthening the argumentation,

---

[1] Other uses include theory construction, grammar construction, sentence construction, level construction and constructional homonymity. None of these will be discussed here.
[2] These are the examples (82a/b) of Syntactic Structures page 75.
[3] Thanks to Charles Yang for sharing this observation with me.

even though Chomsky in *Syntactic Structures* does not attempt to broach such a line of research. Nevertheless, Chomsky makes points about syntax by zooming in on sets of empirical phenomena that exhibit certain specific properties that point the way to conclusions about the structure and functioning of grammar. The fact of the matter is that Chomsky uses the term construction about 35 times in *Syntactic Structures*, but in the vast majority of these cases he uses the word as a process noun: the construction of a grammar, level construction etc. There is no sense, no intention, in other words, to start using the term construction as a technical term. On the contrary, Chomsky in *Syntactic Structures* already envisages the possibility, indeed necessity, of abstracting away from language specific or, for that matter, cross-linguistic constructions, taking the relevant properties of these constructions, linking them with the properties of other constructions, thereby paving the way for the search of general principles of grammatical design.

2 Ways of organizing grammatical knowledge

In current usage, the term 'construction' plays an important role in the way linguists organize grammatical knowledge. It is quite clear that Chomsky's goal in Syntactic Structures is not to organize grammatical facts or insights, but to use them to tell us more about how grammars are constructed in such a way that their principal properties are properly captured. While recursion is not mentioned, the need for transformations, for example, is quite pervasive throughout the book.

When confronted with the term 'construction' the question of definition hardly ever arises. If you take a reference grammar of some language, the ways it might be organized are limited. Many (just limiting ourselves to the syntax) go from category to category, most in terms of syntactic categories[4] (the noun, the verb, the clause, etc.) and some use functional categories (subject, object, etc.). Depending on how sophisticated the grammar is, phrases will also be discussed. Often the organization is determined by more or less semantic notions that are frequently correlated with inflectional morphology. In Jespersen's *Modern English Grammar*, for example, information about various types of embedded clauses is

---

[4] A very good example of this type of structure in a syntactic grammar of a particular language, based on the types of questions and answers that the syntactic theorizing of the past decades have given rise to is the Syntax of Dutch (Broekhuis, 2012-2016). This monumental work is structured as follows: Nouns and Noun Phrases (2 volumes), Adpositions and Adpositional Phrases (1 volume), Adjectives and Adjective Phrases (1 volume), Verbs and Verb Phrases (3 volumes).

found in the chapter on 'mood' (Jespersen, 1940-1949). In Behaghel's *Deutsche Syntax* (Behaghel, 1923), Volume 3 contains a very substantial Part (his 'Book 6') on clausal structure. The discussion of the internal structure of clauses concentrates mainly on grammatical functions (subject, object, etc.) but their typology is largely characterized in terms of mood (indicative and subjunctive). But when these chapters address specifics, we are fed detailed, sometimes very detailed information about question clauses, conditional clauses, relative clauses ... And soon you are in the thicket of what we would now undoubtedly refer to as constructions: headed relative clauses, headless relative clauses, case attraction in relative clauses etc. Any linguist looking for relevant facts about, say, case matching and case mismatching would be perfectly happy finding such a transparent way of navigating through a very substantive grammar of German and its history that is almost one hundred years old.

The same questions of organization of linguistic materials arise today. Modern linguistics is rich in handbooks. These tend to concentrate on an exposition of the central general notions of current (generative) theorizing. While a discussion about Agree, or about the distinction between A-movement and A'-movement, would undoubtedly be abstracting away from specific constructions, as soon as you start illustrating these notions, using constructions is virtually impossible to avoid. The prototypical case of A'-movement is wh-movement, so wh-questions are the construction most likely used to show what the properties of A'-movement are. But for didactic purposes, of course, an extensive discussion of wh-questions in a variety of languages would not be found in such handbooks.

Wh-movement constitutes a huge subdomain of syntax. Writing a book about that topic would be a real challenge, and it is not obvious that it would make a lot of sense to even attempt to compose such a book. This is so because wh-movement is too large a construction to be truly useful. This is not to deny, of course, that modern syntactic theory has been quite successful in discovering a number of very general, possibly universal, properties of wh-movement. But the level of aggregation is way too high to make this a suitably delimited topic for concrete research. This is even true if we limit ourselves to wh-movement in relative clauses, for example. That is so because there are so many different types of relative clauses: headed, headless, amount relatives, correlatives and so on and so forth. And with the rapidly increasing in depth cross-linguistic knowledge the amount of material rapidly attains a gigantic mass that is hard if not impossible for even great minds to handle unless the material is organized in a sensible way. Without unduly generalizing the situation, I think it is fair to say that scientific contributions of importance in linguistics, and syntax in particular, are based not so much on studies of the highest level of aggregation but on in depth investigations at some intermediate level. This is a pragmatic approach to organization of grammatical knowledge as used for theoretical purposes that makes a lot of sense. *Syntactic Structures* make use of this method and it has remained the main method over the past 60 years.

3 The Companion to Syntax

By way of illustration, let me report on what we might call the philosophy of the Companion to Syntax that I coedited with Martin Everaert.[5] This 'philosophy' is outlined concisely in the preface to The Companion to Syntax (Everaert and van Riemsdijk, 2006)

> [...] From its inception in the 1950s, the ambition has been to go beyond observational and descriptive adequacy to reach explanatory bliss. Important work would be about 'conditions on transformations' rather than on 'some properties of wh-movement in English', about the 'transformational cycle' rather than on verb clusters. This is what science should be like. [...] Emphasis on theory has not, of course, altered the fact that linguistics is a thoroughly empirical science, but data and analyses are seen as what they are: tools to help us understand the structure and properties of the human language faculty. It is the fate of tools that when the product is finished they are put away [...].
>
> More generally, the data and analyses that at some point in the history of generative grammar played an important, sometimes even a crucial, role have a tendency to fade into the background rather quickly. This effect is particularly strong when the piece of theorizing they helped to establish becomes obsolete, but it is even true when the theoretical insight persists over time. As time went on, and as generative grammar (using the term in the broad sense, including all its theoretical diversity), in its explosive success, expanded to dozens of countries, hundreds of universities and colleges, and many hundreds of researchers, the muckheap of once useful but then discarded empirical material continued to grow. Old hands in the field may still be served by a good memory, helping them to dig out some of these rejects if they seem useful at some later stage, but successive new generations of young linguists simply don't have access to the wealth of data, generalizations, and analyses that might be terribly important to their research if only they knew about them. But it is not only a problem for younger generations. Researchers who like to keep track of developments, particularly (but not only) in those subfields that are not directly related to their own research, or who work in closely related disciplines such as, for instance, psycholinguistics or sociolinguistics, find it increasingly difficult to keep track. [...]
>
> [...] Having a good, theoretically oriented mind is not enough. You cannot gain an understanding of the abstract properties of Universal Grammar without having any ideas about

---

[5] The first edition appeared a little over 10 years ago (Everaert and van Riemsdijk, 2006) and a revised, updated and substantially expanded edition will appear towards the end of 2017 (Everaert and van Riemsdijk, forthcoming). In the quote from the preface below the footnotes have been omitted.

interesting empirical areas that might provide the crucial evidence (or counter-evidence) for your claims. But these flashes of empirical insight can only come if you have enough knowledge in your head to start the neurons firing away. And you can only have that knowledge if you have been taught about a certain range of phenomena in a variety of languages, or if you have had access to a repository of such materials to work through by yourself.

The term we chose to refer to the rather gigantic collection of materials on syntax was 'Encyclopaedia of syntactic case studies.' And we defined a *case study* as a *didactic, relatively theory-neutral account of some delimited empirical domain of facts in one or several languages whose analysis has played a significant role in the theorizing of the past decades*. A case study, then, is not quite identical, but nevertheless quite similar, to the notion of construction. In order to see this, let us select a small list of chapters taken from the new *Companion to Syntax* (Everaert and Van Riemsdijk 2018 to appear), which will contain 123 chapters:

- Ellipsis in Noun Phrases
- Free Relatives
- Overtly marked wh-paths
- Partial wh-movement
- Pied-Piping
- Right Node Raising
- Split Topicalization
- Verb Clusters, Verb Raising, and Restructuring

It is reasonable, I believe, to say that all these titles refer to a construction or set of constructions. And as we discussed above, the level of aggregation varies. Indeed, Restructuring in Romance languages could easily be termed a construction by itself and might have been the topic of a separate chapter. Similarly, the title 'Free Relatives' actually covers 'normal' headless relative clauses, but also a special type of free relatives called 'transparent free relatives.' The latter might also have been the title of a separate chapter. In these chapter names, the languages covered generally remain implicit. In some cases it will be known to the reader which language is probably prominent, in some it will not. Split Topicalization, for example, is a construction that exists and has been studied extensively in German, Swiss German, and also in a few Dutch dialects. On the other hand, Right Node Raising is a construction that exists in many languages indeed, but for the convenience of the reader, virtually all of the discussion is based on English with just a dash of Polish (the author's native language) thrown in.

The important thing about these constructions is, of course, that they are highly relevant to a number of central theoretical issues that transcend the construction in question. One of the central issues in the case of ellipsis in noun phrases is why ellipsis in noun phrases generally does not require a linguistic antecedent while clausal types of ellipsis (VP-deletion, gapping, etc.) do need a linguistic antecedent. One of the important issues that emerge from the discussion of Right Node Raising is whether multidominant structures are required to handle the relevant facts. In my chapter on Free Relatives, one issue I raise is whether the notion of merge is to be interpreted in such a way that a terminal node of one syntactic tree (or treelet) can be merged with some element in a matrix tree not containing that treelet, an operation that I have called 'grafting' and which I argue is indispensable in a proper account of so-called transparent free relative clauses.

Such considerations, which transpire in every one of the 123 chapters of the Companion to Syntax, are, of course, what modern syntactic theorizing is all about. So the question that arises is, why bother about constructions at all. The answer that I will propose in this short article is, in all its triviality, that constructions are relevant at two levels:
– Heuristics
– Archiving

In other words, constructions are important tools that syntacticians avail themselves of in their endeavor to build explanatory linguistic theories. Starting with the *archiving function*, consider a student who, in a study of long distance wh-movement type dependencies, has come across some strange facts in Selayarese. The facts apparently have to do with morphological markings on the verb when it takes a complement clause. But when long distance wh-movement takes place in Selayarese, these morphological markings seem to disappear. Clearly, this is not only an interesting analytical problem but one that has potentially far-reaching consequences for how long distance wh-movement should be handled by the theory. Having arrived at this point, our student would do well to find a text in which problems of this kind are discussed systematically, where he finds references to the pertinent languages and an overview of theoretical solutions that have appeared in the literature. Marcel den Dikken's contribution to the *Syntax Companion* would give him exactly that, cf. Den Dikken (forthcoming).

Once a certain fact or set of facts has struck you as interesting, promising, intriguing, you will want to dig in further into this, yes, construction. The interesting, intriguing facts that you have noted are presumably properties of this construction. In view of the fact that these properties will quite possibly become part of the complex network of grammatical properties which abstract, possibly universal, principles will be required to account for, there are two ways to proceed. First, you may eagerly jump at some general principle that could explain the property that you have already found, but you could also explore the construction further to discover more properties that are, or seem to be, characteristic of this construction. Both lines of research should ultimately lead to the same goal, namely the identification of one or several general principles of grammatical design that constitute the current best theory. But while researchers tend to be impatient to jump to the higher echelons of the theory, I submit that solid science should not forget to try to establish as complete a picture of the construction in question as possible, not least to avoid embarrassing signal failure at the highest level. Picking up the first interesting properties of a construction and taking them as a point of departure for a search of other possibly significant properties is what I call the *heuristic function* of constructions.

4 An example: Split Topicalization

Being a native speaker of Standard German and Swiss German, I could not fail to come across examples of a type that are now called Split Topicalization. In Split Topicalization, instead of topicalizing a complete noun phrase, what you topicalize is just part of that noun phrase. In the late 80s, 'move α' stood for the idea that movement could be free: 'move anything anywhere', and that general constraints and principles would determine which instances of move α could yield a well-formed sentence. One of the constraints that most people were assuming to be correct was that only heads and maximal projection nodes could be moved, but not intermediate projections of some complex phrase. Clearly a split topicalization sentence such as (2) was going to be a serious problem for such a theory.

(2) [Neue Hosen]$_i$ kann ich mir [keine ___$_i$] leisten
    new pants   can   I   me   none   afford
    'New pants can I afford none' = I cannot afford new pants

Clearly, if [Neue Hosen] is extracted from the complete noun phrase [keine neuen Hosen] we have a problem with the no splitting constraint of move α. Hence it turned out that a simple random observation apparently had a quite far-reaching relevance for the then prevailing theory. But I must confess that once I started thinking about such examples I had not thought that far yet. Rather, I immediately felt that, among the probably dozens of random observations of stray facts that you come across every day, this was one that stood out as being truly important. The next step then is to determine what the major properties of the construction are. I'll make a selection of some of the most salient properties as described in my first paper on this construction (Van Riemsdijk, 1989). There are many important and in part remarkable properties of this construction, some suggesting strongly that the relationship between the fronted part (henceforth the partial topic PT) and the remnant in situ (henceforth RIS) is characteristic of A'-movement, some others causing problems for a movement analysis. Here is a concise overview over a subset of these properties.

1. The PT may contain, in addition to the head noun, either adjuncts or complements or both, and so does the RIS. Here are a few examples:[6]

   (3) a. [Eine Verurteilung des   ersten Verräters] darf man
          a   conviction   of-the first traitor   may one
          [keine ___] erwarten.
          none   expect
          'One should not expect a conviction of the first traitor.'
       b. [Eine Verurteilung] darf man [eine ___ des   ersten
          a   conviction   may one   one   of-the first
          Verräters] nicht erwarten.
          traitor   not   expect
          'One should not expect a conviction of the first traitor.'

   (4) a. [Ein Haus in Italien] würde ich mir [keins ___]
          a   house in Italy   would I   me   none
          kaufen.
          buy
          'A house in Italy I would not buy'
       b. [Ein Haus] würde ich mir [keins ___ in Italien]
          a   house would I   me   none   in Italy
          kaufen.
          buy
          'As for a house, I would not buy one in Italy.'

2. In some dialects both the PT and the RIS require an article. This is also illustrated in the examples (3/4) above.

---

[6] In the translations of these examples the topic – focus distinction is lost. In (3a) 'conviction of the first traitor' is the topic and 'none' is the focus, while in (3b) only 'conviction' is the topic whereas 'of the first traitor' is the focus. The same will be true in the coming examples.

3. In most cases (there are some exceptions that vary from speaker to speaker) the RIS must contain a gap corresponding to the PT. An exception is the following example from Fanselow (1993:63)[7]

   (5) [Raubvögel] glaube ich kennt Gereon nur [Bussarde].
       birds of prey believe I knows Gereon only buzzards
       'As for birds of prey, Gereon knows only buzzards.'

4. While aboutness constructions such as *As for Shakespeare's plays, I have not read a single one* do not require number agreement between the fronted NP and the *in situ* NP, Split Topicalization does require number agreement. This is contested as well, see Van Hoof (2006:418 ex (23)).

   (6) a. [Autos] hat er nur [eins ___].
          cars has he only one
          'As for cars, he has only one

       b. *[(Ein) Auto] hat er sogar [zwei ___].
          (a) car has he even two
          'As for (a) car, he has even two.'

   While (6a) is far from fully grammatical for the present author, there is undeniably an asymmetry, as Van Hoof notes, in that (6b) is completely ungrammatical.

5. The relationship between the PT and the RIS is constrained by the usual island conditions. The Complex Noun Phrase Constraint, for example, cannot be violated, as shown in (7):

   (7) a. [Eine Lösung] hat er [eine bessere ___] als ich.
          a solution has he a better than I
          'He has a better solution than I do.'

       b. *[Eine Lösung] kenne ich keinen, der [eine bessere
           a solution know I noone who a better
           ___] hat als ich
                has than I
          'I know nobody who has a better solution than I do.'

                                              (Van Riemsdijk 1989:114 ex (24))

---

[7] In my variant of German this is not possible.

6. At LF the PT needs to be reconstructed into the RIS positions in order for the binding conditions to work properly. Take the following example illustrating the Principle C effect.
   (8) *[Bücher von ihm$_i$] hat Halle$_i$ [keine ___] im Regal.
         books   by   him$_i$ has Halle$_i$ none   in shelf
         'As for books by him$_i$, Halle$_i$ has none on his$_i$ shelf.'

   (Van Riemsdijk 1989:115 ex (31))

7. Ordering restrictions on adjuncts and complements in the non-split noun phrase are replicated in the split version; for example you can say *ein schöner blauer Ring* ('a beautiful blue ring'), but not (at least in non-contrasting contexts) *ein blauer schöner Ring*. In the split variant this remains constant: *einen blauen Ring hat sie einen schönen* ('as for a blue ring, she has a beautiful one') vs. **einen schönen Ring hat sie einen blauen* ('as for a beautiful ring, she has a blue one').

Among these seven properties, there are quite a number that strongly point in the direction of an A'-movement analysis: 3. 5. 6. and 7. Property 1 is mainly a challenge to the theory of phrase structure: should adjuncts be attached higher than comlements? Property 2. Can probably be solved in terms of late insertion, while the aboutness issue remains somewhat mysterious and has possibly little to do with syntax in the first place. In my article (Van Riemsdijk 1989) I discuss these and a few more properties in detail and propose an actual movement solution.[8]

What is important here is that constructions have properties, and these properties constitute direct links to theoretical issues. Furthermore, these properties are recurrent properties in the sense that most of these properties are likely to be found in other constructions in the same language as well as in constructions in other languages. In that sense such properties are part of a dense network. And in this network certain properties seem to cluster, that is, they seem to co-occur frequently, linking together certain constructions previously not considered to be related. Thereby such networks of properties result in numerous questions that together make up major challenges for theoretical accounts. That is the way things often tend to go: as we learn more about a construction or a cluster of constructions and as we associate a set of properties with that construction, we formulate

---

[8] There is much more to say and there are many more problems to solve. Furthermore, the divergence of speakers' intuitions complicates matters considerably. A very detailed and helpful overview is presented in Van Hoof (2006) which is alo reprinted in (Everaert and Van Riemsdijk 2018 to appear).

a number of serious challenges to some of the core principles of the theory of syntax.

In the above partial list of properties of the Split Topicalization Construction, challenges of very central theoretical principles (or at least beliefs) abound. Let us just single out a few of them. Property 1 suggests strongly that the distinction between complements and adjuncts may well be much less sharp than was hitherto believed: both complements and adjuncts can end up in the PT and in the RIS. Is this a result of radical scrambling? Possibly not if we look at property 7, see below. Property 2 suggests that if Split Topicalization is the result of a movement operation we may end up with a single (split) noun phrase that has two determiners, which is normally speaking excluded. Should we conclude that there is no movemet, or should we invoke the possibility of late insertion of determiners to yield an overt determiner both in the PT and in the RIS? Property 3 is controversial. For many speakers the example (5) is ungrammatical. On a non-movement analysis this would mean that there are cases in which ellipsis, normally thought to be an optional phenomenon, must actually be obligatory, thereby posing some serious questions both for a theory of movement and for a theory of ellipsis. Turning now to property 4, we must conclude that the semantico-pragmatic notion of 'aboutness' is very closely linked with certain distinctions in syntax: how are the interactions between the two domains of grammar at the relevant interface implemented? Properties 5 and 6 both show that Split Topicalization evidences a number of clear movement properties including island sensitivity and reconstruction. But if we conclude from a number of the previous properties such as 2 and 3 that Split Topicalization is not a typical movement process after all, how can we account for the presence of island sensitivity and reconstruction. For proponents of a non-movement solution, property 7 might well be the most vexing of the lot. It says, in short, that the split construction mirrors adjunct and complement ordering constraints found in the non-split variant. No serious attempt at an answer to this question has yet come to my attention.

Let there be no mistake, the situation is often too complex to be able to say that a certain construction, or a certain aspect of that construction, or indeed a cluster of constructions containing the one in question, constitutes a challenge to the theory, any theory, of syntax that is so powerful, so commonly known and understood that we can confidently say: this is the XYZ-Problem, and no one can escape the necessity of not only addressing it but actually solving it if he/she wants to have any hope of successfully presenting a new theoretical proposal. But that is the direction in which we should go. For the time being it is still far too easy to make proposals that may be attractive in many ways but which are simply incompatible with what we know about certain constructions. That incompatibility is likely to be relegated to some footnote in which it is listed among the growing numbers of issues "left for future research." The ease with which we allow ourselves to live with such partial understanding and issues for future research that remain in their footnotes for ages is indicative of the relative immaturity of modern linguistic theory as compared to the natural sciences that have a long and venerable history behind them. There is no question that linguistics will get there, but aiming at a solid understanding of such lowly matters as constructions and their properties is, at least for the time being, an inescapable necessity.

5 Linguistics and Science

It would be wrong, however, to conclude that linguistics is completely different from the natural sciences because it keeps messing around with constructions and their properties. There is a lot of similar messing around of that type in the 'old', well-established sciences as well. The real difference is that in biology, for example, there is no part of the theory of DNA self-replication that is about horses, as Edwin Williams (p.c.) points out. In linguistics the theory of merge is similarly independent of specific constructions, but we cannot, for the time being, escape the fact that in order for merge to work properly in some construction X in language Y, specific parameters connected to X and Y are needed. This is true. But does that mean that in, say, biology you can dispense with detailed knowledge of, for example, horses. Above I said that the role of constructions in linguistics was at the level of archiving and heuristics. And at that level biologists cannot escape the need for detailed knowledge about the objects that biology deals with: specific living creatures.

Take for example a biologist who is interested in birdsong, as many of them are now. Birdsong as an object of research is similar to linguistic constructions being objects of research. But of course, birdsong is an interesting object of research because, among other things it may tell us something about the structure and the functioning of birds' brains: how much variation is possible in the birdsong of a specific type of bird? What properties must be satisfied for a particular bird to learn (or develop) the birdsong typical of its subspecies? Furthermore, if a biologist wants to set up some experiment to study certain properties of birdsong, it is important for him to pick the right type of bird in order to achieve optimal results. Such knowledge has in all likelihood been established on the basis of earlier experiments, be they on birdsong or, perhaps on other properties of various potential candidate birds for his experiment. It is in this sense that the mature sciences must work with the equivalent of constructions. Therefore linguists would be foolish to ignore, neglect or ridicule serious work on constructions, as long as that work is done with the ultimate goal of developing construction-independent theories in mind. And this, along with many other insights that guided me on my meandering through linguistics in search of deep fundamental insight into the human brain, was one of the many eye-openers that stuck with me ever since reading *Syntactic Structures*, the first book on generative grammar that found its way into my hands.

Acknowledgements Thanks are due to Edwin Williams for suggesting ways to approach the topic of 'constructions'. I also want to thank Charles Yang for discussing the first draft of this essay with me.

Bibliography

Behaghel, Otto. 1923. *Deutsche Syntax, eine geschichtliche Darstellung*. Heidelberg, Germany: C. Winter.
Broekhuis, Hans. 2012-2016. *Syntax of Dutch (7 volumes)*. Comprehensive Grammar Resources. Amsterdam, Netherlands: Amsterdam University Press. Series editor: Henk C. van Riemsdijk and István Kenesei.
Chomsky, Noam. 1957. *Syntactic Structures*. The Hague, The Netherlands: Mouton de Gruyter.
den Dikken, Marcel. forthcoming. Overtly marked wh-paths. In *The Wiley Blackwell Companion to Syntax, Second edition*, ed. Martin Everaert and Henk C. van Riemsdijk. Hoboken, NJ: John Wiley & Sons, Inc.
Everaert, Martin, and Henk C. van Riemsdijk, ed. 2006. *The Blackwell Companion to Syntax*. 5 vols. Blackwell Handbooks to Linguistics. Malden, MA: Blackwell.
Everaert, Martin, and Henk C. van Riemsdijk, ed. forthcoming. *The Wiley Blackwell Companion to Syntax, Second revised, updated and expanded edition, 8 volumes and online publication*. The Wiley Blackwell Companions to Linguistics. Hoboken, NJ: John Wiley & Sons, Inc.
Fanselow, Gisbert. 1993. The return of the base generators. *Groninger Arbeiten zur Germanistischen Linguistik* 36:1–74.
Jespersen, Otto. 1940-1949. *A Modern English Grammar on Historical Principles, Volume 7*. Copenhagen, Denmark and London, UK: E. Munksgaard and Allen & Unwin. Reprinted in Great Britain 1961 and 1965 ed. 7 vols.
Van Hoof, Hanneke. 2006. Split Topicalization. In *The Blackwell Companion to Syntax*, ed. Martin Everaert and Henk C. van Riemsdijk, 410–465. Malden, MA: Blackwell.
Van Riemsdijk, Henk C. 1989. Movement and refeneration. In *Dialect variation and the theory of grammar*, ed. Paola Benincà, 105–136. Dordrecht, Netherlands: Foris.

Paul M. Pietroski
Meanings via Syntactic Structures

Chomsky (1957) offered prescient suggestions about how to formulate theories of understanding for the spoken languages that human children can naturally acquire. We can view his proposal as a prolegomenon to a theory of meaning that combines a layered theory of syntax with an account of how humans can naturally use expressions in acts of referring, asserting, querying, and so on; cp. Austin (1961); Davidson (1967); Dummett (1976); Higginbotham (1985). Though crucially, Chomsky's (1957) conception of reference differed from more familiar conceptions of denotation, as in Frege (1892b) or Russell (1905, 1912, 1957); cp. Goodman (1949, 1953), Strawson (1950), Chomsky (1977, 1995b, 2000b, 2017). I think we should develop the kind of semantic theory towards which Chomsky has long been pointing; see Pietroski (2017abc). But in this essay, my aim is simply to articulate a sense in which *Syntactic Structures* outlined a program for semantics, well before Davidson (1967), Montague (1970), and Lewis (1970).

1 Introduction

Human children come equipped with a remarkable resource. Given an ordinary course of experience, an ordinary child can acquire at least one procedure that generates unboundedly many linguistic expressions that are pronounceable and meaningful. Children also tend to acquire procedures that are remarkably similar to those acquired by local peers, even though each child's experience is limited and somewhat idiosyncratic. Correlatively, adults in a linguistic community will agree—if asked—about many subtle linguistic facts.

For example, mature speakers of English can tell that (1) is ambiguous,

(1) the old man was frightened by the new methods

even if they have not previously encountered this string of words. We can hear (1) as a sentence according to which the old man found it scarily hard to deal with some new ways of doing something (e.g., getting books from the library). But on another construal, perhaps less obvious, (1) is a sentence according to which new methods of frightening people were successfully used on the old man.[1] Interestingly, (2) can be understood as a description of a certain man,

(2)   the old man frightened by the new methods

though not as a sentence; while (3) can only be understood as a sentence with a bizarre meaning,

(3)   the old man frightened the new methods

and (4) is a mere string of words with no unified meaning.

(4)   old the was man by frightened new the methods

A monolingual speaker of Japanese will not know such facts, unless she is explicitly told about them—say, in a linguistics class conducted in Japanese. But such a speaker will also fail to know, with regard to (1), what the words and any constituent phrases mean. The important point here is that a speaker of English who knows what the words mean, and how they can be fit together, can recognize that (1) is ambiguous and (4) is gibberish.

A caveat: using words like 'English' and 'Japanese' in this way reflects an idealization that is not always appropriate. The many competent speakers of English do not share a common procedure that connects a public stock of meanings with the very same pronunciations. But in many contexts, including this one, we can abstract away from the relatively minor variations exhibited by the English procedures acquired in London, Sydney, Glasgow, Chicago, etc. Then we can pretend that English is a single language (with a fixed vocabulary). Likewise, we might treat the sundry Japanese procedures as equivalent, perhaps to highlight more dramatic contrasts between any one of them and *any* English procedure. For despite these contrasts, a human infant is prepared to acquire English or Japanese or both, without any special instruction regarding facts like those illustrated with (1–4). So even if we speak of variation across dialects of *a* language—maintaining the pretense that English is *one*, and Japanese another—acquiring a language like English or Japanese is a matter of acquiring a generative procedure of a special kind.

---

[1] The meanings differ, even if the new way of getting books was designed to frighten the elderly. I'll return to this example of what Chomsky (1957, pp. 86–90) calls *constructional homonymity*; see his example (114).

Chomsky (1986) sharpened this point by speaking of I-languages, which he defined as generative procedures, in explicit contrast with sets of expressions. Given this technical notion, one can ask how the I-languages that children naturally acquire *differ* from other procedures that connect signals of some kind with interpretations of some kind. For reasons noted below, Chomsky (1957, p.13) said that a language is a set of sentences, each of which is "finite in length and constructed out of a finite set of elements." But as the restriction and subsequent discussion makes clear, the real issues concerned methods of generation, not sets of generable sentences. More specifically, the assumption was that among the computational procedures characterized by Turing (1936) and Church (1941), there are some that humans can acquire and use to connect pronunciations with meanings—whatever pronunciations and meanings are—in ways that children regard as natural, at least for purposes of formulating and evaluating the relevant options in the course of acquiring languages like English or Japanese.[2]

This invites a research project that Chomsky (1957) initiated. Given a vocabulary that lets us describe the full range of computable procedures, we can try to provide a rough description of the smaller range that corresponds to the spoken languages that humans can naturally acquire. But the terminology we initially use, as we start to delimit the relevant subclass of procedures, is likely to be artificial in the following sense: this subclass may well be arbitrary, at least to some degree, from an abstract computational perspective that ignores requirements imposed by the need for biological implementations in human children; and while part of our initial aim (as theorists) is to locate certain procedures in a larger space that includes many logically coherent options that are *un*available to children, the targeted procedures form a scientifically interesting subclass because they are the ones available to children. So if all goes well, we should expect our theoretical vocabulary to evolve—from Subject/Copula/Predicate, to NP/Aux/VP, to whatever—as linguists make progress towards specifying certain naturally acquirable procedures in terms of notions that are naturally available to children.[3]

---

[2] We can speak of procedures as abstract mappings from elements of a domain to elements of a range. But at least when the functions in question are Turing-computable, we can also speak of physical implementations of the mappings; and implementations of a procedure/program—e.g., as a string of binary numerals, suitably stored on a certain machine—can be acquired and used in various ways. Chomsky's (1986) I-language/E-language contrast echoed Church's (1941) contrast between functions-in-intension and functions-in-extension; cp. Frege (1892a).

[3] Of course, one can hypothesize that the computational character of these procedures is not entirely arbitrary; see Chomsky (1995a, 2000a). And in principle, lucky inquirers might quickly hit on the right terminology for their subject matter; though in actual scientific practice, this never happens. So given that semanticists often use Church's (1941) lambda calculus to describe mean-

Correspondingly, the goal is not to specify and study certain sets of sentences. The goal is to describe the cognitive resources that humans deploy in the acquisition and use of certain generative procedures. Though in terms of making progress, we face an immediate problem, absent clear ideas about what meanings are.

It's hard enough to say what pronunciations are, even if we focus on spoken as opposed to signed languages. But at least we can talk about sequences of phonemes. If we want to talk about *expressions*, however, the phenomenon of homonymy introduces a familiar complication. Consider (5–8); where only (5) and (6) are strings that correspond to meaningful phrases.

(5)   by the new methods

(6)   buy the new methods

(7)   by the knew methods

(8)   buy the knew methods

In many cases, a sequence of phonemes corresponds to more than one word. Still, one might hope to confine this kind of homonymity to a stock of finitely many atomic expressions that can be distinguished formally—i.e., without appeal to their meanings—as when lexicographers use superscripts to distinguish the several words that share the pronunciation indicated with 'bank' or /bæŋk/. But even given a specification of the meaningful sequences of English phonemes, along with a way of disambiguating lexical homonyms, how can we start to describe the procedures that connect these sequences with their meanings if we don't know what meanings are?[4]

---

ings, we should remember that this formalism was invented as a tool for representing the entire space of computable functions. Likewise, the now familiar Fregean hierarchy of types—rooted in basic types that correspond to denotable entities and a pair of truth values—was introduced in the course of inventing a language that can be used to encode mathematical thoughts that humans can entertain, with help, even if the thoughts cannot be expressed in natural languages; see Pietroski (2017b) for discussion.

4 In my view, semanticists still don't have good analogs of phoneme sequences. Invoking sets of possible worlds is obviously inadequate, absent an independent characterization of worlds *and* a method for pairing distinct sets of worlds with nonsynonymous sentences—e.g., 'If there are groundhogs on Venus, then five is an even number' and 'There are finitely many prime numbers if woodchucks exist on Hesperus'.

2 Ambiguities and Analyses

Chomsky's (1957) strategy was inspired. But we should remember how bold it was. As an initial model that he soon modified, Chomsky *replaced* the question of how a computational device could generate (all and only) the pronunciation-meaning pairs of English with the somewhat clearer question of how a computational device could generate certain strings of English words—the "grammatical" strings—without also generating boundlessly many others. This was helpful, in part because given the new question, it was easy to show that some simple devices would overgenerate and/or undergenerate. But the grammatical strings served as first-pass proxies for the corresponding sentential meanings; and as discussed below, equivalence classes of derivational histories—represented as trees—provided better second-pass proxies.

Chomsky knew that a single string of words can correspond to more than one sentence meaning, much as a single string of phonemes can correspond to more than one word meaning. So he introduced a general notion of "constructional homonymity" for cases in which a phoneme sequence "is analyzed in more than one way on some level" (p. 86).

> For example, for many English speakers the phoneme sequence /aneym/ can be understood ambiguously as either 'a name' or 'an aim'. If our grammar were a one-level system dealing only with phonemes, we would have no explanation for this fact. But when we develop the level of morphological representation, we find that, for quite independent reasons, we are forced to set up morphemes 'a', 'an', 'aim' and 'name', associated with the phonemic shapes /a/, /an/, /eym/ and /neym/. Hence, as an automatic consequence of the attempt to set up the morphology in the simplest possible way we find that the phoneme sequence /aneym/ is ambiguously represented on the morphological level (p. 85).

Similarly, even if this ambiguity is resolved in favor of 'a name', intuition suggests that string (9) is ambiguous in a now familiar way indicated with (9a) and (9b);

(9) referred to a star with a name
    a. [$_{VP}$ referred to a [$_{NP}$ star with a name]]
    b. [$_{VP}$ [referred to a star] [$_{PP}$ with a name]]

where 'star with a name' is a constituent on analysis (a), and 'referred to a star' is a constituent on analysis (b). Compare 'saw a teacher with a telescope', which can be understood as implying that some teacher *had* a telescope, or as implying that someone *used* a telescope to see a teacher.

Example (1) is subtler, in part because 'frightened' is morphologically complex.

(10) [(1)] the old man was frightened by the new methods

But the two meanings seem to reflect distinct ways of combining the meaningful elements. Given the details in Chomsky (1957), including his account of passive constructions in terms of transformations (pp. 42–43), one might describe the ambiguity of (1) by positing two Deep Structures that correspond to distinct thoughts about the old man: the new methods (were things that) frightened him; or the new methods were used (by someone) to frighten him. Subsequent work led to other proposals; see, e.g., Pesetsky (1995). But here, the details are less important than the methodological moral Chomsky drew from the phenomenon of nonlexical ambiguity.

> This suggests a criterion of adequacy for grammars. We can test the adequacy of a given grammar by asking whether or not each case of constructional homonymity is a real case of ambiguity and each case of the proper kind of ambiguity is actually a case of constructional homonymity (p.86).

This passage highlights an important point, especially in light of the surrounding chapter ("The Explanatory Power of Linguistic Theory," discussed by Lidz in this volume). In providing a partial grammar for English, Chomsky's goal was not to partially specify a procedure that generates all and only the phoneme sequences that can be understood as English sentences. The aim was to characterize a procedure that generates the English pronunciation-meaning pairs *without also* generating many boundlessly other such pairs; and this was in the service of the larger goal of characterizing such a procedure as one possible choice from the range of diverse but fundamentally similar linguistic options that are available to human children.

The initial presentation in terms of word strings was a pedagogical device—a way of introducing students to the subject. Given the words of English, it's easy to imagine a finite state automaton that yields all the corresponding word strings, and hence each one that can be understood as an English sentence.[5]

---

[5] The procedure below generates every string that can be formed from a lexicon consisting of 'a' and 'b'.

With regard to combining meanings, we (still) haven't discovered the relevant analog of concatenating inscriptions. But we can imagine supplementing a universal string generator with a "semantic procedure" that connects each string of atomic expressions with all the sentence meanings that could be formed from those atoms. Then however one describes the grammatical strings, each one would be connected to the corresponding sentence meanings, though at the cost of massive overgeneration.

Chomsky (1964, 1965) stresses these points more explicitly, using contrastive examples like (11) and (12); where '#' indicates a coherent but unavailable construal of the string.

(11)   John is easy to please
    a. It is easy for us to please John.
    b. # It is easy for John to please us.

(12)   John is eager to please
    a. # John is eager for us to please him.
    b. John is eager that he please us.

Even more interestingly, (13) is three ways ambiguous;

(13)   the boy saw the woman walking towards the church
    a. The boy saw the woman while (he was) walking towards the church.
    b. The boy saw the woman who was walking towards the church.
    c. The boy saw the woman walk towards the church.

and unlike (12b), (12c) implies that the boy *saw an event* of the woman walking. But (13) is unambiguous, having only the interpretation that corresponds to (12c).

(14)   this is the church the boy saw the woman walking towards

We understand (14) as meaning that the church is such that the boy saw the woman *walk* towards it. Yet superficially, (14) is more like (13) and the equally ambiguous (15).[6]

---

[6] As Chomsky (1964) also notes, 'what did Mary see the boy walking towards' can be used to ask which thing is such that Mary saw the boy *walk* towards it—but not which thing is such that Mary saw the boy *who was walking* towards it, or such that Mary saw the boy *while walking* towards it. This suggests a common constraint on the interpretation of relative clauses and questions; see Ross (1967). For discussion of the relevance of event variables in accounting for constraints on

(15) this is the church such that the boy saw the woman walking towards it

Similar remarks apply to (16), one of Chomsky's (1957) examples of constructional homophony.

(16) John found the boy studying in the library

We could invent languages that generate (10–15) in ways that are subject to different constraints—e.g., languages in which (11) is as ambiguous as 'the duck is ready to eat', and (10) has only its English meaning, or vice versa. But naturally acquirable languages connect pronunciations with meanings as they do. Even controlling for morphological and lexical homonymy, a string of (formally disambiguated) words can still be constructionally homonymous in constrained ways. In many cases, it may be hard to know how many ways a given string can be understood. But prima facie, the facts to be accounted for include boundlessly many instances of the following generalization: each grammatical string of English words is constructionally homonymous in exactly n ways for some n, $n \geq 0$. While (12) is three ways ambiguous, it cannot be understood in the fourth way indicated with (12d).

(17) [(12)]
     d. # The boy saw the woman and walked towards the church.

So given Chomsky's proposed criterion of adequacy, a grammar for English cannot merely specify the grammatical strings of phonemes. Each string must be paired with the right number of analyses; and in the case of ambiguous strings, it needs to be plausible that each way of understanding the string is reflected by one of the analyses. But the point is not confined to grammatical strings. For example, (16) is degraded but comprehensible;

(18) the child seems sleeping

cp. (17), which is bizarre yet grammatical.

(19) colorless green ideas sleep furiously

---

homonymity, and arguments that the grammatical strings do not form an interesting class, see Higginbotham (1985) and Pietroski (2017c).

We understand (16) as meaning that the child seems to be sleeping, and not as meaning that the child seems sleepy; see also Higginbotham (1983). So we want a grammar of English to yield a suitable analysis of (16).

Correlatively, the mere ungrammaticality of (18)

(20) * she have might been there

does not yet explain why (18) cannot be understood as synonymous with (19).

(21) she might have been there

The explanandum is not merely that (18) is *defective*, but rather, that it cannot be understood as a sentence—even though the words in (18) can be combined to form a perfectly fine sentence. A good grammar for English should assign some analysis to (19) *and not* assign an equivalent analysis to (18). Seen in this light, examples of constructional homonymity are special cases of strings that have more than zero meanings, and hence strings that should be assigned more than zero grammatical analyses.[7]

Chomsky (1957) left room for levels of semantic analysis other than Deep Structure and Surface Structure. He also noted that (20) and (21), on their obvious construals,

(22) everyone in the room knows at least two languages

(23) two languages are known by everyone in the room

are not remotely equivalent. The former, but not the latter, can be used to describe a situation in which no two people in the room know the same language. Such examples suggest the possibility of "covert" transformations of Surface Structures; see, e.g., May (1985). But given endlessly many examples like (22) and (23),

(24) she could haven't being fly
 a. # She could not have been flying.

(25) Romeo loves Juliet
 a. # Juliet is such that Romeo is such that she loves him.

---

[7] See Berwick et al. (2011) for discussion in the context of responses to corresponding "poverty of stimulus" arguments.

theorists must be careful in adding a new level of analysis. The more complex grammar must not generate unattested pronunciation-meaning pairs that are not generated by the simpler grammar.

A related point is that if one allows for more than one meaning per grammatical analysis, then absent an independent proposal about how analyses are (not) related to meanings, the whole project of providing and evaluating constrained grammars is threatened. If a single analysis can correspond to two or more meanings, then providing a grammar that assigns n analyses to a string with n meanings does yet explain why the string fails to be more ambiguous than it is.

From this perspective, one shouldn't exclude the possibility of a semantic theory that pairs Surface Structures with hypothesized mental representations, as opposed to formal specifications of truth conditions; see Katz and Postal (1964); Katz and Fodor (1963). If theories of meaning are theories of understanding, then *pace* Lewis (1970), one cannot mandate that such theories be truth-theoretic; see Harman (1974). But if the mental representations are said to be the meanings that grammars connect with pronunciations, then the mapping from grammatical analyses to the posited meanings must be suitably constrained to avoid overgeneration. For example, an algorithm that pairs Surface Structures with Katzian disambiguaters must not yield too many meanings for (10–23). And if one posits a level of *grammatical* structure that is specified in terms of meanings, then analyses will not disambiguate strings formally, raising the question of how analyses are individuated for purposes of deciding whether or not a theory assigns n analyses to a given string. Put another way, theorists can posit levels of grammatical analysis that reflect meaning. But if analyses are to serve as proxies for meanings, the former can't be individuated in terms of the latter.[8]

---

8 Montague (1970) adopted a very different view without discussing the issues regarding overgeneration.

> Like Donald Davidson I regard the construction of a theory of truth—or rather, of the more general notion of truth under an arbitrary interpretation—as the basic goal of serious syntax and semantics; and the developments emanating from the Massachusetts Institute of Technology offer little promise towards that end (p. 188).

The talk of "truth under an arbitrary interpretation" suggests misunderstanding of Davidson's (1967) project; see Lepore (1983). More importantly, Montague's conception of serious syntax was remarkably implausible, and yet the basis for his influential decision to ignore Chomsky's (1957; 1964; 1965) conception of how a formal theory of syntax could be part of a substantive theory of understanding. It might be useful to ask how the field would have developed if Montague had been set aside, as irrelevant to the study of natural language, given the arguments (based on actual phenomena) that had emanated from MIT. Cp. Davidson (1967, p. 315), "Recent work by Chomsky and others is doing much to bring the complexities of natural languages within the scope of serious semantic theory." While Davidson's conception of reference differed from Chom-

3 Trees and Transformations

Following Chomsky's lead, I began with some mundane observations about children, and then noted some examples of homonymy. Instead of *starting* with assumptions about what meanings are—and how they are related to use, truth, logic, reference, functions, conventions, possible worlds, or other things—one can initially ground theoretical talk of meaning in specific facts about how many meanings certain strings of phonemes have, and more generally, how natural languages like English do and don't connect pronunciations with meanings. This highlights empirical phenomena that turned out to be theoretically tractable. But given this "syntax first" approach to semantics, it's important to be clear about what expressions and analyses are. In particular, if the idea is to use analyses as formal proxies for meanings—thereby delaying vexed questions about what meanings are, and how to connect a pronunciation with exactly *one* of them—we need a way of deciding how many analyses a proposed grammar assigns to a given sequence of phonemes. Otherwise, we can't assess the degree to which a proposed grammar is (in)adequate by the proposed standards.

If only to fix terminology in a simple way for his initial discussion, Chomsky (1957) took sentences to be strings as opposed to structured objects. Instead of saying that (1)

(26) [(1)] the old man was frightened by the new methods

is homonymous as between two different sentences, he regarded string (1) as a sentence that can be classified in two different ways, each of which corresponds to a certain diagram (or "tree") that represents a certain partial ordering of the relevant lexical items. But the grammar that Chomsky provided did not yield such diagrams, or any other structured objects, as *outputs*. The derivational procedure he described yielded certain strings, and thus distinguished those strings from underivable alternatives.[9] Though typically, there is more than one legitimate derivation of a string, even ignoring homonymy.

As an illustration, consider (23) and the toy grammar (24).

(27) [(23)] Romeo loves Juliet

---

sky's, this could have led to fruitful discussion, with less emphasis on mapping word-strings to expressions of the lambda calculus; cp. Lewis (1970, 1975).
9 The tacit assumption was that being derivable (from a naturally acquirable grammar) is a formally decidable property of strings; cp. being a tautology of first-order logic.

(28) S → NP VP
NP → Romeo
NP → Juliet
VP → V NP
V → V loves

The grammar licenses several derivations of (23), including the two shown below.

(29)
```
            S
     NP         VP
     Romeo      VP
     Romeo   V     NP
     Romeo   loves NP
     Romeo   loves Juliet
```

(30)
```
            S
     NP         VP
     NP      V     NP
     NP      V     Juliet
     NP      loves Juliet
     Romeo   loves Juliet
```

But (25) and (26) correspond to the same "collapsed PS tree," depicted as (27).

(31)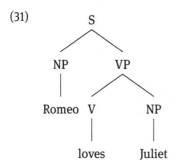

This tree preserves key information about which rules were applied how many times, while abstracting from differences of order across derivations; see Lasnik (1999) for lucid discussion. Note that (25–27) all capture the idea that relative to grammar (24), string (23) *is an* S in which 'loves Juliet' *is a* VP.

On a first reading, one might wonder why Chomsky fussed about defining a particular notion of derivational equivalence. But one important reason was to be explicit about the proxies for meanings, which could not be plausibly identified with strings or derivations. The idea was that (15) has two *analyses*, not that it has two derivations.

(32) [(15)] John found the boy studying in the library

And while (23) has more than one derivation, it doesn't have more than one meaning.

Focusing on equivalence classes of derivations (cp. Goodman (1951)) was a beautiful idea that offered a new way of thinking about how meanings are related to technical notions of extensional equivalence. It was also an empirically fruitful idea about what matters for grammatical distinctions; see Lasnik and Kupin (1977) for discussion and an independent specification of derivational equivalence. But in terms of providing proxies for meanings, the key point is that given a way of saying which derivations are equivalent, Chomsky could identify analyses with classes of equivalent derivations and then say that cases of constructional homonymity are cases in which a string of phonemes has *non*equivalent derivations.

On this view, a formal theory of syntax for a language L—a theory that specifies, without appeal to meanings, how expressions of L are generated—can be a core component of a broader theory of how speakers of L understand expressions of L. Moreover, a theory of syntax for L can help explain how speakers understand expressions of L in structured ways, even if the proposed grammar does not itself generate structured objects.

In distinguishing phrase structure grammars from finite state systems, Chomsky's point was not that the former let us build certain tree-like objects. His aim was to focus on procedures that can at least generate strings in which distant elements were introduced together, and then motivate appeals to transformations (of some kind) in specifying how humans naturally generate linguistic expressions, while recognizing that invoking transformations can easily lead to overgeneration. As Chomsky (1957, p.23) puts it, "there are processes of sentence-formation that finite state grammars are intrinsically not equipped to handle." But likewise, we need to posit grammars that generate strings in ways that phrase structure grammars do not. So we face the empirical question of which other procedures should be invoked for which constructions. And when evaluating proposals, considerations of simplicity are relevant.

> ... if we have a transformation that simplifies the grammar and leads from sentences to sentences in a large number of cases (i.e., a transformation under which the set of grammatical sentences is very nearly closed), then we attempt to assign constituent structure to sentences in such a way that this transformation always leads to grammatical sentences, thus simplifying the grammar even further (p. 83).

Space constraints preclude discussion of the many implications of this point for semantics. But let me offer a reminder that Chomsky's analysis of English auxiliaries, as in (28),

(33) she could have been flying

addressed ancient questions concerning how modes of speech are related to thoughts that seem to exhibit Subject-Copula-Predicate structure. We can describe (33) as a result of transforming a string that exhibits NP-Aux-VP structure, as shown in (28D), into something more like (28S).

(34) [(28D)] [$_S$[$_{NP}$ she] [$_{Aux}$ *past* can have-en-be-ing] [$_{VP}$ fly]]

(35) [(28S)] [$_S$ [$_{NP}$ she] [$_{Aux}$ can-*past* have be-en] [$_{VP}$ fly-ing]]

So we can describe (28) as a generable string that corresponds, via slight grammatical detour, to a thought whose complex Copula links a Subject to a Predicate. Similar remarks apply to (29),

(36)   she flew
    D [$_S$ [$_{NP}$ she] [$_{Aux}$ *past*] [$_{VP}$ fly]]
    S [$_S$ [$_{NP}$ she] [$_{Aux}$] [$_{VP}$ fly-*past*]]

and to (30), given Chomsky's (1957) proposal about 'do' supporting the tense morpheme.

(37)   she did fly
    D [$_S$ [$_{NP}$ she] [$_{Aux}$ *past*] [$_{VP}$ fly]]
    S [$_S$ [$_{NP}$ she] [$_{Aux}$ do-*past*] [$_{VP}$ fly]]

As Chomsky notes, further computation is required to convert Surface Structures into phonemic sequences. More importantly, and as one would expect from the quote above, he treats negation as a transformation: a rule, in this case optional, that converts (29D) into a negated form—she *past*+n't fly—which is converted to (31) via "Do-Support" and morphology (p. 62).

(38) she didn't fly

In this way, we can also describe (31) and (32)

(39) she couldn't have been flying

as generable strings that correspond to Subject-Copula-Predicate thoughts.[10] This is independently interesting because natural language negation doesn't seem to be a prefix that attaches to complete sentences, much less an expression of the Fregean type <t, t>; see Horn (1989) for extended discussion. We can't use (33) to express the thought we can voice with (34).

(40) not she flew

(41) it isn't the case that she flew

Morphemes that signify negation seem to be interwoven with tense and modal auxiliaries, as Aristotle suggested; though as he observed, this leads to puzzles. For example, (35)

(42) Socrates may not speak

can be used to say that it is impermissible for Socrates to speak. We still don't know why.

4 Rules and Reference

Thinking of negation as an optional transformation invites appeal to Chomsky's (1957, p. 45) distinction between the *kernel* of a language, as specified by some grammar G—viz., the set of sentences generated by applying obligatory transformations to the terminal strings of the phrase-structure component of G—and the other sentences generated by G. And if grammars support this distinction, one shouldn't assume that theories of meaning ignore it.

In specifying how strings are understood relative to a grammatical analysis, we may well posit lexical meanings and combinatorial operations that categori-

---

[10] In a different idiom, one might describe *n't* as a functional element that is attracted to tense—see Laka (1994)—with the result that in (31), *n't* blocks tense from hopping further to the right, thus triggering Do-Support; cp. (29).

cally determine many phrasal meanings that correspond to nodes of collapsed PS-trees. But we may also be led to posit various syncategorematic operations—akin to Tarski's (1933; 1944) treatments of negation, connectives, and quantifiers—that convert one meaning into another, in accord with a rule, but not via composition in any interesting sense.[11] In particular, one can imagine rules according to which each instance of NP-Aux-VP has a meaning that is determined by (i) the meanings of the constituent NP and VP, and (ii) the particular connector, which may comprise two or more auxiliary elements; where (ii) need not have a meaning that is determined, node by node, relative to the corresponding equivalence class of derivations. Other things equal, one might want grammars that "minimize mismatches" among meanings, derivations, and pronunciations; see Barker and Jacobson (2007). But other desiderata bear on the questions Chomsky highlighted.

Let me stress that describing expressions as strings (relative to analyses) leaves room for the idea that meanings and/or pronunciations are structured things, perhaps generated via simple operations that don't involve transformations; see Idsardi (forthcoming), Pietroski (forthcoming). In particular, a syntactician can treat equivalence classes of derivations as proxies for meanings, while thinking that psychologically realized grammars connect phonemic strings with structured meanings of some kind. But it is far from the spirit of Chomsky (1957) to suppose that grammars generate labeled phrase markers that await interpretation, like the well-formed formulae of an invented formal language. The idea was not that grammars generate uninterpreted syntactic structures, but rather, that humans enjoy a grammatical competence that lets us connect meanings with pronunciations in (autonomous) ways.[12]

Correlatively, as Chomsky (1957, pp. 103–4) emphasized,

---

[11] Cp. Chomsky's discussion of 'and' on pp. 35–36, and his similar formulation of a rule concerning 'Aux' on p. 43.

[12] In describing his efforts to characterize the syntax of English, Chomsky spoke of "studying language as an instrument or a tool, attempting to describe its structure with no explicit reference to the way in which this instrument is put to use." His motivation "for this self-imposed formality requirement for grammars" is that "there seems to be no other basis that will yield a rigorous, effective, and revealing theory of linguistic structure." Though as he immediately stressed, the formality requirement is "perfectly compatible with the desire to formulate it in such a way as to have suggestive and significant interconnections with a parallel semantic theory (p.103)." Moreover, even if one rejects Chomsky's empirically motivated reasons for his formality requirement, violating it raises questions about how else one can distinguish psychologically realized grammars from all the other aspects of human cognition that influence the use of linguistic expressions.

> To understand a sentence we must know much more than the analysis of this sentence on each linguistic level. We must also know the reference and meaning of the morphemes or words of which it is composed; naturally, grammar cannot be expected to be of much help here. These notions form the subject matter for semantics.

And in a footnote attached to the word 'meaning', Chomsky cites Goodman (1949, 1953).

> Goodman has argued—to my mind, quite convincingly—that the notion of meaning of words can at least in part be reduced to that of reference of expressions containing these words. … Goodman's approach amounts to reformulating a part of the theory of meaning in the much clearer terms of the theory of reference, just as much of our discussion can be understood as suggesting a reformulation of parts of the theory of meaning that deal with so-called "structural meaning" in terms of the completely nonsemantic theory of grammatical structure. Part of the difficulty with the theory of meaning is that "meaning" tends to be used as a catch-all term to include every aspect of language that we know very little about. Insofar as this is correct, we can expect various aspects of this theory to be claimed by other approaches to language in the course of their development.

Chomsky assumed that his professional readers would know about Goodman's work, or follow the citations to it, and recognize that the intended notion of reference was not Russell's (1912) notion of denotation or Frege's (1892b) notion of *Bedeutung*. But given that appeals to denotational "semantic values" have become standard, it may be useful to recall the context—Cambridge Mass. in the 1950s—along with Goodman's main point and his central example.

Goodman assumed that (a) linguistic expressions have interpretations of some kind, but (b) our ordinary notions of meaning are not themselves suitable for use in scientific theories, and (c) simply identifying interpretations/meanings with denotations/extensions is not the way forward. The suggestion was to develop a notion of reference condition such that expressions with the same reference condition—i.e., expressions that impose the same conditions on acts of reference (or predication) across constructions—could be said to have the same meaning, at least to a first approximation that could serve tolerably well in theories of linguistic understanding. Today, the project of "reconstructing" talk of meanings might seem quaint. But fads change.

Prior to Tarski (1933, 1944), one might have thought that *any* substantive notion of "interpretation" will be too vague and interest-relative to do duty in a scientific theory. Given Tarski's discussion of truth, however, matters became quite unclear with regard to meaning. On the one hand, there was pressure to eschew notions of meaning in favor of extensional notions, which apply to whatever things they apply to regardless of how those things are described or depicted in thought; see, e.g., Quine (1951, 1953). On the other hand, one might think that

Tarski showed how at least one commonsense notion of interpretation could be regimented and put to use in a fruitful way.[13]

Goodman offered a proposal for how to replace ordinary notions of meaning with a substitute that was in one sense extensional—without insisting that each word has an extension that is the word's meaning, and hence that 'Hesperus' and 'Phosphorus' are synonymous, along with 'unicorn' and 'centaur'. For Goodman, it was clear that 'unicorn' and 'centaur' have different meanings. The challenge was to defend this truism from skeptical attack without relying on intuitions regarding a vague and interest-relative (or objectionably mentalistic) notion of meaning. The idea was that even a tough-minded physicalist can agree that there are pictures of unicorns, and spatially distinct pictures of centaurs, and hence that the class of unicorn-pictures differs from the class of centaur-pictures. Similarly, Goodman claimed, one need not posit any mythical beasts to distinguish descriptions of unicorns from descriptions of centaurs. But if 'depiction of a unicorn' and 'depiction of a centaur' have different extensions, one can say that 'unicorn' and 'centaur' have different reference conditions—despite having the same (null) extension—because they appear as *constituents* of expressions that have different extensions.

This suggestion exploits a familiar idea in reverse. One might think that the phrases 'creature with a heart' and 'creature with a kidney' have different meanings because they have constituents that have different meanings. Even an extensionalist can agree that 'heart' and 'kidney' differ semantically. Of course, a certain kind of extensionalist might also think that the extension of a phrase is determined by the extensions of the constituent words, given the phrasal syntax. But one can relax this "bottom up" conception of how reference conditions are determined, in favor of a more holistic conception, as suggested by Frege's (1892a; 1892b) notion of abstraction and his claim that words signify things only in sentential contexts.

Suppose you learn that 'picture of a unicorn' and 'picture of a centaur' have different extensions. If you assume that meanings determine extensions, you can conclude that 'unicorn' and 'centaur' have different meanings, and use what you've learned in figuring out what the words mean. This doesn't imply that meaning is reference. But if two expressions are extensionally equivalent across

---

13 Davidson (1967) offered a partly reconstructive proposal that explicitly tied linguistic meaning to Tarski's notion of truth. This sparked objections and illuminating discussions; see, e.g., Davies (1981); Dummett (1976); Evans and McDowell (1976); Foster (1976); Harman (1974). But before this boom, there was even less clarity about a range of questions concerning whether meaningful expressions have meanings, how sentence meanings are related to word meanings, and how meaning is related to understanding, thought, truth, reference, use, etc.

all linguistic contexts (including 'description of a ...') for which sameness of extension can be determined, then in an important sense, the expressions are semantically equivalent. In short, Goodman treated "global" sameness of reference as a proxy for sameness of meaning. Or abbreviating further, "same reference, same meaning."

However, Chomsky's appeal to Goodman figured as one part of a far more interesting proposal: a theory of understanding is a theory of syntax *supplemented* by an account of reference conditions for generable expressions. So in the end, Chomsky's (1957) proposed proxies for meanings were multi-leveled syntactic analyses together with specifications (not yet provided) of reference conditions. But he didn't assume that generable phrases have extensions that are determined by the extensions of their lexical constituents. And as discussed above, in the context of syncategoremata, he avoided assumptions about how meanings can combine. So especially in light of Chomsky's (1977; 1995b; 2000b) discussions of reference—including the many ways in which words like 'water', 'river', and 'London' can be used—we shouldn't read his early references to Goodman as suggesting that ordinary words have classical extensions that somehow determine truth conditions for sentences.[14]

Chomsky (1977) returned to these issues, discussing examples like (36) and (37).

(43) beavers are mammals

(44) beavers build dams

Intuitively, (36) implies that *all* beavers are mammals, while (37) implies only that *typical* beavers—in the wild, with suitable resources and able to express their beaverish nature—build dams. Moreover, (37) differs in meaning from the passive (38),

(45) dams are built by beavers

which falsely implies that typical dams are built by beavers; cp. (39) and the equivalent (40).

---

[14] The conditions imposed by ordinary words on human acts of reference are context sensitive in many ways, as suggested by Wittgenstein (1953), Austin (1961, 1962) and Strawson (1950). See Travis (2008), McGilvray (1991, 1999), Stainton (2008), and Pietroski (2017c) for discussion. Though despite this complexity, grammar can impose formal constraints on coreference (i.e., anaphoric dependence); see, e.g., Chomsky (1986).

(46) beavers built this dam

(47) this dam was built by beavers

Or consider (41) and (42),

(48) poems are written by fools like me

(49) mountains are climbed by fools like me

which imply that all poems are written by fools, but not that all mountains are climbed by fools. While there are systematic form-meaning correspondences that reflect details of lexical meanings, the relevant notion(s) of composition remain unclear.

> Global properties of the sentence, which may be quite involved, seem to play a role. We cannot simply assign a meaning to the subject and a meaning to the predicate (or to a sentence form with a variable standing for the subject), and then combine the two. Rather, the meaning assigned to each phrase depends on the form of the phrase with which it is paired (Chomsky (1977, p, 31).

Chomsky (1957) was already stressing that correlations between grammatical forms and stable features of the environment (including language-independent thoughts) are imperfect. But the "correspondences between formal and semantic features cannot be ignored." They should be studied "in some more general theory of language that will include a theory of linguistic form and a theory of the use of language as subparts (p. 102)." Indeed, he concludes *Syntactic Structures* with a cautiously optimistic remark about semantics.

> Description of meaning can profitably refer to this underlying syntactic framework, although systematic semantic considerations are apparently not helpful in determining it in the first place. The notion of "structural meaning" as opposed to "lexical meaning", however, appears to be quite suspect, and it is questionable that the grammatical devices available in language are used consistently enough so that meaning can be assigned to them directly. Nevertheless, we do find many important correlations, quite naturally, between syntactic structure and meaning; or, to put it differently, we find that the grammatical devices are used quite systematically. These correlations could form part of the subject matter for a more general theory of language concerned with syntax and semantics and their points of connection (p.108).

5 Recap

Chomsky (1957) offered a program for developing theories of understanding—and in that sense, theories of meaning for human languages—that combine formal theories of syntax with proposals regarding what competent speakers know about how expressions can/cannot be used, especially in acts of reference. He envisioned studies of form and meaning that developed in tandem. The phenomenon of constructional homonymity played a key role in formulating and testing his claims about how humans generate linguistic expressions. And in the final chapter, "Syntax and Semantics," he summarized the previous discussion as follows.

> We have now found cases of sentences that are understood in more than one way and are ambiguously represented on the transformational level (though not on other levels) and cases of sentences that are understood in a similar manner and are similarly represented on the transformational level alone. This gives an independent justification and motivation for description of language in terms of transformational structure, and for the establishment of transformational representation as a linguistic level with the same fundamental character as other levels. Furthermore it adds force to the suggestion that the process of "understanding a sentence" can be explained in part in terms of the notion of linguistic level. In particular, in order to understand a sentence it is necessary to know the kernel sentences from which it originates (more precisely, the terminal strings underlying these kernel sentences) and the phrase structure of each of these elementary components, as well as the transformational history of development of the given sentence from these kernel sentences (p.92).

From a contemporary perspective dominated by model theory and truth-theoretic conceptions of meaning, it can be tempting to view Chomsky's contributions to semantics more narrowly—i.e., as an initial specification of the expressions whose semantic properties are to be specified by some other algorithm that pairs sentences (relative to analyses) with representations of truth conditions. But Davidson's (1967) bold conjecture was never the only game in town. Chomsky (1957) had already offered a sophisticated proposal, motivated by his sense that

> There is no aspect of linguistic study more subject to confusion and more in need of clear and careful formulation than that which deals with the points of connection between syntax and semantics (p.93).

Bibliography

Austin, John. 1961. *Philosophical Papers*. Oxford, UK: Oxford University Press.
Austin, John. 1962. *How to Do Things with Words*. Oxford, UK: Oxford University Press.

Barker, Chris, and Pauline I. Jacobson. 2007. *Direct Compositionality*. Oxford, UK: Oxford University Press.

Berwick, Robert C, Paul Pietroski, Beracah Yankama, and Noam Chomsky. 2011. Poverty of the stimulus revisited. *Cognitive Science* 35:1207–1242.

Chomsky, Noam. 1957. *Syntactic Structures*. The Hague, The Netherlands: Mouton de Gruyter.

Chomsky, Noam. 1964. *Current Issues in Linguistic Theory*. The Hague: Mouton.

Chomsky, Noam. 1965. *Aspects of the Theory of Syntax*. Cambridge, MA: MIT Press.

Chomsky, Noam. 1977. *Essays on Form and Interpretation*. New York, NY: North Holland.

Chomsky, Noam. 1986. *Knowledge of Language*. New York, NY: Praeger.

Chomsky, Noam. 1995a. *The Minimalist Program*. Cambridge, MA: MIT Press.

Chomsky, Noam. 1995b. Language and Nature. *Mind* 104:1–61.

Chomsky, Noam. 2000a. Minimalist Inquiries. In *Step by step: Essays on minimalist syntax in honor of Howard Lasnik*, ed. Roger Andrew Martin, David Michaels, and Juan Uriagereka. MIT Press.

Chomsky, Noam. 2000b. *New Horizons in the Study of Language and Mind*. Cambridge, UK: Cambridge University Press.

Chomsky, Noam. 2017. The Galilean Challenge. *Inference* 3.

Church, Alonzo. 1941. *The Calculi of Lambda Conversion*. Princeton, NJ: Princeton University Press.

Davidson, Donald. 1967. Truth and Meaning. *synthese* 17:304–323.

Davies, Martin. 1981. Meaning, structure and understanding. *Synthese* 48:135–161.

Dummett, Michael. 1976. What Is a Theory of Meaning? In *Truth and Meaning: Essays in Semantics*, ed. Gareth Evans and John McDowell. Oxford, UK: Clarendon.

Evans, Gareth, and John McDowell, ed. 1976. *Truth and Meaning*. Oxord, UK: Oxford University Press.

Foster, John. 1976. Meaning and Truth Theory. In *Truth and Meaning*, ed. Gareth Evans and John McDowell. Oxord, UK: Oxford University Press.

Frege, Gottlob. 1892a. Function and Concept. In *Translations from the Philosophical Writings of Gottlob Frege*, ed. Peter Geach and Max Black. Oxford, UK: Blackwell.

Frege, Gottlob. 1892b. On Sense and Reference. In *Translations from the Philosophical Writings of Gottlob Frege*, ed. Peter Geach and Max Black. Oxford, UK: Blackwell.

Goodman, Nelson. 1949. On Likeness of Meaning. *Analysis* 10:1–7.

Goodman, Nelson. 1951. *The Structure of Appearance*. Cambridge, MA: Harvard University Press.

Goodman, Nelson. 1953. On some differences about meaning. *Analysis* 13:90–96.

Harman, Gilbert. 1974. Meaning and Semantics. In *Semantics and Philosophy*, ed. K. Munitz and P. Unger, 1–16. New York, NY: New York University Press.

Higginbotham, James. 1983. The logic of perceptual reports: An extensional alternative to situation semantics. *The Journal of Philosophy* 80:100–127.

Higginbotham, James. 1985. On Semantics. *Linguistic inquiry* 16:547–593.

Horn, Laurence. 1989. *A natural history of negation*. Chicago, IL: Chicago University Press.

Idsardi, William. forthcoming. Why is Phonology Different? No Recursion. In Martin and Gallego, eds.

Katz, Jerrold, and Paul Martin Postal. 1964. *An Integrated Theory of Lingquistic Descriptions*. Cambridge, MA: MIT Press.

Katz, Jerrold J., and Jerry A. Fodor. 1963. The structure of a semantic theory. *Language* 39:170–210.

Laka, Itziar. 1994. *On the syntax of negation*. New York, NY: Garland.
Lasnik, Howard. 1999. *Minimalist Analysis*. Oxford, UK: Blackwell.
Lasnik, Howard, and Joseph J Kupin. 1977. A restrictive theory of transformational grammar. *Theoretical Linguistics* 4:173–196.
Lepore, Ernest. 1983. What Model-Theoretic Semantics Cannot Do. *Synthese* 54:167–187.
Lewis, David. 1970. General semantics. *Synthese* 22:18–67.
Lewis, David. 1975. Languages and Language. In *Minnesota Studies in the Philosophy of Science*, ed. K. Gunderson, volume 7. Minneapolis, MN: University of Minnesota Press.
May, Robert. 1985. *Logical Form: Its structure and derivation*. Cambridge, MA: MIT Press.
McGilvray, James A. 1991. *Tense, Reference, and Worldmaking*. McGill-Queen's Press.
McGilvray, James A. 1999. *Chomsky: Language, Mind and Politics*. Cambridge, UK: Polity Press.
Montague, Richard. 1970. Universal grammar. *Theoria* 36:373–398.
Pesetsky, David. 1995. *Zero Syntax*. Cambridge, MA: MIT Press.
Pietroski, Paul. 2017abc. Semantic Internalism. In *The Cambridge Companion to Chomsky*, ed. J McGilvray, 196–216. Cambridge, UK: Cambridge University Press.
Pietroski, Paul. 2017b. Semantic Typology and Composition. In *The Science of Meaning*, ed. B. Rabern and D. Ball. Oxford, UK: Oxford University Press.
Pietroski, Paul. 2017c. *Conjoining Meanings: Semantics without Truth Values*. Oxford, UK: Oxford University Press.
Pietroski, Paul. forthcoming. Limiting Semantic Types. In Martin and Gallego, eds.
Quine, Willard Van Orman. 1951. Two Dogmas of Empiricism. *Philosophical Review* 60:20–43.
Quine, Willard Van Orman. 1953. *From a Logical Point of View*. Cambridge, MA: Harvard University Press.
Ross, John Robert. 1967. Constraints on variables in syntax. Doctoral Dissertation, MIT, Cambridge, MA. Published as *Infinite Syntax!* Norwood, N.J.: Ablex (1986).
Russell, Bertrand. 1905. On denoting. *Mind* 14:479–93.
Russell, Bertrand. 1912. *The Problems of Philosophy*. London, UK: Butterworth.
Russell, Bertrand. 1957. Mr. Strawson on Referring. *Mind* 66:385–89.
Stainton, Robert. 2008. Meaning and Reference: Some Chomskyan Themes. In *Oxford Handbook of Philosophy of Language*, ed. Ernest Lepore and Barry C. Smith. Oxford, UK: Oxford University Press.
Strawson, Peter F. 1950. On referring. *Mind* 59:320–344.
Tarski, Alfred. 1933. The Concept of Truth in Formalized Languages. In *Logic, Semantics and Metamathematics*, ed. John. Corcoran. Indianapolis, IN: Hackett, 2 edition.
Tarski, Alfred. 1944. The Semantic Conception of Truth. *Philosophy and Phenomenological Research* 4:341–75.
Travis, Charles. 2008. *Occasion-sensitivity: Selected essays*. Oxford, UK: Oxford University Press.
Turing, Alan. 1936. On Computable Numbers with an Application to the Entscheidungs problem. In *Proceedings of the London Mathematical Society 2*, volume 42, 230–265.
Wittgenstein, Ludwig. 1953. *Philosophical Investigations*. New York, NY: MacMillan.

Omer Preminger
Back to the Future: Non-generation, filtration, and the heartbreak of interface-driven minimalism

1 Introduction

This paper argues that the filtration-based approach to syntactic competence adopted in the context of minimalist syntax (Chomsky 1995, 2000, 2001), where freely-assembled syntactic outputs are filtered at the interfaces with the sensori-motor (SM) and conceptual-intentional (C-I) systems, is empirically wrong. The solution, I argue, is a return to a non-generation alternative, of the kind put forth in *Syntactic Structures* (Chomsky 1957).

2 The beginning: non-generation as the only source of ill-formedness in syntax

Early on in *Syntactic Structures*, Chomsky proposes a *generative* way to think about the grammar of a given language:[1]

> The fundamental aim in the linguistic analysis of a language L is to separate the grammatical sequences which are the sentences of L from the ungrammatical sequences which are not sentences of L and to study the structure of the grammatical sequences. The grammar of L will thus be a device that generates all of the grammatical sequences of L and none of the ungrammatical ones.
>
> *[Chomsky 1957:13]*

This way of thinking about language and grammar laid the groundwork for serious inquiry into that which was systematically absent: patterns and structures

---

[1] This way of framing things, and in particular the implied bifurcation of sentences into exactly two categories (grammatical and ungrammatical), has come under a variety of criticisms in the decades since. But virtually all such criticisms conflate *performance* with *competence*—and, more generally, fall into the trap of inferring gradient representations from gradient behavior. This, as already demonstrated in Armstrong et al. 1983, is by no means guaranteed to be a valid inference.

that could have, logically speaking, been part of natural language, but which are systematically excluded from it. Perhaps the greatest and most seminal example of such work, in the wake of *Syntactic Structures*, was Ross' 1967 study on kinds of movement dependencies that are systematically excluded from language.

This way of characterizing the goals of a grammatical theory brings into focus the question of how those outputs which we want the grammar to never generate (i.e., ungrammatical ones) are excluded by the generative procedure.

In *Syntactic Structures*, the answer to this question was *non-generation*. There were two sub-cases worth noting. First, some outputs were excluded because the phrase-structure component did not contain the relevant rewrite rules necessary to generate them. More precisely, the phrase-structure component did not contain rewrite rules that could produce anything that could be related to the output in question by the extant transformations in the grammar of L. For example, the absence of rewrite rules that could be combined to yield the effect in (1a) underpinned the fact that (1b) is not generated by the grammar. (The phrase-structure symbol 'T' corresponds to what we would now call 'D' or 'Det'.)

(1)   a.   *unavailable*: S → ... → N N T P
        b.   * convection legume the of.

There is a second way in which the generative procedure used in Chomsky (1957) could exclude a particular output. This is when the phrase-structure component produced something that could, in principle, be related to the output in question by the extant transformations in the grammar of L, but the STRUCTURAL DESCRIPTION was not met for one or more of the transformations in question.[2] For example, the output in (2a) was generable by the phrase-structure component of the grammar of English. And there was a transformation (an obligatory one, in fact) of the form in (2b) (p. 112). But because (2a) did not meet the STRUCTURAL DESCRIPTION for (2b) (shown in (2c)), the output in (2d) could not be generated by the grammar.[3]

---

2 In *Syntactic Structures*, Chomsky uses the term STRUCTURAL ANALYSIS (76, 111, *i.a.*), rather than the now more familiar STRUCTURAL DESCRIPTION.

3 Technically, this is only part of the explanation for (2d) not being generated by the grammar. Another necessary part of the explanation is that (2d) cannot be related to (2a)—nor to any other possible output of the phrase-structure component—by any other, applicable transformation (or series of applicable transformations).

(2) a. John — C — see – stars
 b. $X_1 - X_2 - X_3 - X_4 \to X_1 - X_2 - X_4 - X_3$
 c. STRUCTURAL DESCRIPTION for (b): $\left\{ \begin{array}{l} X - V_1 - Prt - Pronoun \\ X - V_2 - Comp - NP \end{array} \right\}$
 d. *John stars see.

For close to two decades, even as the theory of syntax developed, non-generation remained the primary mode of excluding ungrammatical outputs. Ross' (1967) findings, for example, were integrated into the theory of grammar by Chomsky (1973) (in the aptly-named *Conditions on Transformations*) through the mechanism of *Subjacency*, whose function was to restrict possible rule applications. In particular, an extraction rule could not relate two positions separated by more than one *cyclic* node (NP, S). Accordingly, an output like (3) was not ruled out because it violated some output filter. It was ruled out because the only way to derive it (given the assumptions in Chomsky 1973) involved the application of the wh-Movement transformation across two cyclic nodes at once (Chomsky 1973:23ff.).

(3)   * Who does she believe [NP the claim [S that John saw ___]]

More succinctly, (3) was excluded because the grammar—beholden, as it was, to the Subjacency constraint—had no way of generating this kind of structure.

At this stage in the theory's development, there was a concerted attempt, at least in some circles, to restrict the possible sources of syntactic ill-formedness to non-generation alone. As an example, see Baker & Brame's (1972) position in the *Global Rules* debate (Baker and Brame, 1972; Lakoff, 1970, 1972). But a sea change was coming: soon thereafter, Chomsky and Lasnik (1977) *Filters and Control* ushered in the golden era of filtration, which I discuss in the next section.

3 The rise of filtration

Chomsky and Lasnik (1977) influential study centered on a series of environments in which overt noun phrases are unable to occur in English.[4] These environments, however, did not readily lend themselves to a non-generation account, at least

---

4 In the years since, it has become quite clear that most languages do not manifest anything resembling this set of restrictions. It may very well be the case that, in the end, the phenomenon in question is a fairly marginal one, restricted to a small group of Western European languages.

not against the backdrop of the syntactic theory of the time. Instead of non-generation, Chomsky & Lasnik adopt Perlmutter's (1968; 1971) proposal that the generative mechanism includes a set of *Surface Filters*. These are constraints that potential outputs of the generative procedure must meet before those outputs can be deemed well-formed.

Of the filters that Chomsky & Lasnik proposed, the one that had perhaps the greatest influence on the field is the *[NP to VP] filter, whose full form is given in (4):

(4) THE NON-FINITE SUBJECT FILTER
* [$_\alpha$ NP to VP], unless α is adjacent to and in the domain of a verb or *for*.
[Chomsky & Lasnik 1977:479]

Upon reading a draft of Chomsky & Lasnik's paper, Jean-Roger Vergnaud wrote a letter to the authors. In this letter, he suggests that a filter like (4) could actually be subsumed under Case, a mechanism inspired by the different forms that noun phrases take on depending on the different positions in which they occur (in some languages). This suggestion was itself very influential, and within a few years, took hold in the form of the *Case Filter*, given in (5):

(5) THE CASE FILTER
* NP, if NP has phonetic content and has no Case
[Chomsky 1981:49]

This shift, whereby ungrammatical outcomes were increasingly excluded through filters rather than non-generation, did not take place in a vacuum. The rise of filters was intertwined with a concomitant effort to simplify the form of transformations, culminating in the unification of all movement transformations under a single rule, Move-α:

(6) THE TRANSFORMATION *Move-α*
Move some category α to some position
[Chomsky 1980:3–4, see also Chomsky 1981]

With this unification, the STRUCTURAL DESCRIPTIONS and STRUCTURAL CHANGES of movement transformations were eliminated altogether. They were replaced with a single, freely applying, fully general movement transformation (6), whose application was constrained only by the requirement that the eventual output comply with Surface Filters of the kind exemplified in (4)/(5).

If the formal complexity of transformations was to be simplified in this manner, it seems rather inescapable that much of the explanatory burden would have to be offloaded to filters. Inevitably, then, the developments touched on here ushered in what might be thought of as the *golden era of filtration*. Many subsequent proposals were widely adopted that made crucial reference to filters as the source of syntactic ill-formedness. Alongside the Case Filter (5), there emerged the Empty Category Principle (ECP; Chomsky 1981:248); the principles of Binding Theory, now construed as filters (Chomsky 1981:188ff. cf. Lees and Klima 1963 for an early, non-generation approach to binding); the Theta Criterion (Chomsky 1981:36); and others.

A crucial question is whether the choice to parcel out explanatory burden this way can be adjudicated empirically—and if so, what the empirical verdict is. It is this question that I will tackle in section 5. But before that, let us survey some of the more recent history of non-generation and filtration in syntactic theory.

4 Non-generation and filtration in contemporary syntactic theory

In the wake of Chomsky's (1995) *The Minimalist Program*, the trend towards a filtration-based theory became reified in the grammatical architecture. To see why, consider Chomsky's (2004:106) Strong Minimalist Thesis (SMT):

(7) POSSIBLE SOURCES OF PROPERTIES OF NATURAL LANGUAGE SYNTAX
  i. factors specific to natural language
  ii. interface conditions: properties imposed by the very fact that syntax is connected to sensorimotor (SM) and conceptual-intentional (C-I) cognitive systems
  iii. general properties (of cognition, or of the physical world more generally)

(8) THE STRONG MINIMALIST THESIS
  There are no properties that fall under (7i).

The SMT is the assumption that there are no proprietary characteristics of syntax, whose etiology is specific to natural language (besides the basic combinatorial operation, *Merge*). If we assume—as do most scholars working in this research tradition—that syntax is modularly encapsulated from other cognitive systems, then the sensorimotor (SM) and conceptual-intentional (C-I) systems cannot exert their influence in the form of non-generation. Instead, these systems must exert their influence by way of filtration, scrutinizing the structure that syntax has built and checking whether it meets the relevant well-formedness criteria at the interfaces.

On this view, the freely-applying nature of Move-α, now recast as freely-applying *Merge*, is no longer a theoretical choice-point. It is forced by the very architecture of the system. An operation that could not apply freely, and instead had linguistically-proprietary conditions on its application, would constitute a violation of (8).[5]

Note that, technically speaking, what is submitted to the interfaces for filtration need not be the putative syntactic structure of the utterance in its entirety. On a view where syntactic structure is shipped to the interfaces in chunks such as *phases* (Chomsky, 2004; Uriagereka, 1999), the evaluation of well-formedness can apply to each chunk separately. At the limit, if the chunks are the size of individual syntactic projections (cf. Müller 2004), this dissolves the distinction between non-generation and filtration entirely (as well as, arguably, the modular encapsulation of syntax in the first place). However, for the purposes of the current paper, I will assume that syntax is capable of building a non-trivial amount of structure before the result is inspected by extra-syntactic systems.

Having said all this, and despite the aforementioned architectural commitments, it turns out that minimalist syntax still harbors a significant residue of non-generation, in the form of so-called economy principles. As an example, consider minimality effects. These are scenarios of the kind schematized in (9), where there are two putative targets for some syntactic relation, which stand in an asymmetric c-command relation to one another. As observed by Rizzi (1990), syntax quite generally disallows relations that target the (structurally) farther away of the two putative targets in such cases.

(9) If α ≫ β,γ; β ≫ γ; and β and γ are both putative targets for α:
     [where '≫' denotes asymmetric c-command]
  a. α ... β ... γ
  b. *α ... β ... γ

---

[5] In this light, appeals to syntactically proprietary principles like *Greed* in earlier versions of minimalism (Chomsky, 1995, 2000) are very much in violation of (8). The only hope would be to derive principles of this sort from so-called economy considerations, but the prospects for such a derivation seem to me to be very bleak; see the discussion below.

It seems unlikely that configurations like (9b) are ruled out because of some incompatibility with the SM or C-I systems. There is some promissory discussion in Chomsky 1995 *et seq.*, suggesting that restrictions like (9) might ultimately derive from more general principles of efficient computation, which are not specific to language (see, e.g., Chomsky 2000:135). Promissory discussion aside, I know of no explicit proposal that would tell us why (9) is an attested restriction, but a myriad of other restrictions—which could just as easily be tied to efficient computation in the same vague manner—are not. Pending such explication, I see no other concrete option than to treat the ill-formedness of configurations like (9b) as an instance of non-generation *per se*.

The state of affairs with respect to other so-called economy principles seems similar. Chomsky (2001) cites efficient computation as the explanation behind a particular reformulation of Pesetsky's (1989) *Earliness Principle*, given in (10).

(10)   Perform computations as quickly as possible.   [*Chomsky 2001:15*]

To see just how tenuous the argument from efficient computation to (10) is, one needs to look no further than Chomsky 2008, where the same premises are used to argue for a conclusion that stands in direct contradiction to (10):

(11)   Operations are at the phase level only.   [*Chomsky 2008:156*]

Clearly, whatever overtures to efficient computation are made in these works, according them the status of 'explanations' would be very misleading. Thus, to the extent that there are any derivations that are ruled out by (10) or by (11) (see Chomsky 2001 and Chomsky 2008, respectively, for some putative examples), these must also be taken for the time being as instances of non-generation.[6]

The examples in (9) and in (10–11) are important for the following reason: one could attempt to mount an argument against non-generation on the grounds that a theory resorting to filtration alone would be more uniform, and thus simpler. (In the context of minimalism, this would depend on the extra step of showing that the filters in question fall under (7ii), i.e., that they are good candidates to be something that the SM & C-I systems would care about; see the discussion in §5.1.) What these examples show is that, at the present time, no extant theory can seriously claim to be uniformly filtration-based, and free of non-generation as a

---

[6] This discussion is not meant to add support to one of (10–11) over the other. It is merely a demonstration that, in the context of a theory of syntactic competence, the current understanding of efficient computation and related concepts appears to be an insufficient basis upon which to build argumentation of this sort.

mechanism for excluding ungrammatical outcomes. This sets the stage for investigating the choice between these two mechanisms from an *empirical* perspective. It is this type of investigation that is the topic of the next section.

5 The case against filtration-based minimalism

5.1 Some background

There is not—and cannot be—an empirical argument against filtration in its most general form. That is because one can always enrich the syntactic representation using devices like traces, indices, etc., to the point that any relevant aspect of a structure's derivational history can be read directly off of the final representation. Given a sufficiently enriched representation, then, any effect of non-generation can be recast as a filter on the occurrence of the relevant history-encoding devices.[7] Accordingly, the arguments in the remainder of this section are not about filtration in general, but rather about a particular filtration-based approach: the one that has been put forth in the context of minimalist syntax. The approach in question involves "free generation" by the syntactic component, which then submits its putative output to filtration at the interfaces with the SM & C-I systems.

The arguments rest on the following two premises:

(12) **PREMISE 1**: A filter on the output of syntax imposed by some system S must be statable in a plausible manner using the primitives of S.

(13) **PREMISE 2**: Both agreement in ϕ-features[8] ("ϕ-agreement") and configurationally-assigned case ("m-case") are computed within syntax proper.

---

[7] A variant of this argument can be applied to the relation between derivational approaches to syntactic competence and representational ones. Any derivational approach can be recast in representational terms by, for example, taking the set of licit derivational operations in the former model, and recasting them as representational well-formedness conditions on adjacent pairs of syntactic trees in an ordered sequence. (Each individual tree in this ordered-sequence model would correspond to an intermediate derivational step in the derivational model.) Thus, if one places zero restrictions on what syntactic representations might look like (e.g. n-tuples of syntactic trees), then—somewhat unsurprisingly—there is nothing that cannot be modeled in representational terms.

[8] The term 'ϕ-features' is shorthand for "a non-empty subset of {PERSON, NUMBER, GENDER/NOUN-CLASS}."

Premise (12) amounts to the assumption that different cognitive modules traffic in different informational primitives. Insofar as the SM & C-I systems are modularly distinct from syntax—which, it seems to me, is a fairly innocuous and widespread assumption—it would be quite the coincidence if the basic vocabulary of one or both of these distinct modules happened to be the same as the basic vocabulary of syntax. This premise still leaves room for filters that examine, for example, the featural content of a given syntactic node (this includes Chomsky's 2000, 2001 *uninterpretable features* proposal, though we will see shortly that this proposal fails for independent, empirical reasons). Some subset of syntactic features have effects on phonology and semantics, and are thus part of the vocabularies of the latter systems; filters stated over such features are therefore not problematic, from the perspective of (12). What this premise would exclude, for example, is a filter demanding that every node bearing some feature f stand in some syntactic relation to some other node bearing some particular featural specification. That is because syntactic relations are, by definition, the purview of syntax, not of other systems.

As for premise (13), this has been explicitly argued in Preminger 2014:177–213. In brief, the argument goes as follows. First, Bobaljik (2008) has shown that φ-agreement tracks m-case, rather than Abstract Case or grammatical function. Second, φ-agreement is causally implicated in movement to canonical subject position (at least in some languages; see Preminger 2014:157–170). Finally, since movement to canonical subject position is inescapably syntactic (it has effects on scope, for example), it follows that both m-case and φ-agreement must be in syntax, as well (contra Marantz 1991, McFadden 2004, as well as Bobaljik's own 2008 claim concerning the modular loci of the relevant operations).

5.2 Two arguments

In this subsection, I will review two arguments against the kind of filtration approach outlined above: one from φ-agreement, and one from m-case.

5.2.1 Argument 1: φ-agreement

The following discussion applies to a fairly broad range of theories—namely, any that enforce the obligatory nature of agreement using a condition evaluated at the interfaces. Nevertheless, a useful straw man to keep in mind throughout the current discussion is the *uninterpretable features* proposal of Chomsky (2000, 2001). According to Chomsky's proposal, some features are illegible at the interfaces with the SM & C-I systems. And, for some reason—which, as far as I can tell, is never really given—these extra-syntactic systems cannot simply ignore illegible features.[9] Instead, if such features reach the interfaces untouched, this results in a "crash" (i.e., ungrammaticality).

Let us adopt the following labels:

(14) i. H^0 = some head (e.g. a finite verb)
      ii. α = some phrase (e.g. a nominal/DP argument) whose features control agreement morphology on H^0

There is, by now, substantial evidence that φ-agreement is subject to the structural condition in (15) (see Preminger 2014; Preminger and Polinsky 2015 for a review):

(15) φ-AGREEMENT
      A head H^0 can enter into agreement in some φ-feature *f* with a DP α **only if**:
      i. H^0 c-commands α
      ii. H^0 and α are in the same locality domain
      iii. there is no bearer of valued *f* c-commanded by H^0 that asymmetrically c-commands α

Now, suppose that we observe an instance in which φ-agreement between some particular H^0 and some particular α appears to be obligatory (i.e., its absence yields ungrammaticality). By hypothesis, operations within syntax, such as agreement, are supposed to be freely-applying. Thus, derivations in which the relevant agreement relation has not obtained would have to be ruled out at (one or both of) the interfaces between syntax and the SM & C-I systems. The question, then, is how the SM & C-I systems could identify the offending derivations (i.e., those in which φ-agreement has failed to apply).

Following (12), evaluating whether a particular pair <H^0, α> satisfies (15) with respect to some φ-feature *f* is something only syntax can do. Giving the SM or C-I systems access to the primitives necessary to evaluate (15) would amount to undo-

---

[9] Norbert Hornstein (p.c.) suggests that the SM & C-I systems' inability to ignore illegible (or 'uninterpretable') features could be attributed to the principle of Full Interpretation. This principle demands that all syntactic material be interpreted, and could be used to rule out, e.g., sentences like *Who did Kim hug Sandy? But it is entirely unclear to me that we have any reason to think individual *features* should be subject to Full Interpretation. For example, it is unclear that the syntactic feature that prevents the English *hug* from undergoing *v*-to-T movement is interpreted anywhere outside of syntax.

ing the modular separation between syntax and the SM & C-I systems, in the first place (see §5.1)—especially as it concerns c-command-based minimality. Consequently, the most that the SM & C-I systems could do is inspect H^0 and/or α on their own. Not coincidentally, perhaps, both of these options have been pursued in the minimalist literature. The proposal that φ-features are 'uninterpretable' at the interfaces (Chomsky 2000, 2001) amounts to an "inspect H^0" approach. The proposal that abstract case is assigned as a side effect of agreement in φ-features (Chomsky 1995), coupled with the idea that noun phrases are subject to the Case Filter (Chomsky 1981), amounts to an "inspect α" approach.[10] As we will see below, however, neither of these options (nor a combination of the two) is empirically adequate.

The crucial evidence comes from patterns of omnivorous agreement in the K'ichean Agent-Focus construction.[11] There is much more to say about the syntax of K'ichean in general, and about the Agent-Focus construction in particular, than I am able to say in this space.[12] The crucial data, however, are given below:

(16) 3PL "WINS" OVER 3SG
    a. *ja   rje'   x-e/*φ-tz'et-ö   rja'*
        FOC them COM-**3pl/*3sg.ABS**-see-AF him
        'It was them who saw him.'
    b. *ja   rja'   x-e/*φ-tz'et-ö   rje'*
        FOC him COM-**3pl/*3sg.ABS**-see-AF them
        'It was him who saw them'

---

[10] The idea that case (whether abstract or otherwise) is assigned as a side effect of agreement has turned out to be wrong (see Bittner and Hale 1996; Bobaljik 2008; Preminger 2011a; Preminger, 2014 and, in particular, Preminger 2011b:929–930). But as we will see, the interface-driven approach to the obligatoriness of agreement fails even if we counterfactually grant this assumption.

[11] The term *omnivorous agreement* is due to Nevins (2011), and refers to patterns in which the appearance of a given agreement marker is triggered whenever a particular feature f is found on the subject or on the object (or both).

[12] For discussion of the syntax of K'ichean and of K'ichean Agent Focus, see Aissen (1999, 2011); Campbell (2000); Coon et al. (2014); Craig (1979); Davies and Sam-Colop (1990); Dayley (1978, 1985); Erlewine (2016); Henderson and Coon (to appear); López Ixcoy (1997); Mondloch (1981); Norman and Campbell (1978); Preminger (2014); Pye (1989); Sam-Colop (1988); Stiebels (2006).

(17) 1(/2) "WINS" OVER 3
    a. *ja   rat   x-**at**/****e***-ax-an   rje'*
       FOC you(sg.) COM-**2sg/*3pl.ABS**-hear-AF them
       'It was you(sg.) who heard them.'
    b. *ja   rje'   x-**at**/****e***-ax-an   rat*
       FOC them COM-**2sg/*3pl.ABS**-hear-AF you(sg.)
       'It was them who heard you(sg.).'

(18) OKAY TO HAVE TWO PLURALS, OKAY TO HAVE NO PLURALS
    a. *ja **röj** x-oj-tz'et-ö   rje'*
       FOC **us** COM-1pl.ABS-see-AF **them**
       'It was us who saw them'
    b. *ja ri **xoq**   x-ɸ-tz'et-ö   ri   achin*
       FOC **the woman** COM-3sg.ABS-see-AF **the man**
       'It was the woman who saw the man.'

Several prima facie candidates for an analysis of these facts can be ruled out. These include: **Multiple Agree** (Anagnostopoulou 2005; Hiraiwa 2001, 2004, i.a.); **feature-percolation** (Chomsky 1973; Cowper 1987; Gazdar et al. 1985; Grimshaw 2000; Kayne 1983; Webelhuth 1992, i.a.); **a portmanteau** (i.e., a single morpheme reflecting agreement with both arguments); **the effects of a scale/hierarchy** (e.g. one that reflects "cognitive salience"; Dayley 1978; Mondloch 1981; Norman and Campbell 1978; Smith-Stark 1978, i.a.; see also Stiebels 2006); and **multiple lexical variants of the probe** (cf.: C^0[+decl] vs. C^0[+decl, +*wh*]). See Preminger 2014 (pp. 18–20, 67–73, 89, 123–128) for the relevant argumentation.

Let us consider what a viable account of these K'ichean data must deliver. What follows are schemata of a few relevant derivations, along with what we would need the verdict of interface-based filtration to be in each case:

(19)

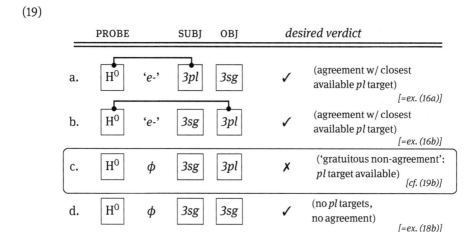

The question I would now like to focus on is: **What rules out 'gratuitous non-agreement', as schematized in (19c)?** In a model where syntactic operations are freely-applying, the mere availability of an appropriate agreement target (the *3pl* object) is not, in and of itself, enough to guarantee that agreement will apply. The derivation in which agreement has not applied would have to fail some criterion enforced by the SM & C-I systems.

Can (19c) be ruled out because of some property of the probe (H^0)? There are two possibilities to consider. If *3sg* targets can remove the offending property from the probe—e.g. "check the uninterpretable feature(s)"—then (20) should be grammatical, contrary to fact:

(20)

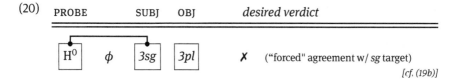

Alternatively, if *3sg* targets cannot remove the offending property, then (19d) above should be ungrammatical—again, contrary to fact.

Overall, the conclusion is that deriving the obligatoriness of agreement from representational properties of the probe (e.g. 'uninterpretable' features) leads to a contradiction.[13]

Can (19c) be ruled out because of a property of one the DP goals? If DPs in this language/construction needed to be agreed with—e.g. to check their "Case"— then (19a–b) would be ungrammatical, contrary to fact. The same is true for (21), as well:

(21)

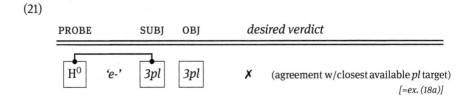

PROBE	SUBJ	OBJ	*desired verdict*
H⁰ 'e-'	3pl	3pl	✗ (agreement w/closest available *pl* target) [=ex. (18a)]

To summarize, inspecting properties of the probe and/or the goals unto themselves is insufficient to account for the obligatoriness of agreement in the K'ichean Agent-Focus construction.

A successful account of agreement is one where agreement involving a feature f takes place *as soon as the condition in (15) is satisfied*, and only if it is satisfied. (For reasons of space, I will not go through the relevant derivations here; the reader is referred to Preminger 2014:85–100, 129–175 for details.) In those derivations where the condition is never satisfied (e.g. (18b)/(19d), for f = [plural]), agreement simply does not apply, and no ungrammaticality (or "crash") arises. But evaluating (15) requires reference to primitives that are crucially syntactic. Therefore, the SM & C-I systems cannot ensure that agreement happens in the correct subset of cases, and thus, filtration at the interfaces with these systems cannot be what gives rise to the obligatoriness of agreement.

---

[13] The same contradiction obtains even if we avail ourselves of covert expletives and/or other undetectable agreement targets. Suppose H⁰ in (19d) successfully agrees with some XP β (e.g. a covert expletive). If H⁰ could target singular DPs, (20) would be okay, contrary to fact—so β cannot be singular. But if β, targeted by H⁰, is formally plural, we predict that H⁰ in (19d) would be spelled out as *e-* ("pl."), again contrary to fact.

5.2.2 Argument 2: case[14]

As in the previous subsection, this discussion is intended to apply to any theory that enforces the obligatory nature of case assignment using a condition evaluated at the interfaces with the SM & C-I systems. But a useful straw man to keep in mind is the Case Filter proposal (Chomsky 1981), where valuation of a nominal's case features is enforced via a late-applying representational condition (see also Chomsky and Lasnik 1977, as well as the discussion in section 3).

The crucial evidence against this family of approaches comes from accusative case assignment in Sakha (Turkic). As shown by Baker and Vinokurova (2010), the conditions on the assignment of accusative in Sakha are as follows:

(22) ACCUSATIVE
A nominal/DP α can be assigned ACC **only if** there is a nominal/DP β such that:
  i. β c-commands α
  ii. β and α are in the same locality domain
  iii. β is caseless

See Baker & Vinokurova 2010:599–620 for several arguments that accusative in Sakha is indeed assigned in this fashion, rather than by some head in the extended verbal projection (e.g. v^0 or V^0). Recall also that the assignment of case in Sakha—as in other languages—is part of syntax proper (see also Preminger 2014:177–213).

Now, suppose that we observe a scenario in Sakha in which accusative case is, empirically speaking, obligatory. By hypothesis, operations within syntax (such as case assignment) are supposed to be freely-applying. Thus, derivations in which accusative case has not been assigned would have to be ruled out at (one or both of) the interfaces between syntax and the SM & C-I systems.

As with (15), giving the SM or C-I systems access to the primitives necessary to evaluate (22) would amount to undoing the modular separation between syntax and the SM & C-I systems, in the first place (see (12), above). Thus, evaluating whether there is any nominal β that satisfies (22) with respect to a given nominal α is something only syntax can do. The most that the SM & C-I systems could do is inspect α itself. The interfaces with the SM and/or C-I systems could flag any derivation in which a given nominal α did not receive case as ungrammatical (e.g. due to "unchecked" case features). If the only opportunity for this particular α to

---

[14] This subsection builds on joint work with Theodore Levin and with Jaklin Kornfilt; see Levin and Preminger 2015 and Kornfilt and Preminger 2015.

get case was via the configuration in (22), then the obligatoriness of this instance of accusative could be derived via filtration at the interfaces. As we will see below, however, this approach is empirically inadequate.

The crucial evidence comes from raising-to-accusative constructions in Sakha:

(23) a. Sardaana **Aisen-*(y)** beqehee [bügün t kel-er
       Sardaana **Aisen-*(ACC)** yesterday today   come-AOR
       dien] ihit-te
       COMP hear-PAST.3

                                                           (Sakha)

    'Sardaana heard yesterday that Aisen is coming today.'

  b. Sardaana beqehee [bügün **Aisen-(*y)** kel-er   dien]
       Sardaana yesterday today **Aisen-(*ACC)** come-AOR COMP
       ihit-te
       hear-PAST.3

    'Sardaana heard yesterday that Aisen is coming today.'
                                  [Vinokurova 2005:363; annotations added]

As (23a) illustrates, accusative case on the raised embedded subject is obligatory. (See Baker and Vinokurova 2010:616–617 for evidence that this is raising *per se*, and not a base-generated argument in the matrix clause coindexed with a null category of some sort in the embedded clause.)

The question I would now like to focus on is: **What rules out 'gratuitous non-accusative' on *Aisen* in (23a)**? If this is to be derived as a filter imposed by the SM & C-I systems, then—given the discussion above—there must be a way to detect the ill-formedness of the accusative-less version of (23a) by inspecting [$_{DP}$ *Aisen*] alone.

It would appear, based on (23b), that there is nothing wrong with an instance of [$_{DP}$ *Aisen*] that has not been assigned accusative. The interface-driven approach to case is therefore forced into the following position: the embedded clause in (23b) must have some property p (e.g. the ability to "assign nominative" to [$_{DP}$ *Aisen*]) that ameliorates whatever representational lacuna the accusative-less version of [$_{DP}$ *Aisen*] in (23a) has. At the same time, the embedded clause in (23a) must lack property p, otherwise the accusative-less variant of (23a) would be predicted to be grammatical.

But this alone still would not suffice. Whether the embedded clause has property p must covary with whether or not [$_{DP}$ *Aisen*] moves out of the embedded clause, otherwise the biconditional relationship in (23a–b) between the position of [$_{DP}$ *Aisen*] and its case-marking would not be accurately captured.

This is where the approach runs into problems. Consider the acceptability of the accusative-less variant of *ehigi* ("you") in (24b):[15,16]

(24) a. min **ehigi-ni** bügün t kyaj-yax-xyt dien erem-mit-im
    I **you-ACC** today   win-FUT-2pl.S that hope-PST-1sg.S
    'I hoped you would win today.'
  b. min **ehigi** bügün t kyaj-yax-xyt dien erem-mit-im
    I **you** today   win-FUT-2pl.S that hope-PST-1sg.S
    'I hoped you would win today.'

[Vinokurova 2005:361]

This suggests that the kind of movement involved in the alternation between (23a) and (23b) is not, in and of itself, a sufficient condition for the assignment of accusative in this construction. To put this another way: raising out of the embedded clause is not restricted to those nominals that will ultimately receive accusative case (as the account where p = "the ability of the embedded clause to assign nominative" would falsely predict).

The distinction between (23a) (where accusative on the raised subject is obligatory) and (24a–b) (where it seems as though accusative is optional) is likely the result of (24) having two slightly different structures, one of which is ruled out in (23a). Consider (25a–b):[17]

---

15 The placement of the traces in the annotation of (24a–b) assumes that the position of modifiers is fixed, and arguments move around them. This is standard practice in syntactic theory (cf. Pollock 1989, among many others). Note the relative position of bügün ("today") and *Aisen* in (23b).

16 The embedded verb in (24) shows full agreement with the raised embedded subject, in both number and person. Sakha also allows for partial agreement (in number but not in person) on the embedded verb, in which case accusative on the raised embedded subject becomes obligatory (rather than optional, as it is in (24)); see Vinokurova (2005:361). Note, however, that the subject in (23a) is 3rd person, meaning the string in question is compatible with both a full agreement parse and a partial agreement parse (as far as the agreement morphology in the embedded clause is concerned). Therefore, the possibility of partial agreement does not explain the obligatoriness of accusative in (23a) (cf. Baker 2011:893–896).

17 As Baker & Vinokurova (2010:602) note, accusative in (25b) is possible only if the object bears contrastive focus, hence the '#' annotation (relative to a neutral/out-of-the-blue context).

(25) a. *Masha salamaat-*(y)* **turgennik** t *sie-te*
Masha porridge-*(ACC) **quickly** eat-PAST.3sg.S
'Masha ate the porridge quickly'
b. *Masha* **turgennik** *salamaat-(#y) sie-te*
Masha **quickly** porridge-(#ACC) eat-past.3sg.S
'Masha ate porridge quickly.'

[Baker & Vinokurova 2010:602]

In (25a), the nominal *salamaat* ("porridge") has moved out of the verb phrase; in (25b), however, it has not. Crucially, the presence of accusative case covaries with this movement (see also Baker & Vinokurova 2010:602–604).

It is likely, then, that this is precisely the source of apparent optionality in (24a–b): the examples in (24) contain no matrix-clause modifier (*bügün* "today" is an embedded-clause modifier, as the tense of the respective verbs makes clear). Thus, there is no overt material in (24) to delimit the edge of the matrix verb phrase. Crucially, then, the difference between (24a) and (24b) involves movement *within the matrix clause* (on a par with movement in the monoclausal (25)).

This means that there is no property *p* that satisfies the requirements stated earlier: regulating both the assignment of accusative *and* movement out of the embedded clause.[18] Crucially, the existence of such a property was a necessary condition for an account of (23a–b) in which the obligatoriness of accusative is enforced at the interfaces with the SM & C-I systems. (I.e., an account that rules out the accusative-less variant of (23a) by inspecting the status of [$_{DP}$ Aisen] itself, without needing to (re-)evaluate a condition like (22) outside of narrow syntax.)

To summarize, inspecting the properties of the nominal alone is insufficient to account for the obligatoriness of the assignment of accusative in Sakha raising-to-object constructions.

A successful account of the assignment of accusative (in Sakha, and likely in most other languages) is one where accusative is assigned to a nominal *as soon as it meets the condition in (22)*, and only if it meets this condition. (Once again, space considerations prevent me from going through the relevant derivations here; see Preminger 2014:187–208 for details.) In those derivations where the condition is never satisfied (e.g. (24b, 25b)), accusative is simply not assigned, and no ungrammaticality (or "crash", or fatal violation of the Case Filter) arises. But evaluating (22) requires reference to primitives that are crucially syntactic. Therefore, the SM & C-I systems cannot ensure that accusative is assigned in the correct subset of

---

[18] The same facts cast considerable doubt on the already dubious *Activity Condition* (Chomsky, 2001); see also Nevins (2004), as well as Preminger 2014:134–136.

cases, and thus, filtration at the interfaces with these systems cannot be what gives rise to the obligatoriness of accusative in those instances where it is obligatory.

6 The solution: a return to STRUCTURAL DESCRIPTIONS

In the minimalist model, the obligatoriness of an operation $\mathcal{R}$ is enforced by means of one or more representational filters, imposed by the sensorimotor (SM) and conceptual-intentional (C-I) systems, which rule out the end results of those derivations in which $\mathcal{R}$ has not applied. In *Syntactic Structures* (as well as in Chomsky and Halle 1968, and many others), on the other hand, the obligatoriness of an operation $\mathcal{R}$ is enforced by automatically triggering $\mathcal{R}$ whenever (and as soon as) its STRUCTURAL DESCRIPTION is met. Derivations in which $\mathcal{R}$ has gratuitously not applied are ruled out as a simple case of non-generation: the grammar simply does not entertain derivations in which the relevant structural description is met but $\mathcal{R}$ is not triggered.

In the previous section, we saw two case studies showing that the latter model is empirically preferable to the former. These case studies can be seen as specific instances of a broader strategy that can be used to empirically distinguish these two models of obligatoriness:

(26) FILTRATION   *[Chomsky & Lasnik 1977, Chomsky 1995, among many others]*

		structural conditions on $\mathcal{R}$ met?	
		YES	NO
$\mathcal{R}$ happens?	YES	*grammaticality* (definitional)	*ungrammaticality* (definitional)
	NO	*ungrammaticality* (obligatoriness)	**ungrammaticality**

(27) NON-GENERATION [Chomsky 1957, Chomsky and Halle 1968 among many others; but also: López 2007, Preminger 2014, i.a.]

		structural conditions on ℛ met?	
		YES	NO
ℛ happens?	YES	grammaticality (definitional)	ungrammaticality (definitional)
	NO	ungrammaticality (obligatoriness)	**grammaticality**

The tables in (26–27) are meant to show the relationship between whether the structural conditions on some obligatory operation ℛ are met, whether the operation itself applies, and whether the result is well-formed. The cells in the first row of each table are definitional: what it means for the structural conditions on ℛ to be met is that applying ℛ is licit; what it means for them not to be met is that applying ℛ is illicit. Since we are interested in obligatory operations, the bottom-left cell of each table (the structural conditions on ℛ are met, but ℛ does not apply) must yield ungrammaticality.

The interesting case is when the structural conditions on ℛ are not met, and ℛ does not apply. On the filtration approach, what is important is that ℛ apply (e.g. that the 'uninterpretable' features on the probe and/or goal be checked), and so this state of affairs should result in ill-formedness. On the non-generation approach, a scenario where the structural conditions on an operation are not met is simply a scenario where the operation is not triggered (cf., for example, the failure of *final devoicing* to apply to words that end in a phonological segment of the wrong type). No ill-formedness should arise, in the latter case.

A way to think about the two case studies in section 5.2, then, is as explorations of scenarios of precisely this type. In §5.2.1, we looked at scenarios like (19d), where the operation of *φ-agreement in [plural] features* is inapplicable because there was no accessible argument bearing this feature. (Recall that, in this construction, 3rd person singular arguments cannot be treated as viable targets for number agreement; see the discussion in §5.2.1.) And the result is well-formed, as shown in (18b). In §5.2.2, we looked at scenarios where the operation of *accusative case assignment* is inapplicable because the nominal in question is not in sufficient proximity to the next higher nominal (see (22)). And the result is well-formed, as shown in (24b) and (25b).

Both φ-agreement (at least as it concerns [plural] in K'ichean) and case assignment (at least as it concerns accusative in Sakha) must therefore be obligatory operations of the (27) type. In section 5, the two were formulated in a filtration-oriented way:

(28) [(15)] ɸ-AGREEMENT
A head H⁰ can enter into agreement in some ɸ-feature f with a DP α **only if**:
   i.   H⁰ c-commands α
   ii. H⁰ and α are in the same locality domain
   iii. there is no bearer of valued f c-commanded by H⁰ that asymmetrically c-commands α

(29) [(22)] ACCUSATIVE A nominal/DP α can be assigned ACC **only if** there is a nominal/DP β such that:
   i.   β c-commands α
   ii. β and α are in the same locality domain
   iii. β is caseless

But (15, 22) can easily be reformulated as obligatory operations, as required by the non-generation mode of explanation (crucial changes are indicated by underlining):

(30) [(15')] ɸ-AGREEMENT
A head H⁰ <u>enters</u> into agreement in some ɸ-feature f with a DP α **as soon as**:
   i.   H⁰ c-commands α
   ii. H⁰ and α are in the same locality domain
   iii. there is no bearer of valued f c-commanded by H⁰ that asymmetrically c-commands α

(31) [(22')] ACCUSATIVE
A nominal/DP α <u>is</u> assigned ACC **as soon as** there is a nominal/DP β such that:
   i.   β c-commands α
   ii. β and α are in the same locality domain
   iii. β is caseless

What we have seen is that (15') and (22') are preferable to (15) and (22) on empirical grounds. And if we think of operations as being triggered immediately when their structural description is met, the "as soon as" portion of (15'–22') can be factored out of their definition:

(32) [(15")] ϕ-AGREEMENT
   a. STRUCTURAL DESCRIPTION:
      i. H^0, a seeker of valued f, c-commands α, a bearer of valued f
      ii. H^0 and α are in the same locality domain
      iii. there is no bearer of valued f c-commanded by H^0 that asymmetrically c-commands α
   b. STRUCTURAL CHANGE:
      associate the instance of valued f on α with H^0

(33) [(22")] ACCUSATIVE
   a. STRUCTURAL DESCRIPTION:
      i. β, a caseless nominal/DP, c-commands α, a caseless nominal/DP
      ii. β and α are in the same locality domain
   b. STRUCTURAL CHANGE:
      assign ACC to α

In other words, we can view these results as an indication that ϕ-agreement and case are better understood as transformations (in the *Syntactic Structures* sense), and not as interface conditions (in the minimalist sense).

7 Conclusion

In this paper, we have seen evidence against the way certain ungrammatical outcomes are ruled out in minimalist syntax, via freely-applying operations coupled with filtration at the interfaces with the sensorimotor (SM) and conceptual-intentional (C-I) systems. It was argued that an empirically preferable approach is the one taken in *Syntactic Structures*, involving obligatory operations and non-generation.

Acknowledgements I thank Mark Baker, Norbert Hornstein, and David Pesetsky for many illuminating discussions over the years that have fed into this work, and again to Norbert Hornstein for comments on an earlier draft. Thanks also to Dennis Ott and Radek Šimik, organizers of the workshop on *What drives syntactic computation?* at the 37th Annual Meeting of the German Society of Linguistics (DGfS 37), and Rajesh Bhatt and Vincent Homer, organizers of the workshop on *How to Make Things Happen in the Grammar: the Implementation of Obligatoriness* at the 11th International Tbilisi Symposium on Language, Logic and Computation (TbiLLC 2015), and to audiences at both workshops, for their comments and suggestions. Any errors or misconstruals are my own.

Bibliography

Aissen, Judith. 1999. Agent focus and inverse in Tzotzil. *Language* 75:451–485.
Aissen, Judith. 2011. On the syntax of agent focus in K'ichee'. In *Proceedings of FAMLi: Formal Approaches to Mayan Linguistics*, ed. Kirill Shklovsky, Pedro Mateo Pedro, and Jessica Coon, number 63 in MIT Working Papers in Linguistics, 1–16. Cambridge, MA: MITWPL.
Anagnostopoulou, Elena. 2005. Strong and weak person restrictions: A feature checking analysis. In *Clitic and affix combinations: Theoretical perspectives*, ed. Lorie Heggie and Francisco Ordonez, number 74 in Linguistics Today, 199–235. Amsterdam: John Benjamins.
Armstrong, Sharon Lee, Lila R. Gleitman, and Henry Gleitman. 1983. What some concepts might not be. *Cognition* 13:263–308.
Baker, C. L., and Michael K. Brame. 1972. Global rules: A rejoinder. *Language* 48:51–75.
Baker, Mark C. 2011. When agreement is for number and gender but not person. *Natural Language & Linguistic Theory* 29:875–915.
Baker, Mark C., and Nadya Vinokurova. 2010. Two modalities of Case assignment: Case in Sakha. *Natural Language & Linguistic Theory* 28:593–642.
Bittner, Maria, and Ken Hale. 1996. The structural determination of Case and Agreement. *Linguistic Inquiry* 27:1–68.
Bobaljik, Jonathan David. 2008. Where's phi? Agreement as a post-syntactic operation. In *Phi Theory: Phi-features across interfaces and modules*, ed. Daniel Harbour, David Adger, and Susana Béjar, 295–328. Oxford: Oxford University Press.
Campbell, Lyle. 2000. Valency-changing derivations in K'iche'. In *Changing valency: Case studies in transitivity*, ed. R. M. W. Dixon and Alexandra Y. Aikhenvald, 236–381. Cambridge University Press.
Chomsky, Noam. 1957. *Syntactic structures*. The Hague: Mouton.
Chomsky, Noam. 1973. Conditions on transformations. In *A festschrift for Morris Halle*, ed. Stephen R. Anderson and Paul Kiparsky, 232–286. New York, NY: Academic Press.
Chomsky, Noam. 1980. *Rules and representations*. New York, NY: Columbia University Press.
Chomsky, Noam. 1981. *Lectures on government and binding*. Dordrecht: Foris.
Chomsky, Noam. 1995. *The Minimalist Program*. Cambridge, MA: MIT Press.
Chomsky, Noam. 2000. Minimalist inquiries: The framework. In *Step by step: Essays on minimalist syntax in honor of Howard Lasnik*, ed. Roger Martin, David Michaels, and Juan Uriagereka, 89–155. Cambridge, MA: MIT Press.
Chomsky, Noam. 2001. Derivation by phase. In *Ken Hale: A life in language*, ed. Michael Kenstowicz, 1–52. Cambridge, MA: MIT Press.
Chomsky, Noam. 2004. Beyond explanatory adequacy. In *Structures and beyond*, ed. Adriana Belletti, number 3 in The Cartography of Syntactic Structures, 104–131. New York, NY: Oxford University Press.
Chomsky, Noam. 2008. On phases. In *Foundational issues in linguistic theory*, ed. Robert Freidin, Carlos Otero, and Maria-Luisa Zubizarreta, 133–166. Cambridge, MA: MIT Press.

Chomsky, Noam, and Morris Halle. 1968. *The sound pattern of English*. New York, NY: Harper and Row.

Chomsky, Noam, and Howard Lasnik. 1977. Filters and control. *Linguistic Inquiry* 8:425–504.

Coon, Jessica, Pedro Mateo Pedro, and Omer Preminger. 2014. The role of case in a' extraction asymmetries: Evidence from Mayan. *Linguistic Variation* 14:179–242.

Cowper, Elizabeth. 1987. Pied piping, feature percolation and the structure of the noun-phrase. *Canadian Journal of Linguistics* 32:321–338.

Craig, Colette Grinevald. 1979. The antipassive and Jacaltec. In *Papers in Mayan linguistics*, ed. Laura Martin, 139–165. Columbia, MO: Lucas Bros. Publishers.

Davies, William D., and Luis Enrique Sam-Colop. 1990. K'iche' and the structure of antipassive. *Language* 66:522–549.

Dayley, Jon P. 1978. Voice in Tzutujil. *Journal of Mayan Linguistics* 1:20–52.

Dayley, Jon P. 1985. *Tz'utujil grammar*. Number 107 in University of California Publications in Linguistics. Berkeley, CA: University of California Press.

Erlewine, Michael Yoshitaka. 2016. Anti-locality and optimality in Kaqchikel Agent Focus. *Natural Language & Linguistic Theory* 34:429–479.

Gazdar, Gerald, Ewan Klein, Geoffrey K. Pullum, and Ivan A. Sag. 1985. *Generalized Phrase Structure Grammar*. Cambridge, MA: Harvard University Press.

Grimshaw, Jane. 2000. Locality and extended projections. In *Lexical specification and insertion*, ed. Peter Coopmans, Martin Everaert, and Jane Grimshaw, 115–134. Amsterdam: John Benjamins.

Henderson, Robert, and Jessica Coon. to appear. Adverbs and variability in Kaqchikel Agent Focus: A reply to Erlewine (2016). *Natural Language & Linguistic Theory* .

Hiraiwa, Ken. 2001. Multiple Agree and the defective intervention constraint in Japanese. In *The Proceedings of the MIT-Harvard joint conference (HUMIT 2000)*, ed. Ora Matushansky, number 40 in MIT Working Papers in Linguistics, 67–80. Cambridge, MA: MITWPL.

Hiraiwa, Ken. 2004. Dimensions of symmetry in syntax: Agreement and clausal architecture. Doctoral dissertation, MIT, Cambridge, MA.

Kayne, Richard S. 1983. Connectedness. *Linguistic Inquiry* 14:223–249.

Kornfilt, Jaklin, and Omer Preminger. 2015. Nominative as *no case at all*: An argument from raising-to-ACC in Sakha. In *Proceedings of the 9th Workshop on Altaic Formal Linguistics (WAFL 9)*, ed. Andrew Joseph and Esra Predolac, number 76 in MIT Working Papers in Linguistics, 109–120. Cambridge, MA: MITWPL.

Lakoff, George. 1970. *Irregularity in syntax*. New York, NY: Holt, Rinehart and Winston.

Lakoff, George. 1972. The arbitary basis of transformational grammar. *Language* 42:76–87.

Lees, Robert B., and Edward S. Klima. 1963. Rules for English pronominalization. *Language* 39:17–28.

Levin, Theodore, and Omer Preminger. 2015. Case in Sakha: Are two modalities really necessary? *Natural Language & Linguistic Theory* 33:231–250.

López, Luis. 2007. *Locality and the architecture of syntactic dependencies*. New York, NY: Palgrave MacMillan.

López Ixcoy, Candelaria Dominga. 1997. *Gramática K'ichee'*. Guatemala City: Cholsamaj.

Marantz, Alec. 1991. Case and licensing. In *Proceedings of the 8th Eastern States Conference on Linguistics (ESCOL 8)*, ed. German Westphal, Benjamin Ao, and Hee-Rahk Chae, 234–253. Ithaca, NY: CLC Publications.

McFadden, Thomas. 2004. The position of morphological case in the derivation: A study on the syntax-morphology interface. Doctoral dissertation, University of Pennsylvania, Philadelphia, PA.

Mondloch, James L. 1981. Voice in Quiche-Maya. Doctoral dissertation, State University of New York, Albany, NY.

Müller, Gereon. 2004. Phrase impenetrability and -intervention. In *Minimality effects in syntax*, ed. Arthur Stepanov, Gisbert Fanselow, and Ralf Vogel, 289–325. Berlin: Mouton de Gruyter.

Nevins, Andrew Ira. 2004. Derivations without the Activity Condition. In *Perspectives on phases*, ed. Martha McGinnis and Norvin Richards, number 49 in MIT Working Papers in Linguistics, 287–310. Cambridge, MA: MITWPL.

Nevins, Andrew Ira. 2011. Multiple Agree with clitics: Person complementarity vs. omnivorous number. *Natural Language & Linguistic Theory* 29:939–971.

Norman, William M., and Lyle Campbell. 1978. Towards a Proto-Mayan syntax: A comparative perspective on grammar. In *Papers in Mayan linguistics*, ed. Nora C. England, number 6 in University of Missouri Miscellaneous Publications in Anthropology, 136–156. Columbia, MO: University of Missouri.

Perlmutter, David M. 1968. Deep and surface structure constraints in syntax. Doctoral dissertation, MIT, Cambridge, MA.

Perlmutter, David M. 1971. *Deep and surface structure constraints in syntax*. New York, NY: Holt, Rinehart and Winston.

Pesetsky, David. 1989. Language-particular processes and the Earliness Principle. Ms.

Pollock, Jean-Yves. 1989. Verb movement, UG and the structure of IP. *Linguistic Inquiry* 20:365–424.

Preminger, Omer. 2011a. Agreement as a fallible operation. Doctoral dissertation, MIT, Cambridge, MA.

Preminger, Omer. 2011b. Asymmetries between person and number in syntax: A commentary on Baker's SCOPA. *Natural Language & Linguistic Theory* 29:917–937.

Preminger, Omer. 2014. *Agreement and its failures*. Number 68 in Linguistic Inquiry Monographs. Cambridge, MA: MIT Press.

Preminger, Omer, and Maria Polinsky. 2015. Agreement and semantic concord: a spurious unification. URL http://ling.auf.net/lingbuzz/002363, Ms.

Pye, Clifton. 1989. The focus antipassive in K'iche' Mayan. In *Studies in native american languages V*, ed. Jong-Seok Ok and Mubeccel Taneri, volume 14 of *Kansas Working Papers in Linguistics*, 88–98. Lawrence, KS: University of Kansas Linguistics Graduate Student Association.

Rizzi, Luigi. 1990. *Relativized minimality*. Cambridge, MA: MIT Press.

Ross, John R. 1967. Constraints on variables in syntax. Doctoral dissertation, MIT, Cambridge, MA.

Sam-Colop, Luis Enrique. 1988. Antipassive and *2-3 retreat* in K'iche'. Master's thesis, University of Iowa, Iowa City, IA.

Smith-Stark, Thom. 1978. The Mayan antipassive: Some facts and fictions. In *Papers in Mayan linguistics*, ed. Nora C. England, number 6 in University of Missouri Miscellaneous Publications in Anthropology, 169–187. Columbia, MO: University of Missouri.

Stiebels, Barbara. 2006. Agent Focus in Mayan languages. *Natural Language & Linguistic Theory* 24:501–570.

Uriagereka, Juan. 1999. Multiple spell-out. In *Working minimalism*, ed. Samuel Epstein and Norbert Hornstein, 251–282. Cambridge, MA: MIT Press.

Vinokurova, Nadya. 2005. Lexical categories and argument structure: A study with reference to Sakha. Doctoral dissertation, UiL-OTS, Utrecht. LOT dissertation series.

Webelhuth, Gert. 1992. *Principles and parameters of syntactic saturation*. Oxford University Press.

Mark Aronoff
English verbs in *Syntactic Structures*

Beauty is truth, truth beauty—that is all
Ye know on earth, and all ye need to know.

John Keats, Ode on a Grecian Urn (1820)

1 Introduction

The formally inclined take comfort in the last two lines of Keats's Ode on a Grecian Urn. We judge an analysis by its beauty, or elegance, or simplicity. In linguistics, there is no clearer demonstration of Keats's maxim than the analysis of English verbs in *Syntactic Structures* (henceforth SS). I am not alone in my belief that the beauty of this analysis played a large part in leading the field to accept the truth of Chomsky's claim that the description of human language calls for the use of transformations.

The system of English verbs provides one of the core pieces of evidence in SS for the value of transformations in grammatical theory and description. In this article, I will review Chomsky's analysis of English verbs and use it to partially reconstruct the (largely implicit) view of morphology that lies behind it—most centrally, the role that the morpheme played in SS and just what the term *morpheme* meant in that work. I will explore the roots of this view in structuralist linguistics, especially in the morphological theory of Chomsky's mentor, Zellig Harris. Chomsky's analysis of English verbs and their morphology might have been possible within another framework, but a deeper understanding of the assumptions that undergird it makes the analysis even more beautiful.

In his preface, Chomsky described SS as a comparison of "three models for linguistic structure" (p. 6) and a demonstration "that a certain very simple communication theoretic model of language and a more powerful model ... 'immediate constituent analysis' cannot properly serve the purposes of grammatical description" (ibid.). He showed that the even more powerful transformational model that he developed "provides a good deal of insight into a wide range of phenomena" (ibid.).

I had always accepted Chomsky's presentation of SS as a single argument in favor of the need for the mathematical power of transformations in linguistics, and I have taught that to my students. I now understand that the book also resembles Darwin's *Origin of Species* (1859), which Darwin called one long argument for the theory of evolution by natural selection. Darwin was no mathematician. His arguments were all grounded in the insights that his deceptively simple theory made possible. I now understand that much the same is true of SS. The value of transformational method lies especially in the beautiful truths that it allows us to express in a simple fashion. In terms that Chomsky would use later, while it might be possible to describe English verbs without resorting to a transformation, the transformation allows us to gain understanding, and there are no formal methods for determining whether we have understood anything.

I will not relate *Syntactic Structures* to later developments in morphology. My goal is to understand the morphology of *Syntactic Structures* on its own terms, in its own time, and in relation to what came before it. I am especially interested in how Chomsky's abandonment of discovery procedures led him to construct an analysis that could be judged in terms of beauty and truth.

The morpheme of SS lies within the post-Bloomfieldian tradition of what Peter Matthews (1993) and others have termed *distributionalism*. This primarily methodological movement arose in the wake of Bloomfield's *Language*; Bloomfield may have been an inspiration but he was not an adherent. The movement formed the core of American structuralist linguistics from around 1940. Its adherents advocated doing linguistic analysis based solely on distribution and without resorting to lexical semantics. This was no empty exercise, but rather stemmed from the deep belief that one's practice must have a firm foundation. The scientific study of meaning had none. Even today, although much progress has been made in understanding how the meanings of complex utterances are built up from the meanings of their parts, the meanings of the most basic parts, individual lexical words, remain largely a mystery.

2 What the thunder said

Chomsky is famous for his footnotes. This article was sparked by my attempt to understand two enigmatically startling footnotes in SS. If we think of Chomsky's footnotes as a kind of gemara to the text, then the purpose of the article is commentary on the specific gemara that these two notes make up.

The first footnote is found on page 29. A couple of pages earlier, Chomsky had introduced a set of rewrite rules for very simple sentences, one of which, (13ii), rewrites NP as T + N. Two pages later, in observing that some rewrite rules must be context sensitive, he writes the following (pp. 28–29):[1]

> One generalization of (13) is clearly necessary. We must be able to limit application of a rule to a certain context. Thus T [article] can be rewritten *a* if the following noun is singular, but not if it is plural; similarly, Verb can be rewritten "hits" if the preceding noun is *man*, but not if it is *men*. In general, if we wish to limit the rewriting of X as Y to the context Z — W, we can state in the grammar the rule
>
> (1)   [(16)] $Z + X + W \to Z + Y + W$
>
> For example, in the case of singular and plural verbs, instead of having *Verb* → *hits* as an additional rule of (13). we should have
>
> (2)   [(17)] $NP_{sing} + Verb \to NP_{sing} + hits$
>
> indicating that *Verb* is rewritten *hits* only in the context NP_{sing}—.
> Correspondingly, (13 ii) will have to be restated to include NP_{sing} and NP_{pl}. This is a straightforward generalization of (13).

The first of our footnotes (fn. 3) is appended to this last sentence:

> Thus in a more complete grammar, (13ii) might be replaced by a set of rules that includes the following:
>
> $NP \to \left\{ \begin{array}{c} NP_{sing} \\ NP_{pl} \end{array} \right\}$
>
> $NP_{sing} \to T + N + \emptyset \ (+ \textit{Prepositional Phrase})$
>
> $NP_{pl} \to T + N + S \ (+ \textit{Prepositional Phrase})$
>
> where S is the morpheme which is singular for verbs and plural for nouns ("comes," "boys"), and ø is the morpheme which is singular for nouns and plural for verbs ("boy," "come"). We shall omit all mention of first and second person throughout this discussion. Identification of the nominal and verbal number affix is actually of questionable validity.

These two morphemes each have one form and share two contextually distributed meanings, singular and plural. They share these meanings in a crossing manner, as in Table 1:

---

[1] I preserve the numbering of SS throughout, since subsequent cited passages will refer to that numbering. All otherwise unattributed quoted passages are from SS.

Tab. 1: the two morphemes S and ø

morpheme	ø	S
Context	meaning	
Noun	SINGULAR	PLURAL
Verb	PLURAL	SINGULAR

Misgivings about such a crossing pattern may be what led to the last line of the note, which ascribes 'questionable validity' to the identification of the nominal and verbal affix. But the analysis was tempting enough for Chomsky to return to it a few pages later, in a footnote to the centerpiece of the book, the analysis of English verbs (pp. 38–40). I present the analysis here in full:

> Consider first the auxiliaries that appear unstressed; for example, "has" in "John has read the book" but not "*does*" in "John *does* read books." We can state the occurrence of these auxiliaries in declarative sentences by adding to the grammar (13) the following rules:
>
> (3)   [(28)]
> (i)   *Verb* → *Aux + V*
> (ii)   *V* → *hit, take, walk, read,* etc.
> (iii)   *Aux* → *C(M)(have + en)(be + ing)(be + en)*
> (iv)   *M* → *will, can, may, shall, must*
>
> (4)   [(29)]
> (i) $C \rightarrow \begin{Bmatrix} S \text{ in the context } NP_{sing}- \\ \text{ø in the context } NP_{pl}- \\ past \end{Bmatrix}$
> (ii)   Let *Af* stand for any of the affixes *past*, ø, *en*, *ing*. Let *v* stand for any *M* or *V* or *have* or *be* (i.e., for any non-affix in the phrase Verb). Then:
>   *Af + v → v + Af#,*
> Where # is interpreted as a word boundary
> (iii)   Replace + by # except in the context *v — Af*. Insert # initially and finally.

The interpretation of the notations in (28iii) is as follows: we must choose the element *C*, and we may choose zero or more of the parenthesized elements in the given order. In (29i) we may develop *C* into any of three morphemes, observing the contextual restrictions given. As an example of the application of these rules, we construct a derivation in the style of (14), omitting the initial steps.

(5) [(30)] *the + man + Verb + the + book*   from (13i–v)

the + man + Aux + V + the + book   (28i)

the + man + Aux + read + the + book   (28ii)

the + man + C + have + en + be + ing +   (28iii)—we select the
read + the + book   elements *C, have + en,* and *be + ing*.

the + man + S + have + en + be + ing + read + the + book   (29i)

the + man + have + S# be + en#read + ing#the + book   (29ii)—three times

#the# man# have + S#be + en# + read + ing#the + #book#   (29iii)

The morphophonemic rules (19), etc., will convert the last line of this derivation into:

(6) [(31)] the man has been reading the book

(29i) sets the stage for (29ii), a transformation, which we now call affix hopping. (29i) also bears our second footnote of interest, which is short:

> We assume here that (13ii) has been extended in the manner of fn. 3, above, p. 29, or something similar.

We don't know what "something similar" might be, but morphemes like *S* and ∅ of fn. 3 are astonishing to almost any morphologist because they contradict two fundamental tenets. First, every morpheme must have a single meaning (though we may not always know what that meaning is), though it may have many forms. Second, no two morphemes can have the same meaning.[2] As shown in Table 1, these two morphemes each have only one form but two meanings, depending on context, and they share these meanings. If we are to understand how Chomsky could have entertained morphemes with such strangely-crossed meaning patterns, we must review the history of the use of the term *morpheme* since its invention, with special attention to the place of meaning in its definition.

---

[2] The claim that there are no synonymous words dates to Girard (1718). Bloomfield accepted it for morphemes (see below) and the notion of allomorphy depends on it, as does morphological blocking. Not everyone understands its value or ubiquity. Fought, for example, noted: "I have not found any effort in his [Bloomfield's] published work to justify his unusual position on synonymy … Indeed, the outright rejection of synonymy is a position not often taken" (1999, p. 323). The opposite is true.

3 The morpheme through time[3]

The term *morpheme* was coined by Baudouin de Courtenay before 1880, on the model of the term *phoneme*.[4] He defined the morpheme as follows (1895/1972, p. 153):

> ... that part of a word which is endowed with psychological autonomy and is for the very same reason not further divisible. It consequently subsumes such concepts as the root (radix), all possible affixes, (suffixes, prefixes), endings which are exponents of syntactic relationships, and the like.

3.1 Morphemes and meaning: Bloomfield's quandary

We cannot know exactly what Baudouin meant by 'psychological autonomy'. Fifty years later, in his (1933) the bible of American structuralist linguistics, Leonard Bloomfield, who by then had given up on the utility of psychological interpretation of language for linguists, defined morphemes in terms of meaning or semantics instead of psychological autonomy. He declared that "each linguistic form has a constant and specific meaning" (p. 145) and a few pages later that "[a] linguistic form which bears no partial phonetic-semantic resemblance to any other form is a *simple* form or *morpheme*" (p. 161). Although Bloomfield defined the morpheme in terms of meaning, he cautioned in the next paragraph that "[a] morpheme can be described phonetically, since it consists of one or more phonemes, **but its meaning cannot be analyzed within the scope of our science** [emphasis mine]." And on the next page:

> The meaning of a morpheme is a *sememe*. The linguist **assumes** [emphasis MA] that each sememe is a constant and definite unit of meaning, different from all other meanings, including all other sememes, in the language, but **he cannot go beyond this** [emphasis MA]. There is nothing in the structure of morphemes like *wolf*, *fox*, and *dog* to tell us the relation between their meanings. This is a problem for the zoölogist. The zoölogist's definition of these meanings is welcome to us as a practical help, but it cannot be confirmed or rejected on the basis of our science. (ibid., p. 162)

---

[3] Anderson (2015) provides an insightful comprehensive survey of the morpheme since the term and notion were first created. Matthews (1993) is broader in scope but his treatment of the history of the American structuralist conception of the morpheme and its place in both structuralist theory and early generative grammar is masterful.

[4] Jakobson (1971) traces Baudouin's first use of the term to his lectures of 1877–78. A program of these lectures was published in 1880.

An entire chapter of *Language* bears the title *Meaning*, but this chapter consists mainly of an apologia for not discussing meaning more precisely. Bloomfield believed: "In order to give a scientifically accurate definition of meaning for every form of a language, we should have to have a scientifically accurate knowledge of everything in the speaker's world" (p. 139). He concludes: "The statement of meaning is therefore the weak point in language-study, and will remain so until human knowledge advances very far beyond the present state" (p. 140). Nonetheless, although he cannot define meanings, he makes the following axiomatic declaration:

> Since we have no way of defining most meanings [of morphemes MA] and of demonstrating their constancy, we have to take the specific and stable character of language as a presupposition of linguistic study, just as we presuppose it in our everyday dealings with people. We may state this presupposition as the *fundamental assumption of linguistics* (§5.3), namely:
>
> *In certain communities (speech-communities) some speech-utterances are alike as to form and meaning.* (p. 144).

Bloomfield's attitude towards meaning is a classic case of taboo: he assumes that each morpheme is a distinct pairing of a meaning and a form, but he insists that meaning is so powerful a notion that he can't talk about or even think about what it is.[5] It is true that Bloomfield favored what he called a materialist or mechanistic theory of psychology in the analysis of meaning over what he memorably termed mentalistic psychology, but that had no effect on his attitude towards meaning itself or towards his practice. As Bernard Bloch so cogently remarked of Bloomfield in his obituary, "He had convinced himself ... that it does not matter what particular brand of psychology a linguist finds attractive, so long as he keeps it out of his linguistic writing" (Bloch 1949/1970, p. 526).

---

5 This taboo surrounding meaning most closely resembles the taboo that has long surrounded the name of the god of the Hebrews: we know that this god has a name, and we even know how to spell the name in letters (יהוה the *tetragrammaton* 'four-letter word'), but we have never been permitted to speak it, because the name is so sacred as to be taboo. According to tradition, if anyone ever were to successfully pronounce the complete true name of the deity, the world would end immediately.

3.2 The triumph of distributionalism [6]

The small band of Sapir and Bloomfield's immediate successors in American Structural linguistics came to be called the post-Bloomfieldians. They treated his *Language* as their bible. The boldest among them dealt with the taboo on meaning in a more radical way than their mentor: by banishing meaning from linguistics entirely and putting their faith in distribution alone.[7] The result was what Matthews (1993) calls distributionalism. Most prominent among the distributionalists was Chomsky's mentor, Zellig Harris, and most radically in his *Methods in Structural Linguistics* (Harris, 1951). The distributionalists themselves regarded Harris as their leading theoretician. For example, in his review of *Methods in Language*, Norman McQuown (1952) calls it "epoch-making" and declares: "Not since Bloomfield's Language has there been such an ambitious attempt to cover a whole field." And we are still in the first paragraph of a laudatory ten-page review! In the next sentence, McQuown cautions: "Unlike Bloomfield's, however, this book is limited to the presentation of one principle and one method of linguistic analysis and description. The principle is that of relative distribution, the method that of controlled substitution." The entertainment of morphemes like Chomsky's *S* and ∅ makes sense only in the context of Harris's version of distributionalism. The entire treatment of the English verb in SS is profoundly distributionalist. I will now turn to the roots of distributionalism. Its connection to the phoneme is well known but worth rehearsing. The tie to Whorf, especially Whorf (1945) is new.

---

[6] My discussion of the post-Bloomfieldians and distributionalism relies heavily on the sections devoted to those topics in Matthews (1993). Matthews does not discuss Whorf's abstractionism, which I propose as an important factor in the rise of distributionalism.

[7] The idea of exploring lexical semantics in terms of use rather than definition was not confined to linguistics. Ludwig Wittgenstein, for instance, who had no known contact with linguists, came to similar conclusions in the second half of his career, with his famous dictum: "For a large class of cases of the employment of the word 'meaning'—though not for all—this word can be explained in this way: the meaning of a word is its use in the language" (Wittgenstein 1953, §43). Wittgenstein had worked on the ideas in Philosophical Investigations since returning to philosophy and to Cambridge in 1929. He submitted a complete draft to the publisher in 1945, but withdrew the final version in 1946, authorizing posthumous publication. Among American linguists, only Harris, who was steeped in formal logic, might possibly have known of Wittgenstein, but none of Wittgenstein's work on ordinary language was published until after Harris had completed his book in 1946, making even this implausible. In short, there was likely no direct contact between the two. In any case, Wittgenstein never formulated any specific methods for exploring his use theory of meaning in the way that Harris did. The ordinary language philosophers who followed his lead suffered from a similar absence of explicit methodology and the effort sadly dissipated.

3.3 The abstract phoneme, Whorf's covert categories, and distributional methods

The greatest achievement in the field of linguistics in the second quarter of the 20th century was the discovery of the phoneme as a distinctive sound unit of individual languages, vindicating Saussure's structuralist approach to language.[8] The phoneme, no matter how one attempts to define its essence, is defined in practice by the two distributional methods by which the phonemes of a language are found or discovered. These are substitution/contrast and complementary distribution. If two sounds contrast (are judged by native speakers of the language to result in distinct words) when substituted for one another (as with /p/ and /b/ in English *pat* and *bat*), they belong to separate phonemes. If linguists discover that they are in complementary distribution (as with [p^h] and [p] in *pit* and *spit*), they are variants or allophones of the same phoneme. The allophones of a single phoneme are gathered together into a set. The phoneme is the name of the set. So, we may say that the set called the English phoneme /p/ has the members { p, p^h, ...}. In the 1930's and later, there was much discussion over the 'reality' of the phoneme and over whether one variant of each phoneme had a privileged status in the mind of the language user or otherwise. But the methods for discovering phonemes and allophones were not touched by this discussion: the methods were entirely distributional. It was crucial to know whether two words meant different things, but their actual meanings were irrelevant. The phoneme was a true breakthrough, a property of all languages, and though the debate over whether a phoneme was a single 'real' sound or simply the name of a set of allophones persisted well after the structuralist phoneme succumbed to the generative underlying representation, the debate had no effect on the distributional method and this remarkable result.

Benjamin Lee Whorf was a central member of the group of linguists who had gathered around Edward Sapir at Yale in the 1930's. Sapir's coterie constituted the first critical mass of modern linguists in North America. It continued to thrive after Sapir's death in 1939 under Bloomfield (who arrived the next year and was active until his stroke in 1949) and Bloch (from 1943). This group formed the core of American structuralist linguistics. Whorf's influence during his short lifetime (he died at age 44 in 1941) is evinced most by terms that he coined that were later to become standard, notably *allophone* and *lexeme*.

---

8 Readers interested in details of the history of the concept of the phoneme should consult Anderson (1985) and Dresher (2011)

Whorf's article, "grammatical categories," was published in *Language* in 1945. John Carroll writes the following about its provenance:

> According to a note supplied by the editor of Language [Bernard Bloch], "This paper was written late in 1937 at the request of Franz Boaz, then editor of the *Int. J. Amer. Linguistics*. The manuscript was found in the Boaz collection by C. F. Voegelin and Z. S. Harris." (Whorf 1956, p. 87).

The fact that Bloch, the editor of *Language* for over a quarter century and a major gatekeeper of American structural linguistics, chose to publish this, the most theoretical of Whorf's articles, posthumously almost ten years after it had been written and over four years after Whorf's death, tells us that Bloch believed it was important to the structuralist program. The central innovation of the article is the notion of a *covert category*, for which, as opposed to an *overt category*, there is no overt identifiable mark of category membership. Instead, membership can be determined by what Whorf (ever a chemist) called the *reactance* of the category, its distribution. His first example of a covert category is the English intransitive verb, and his definition is a masterpiece of distributional analysis:

> In English, intransitive verbs form a covert category marked by the lack of the passive participle and the passive and causative voices; we cannot substitute a verb of this class (e.g., 'go, lie, sit, rise, gleam, sleep, arrive, appear, rejoice') into such sentences as 'It was cooked, It was being cooked, I had it cooked to order.' An intransitive thus configurationally defined is quite a different thing from the "dummy" intransitive used in traditional English grammar. It is a true grammatical class marked by these and other constant grammatical features, such as nonoccurrence of nouns or pronouns after the verb; one does not say 'I gleamed it, I appeared the table.' Of course compound formations involving these same lexemes may be transitive, e.g., 'sleep (it) off, go (him) one better.' In the American colloquial forms, 'go haywire, go South Sea Islander,' etc., the word or phrase after the verb is a covert adjective, cf. 'go completely haywire.' (Whorf 1956, pp. 89–90)

This passage, in which a category of elements is defined solely in terms of its privileges of occurrence, is perfectly understandable to any modern syntactician. It is modern syntax. As always with Whorf, it is beautifully written. This is distributionalism at its finest.

And it does not depend in any way on meaning, only on reactance. Whorf provides two examples showing that covert categories are "not reflections in speech of natural and noncultural differences." (p. 91). The first is English gender, revealed only in the choice of coreferent pronoun, which must be feminine, masculine, or neuter, and which does not depend on "knowledge of any 'natural properties" (p. 90). The second is Navajo nouns "based actually or ostensibly on shape":

Some terms belong to the round (or roundish) class, others to the long object class, others fall into classes not dependent on shape. No overt mark designates the class in every sentence. The class mark as in English gender is a reactance; not a pronoun, however, but a choice between certain verb stems that go definitely with one class and no other, although there are very many verb stems indifferent to this distinction. I doubt that such distinctions, at least in Navaho, are simply linguistic recognitions of nonlinguistic objective differences that would be the same for all observers, any more than the English genders are; they seem rather to be covert grammatical categories. Thus, one must learn as part of learning Navaho that 'sorrow' belongs in the "round" class. (ibid. p. 91).

Whorf wrote this article at the request of Franz Boaz and his covert categories are Boazian. They are not given in advance (by nature, Whorf would say) but rather emerge from the structure of each language. Sorrow belongs in the round class because it shares a distribution with the other members of that category. So too with English gender, which is a covert distributional category of English and no other language. Every language has its own categories, many of them covert, which lie hidden in the linguist's data, waiting to be discovered. Chomsky's analysis of English verbs lies squarely within this Boazian tradition.

Both phonemes and Whorf's covert categories demonstrate the success of an objective distributional method that, as Bloomfield had proposed, depend only on words and categories having distinct meaning, not on having to know what these meanings are. The method is also objective and reliant only on the linguist's ability to collect reliable data from a fluent speaker/hearer. It made synchronic linguistics a successful science. The obvious next step was to extend the method to morphology.

3.4 Harris' Method

The structuralist phoneme and Whorf's covert categories demonstrated the power of structure over substance. Zellig Harris struck the final blow. Harris was an outsider, who spent his academic life from the age of 18 at the University of Pennsylvania. For a decade or so, though, he was the standard bearer of the distributional method. He published numerous articles on distribution beginning in 1942 and his major book (Harris, 1951) bore the title *Methods in Structural Linguistics*. It was devoted entirely to this method.[9]

Harris started out as a Semitist and published two well-received philological monographs early on, one on Phoenician (1936) and the other on Canaanite di-

---

[9] The title of later editions was shortened to *Structural Linguistics*. One can only speculate on the reasons for the change.

alects (1939). He was famously private all his life and had little personal contact with other American descriptive linguists. Beginning in 1942, though, and continuing for more than a decade, he published a series of articles in *Language* that were tremendously influential in the theoretical mainstream. The first of these set the tone. Harris tells the reader in the first sentence: "The purpose of this paper is to suggest a technique for determining the morphemes of a language, as rigorous as the method used now for finding its phonemes." (Harris 1942, p.169). He begins with what he calls "the present treatment of morphemes" (ibid.), for which he cites Bloomfield: "Every sequence of phonemes which has meaning, and which is not composed of smaller sequences having meaning, is a morpheme." (ibid.). He calls Bloomfield's morphemes morpheme alternants but extends the possible signifiers "by taking sequence to mean not only additive sequence (the addition of phonemes), but also zero (the addition of no phonemes), negative sequence (the dropping of a phoneme), and phonemic component sequence (the addition of a physiological feature of phonemes." (ibid. 170). He encapsulates his tripartite method for finding morphemes in the summary section of the book:

> The method of arranging the phonemes of a language consists of three steps: 1. dividing each phonemically written linguistic expression into the smallest parts which recur with the same meaning in different expressions, each such part to be called a morpheme alternant; 2. grouping into a distinct morpheme unit all alternants which satisfy the following conditions: (a) have the same meaning, (b) never occur in identical environments, and (c) have combined environments no greater than the environments of some single alternant in the language; 3. making general statements for all units which have identical difference between their alternants. (ibid. 179–180)

The morpheme that results from this method does not have a single signifier in the form of concrete sequence of phonemes, à la Bloomfield. Instead, analogous to the post-Bloomfieldian phoneme and allophone, each morpheme names a set of signifiers (allomorphs) in complementary distribution. And some of these signifiers (such as ablaut) are sequences in name only, as noted above. The resulting morpheme is even more abstract than the structuralist phoneme and close to Whorf's covert category. The members of the distributionalist phoneme are at least tethered to one another by the concrete criterion of phonetic similarity, which famously prevents uniting English [h] and [ŋ] under a single phoneme, even though [h] occurs only syllable initially and [ŋ] in the coda. But morphological variants are free from substantive relations. As Eugene Nida (1949) declared in his seminal textbook on morphological analysis in American structuralist linguistics, "There are absolutely no limits to the degree of phonological difference between allomorphs" (44). All that matters are complementary distribution and synonymy.

4 Meaning and method in *Syntactic Structures*

Harris (2002) recognized Noam Chomsky as his most successful student. In the Preface to Harris (1951), dated January 1947, he noted that "N. Chomsky has given much-needed assistance with the manuscript" (p.v). Chomsky similarly wrote: "My introduction to the field of linguistics was in 1947, when Zellig Harris gave me the proofs of his Methods in Structural Linguistics to read" (Chomsky (1975a), p. 25). In the same article, he noted: "While working on LSLT [Chomsky 1955/1975b] I discussed all aspects of this material frequently and in great detail with Zellig Harris, whose influence is obvious throughout" (1975a, p. 4). SS is, in his own words, "a sketchy and informal outline of some of the material in LSLT" (ibid., p. 3). We find homage to Harris in the symbol C in rule (28iii), which became T (for tense) in later work. Harris (1948) named the set of person, number, gender, and tense affixes in Modern Hebrew C. The name is as opaque in Harris as it is in Chomsky but it is the same name.

4.1 Meaning

In SS, Chomsky followed Harris in insisting on the independence of linguistic analysis from semantics. He explicitly refused to rely on meaning in defining morphemes or even in doing linguistics. Chapter 9 of SS is entitled "Syntax and Semantics" and is devoted to the question "whether or not semantic information is required for discovering or selecting a grammar" (p. 93). For morphology specifically, he lists the claim that "morphemes are the smallest elements that have meaning" as "[a]mong the more common assertions put forth as supporting the dependence of grammar on meaning" (p. 94). He concludes that not all morphemes can be usefully defined as minimal meaning-bearing units:

> Such morphemes as "to" in "I want to go" or the dummy carrier "do" in "did he come?" (cf. §7.1) can hardly be said to have a meaning in any independent sense, and it seems reasonable to assume that an independent notion of meaning, if clearly given, may assign meaning of some sort to such non-morphemes as gl- is "gleam," "glimmer," "glow." Thus we have counterexamples to the suggestion (117ii) that morphemes be defined as minimal meaning-bearing elements. (p. 100)

In asserting his freedom from semantics, Chomsky emphasizes in this summary chapter that the entire framework of SS is purely formal:

> In §§3–7 we outlined the development of some fundamental linguistic concepts in purely formal terms. We considered the problem of syntactic research to be that of constructing a

device for producing a given set of grammatical sentences and of studying the properties of grammars that do this effectively. Such semantic notions as reference, significance, and synonymity played no role in the discussion. (pp. 102–103)

In §§3–7, then, we were studying language as an instrument or a tool, attempting to describe its structure with no explicit reference to the way in which this instrument is put to use. (p. 103)

4.2 Method

Chomsky's most lasting innovation in SS was to cast off the shackles by which Harris had so tightly bound distribution to discovery. Harris and his distributionalist colleagues truly believed that they could formulate (and perhaps had formulated) a purely inductive distributional method free of semantics, which, when carefully applied to a large enough set of data, would supply the linguist with the correct analysis of linguistic phenomena, or at least decide which analysis was correct. Harris set all this out carefully at the start of his 1951 book, where, on page 6, he declared: "The whole schedule of procedures outlined in the following chapters ... is designed to begin with the raw data of speech and end with a statement of grammatical structure."

In the 1975 preface to Chomsky (1955/1975b), Chomsky describes how, by 1953, he had "abandoned any hope of formulating taxonomic 'discovery procedures'" (p. 33), under the influence of Nelson Goodman and W.V.O. Quine. In Chapter 6 of SS, entitled *On the Goals of Linguistic Theory*, Chomsky rejected the quest for a discovery procedure or even a *decision procedure* that would determine whether a proposed grammar "is, in fact, the best grammar of the language from which this corpus is drawn" (SS p. 51), in favor of what he called a *practical evaluation procedure*, which would choose which of two grammars was better.[10] Characteristically, he makes the argument most cogently in a footnote: "Our main point is that a linguistic theory should not be identified with a manual of useful procedures, nor should it be expected to provide mechanical procedures for the discovery of grammars" (p. 55).

In LSLT, in SS, and for the next decade, Chomsky advocated using a simplicity measure to compare between grammars, but any such measure was more honored in the breach than in the observance. In practice, the most important consequence of abandoning discovery procedures was to free the analyst from any need for self-justification:

---

[10] The use of the term *procedure* throughout this passage shows that the theory of SS was constructed against the backdrop of Harrisian linguistic method.

> In short, we shall never consider the question of how one might have arrived at the grammar whose simplicity is being determined; e.g., how one might have discovered the analysis of the verb phrase presented in §5.3. Questions of this sort are not relevant to the program of research that we have outlined above ... We are thus interested in describing the forms of grammars ... rather than in showing how, in principle, one might have arrived at the grammar of a language. (p. 56)

This stance, more than any technical or analytical innovations, was revolutionary. Combined with the absence of either a practical simplicity measure or any ties to semantics, it freed the analyst to posit whatever structures lay hidden within the language. The primary justification left for defending these structures was beauty. The analysis of the verb phrase in §5.3 is beautiful.

5 Beauty and Truth

The task that Chomsky had assigned to himself beginning in the mid 1950s was to "provide simple and revealing grammars that generate all of the sentences of English and only these" (Chomsky 1956, p. 113). The key phrase is *simple and revealing*. There is a myth that Chomsky proved in SS that transformations are mathematically necessary for the description of natural languages. The roots of this myth lie in such direct claims in the book as that "discontinuities cannot be handled with [Σ, F] grammars" (p. 41) but Chomsky immediately tempered this claim in the very long footnote that follows it:

> We might be tempted to extend the notions of phrase structure to account for discontinuities. It has been pointed out several times that fairly serious difficulties arise in any systematic attempt to pursue this course ... If we were to attempt to extend phrase structure grammar to cover the entire language directly, we would lose the simplicity of the limited phrase structure grammar and of the transformational development." (pp. 41–42)

Here, Chomsky is acknowledging that his argument for the truth of his approach is rooted in beauty and not in mathematical necessity. His term is *simplicity*, which he says we would lose without transformations. Indeed, a quarter century later, Gazdar et al. (1982) famously showed that a phrase structure grammar could account for the English verb. No one who has read that account, however, would argue that it is anywhere close to beautiful. Like all subsequent accounts that dispense with affix hopping (e.g., Chomsky 1995; Lasnik 2005), its complexity cannot pin down the central observations that the SS analysis puts front and center: the form of each verb in the English verb complex is dictated by the preceding verb word; and, since no verb word precedes the first verb in the complex, the form of the first verb cannot be determined by its predecessor. Within the SS analysis, a single operation is at play in both. The operation is *affix-hopping*: the affix immediately preceding a verb 'hops over' that verb and attaches to it. The form of the first verb in the complex is made to conform to the hopping generalization by having its affix start off in front of the verb, as the tense marker for the entire complex. Do-support provides further support for this placement of the tense marker.

The affix-hopping analysis is no simpler than a PS analysis in any measurable technical or mathematical sense. The whole of SS is constructed around the fact that transformations constitute a third dimension that considerably extends the analytical power of the theory. The affix-hopping analysis is therefore less simple than the PS analysis. Its virtues are beauty and truth. Chomsky remarks on "the simplicity of the limited phrase structure grammar and of the transformational development" (ibid.). The PS rule in (28) and the transformation in (29ii) split the structure of the complex verb into two parts, each of which is succinct and straightforward. Their beauty lies in their combination. I repeat (28) and (29) here:

(7) [(28)]
(i) $Verb \rightarrow Aux + V$
(ii) $V \rightarrow hit, take, walk, read$, etc.
(iii) $Aux \rightarrow C(M)(have + en)(be + ing)(be + en)$
(iv) $M \rightarrow will, can, may, shall, must$

(8) [(29)]
(i) $C \rightarrow \begin{Bmatrix} S \text{ in the context } NP_{sing}- \\ \emptyset \text{ in the context } NP_{pl}- \\ past \end{Bmatrix}$
(ii) Let Af stand for any of the affixes *past*, $\emptyset$, *en*, *ing*. Let v stand for any M or V or *have* or *be* (i.e., for any non-affix in the phrase Verb). Then:
$$Af + v \rightarrow v + Af\#,$$
Where $\#$ is interpreted as a word boundary
(iii) Replace + by $\#$ except in the context $v - Af$. Insert $\#$ initially and finally.

Chomsky shows at some length that (29) "violates the requirements" of PS grammars. He defends the entire analysis by arguing that a PS grammar with the same coverage would be less revealing, though he never uses that word:

> The reader can easily determine that to duplicate the effect of (28 iii) and (29) without going beyond the bounds of a system [Σ, F] of phrase structure, it would be necessary to give a fairly complex statement. ... [S]ignificant simplification of the grammar is possible if we

are permitted to formulate rules of a more complex type than those that correspond to a system of immediate constituent analysis. By allowing ourselves the freedom of (29ii) we have been able to state the constituency of the auxiliary phrase in (28iii) without regard to the interdependence of its elements, and it is always easier to describe a sequence of independent elements than a sequence of mutually dependent ones. To put the same thing differently, in the auxiliary verb phrase we really have discontinuous elements—e g., in (30), the elements *have...en* and *be...ing*.... In (28iii) we treated these elements as continuous, and we introduced the discontinuity by the very simple additional rule (29ii). (pp. 41–42).

The key phrase here is "in the auxiliary verb phrase we really have discontinuous elements." This is a claim about truth, not about simplicity or complexity. The SS analysis won the day because it appeared to reveal a truth, discontinuous dependency, and it represented that revealed truth in a simple and elegant way by splitting it into two parts: (28iii) expressed the dependency and (29ii) expressed the linear discontinuity.

5.1 Chomsky's morphemes and the end of certainty in the search for truth

SS was the work of a post-Bloomfieldian distributionalist freed from discovery procedures. Its morphemes were analytical elements unified only by their distribution and their utility in an analysis. Without discovery procedures, though, there could be no way to know whether the analysis was correct, no certainty. The hope of finding an evaluation metric might provide some solace, but, truth be told, no useful concrete evaluation metric was ever found, and certainly none played a role in SS. The value of an analysis was, we now see, determined largely by the criteria of beauty and truth.

Chomsky uses the word *morpheme* 58 times and *affix* 6 times in SS. What did Chomsky mean by these terms and how did he use what he called morphemes and affixes? Chomsky does not discuss in SS what he means by affix. He has a bit to say about morphemes. For one, he follows Harris in explicitly rejecting the traditional Bloomfield definition of the morpheme as "having actual phonemic 'content' in an almost literal sense" (p. 58) in favor of a more abstract entity:

> This leads to trouble in such well-known cases as English "took" /tuk/, where it is difficult without artificiality to associate any part of this word with the past tense morpheme which appears as /t/ in "walked" /wɔkt/, as /d/ in "framed" /freymd/, etc. We can avoid all such problems by regarding morphology and phonology as two distinct but interdependent levels of representation, related in the grammar by morphophonemic rules such as (19). thus "took" is represented on the morphological level as *take + past* just as "walked" is represented as *walk + past*. The morphophonemic rules (I9ii), (19v), respectively, carry these

strings of morphemes into /tuk/, /wɔkt/. The only difference between the two cases is that (19v) is a much more general rule than (19ii). (p. 58)

The footnote to this passage is even more revealing:

Hockett gives a very clear presentation of this approach to levels in *A manual of phonology* (1955), p. 15. In "Two models of grammatical description," *Linguistics Today, Word* 10.21033 (1954), Hockett rejected a solution very much like the one we have just proposed on the grounds that "*took* and *take* are partly similar in phonemic shape just as are *baked* and *bake*, and similar in meaning also in the same way: this fact should not be obscured" (p. 224). But the similarity in meaning is not obscured in our formulation, since the morpheme *past* appears in the morphemic representation of both "took" and "baked." And the similarity in phonemic shape can be brought out in the actual formulation of the morphophonemic rule that carries *take* + *past* into /tuk/. We will no doubt formulate this rules [sic] as
ey → u in the context t—k + *past*[11] in the actual morphophonemic statement. This will allow us to simplify the grammar by a generalization that will bring out the parallel between "take"–"took," "shake"–"shook," "forsake"–"forsook," and more generally, "stand"– "stood," etc.

Chomsky lists "the affixes *past, S, ∅, en, ing*" in the affix hopping transformation. Of these affixes, only *S* and *ing* can be called phonologically concrete in any sense. We must conclude that affixes are morphemes (perhaps bound morphemes) and that morphemes are abstract entities made up of synonymous allomorphs in complementary distribution, as Harris had shown in 1942. Since Chomsky rejects semantics as a criterion, these abstract morphemes can only be determined through distributional analysis, again as Harris had shown.

The abstract 'affixes' that Chomsky names *past* and *en* have no reality outside his analysis of English verbs. What makes the analysis even possible is that each 'affix' is an abstract entity defined entirely in distributional terms. Each one comprises several phonologically distinct variant forms, including non-affixal morphological operations like the ablaut relating *take* and *took*. Also, for the overwhelming majority of verbs the two morphemes are homophonous, realized as <-ed>. We can unify the realizations of each under one morpheme and gather the morphemes under the category affix only within this specific very abstract analysis.[12] What, then, made this analysis so compelling? It's beauty and the belief on the part of readers that this beautiful analysis helped them to understand the phenomenon in a new way.

---

11 This is Bloch's (1947) analysis of the relation between *take* and *took*, and it has been repeated many times, even recently, often, as here, without attribution.
12 Affix-hopping is the evidence that these elements are all affixes, but affix-hopping has no validity outside the analysis in SS.

Which brings us back to the analysis of *S* and ∅ in footnote 3 and its "questionable validity." A decade earlier, in his warning against the use of purely distributional methods without regard for semantics, Nida had presented this same analysis as a *reductio ad absurdum* argument:

> Hockett considers that complementary distribution is all that fundamentally counts. But the implications of this method seem to be greater than he may have anticipated. For example, consider what could be done on that basis with number distinctions in English. Not only would it be possible to combine all the plural affixes of nouns in one morpheme (a step which we should all agree to), but one could say that these are in complementary distribution with the partly homophonous third-singular suffix of verbs. A single morpheme could then be set up with the meaning 'number distinctiveness' and with the additional distributional characteristic that if an alternant occurs after the noun it does not occur after the verb, and vice versa, e.g. /ðə boyz rən/ the boys run vs. /ðə boy rənz/ the boy runs. By slight extensions it might be possible to construct a descriptive system by which practically all the features of concord, government, and cross-reference could be treated on a submorphemic level. If this were done, we should only have succeeded in changing the meaning of the word 'morpheme' to apply it to certain distributionally related forms. (Nida 1949 p. 418).

Nida only hinted at the fatal flaw of this analysis, the wish to have one's cake and eat it too: if we combine all the plural affixes of nouns in one abstract noun-plural morpheme on the grounds of complementary distribution, which is indeed "a step which we should all agree to," then *S* cannot be a morpheme on its own, but must rather be one of the allomorphic realizations of the abstract noun-plural morpheme, along with the *–en* of *oxen*, the ablaut of *geese*, the ∅ of *deer*, and many others. Identifying this allomorphic *S* with the *S* of the third person singular is either comparing apples (if the verbal *S* is an abstract morpheme) and oranges (the plural *S* is an allomorphic realization, the output of morphophonemic rules in the framework of SS), or both instances of *S* (noun plural and verb singular) are allomorphs, in which case the likeness of the two affixes is no more than a curiosity, driven, as Nida so discreetly hints, by distributionalist zealotry and deliberate disregard for meaning. It is as accidental as the overwhelming homophonic realization of *past* and *–en* as <-ed>. This raises an entirely different question, about syncretism of morphs rather than morphemes, which has been entirely ignored.

Besides overzealousness, though, this curio of an analysis reveals the risk inherent in Chomsky's daring discard of the safety net of discovery procedures within a distributionalist ethos. Those who truly believed in discovery procedures had the comfort of faith: they knew that their distributionalist methods would always lead to the correct analysis. Without this net, there is no certainty. Some analyses will always fail because they are wrongly constructed, as is this one. Other analyses, including the analysis of English complex verbs, must be judged only in the court of academic opinion, for their beauty and their truth. Few will succeed there and even fewer masterpieces will endure for the ages, as this one has.

6 One: Number 31, 1950

Why do we sit transfixed in front of Jackson Pollock's *One: Number 31, 1950* at the Museum of Modern Art in New York? Its crushing beauty moves us to tears. Giotto's Scrovegni Chapel in Padua has the same effect. Both reveal a truth that the viewer has never experienced before. The same holds for the analysis of English verbs in (28) and (29) of *Syntactic Structures*. Chomsky writes of its simplicity, but simplicity alone is not enough to explain it. Rather it is the simplicity with which the analysis expresses what we quickly grasp as a new truth. The simplicity of the analysis is beautiful because, like the Pollock and the Giotto, it reveals a truth that we have never experienced before. All three share one common feature: their creators discovered an entirely novel technique and, more rarely, they used this technique to express a beautiful truth that no one had revealed before. For Pollock, it was the drip method that came to be called action painting. For Giotto it was naturalism augmented by perspective. For Chomsky it was the formal generative transformational technique exemplified in affix-hopping. But technique alone does not make a masterpiece and it does not make us weep.

Acknowledgements Thanks to the editors of this volume for suggesting the topic of affix hopping with special emphasis on questions of esthetics. Thanks to the members of my Spring 2017 graduate seminar and to Jiwon Yun for editorial help. Thanks especially to Richard Larson for his patience with my regular declarations that "now I understand."

Bibliography

Anderson, Stephen R. 1985. *Phonology in the twentieth century: Theories of rules and theories of representations.*. Chicago, IL: University of Chicago Press.
Anderson, Stephen R. 2015. The Morpheme: Its Nature and Use. In *The Oxford Handbook of Inflection*, ed. Matthew Baerman, 11–33. Oxford, UK: Oxford University Press.
Bloch, Bernard. 1947. English verb inflection. *Language* 23:399–418.
Bloch, Bernard. 1949. Leonard Bloomfield obituary. *Language* 25:87–94. Reprinted in Charles F. Hockett, ed., A Leonard Bloomfield Anthology. 525-532. Bloomington: Indiana University Press.
Bloomfield, Leonard. 1933. *Language*. New York, NY: Harcourt Brace.

Chomsky, Noam. 1955/1975b. The Logical Structure of Linguistic Theory. MS, MIT.
Chomsky, Noam. 1957. *Syntactic Structures*. The Hague, The Netherlands: Mouton de Gruyter.
Chomsky, Noam. 1975a. Preface to The Logical Structure of Linguistic Theory. In Chomsky 1975b.
Chomsky, Noam. 1995. *The Minimalist Program*. Cambridge, MA: MIT Press.
Darwin, Charles. 1859. *On the Origin of Species by Means of Natural Selection*. London, UK: John Murray.
Dresher, B. Elan. 2011. The Phoneme. In *The Blackwell Companion to Phonology, Volume 1*, ed. Marc van Oostendorp, Colin J. Ewen, Elizabeth Hume, and Keren Rice, 241–266. Malden, MA: Wiley Blackwell.
Fought, John G. 1999. Leonard Bloomfield's Linguistic Legacy: Later uses of some technical features. *Historiographia Linguistica* 26:313–332.
Gazdar, Gerald, Geoffrey K Pullum, and Ivan A Sag. 1982. Auxiliaries and related phenomena in a restrictive theory of grammar. *Language* 591–638.
Girard, Gabriel. 1718. *la justesse de la langue francoise ou les différentes significations des mots qui passent pour synonimes*. Paris, France: Laurent d'Houry.
Harris, Zellig S. 1936. A Grammar of the Phoenician Language. Doctoral Dissertation, University of Pennsylvania.
Harris, Zellig S. 1939. *Development of the Canaanite Dialects: An Investigation in Linguistic History*. American Oriental Series. New Haven, CT: American Oriental Society.
Harris, Zellig S. 1942. Morpheme alternants in linguistic analysis. *Language* 18:169–180.
Harris, Zellig S. 1948. Componential analysis of a Hebrew paradigm. *Language* 24:87–91.
Harris, Zellig S. 1951. *Methods in Structural Linguistics*. Chicago, IL: University of Chicago Press.
Harris, Zellig S. 2002. The background of transformational and metalanguage analysis. In *The Legacy of Zellig Harris: Language and Information into the 21st Century. Volume 1: Philosophy of Science, Syntax, and Semantics*, ed. Bruce E. Nevin, 1–15. Amsterdam, Netherlands: John Benjamins.
Jakobson, Roman. 1971. The Kazan' school of Polish linguistics and its place in the international development of phonology. In *Word and Language: Selected Writings, vol 2*, ed. Roman Jakobson, 394–428. The Hague, Netherlands: Mouton.
Lasnik, Howard. 2005. *Minimalist investigations in linguistic theory*. London, UK: Routledge.
Matthews, Peter Hugo. 1993. *Grammatical theory in the United States: from Bloomfield to Chomsky*. Cambridge, UK: Cambridge University Press.
McQuown, Norman A. 1952. Review of *Methods in Structural Linguistics* by Zellig S. Harris. *Language* 28:495–504.
Nida, Eugene A. 1949. *Morphology: The Descriptive Analysis of Words (2nd edition)*. Ann Arbor, MI: University of Michigan Press.
Whorf, Benjamin Lee. 1945. Grammatical categories. *Language* 21:1–11.
Whorf, Benjamin Lee. 1956. *Language, Thought and Reality, edited by John B. Carroll*. London, UK: John Wiley & Sons.
Wittgenstein, Ludwig. 1953. *Philosophical Investigations*. London, UK: John Wiley & Sons.

Artemis Alexiadou, Elena Anagnostopoulou and Florian Schäfer
Passive

1 Introduction: Chomsky (1957)

The starting point of any investigation of the passive is the observation that active and passive sentences are related. Unlike other Voice alternations, e.g. the causative alternation, the relationship between the active and the passive seems to be pretty systematic. To illustrate this, consider the examples in (1)

(1) a. John destroyed the manuscript.
    b. The manuscript was destroyed (by John).

The two sentences have basically the same meaning, but they differ in word order and the form of certain elements (e.g. the form of the verb and the (however optional) inclusion of the *by*-phrase in the passive). Unlike the causative-inchoative alternation, the active-passive alternation in English and many other languages is fully productive, does not show gaps and is always associated with special morphology.

The relationship between actives and passives is discussed in Chomsky (1957:42f.), where passive formation is presented as an example of the limitation of phrase structure grammars. Chomsky argues that passive formation should be excluded from the grammatical kernel of phrase structure rules and, instead, be derived from a phrase marker by the transformational rule in (2):[1]

---

[1] Chomsky (1957: 79f.) briefly entertains the hypothesis how the grammar would be like if passives were to be seen as the kernel sentences instead of actives and rejects it as it would lead to a more complex grammar. The simplest grammar is one in which the kernel contains simple, active, declarative sentences and all other sentences are the result of transformations. Note that there are two conceptions of the term kernel. For Chomsky, a kernel sentence is crucially generated without the application of optional transformations. Specifically, in Chomsky's conception of the kernel, transformations apply to abstract structures to generate other structures. This differs from Harris's 1957 conception of the kernel, where a kernel sentence is a sentence that is not derived by any transformations, and transformations apply to sentences to generate other sentences. Thus, crucially for Harris passive sentences are derived from active sentences, while this does not literally hold for Chomsky's interpretation of the term (Chomsky 1957: 44f.). We would like to thank Norbert Hornstein for discussing this issue with us.

(2) If S_1 is a grammatical sentence of the form
$NP_1 - Aux - V - NP_2$
then the corresponding string of the form
$NP_2 - Aux+be+en - V - by+NP_1$
is also a grammatical sentence.

Chomsky argues that the grammar of English would have to be a lot more complicated if passives were formed by phrase structure rules instead of the transformation in (2). Assume the basic phrase structure rules in (3) (Chomsky 1957: 26), auxiliaries can be included if we add (4) (Chomsky 1957:39), where M stands for modals, C reflects inflectional affixes (zero, 3rd person -s or past tense -ed), which are lowered, just as the affixes -en and -ing, to the next verbal head to the right. Passive sentences in English would be formed by choosing the third auxiliary-affix combination be+en from the phrase structure rule in (4iii).

(3) (i) Sentence → NP + VP
    (ii) NP → T + N
    (iii) VP → V + NP

(4) (i) Verb → Aux + V
    (ii) V → hit, take, walk, read, etc.
    (iii) Aux → C(M) (have+en) (be+ing) (be+en)

However, as Chomsky points out, the passive discontinuous element *be+en* shows a number of unique properties among auxiliaries. On the one hand, it can only be selected if the following V is transitive (*was eat-en* is permitted, but not the unaccusative **was occur-ed* or the plain unergative **was danced*). On the other hand, it can also not be selected if V is immediately followed by an NP, i.e. *lunch was eaten John* is not possible. Next, while the other auxiliaries can optionally be inserted, the passive auxiliary is obligatory in the sense that it must be selected if V is transitive and the preposition *by* follows V (*Lunch is eat-en by John; *Lunch eats by John; *Lunch is eat-ing by John*). Finally, a full-fledged grammar must enrich (3) with selectional restrictions on part of individual verbs to reflect that e.g. *John admires sincerity* and *Sincerity frightens John* are OK sentences but *Sincerity admires John* and *John frightens sincerity* are not. In later stages of the theory (Chomsky 1981, 1986), these restrictions were implemented by the interplay of lexical θ-roles, the projection principle and a mapping theory that culminated in UTAH Baker (1988, 1997). As Chomsky (1957) furthermore points out, active and passive sentences show exactly the same selectional restrictions on their NPs, with the crucial difference that these apply in exactly the opposite order in passives than in actives (consider NP_1 and NP_2 in (2)). If both actives and passives are formed by phrase structure rules, then a verb's selectional restrictions would have to be stated twice, once for the NPs in active sentences, and a second time in exactly the opposite order for the NPs in sentences involving the passive auxiliary *be+en*.

Chomsky concludes that all these complications can be overcome if passives are not formed by phrase structure rules but by the transformational rule in (2). This rule "interchanges the subject and object of the active, and replaces V by *is+V+en+by*" (Chomsky 1957: 77). Consequently, *be+en* can be dropped from (4iii), and all restrictions on passive formation mentioned above are reflected by the well-formedness of the base sentence and the properties of this rule. Thus, if *John admires sincerity* is a sentence, so is *Sincerity is admired by John*.

Two further operations need to be considered in order to cover the full treatment of passives in Chomsky (1957). First, the substring $by + NP_1$ in (2) behaves like a constituent, as it can be the input to further transformations like WH-movement or topicalization. Chomsky (1957: 73f.) proposes the general condition on derived constituent structure in (5). Applied to passives, (5) says that the sub-string $by + NP_1$, formed by the transformation in (2), has the status of a PP because a string *by+NP* is otherwise also characterized as a PP by the phrase structure grammar.[2]

(5) If X is a Z in the phrase structure grammar, and a string Y formed by a transformation is of the same structural form as X, then Y is also a Z.

Second, since passive *by*-phrases are optional, Chomsky (1957: 89f.; see also p. 81, fn. 7) assumes that this PP can be deleted by an "elliptical transformation ... that drops the agent in the passive".

In this chapter, we will address the following question: after 60 years of syntactic research, what aspects of this analysis of English passives do we definitely have to capture in our current models? In other words, which aspects of this analysis (both (morpho-)syntactic and semantic) should any theory of the passive in English, but also cross-linguistically to the extent that other languages have English-type passives, offer an account for?

First, every theory must capture the generalization that at least in English basically every transitive verb can passivize (though we will refine this below), that active and passive sentences differ in word order (and/or in case/agreement morphology) and that verbal passives come with a particular morphological marking (in English the passive auxiliary and the participle).

---

[2] "In particular, even when passives are deleted from the kernel we will want to say that the *by*-phrase (as in "the food was eaten - by the man") is a prepositional phrase (PP) in the passive sentence." (Chomsky 1957: 74).

Second, (2) expresses the fundamental insight that the selectional restrictions in active and passive sentences are two sides of the same lexical-semantic coin; the argument NPs of a passive sentence are the very same arguments that we find in the active sentence, which surface, however, in the opposite order in English.

This insight is taken care of in (2) via the hypothesis that the argument NPs are generated in a fixed position by the kernel rules, and the passive transformation consists of what could be called today an instance of leftwards movement plus an instance of rightward movement. Indeed, most modern grammatical theories employ (different versions of) leftward movement, and there is robust and extensive cross-linguistic evidence that the subject of the passive is merged as an internal argument of the verb eventually undergoing A-movement to a derived subject position for Case/EPP reasons.

The hypothesis that the external argument NP_1 undergoes rightward movement, however, has turned out to be problematic as it is generally accepted that rightward movement, in particular rightward A-movement, does not exist. And, indeed, the question of how exactly to treat the external argument in passive *by*-phrases remains one of the main controversies in the discussion of passives, as will be seen.

In this connection, two further aspects in the treatment of the external argument of passives in Chomsky (1957) are clearly not satisfactory from today's perspective. One concerns the formation of the *by*-phrase via the rule in (5); as (Collins 2005:107) points out (5) "violates a general economy condition that states that constituent structure that is already built cannot be changed at a later point in the derivation." Furthermore, the idea that in so-called short passives (i.e. passives without the *by*-phrase) the *by*-phrase is deleted by a rule of ellipsis cannot be maintained. First, it does not obey any considerations of recoverability. Second, it is unclear how to preclude such a rule from over-generation by deleting other arguments, e.g. the external arguments of active clauses. These points of criticism are relevant in so far as the treatment of *by*-phrases remains one of the most problematic issues in more recent theories of passivization.

Finally, rule 2 was introduced as to capture the properties of English passivization and was not necessarily meant as a theory of passivization that holds universally. We observe the following. First, the generalization that only transitive predicates can form passives is not even fully correct for English.[3] Importantly, rule (2) does not necessarily have to be transferred as is to other languages, lead-

---

[3] In *Aspects*, it is pointed out that the passive rule does not hold for all transitive predicates. Chomsky (1965: 103f.) notes that the passive transformation can apply to verbs that are positively specified in the lexicon for the subcategorization frame [__ NP Manner], i.e. verbs that allow a manner adverb. By doing this, Chomsky captures Lees' 1960 observation that only verbs that

ing to a state of affairs in which for each language X, a new and different passive rule should be formulated. And indeed, as is well-known, there are languages like German or Icelandic where transitive and unergative verbs productively passivize. The relevant generalization in view of this seems to be that any verb with an external argument can, in principle, passivize and there are differences across languages concerning the availability of impersonal passives.[4] It has been argued that even unaccusatives can passivize in some languages.[5]

There is another, less widely acknowledged point of variation, however, which we will discuss in section 3, namely that there are also languages where passivization is not fully productive and applies only to what seems to be an at least partially idiosyncratic subset of active verbs. Thus, cross-linguistic research has shown that passivization is a very general rule across languages but is nevertheless not a fully uniform phenomenon and that at least two modes of passive-formation need to be identified. As will be seen in the next sections, this second point of variation has occasionally been observed for individual languages but has not figured prominently in analyses of the passive within the P&P framework and subsequent work.

In the next section, we will describe in some detail a modern incarnation of Chomsky (1957) in Collins (2005); see also Müller (2016) for a different approach in the same spirit.

---

can combine with manner adverbials can freely form a passive, e.g. reciprocal marry, resemble, have, weight etc. do not form passives in English. The passive rule in Chomsky (1965: 104) also captures pseudo-passives (*the proposal was vehemently argued against*). Still this account offers no explanation for impersonal passives with embedded complement clauses and the pronoun *it* in subject position (*it was decided/concluded that ...*).

4 It seems that the question whether unergatives can passivize relates to the EPP-properties of the language combined with the availability of a suitable expletive and/or default agreement (e.g. Ruys 2010).

5 Zaenen (1993), Primus (2011), Kiparsky (2013) among others cast doubt on the unavailability of impersonal passives of unaccusatives predicates. As summarized in (Kiparsky 2013:10), two conditions seem to guide passivization of such intransitive predicates. The first one is whether the language allows the EPP to be violated, i.e. no languages that disallow subjectless sentences allow for impersonal passivization of unaccusatives (c.f. the previous footnote). Second, the implicit argument of such predicates is interpretable as human or agentive/volitional.

2 Passives in syntactic theory with a focus on problems caused by *by*-phrases

The Chomskyan framework has undergone several important shifts in its 60 years of existence. With the rise of Government & Binding (GB) theory, the model moved away from construction specific rules such as the passive transformation towards a theory of interacting general and abstract Principles across different modules of the grammar. θ-theory provided the module for making statements about lexical properties (of verbs and their arguments) in the lexicon, which was abandoned in much later work that adopted configurationally determined thematic roles (see Borer 2005; Ramchand 2008 for alternative ways to capture lexical properties). Abstract Case-theory provided an explanation for A-movement, i.e. the observation that NPs occur in surface positions different than their thematic ones. In a lot of work on Parameters, cross-linguistic variation has been tied to what came to be labeled as the Chomsky-Borer Conjecture, i.e. reducible to differences in the Lexicon of different languages and specifically the elements of their functional vocabulary.

The standard analysis of passives put forth within the P&P framework makes crucial use of the following two assumptions:

(6) a. The passive suffix *-en* absorbs accusative Case.
    b. The passive suffix *-en* absorbs the external θ-role. (Collins 2005:82)

Jaeggli (1986) and Baker et al. (1989) suggest that these two properties coincide in the passive suffix because this suffix actually is an argument in the technical sense, and as such it needs to be assigned a θ-role and Case (the former follows from the θ-Criterion; the latter from the Visibility Condition; Chomsky 1981). On this line of analysis, *-en* is like a clitic base generated under I(nfl), where it receives the external θ-role, and lowers onto the verb, from which it receives accusative. Consequently, the internal argument cannot be assigned (accusative) Case *in situ*, and it moves to the subject position (Spec,IP at that time), where it receives nominative Case. The derivation of passives is thus subsumed under Move-α. This reflects the general shift in the theory away from construction specific transformations.

One further aspect of this analysis is the treatment of *by*-phrases. According to Jaeggli (1986), the passive suffix not only absorbs (or better receives) the external θ-role, but it can also transmit the external θ-role to the *by*-phrase (a process called θ-role transmission). The θ-role transmitted to the PP percolates to *by* and *by* assigns the external θ-role to its complement DP. Baker et al. (1989) view this relationship between the suffix and the *by*-phrase similar to that of a clitic-doubling. Both these accounts then assume a kind of non-movement chain between the passive suffix and the DP inside the *by*-phrase.

Collins (2005: 83f.) criticizes this approach and related approaches from that period because the external θ-role is not assigned uniformly in the active and in the passive; in the active it is assigned to a DP in Spec,IP. The passive morpheme, however, is located in the I(nfl)-head when it is assigned the external θ-role, and a DP inside the *by*-phrase receives its θ-role by a special mechanism of θ-role transmission from the passive morpheme. Thus, such theories appear to violate UTAH (Baker 1988: 46), which states that "identical thematic relationships between items are represented by identical structural relationships between these items at the level of D-structure." Collins adds the consideration that such theories are also incompatible with the so-called configurational theory of θ-role assignment which replaced UTAH in minimalist theorizing once D-structure as an independent representational level was dispensed with and the existence of the lexicon as a level where lexical relationships are stated was questioned. Within the configurational theory of θ-role assignment "each syntactic position (e.g. Spec,vP, complement of V) is associated with a particular θ-role (or set of θ-roles)" (Collins 2005: 84). Collins concludes that "from the point of view of the Minimalist Program it is necessary that the θ-role of the external argument in the passive be assigned in exactly the same way as the external θ-role in the active" (Collins 2005: 84).

While we only partially agree with this last statement (see below), recall that the assumption that the θ-role of the external argument is assigned in exactly the same way in the active and in the passive, is a central assumption underlying Chomsky's transformational analysis of the Passive in English. It is from this perspective that Collins's analysis of the passive (2005) could be called a modern incarnation of (2), as we detail right below.

Based on UTAH Collins proposes that the external argument is always merged in the canonical subject position, Spec,vP, both in the active and in the passive (v is similar to Kratzer's (1996) Voice-head in that it severs the external argument θ-role from the lexical verb, which is located in V). Furthermore, Collins treats the passive participial suffix *-en* (*John was seen*) as identical to the past participial suffix *-en* (*I have seen John*). Both participles involve the same Participle Phrase (PartP) headed by the *-en* affix which is sandwiched between vP and VP, as in (7) (but see Embick (2004), who labels the projection headed by *-en* AspectP, and places it above vP). The lexical verb in V raises to Part to form the participle. Spec,vP is filled by the external argument, and the participial affix *-en* does not absorb any thematic role, nor does it absorb Case for reasons having to do with the way Collins treats the Active-Passive distinction discussed below (see the discussion below (11); he actually claims that absorption of accusative Case in passives is an illusion).

(7)   [vP DP₁ v [PartP -en [VP V DP₂]]]

The difference in word order between passives and actives follows from this analysis because it is hypothesized that participles need to be licensed and there is one way to license them as active past participles and a different way to license them as passive participles, as described in (8) (Collins 2005: 90).[6]

(8)   A participle (PartP) must be licensed by
    a. being c-selected by the auxiliary *have* or
    b. moving to Spec, VoiceP

We concentrate here on (8b). In passives, a VoiceP (which differs from Kratzer's VoiceP in that it is especially dedicated to formal passive formation and does not carry any semantic impact) must merge on top of vP, and PartP is attracted to Spec,VoiceP, thereby smuggling the internal argument across the external argument in Spec,vP. That is, the rightward-movement aspect of NP₁ in rule (2) is replaced in Collins (2005) by phrasal movement to the left, and this phrasal movement can take place only if Voice is present to provide a thematically empty specifier as an escape hatch, i.e. if a passive is formed.

(9)   [VoiceP **[PartP -en [VP V DP₂]]** Voice [vP DP₁ v [<PartP>]]]

Finally, an auxiliary *be* and I(nfl) are merged as in (10), and DP₂ is attracted to Spec,IP. Note that without the smuggling of PartP across the subject, movement of DP₂ to Spec, IP would be blocked due to a violation of the Minimal Link Condition, as DP₁ would intervene.[7]

---

6 (8a, b) are counterbalanced by (ia, b), in order to avoid overgeneralization (Collins 2005: 91, (25a, b)):
(i) a.   The auxiliary verb *have* obligatorily c-selects for a participle.
      b.   Voice requires a participle (PartP) to move to Spec,VoiceP.

7 Collins is aware of the fact that other instances of XP-movement trigger Freezing effects. He suggests that there are two types of XP-movement that differ in this respect. He also provides empirical evidence that XP-movement has taken place in English passives, which we will not review here. If XP-movement obligatorily triggers freezing effects, then an alternative account should be provided for the empirical evidence he discusses.

(10)   [$_{IP}$ **DP$_2$** [$_{I'}$ I [$_{VP}$ be [$_{VoiceP}$ [$_{PartP}$ -en [$_{vP}$ V <DP$_2$>]] Voice [$_{vP}$ DP$_1$ v <PartP>]]]]]

The derivation in (10) does not feature yet the preposition *by* and its relation to DP$_1$. In (9), (10), DP$_1$ is merged in Spec,vP, exactly as in active clauses.

In his discussion of *by*, Collins (2005: 93f) raises a further point (which has not drawn much attention in the GB-literature) beyond the UTAH issue in connection to the *by*-phrase discussed above: how to ensure that the preposition *by* only introduces external arguments in passives, and not, for example, an internal argument (**John was written by the book*) or the external argument in actives? He concludes that this distributional fact about passive *by* suggests that *by* selects for a vP (not the other way around, as would be the case if Spec,vP could be filled by the *by*-phrase). He then proposes that *by* is the head of VoiceP, as in (11), an updated version of (9) above.

(11)   [$_{VoiceP}$ PartP by$_{Voice}$ [$_{vP}$ DP$_1$ v [<PartP>]]]

As mentioned, Voice for Collins is a functional head that lacks any interpretational features, in contrast to the lower v head introducing the external argument. Consequently, Collins characterizes *by*, the head of VoiceP, as a dummy linker, and not as a lexical preposition. Furthermore, he assumes that accusative Case is checked by v in active clauses; in passive clauses, however, "the case feature of v is divorced from v and is projected as part of VoiceP" (Collins 2005: 96). ACC-absorption in passives is thus just an illusion as *by*$_{Voice}$ then checks the structural ACC feature of the DP$_1$ in Spec,vP (similarly to the prepositional complementizer *for* checking ACC on the DP in Spec,IP in ECM constructions of the type [$_{CP}$ *For John to win would be nice*]). DP$_2$ then receives NOM from T.

But note that the structure in (11) raises the same question as Chomsky's rule (2): how do *by+DP$_1$* form a constituent? Recall that Collins rejects a solution along the lines of (5). Instead, he argues that the PP-constituency of *by*-phrases is an illusion. For example, he suggests that (12a) does not have the structure (12b) but it is derived from (13a), where two VoicePs are coordinated. Each VoiceP has the identical PartP moved to its specifier. DP$_2$ is extracted by ATB-movement and the second PartP is deleted under identity.

(12)   a.   The book was written by John and by Bill.
       b.   The book was written [$_{ConjP}$ [$_{PP}$ by John] and [$_{PP}$ by Bill]]

(13)   a.   The book was written by John and written by Bill.
       b.   The book was [[$_{VoiceP}$ [$_{PartP}$ written <the book>] by$_{Voice}$ John] and
                  [$_{VoiceP}$ [$_{PartP}$ ~~written <the book>~~] by$_{Voice}$ Bill]]

While we agree that he offers convincing arguments for the claim that (12a) can, in principle, be derived by coordinating two VoicePs and deleting material in the second one, the claim that *by* + DP_1 do not form a constituent-PP has been criticized by many (e.g. Kiparsky 2013; Müller 2016) and we agree with these criticisms. Kiparsky, for example, points out that if *by* is the head of Voice, then we have no explanation for *by*'s adnominal functions. Moreover, an analysis along the lines of (13b) becomes impossible if the coordinated *by*-phrases are topicalized as in (14), and similar phenomena can be found in other languages.

(14) Neither by John nor by Mary could such a book ever have been written.

On the basis of the discussion so far, we would like to conclude that, while DP_1 in passives indeed receives the external argument θ-role of v, *by* still behaves like a preposition that takes DP_1 as its complement. Case considerations strongly support this conclusion. In languages with morphological case, *by* does not typically assign the verb's objective case (ACC) to DP_1 but rather lexical case, e.g. in German dative, as shown in (15), while in Slavic languages agents appear bearing instrumental Case. Moreover, note that the presence of lexical case is rather unexpected if *by* is really void of any meaning and of (DP-related) argument structure, contra Collins (2005).[8]

But then the question how ACC is absorbed in passives resurfaces. We hold that Case absorption should not be allowed as a special mechanism in the grammar and we follow what we think is the simplest account of Case based on a particular interpretation of Burzio's generalization: ACC depends on the presence of a syntactically projected external argument. If passive vP lacks a specifier (see Alexiadou et al. 2015 for detailed argumentation why passives include a light head lacking a specifier), the internal argument DP of passives (just as the internal argument of unaccusatives) will get nominative case in nominative-accusative languages following a dependent case approach (Marantz 1991 and many others following him).[9]

---

[8] Note that we are not suggesting that *by* assigns its own θ-role. *By* allows transferring the canonical external argument role provided by v to its complement DP in a compositional way via the semantics in (28a) to be discussed below.

[9] But see Schäfer (2012) for a discussion of certain complications.

(15) a. Der   Junge las   den   Roman
         the.NOM boy   read the.ACC novel

   b. Der   Roman wurde von dem   Jungen / *den
       the.NOM   novel was   by   the.DAT   boy   / *the.ACC
       Jungen   gelesen
       boy   read

Collins furthermore assumes that the external argument is syntactically present even in short passives. In this case, the head of passive VoiceP is phonologically zero, the external argument is merged in Spec,vP as PRO and zero Voice checks whatever case PRO has, possibly null Case (Chomsky, 1995, chapter1). We find this view on short passives rather problematic for a number of reasons.

First, it has to be stipulated that this PRO has to be arbitrary and, unlike ordinary PRO, can never be controlled (cf. (16) from Bhatt and Pancheva 2006). Crucially, (16a) can only have the interpretation in (16b) and not the one in (16c); this must be stipulated if the implicit argument in (16a) is ordinary PRO.

(16) a. Every journalist wants Kylie to be interviewed.
     b. Every journalist wants Kylie to be interviewed by someone.
     c. Every journalist$_1$ wants Kylie to be interviewed by him$_1$.

Second, if the implicit argument is PRO, it remains unclear why impersonal passives (of unergative verbs or of verbs with objects carrying lexical case), cannot appear in infinitives. For instance, the German example in (17a) shows that an infinitival subject clause with the active version of the dative verb *helfen* (help) is well-formed. Here the subject is arguably PRO. Since the verb *helfen* selects an object with lexical dative case, it can only form an impersonal passive. In (17b), we see that the impersonal passive can appear in a subject clause if the clause is finite. But if the subject clause is non-finite, the passive of *helfen* is no longer possible (17c). This is unexpected if the external argument of the passive is (arbitrary) PRO.

(17) a. [PRO dem   Mann zu helfen] ist gut.
              the.DAT man   to help   is   good

     b. [Dass dem   Mann geholfen wird] ist gut.
         that   the.DAT man   helped   is   is   good

     c. *[Dem   Mann geholfen zu werden] ist gut.
          the.DAT man   helped   to be   is   good

Third, Collins claims that passives license reflexive pronouns as in (18a), and that this is expected because PRO is known to license anaphors (18b).

(18) a. Such privileges should be kept to oneself.
     b. To be nice of oneself is a priority.

However, across languages, binding of reflexive pronouns by the implicit external argument of passives seems to be rather impossible. A few languages indeed allow strings such as (18a), e.g. German, but Schäfer (2012) provides experimental evidence that the passivized verb in such cases must be inherently or naturally reflexive; with ordinary transitive verbs, the construction is rejected in German. Concerning English, Collins mentions that examples like (18a) show lots of speaker variation. Furthermore, note that the more acceptable examples in the literature all involve modality (or negation, as pointed out to us by Norbert Hornstein); when this condition is not met, the result is ungrammatical (cf. (19) adapted from Kastner and Zu (2014)). Since active infinitive clauses do not show such variation and restriction we tend to conclude that a close look at Principle A phenomena actually suggests that the implicit argument of passives is not a licenser of reflexive pronouns.[10]

(19) a. *A book was being sent to himself/oneself.
     b. *Mary was shown [a picture of himself/oneself].

A further reason to reject the PRO-analysis comes from depictives. Collins argues that the implicit argument of passives is PRO, as it can license depictives, see (20). Data similar to (20) received quite different judgments in the literature (cf. Chomsky 1986, Landau 2010). As Pitteroff and Schäfer (2017) show, adjectival depictives relating to the implicit agent of passives are, in principle, acceptable in many languages (including English).[11] However, they are illicit in passives of

---

10 Collins suggests that speaker variation and marginality of examples such as (18a) results because PartP must be reconstructed. However, the same marginality, or even ungrammaticality, holds in SOV languages (German, Dutch, etc.) where word order suggests that smuggling is not a reasonable option to begin with.

11 Such depictives seem to be subject to a kind of acceptability hierarchy. They are best in impersonal passives lacking any overt DP. With personal passives, they are better if the nominative DP is non-human than if it is human. In the latter case, speakers tend to relate the depictive to the human DP, even if this results in a rather nonsensical interpretation. Again, this suggests to us that the implicit argument is not a syntactic entity in passives, as it should then be on a par with overt DPs, as in infinitives where PRO can easily be accessed by depictives despite the presence of overt DPs.

exactly those languages where the secondary depictive adjective overtly inflects for phi-features of its antecedent (e.g. in Icelandic, Russian or Hebrew passives). This suggests that (uninflected) depictives can be licensed in a purely semantic way and that the implicit argument of passives is not projected as PRO, because PRO should have phi-features and hence depictives in Icelandic, Russian and Hebrew passives should be grammatical.

(20) The book was written drunk.

To sum up, the main insight from Chomsky (1957) is that English active and passive sentences are the two sides of the same coin as they impose exactly the same selectional restrictions on their NPs, though in exactly the opposite linear order. Chomsky derives this thematic parallelism with the transformation in (2) and Collins rephrases this approach in modern syntactic terms. Collins correctly rejects the rule in (5), which forms the *by*-phrase in Chomsky (1957), as incompatible with minimalist reasoning, but then he makes two assumptions which, as we argued, are empirically not warranted, neither within English nor beyond, namely that the *by*-phrase does not exist as a structural unit and that short passives involve a PRO subject. Above, we have explicitly argued against these claims: we believe that *by*-phrases really are prepositional phrases. Furthermore, the empirical picture suggests to us that the implicit external argument is not projected in the syntax (e.g. as PRO).[12] Consequently, we cannot assume that the external argument of short or long passives enters the syntactic structure in exactly the same way as in active sentences.

Recall now that the reasoning behind Collins's set-up derives from his view on the lexicon-syntax mapping and specifically on the way he views the concept of configurational θ-role assignment. However, we are hesitant to follow Collins's ultimate reasoning, which says: "From the point of view of the Minimalist Program it is necessary that the θ-role of the external argument in the passive be assigned in exactly the same way as the external θ-role in the active" (Collins 2005: 84). In fact, this conclusion does not directly follow from the theory of configurational θ-role assignment: nothing prohibits the external θ-role (i) to remain without syntactic realization (implicit, i.e. as an existentially bound variable only semantically represented in the meaning of v/Voice), or (ii) to be realized by an adjunct

---

[12] Landau (2010) also argues that implicit arguments are syntactically projected not as PRO but as so-called *phiP* (see also Legate 2014). His argument, which is developed on the basis of implicit arguments of adjectives, is not directly transferable to passives and, as discussed in Pitteroff and Schäfer (2017), became obsolete for theoretical reasons. In general, we would like to refrain from postulating covert categories that seem to appear only in construction specific contexts.

to vP/VoiceP, i.e. as the *by*-phrase, unless we limit configurational θ-roles to *Set-Merge* (Chomsky, 2000). Instead, it seems to implicitly rely on the second clause of the θ-criterion in (21), which could be read in such a way that a semantic argument slot comes into existence by external merge:[13]

(21) Each argument bears one and only one θ-role, and each θ-role is assigned to one and only one argument. (Chomsky 1981: 36)

The theory of configurational θ-role assignment relates to the first sentence of (21): If an argument (DP) is merged in the syntax, the position of merge determines its interpretation/thematic role; if, for example, a DP is merged in Spec,vP, it will be interpreted as agent/causer. We do not see, however, how such a principle could enforce that each semantic argument/θ-role is necessarily projected to syntax; it does not enforce, for example, that Spec,vP of a transitive verb is always filled with a DP. Furthermore, it does not ensure that a semantic argument/θ-role can only be realized by a syntactic element merged in one particular position.

In fact, lexical theories, which underlie UTAH and the θ-Criterion, assumed that the external argument of passives is existentially bound in the lexical-semantic representation—the level of argument structure—and consequently it is not projected to syntax. In that sense, the (θ-role of the) external argument of passives is exempt from the second clause of (21) (under the interpretation that 'argument' means 'syntactic argument'). While Minimalism does not per se do away with a level of argument structure, at least within those frameworks such as Distributed Morphology (DM) that seek to reduce the burden on the lexicon we need to find a way to rephrase this lexical treatment of the external argument of passives in more syntactic terms. Verbal decomposition, in particular the idea that the external argument variable is semantically introduced by a semi-functional projection above the verbal phrase (Kratzer, 1996), allows us to analyze passives in a way that they do not include a syntactically projected external argument while at the same time being able to account for the fact that the external argument is interpreted in the same way in the active and in the passive. In some sense, Kratzerian Voice, with its semantic variable (agent(e, x), causer(e, x), holder(e, x)) could be understood as doing the job of Chomsky's (1957) kernel, while the active-passive opposition derives from whether Voice projects a DP-specifier saturating the variable introduced by Voice or not.

---

[13] We find Collins's idea according to which argumenthood is fully driven by syntactic realization of arguments inherently consistent; it is just that we do not see it confirmed by the empirical picture.

On the other hand, we will see in the next section that both an account along the lines of Collins (who thereby follows Chomsky 1957) that projects the external argument in passives in the canonical subject position, and an account along the lines of Kratzer (1996) that represents the implicit argument of passives only at the semantic level introduced by Voice, undergenerate from a cross-linguistic perspective. It turns out that there are actually two ways to form a passive across languages, a productive and a semi-productive way, and we will suggest an account for this distinction in terms of the hypothesis that passivization might either apply inside of the verbal phase or outside and on top of the verbal phase.

3 Passive formation across languages

Recall that Chomsky's analysis of English passives predicts that passivization is a fully productive process, in that basically every transitive verb should give rise to a passive. This holds (more or less; see footnote 3) for English and many more languages, suggesting that rule (2) could be seen as rule of UG instead of just a rule of the English grammar. However, it has been pointed out in the literature that passive formation is not equally productive across languages, pointing to the non-generality of rule (2).

Greek is a case in point. As Zombolou (2004) and Alexiadou et al. (2015) report, there are several, sometimes poorly understood, restrictions on Greek passive formation. For one, many and perhaps most change-of-state verbs strongly resist the combination with the non-active (NAct) ending which is necessary to form a passive in Greek, e.g. *kriono* 'cool-1sg', **kriono*me* 'cool-NAct'; *vatheno* 'deepen-1sg', **vathenome* 'deepen-NAct'; *adinatizo* 'thin-1sg', ?**adinatizime* 'thinen-NAct'; *gernao* 'age-1sg', **gerazome* 'age-NAct', etc. Arguably some of these verbs belong to the group of "internally-caused verbs" (Levin and Rappaport Hovav, 1995), i.e. they are unaccusative verbs, which simply do not combine with an external argument. However, other predicates such as the Greek counterparts of *break*, *deepen*, *cool* and many others clearly have active transitive uses. Nevertheless, they resist passivization.[14] Moreover, Zombolou (2004) observed that passivization is quite restricted with other verb classes as well. For example, several mono-eventive

---

14 As pointed out in Alexiadou et al. (2015), some of these verbs lack passives just for reasons of a phonological clash that results from the combination of their stem with the non-active affix (e.g: **vathinome* 'deepen-NAct', **kontenome* 'shorten-NAct', **leptenome* 'thinen-NAct', **makrenome* 'lenghten-NAct').

verbs cannot form a passive in Greek or can do so very marginally, unlike English and German: *haidevo* 'stroke', *derno* 'beat', *klotsao* 'kick', *frondizo* 'take care of'.

Furthermore, Alexiadou et al. (2015) noted that many Greek verbs are allowed to combine with non-active morphology (e.g. the translation equivalents of *burn*, *cut* or *kill*), but only yield an anticausative, not a passive interpretation (they do not accept the Greek counterparts of *by*-phrases, for example). Similar gaps have been described for other languages as well, e.g. Palestinian Arabic (Laks, 2009).

Such languages pose a problem for theories that assume that every transitive verb should have a passive counterpart, as they make it impossible to exclude individual verbs and verb classes from passive formation. In fact, such restrictions have been taken by many to signal a lexical approach to passivization. Lascaratou and Philippaki-Warburton (1984) and Smirniotopoulos (1992) argued that the limited productivity of the passive in Greek seems to have properties associated with a lexical operation (see e.g. the discussion in Wasow 1977; cf. the Lexicon-Syntax parameter in Reinhart and Siloni 2005 which is in the same spirit).

The above contrast between Greek and English-like languages suggests that there are two ways in which a passive can come about, see also Alexiadou and Doron (2012): passives are either amenable to what has been analyzed as a lexical and a syntactic derivation in weak lexicalist approaches. Adapting a line of analysis pursued in Kratzer (1996) and Marantz (2001) for different types of adjectival passives within languages, in Alexiadou et al. (2015) we argued that the Greek vs. English contrast in the productivity of verbal passives can be understood and implemented in a syntactic framework of word formation in general and passive formation in particular if (parts of) the building blocks of passive formation are located either inside or outside the verbal phase (Chomsky, 2001). In the first case, passivization will be sensitive to (eventually idiosyncratic) properties of lexical items, in the latter case, the only restriction on passivization would relate to the (un-)availability of an active/transitive verbal phase. In other words, in a syntactic approach to word formation the two types of passives differ in how much structure they contain. In the rest of this section, we sketch in some more detail the analysis pursued in Alexiadou et al. (2015) for English and Greek passives, respectively, and see Alexiadou and Doron (2012) for Hebrew passives.

Kratzer (1996) proposed that the external argument is severed from the lexical verb as in (22a). The VP in (22b) provides a predicate of events where the object variable of the lexical verb is saturated by the VP-internal DP_2. The Kratzerian Voice-head in (22c), which provides a neo-Davidsonian thematic predicate (e.g. *agent*) that relates an event variable with an argument variable combines with the VP via event identification, resulting in (22d). Active Voice (similar to Collins' v) selects a DP in its specifier. Technically this is implemented by the assumption that active Voice is lexically equipped with a D-feature (Embick, 2004). θ-role assignment boils then down to merge followed by variable saturation. Since argument saturation is an automatic process, the DP in Spec,VoiceP, being the first DP merged in the context of Voice, will necessarily saturate the agent variable provided by Voice as in (22e). This derives, at the level of VoiceP, the effect of a theory of configurational θ-role assignment.[15]

(22) a. [T ... [$_{VoiceP}$ DP$_1$ Voice$_{\{D\}}$ [$_{VP}$ V DP$_2$]]]
 b. 〚 VP 〛 = λe[V(e, DP$_2$)]
 c. 〚 Voice 〛 = λxλe[agent(e, x)]
 d. 〚 Voice′ 〛 = λxλe([agent(e, x)] & [V(e, DP$_2$)])
 e. 〚 VoiceP 〛 = λxλe([agent(e, x)] & [V(e, DP$_2$)])DP$_1$
  = λe([agent(e, DP$_1$)] & [V(e, DP$_2$)])

The lexicon can provide two variants of the semi-functional Voice-head, which differ in their syntax and semantics. Languages can provide a passive Voice as in (23a), which does not select for a DP-specifier (it lacks a D-feature; see Alexiadou et al. 2015; Embick 2004; Schäfer 2017 for discussion). Semantically, passive Voice introduces an existentially bound agent variable (23b). Voice and VP combine as in (23c).

(23) a. [T ... [$_{VoiceP}$ Voice$_{\{\emptyset\}}$ [$_{VP}$ V DP$_2$]]]
 b. 〚 Voice$_{PASS}$ 〛 = ∃xλe[agent(e, x)]
 c. 〚 VoiceP 〛 = ∃xλe([agent(e, x)] & [V(e, DP$_2$)])

Since no DP$_1$ is merged in the specifier of passive Voice, no DP will intervene between T and DP2; the leftward-movement aspect of passives thus follows rather trivially. Furthermore, any version of a dependent case approach (cf. Marantz 1991) will rather easily derive the effect of Case absorption, i.e. that DP$_2$ receives unmarked nominative case.

Do actives as in (22) and passives as in (23) then share the same argument structure? In semantic terms they do, as the very same number of arguments with the very same thematic and ontological restrictions are involved. However, the syntax, in particular the syntactic shape of the VoiceP is not identical in actives

---

[15] Since Voice combines with VP via event identification, DP$_2$ must have merged with the verb inside the VP before Voice enters the derivation. Many authors proposed that indirect objects are severed from the verb by an ApplP (e.g. Pylkkänen 2008) and some suggested something similar for direct objects (e.g. Borer 2005; Lohndal 2014). While such proposals go beyond our main interest here, they have important consequences for a configurational theory of θ-role assignment.

and passives; only the former is projected by a Voice-head with a D-feature, which in turn is checked by merging a DP in Spec,VoiceP.

This syntactic difference has been argued to trigger active vs. passive morphology on Voice. Embick (2004), for example, proposes that NAct-morphology found on Greek passives as in (24) follows from the PF spell-out rule in (25) which states that Voice heads that lack a specifier receive the spell-out 'NAct':

(24) O   Janis katijori-thike
     the John accused-NAct
     'John was accused'

(25) Voice →Voice[NAct]/___ No DP specifier   (Greek)

Crucially, on the above account passives and actives are not transformationally related as they involve different functional heads, Voice$_{active}$ and Voice$_{passive}$. Since VoiceP is a phase (Chomsky, 2001), we can rephrase the "lexical behavior" of Greek passives by stating selectional restrictions on individual lexical verbal items (or on verbal classes) to combine only with Voice active, with both active or passive or none (the latter unaccusatives).

However, at the same time and by the same reasoning, the Kratzerian Voice-theory to passivization outlined so far leaves it unexplained (or at least as a matter of chance), that many languages in fact anti-restrict passivization in that every active verb can productively form a passive. This empirical fact about English and many other languages is captured by Chomsky's transformation in (2), but also in Collins's theory, where the specifier of v is filled by PRO. But above, we argued against the projection of the external argument in passives as a PRO in English. And yet we do need a passive built on an active for English-type languages, if we want the express the difference between Greek and English.

A solution to this apparent contradiction, an active Voice/v without a specifier for English-type languages, is provided in the passive theory of Bruening (2012). According to this theory, English-type passives involve the structure in (26) with a Passive projection (Pass) on top of a VoiceP. In particular, PASS selects for a basically active VoiceP with an unchecked D-feature, that is, for an active VoiceP, yet without a specifier. Bruening (2012: 22) proposes that "a head that selects a head with an unchecked feature will check that feature when it combines with it."

(26) [$_{TP}$ T [$_{PassP}$ Pass [$_{VoiceP}$ Voice $_{\{D\}}$ [$_{vP}$ V DP$_2$]]]]

The Voice head in (26) introduces an unsaturated agent variable. The semantics of PASS, given in (27) impose existential quantification over the open argument slot introduced by the Voice head below it. (27a) applied to the open VoiceP in (27b) derives a standard passive meaning in (27c).

(27) a. ⟦ Pass ⟧ $= \lambda f_{e,st}\lambda e[\exists x.f(x)(e)]$
b. ⟦ VoiceP ⟧ $= \lambda x\lambda e([\text{agent}(e, x)] \& [V(e, DP_2)])$
c. ⟦ PassP ⟧ $= \exists x\lambda e([\text{agent}(e, x)] \& [V(e, DP_2)])$

To conclude, in this approach, English-style passives and Greek-style passives have exactly the same meaning (compare English (27c) with Greek (23c)). However, Greek-style languages introduce existential closure at the level of Voice while English-style passives introduce existential closure at the level of a functional PASS head that selects for an active VoiceP. Thereby, existential closure either is or is not introduced in the domain of idiosyncratic lexical selection (the lexical VoiceP-phase).

Finally, we need to account for *by*-phrases in both types of passives. Above, we expressed our conviction that *by* projects a prepositional phrase involving DP_1. Next, *by*-phrases seem to transmit the verb's external argument role to DP_1. Furthermore, *by*-phrases are optional. All these properties followed in Chomsky (1957) from the transformation in (2) combined with the condition on derived constituent structure in (5) and the ellipsis transformation deleting *by*-phrases. Finally, Collins (2005) arrives at the interesting conclusion that *by* selects for a vP (a VoiceP in Kratzer's terms), and, therefore, it cannot be that the *by*-phrase is located in Spec,VoiceP.

Once again, Bruening (2012: 23f.) seems to us to formulate an interesting response to this bundle of empirical and theoretical requirements. He suggests that *by* combines with DP_1 to form a PP. This *by*-PP is an adjunct, however an adjunct that strictly selects the syntactic category of the phrase it adjoins to, namely VoiceP. Furthermore, while *by* does not introduce a thematic relation itself, *by* is also not semantically empty but has the meaning in (28a).

As depicted in (28), *by* first selects DP_1 as its complement, projecting the PP with the meaning in (28b). Next, PP selects, as an adjunct, VoiceP. This VoiceP must come with an open, unsaturated argument slot as in (28c), so that it can functionally apply to (28b) as in (28d). This last interpretative step ensures that the DP_1 saturates the variable provided by Voice. Thereby, it comes about that DP_1 in the *by*-phrase has exactly the same semantic relation to the verbal event as a DP in the specifier of active VoiceP would have. Consequently, an active sentence and a long passive sentence do not differ in meaning.

(28) a. 〚 by 〛 = $\lambda x \lambda f_{\langle e, st \rangle} \lambda e.f(e, x)$
 b. 〚 PP 〛 = $(\lambda x \lambda f_{\langle e, st \rangle} \lambda e.f(e, x))(DP_1)$
    = $\lambda f_{\langle e, st \rangle} \lambda e.f(e, DP_1)$
 c. 〚 VoiceP 〛 = $\lambda x \lambda e([agent(e, x)] \& [V(e, DP_2)])$
 d. 〚 PP+VoiceP 〛 = $\lambda f_{\langle e, st \rangle} \lambda e.f(e, DP_1)(\lambda x \lambda e([agent(e, x)] \& [V(e, DP_2)]))$
    = $\lambda e([agent(e, DP_1)] \& [V(e, DP_2)])$

Because the *by*-PP is an adjunct to VoiceP, VoiceP will project and DP_1 will also not intervene for A-movement of DP_2 and agreement. Finally, since *by* has meaning and selects DP_1, it is not surprising that it assigns lexical case to DP_1.

4 Summary

In this paper, we discussed the passive from the perspective of Chomsky's (1957) original transformational analysis asking the question how many insights expressed in Chomsky (1957) have survived today, after 60 years of history of the Chomskian framework. The modern analysis that is closest to Chomsky's insights in maintaining that the passive is literally derived from an active syntax is the one developed in Collins (2005). We reviewed in detail Collins's theory pointing to a number of limitations that relate specifically to his treatment of external arguments either expressed as *by*-phrases or as implicit arguments in the absence of a *by*-phrase. Moreover, we selectively reviewed some of the most influential treatments of the passive in the GB framework and Minimalism and we reached the conclusion that the most problematic aspect of the passive in all of these approaches is the representation of implicit external arguments, *by*-phrases and their relationship. While Chomsky's (1957) original rightward movement-type approach is clearly untenable today, it seems to us that no approach so far has been completely successful in dealing with this complex set of questions. Although Chomsky in 1957 did not explicitly address cross-linguistic variation, it is conceivable to think that certain rules could be viewed as general rules applying to all languages and subsequent research in the Principles & Parameters theory showed that indeed the passive is a very general (though not universal) crosslinguistic rule. However, as differences in passive formation among languages exist, we argued for the existence of two types of passives across languages, a fully productive and a semi-productive one showing various gaps, as found in Greek. We showed that a promising way of dealing with this difference in a configurational approach to argument structure alternations is in terms of decomposition combined with the view that the passive Voice domain constitutes a phase in Greek-type languages. On the other hand, in languages like English, the passive is built on the active, as originally proposed by Chomsky. We argued that the best way to express this in a decomposition framework is in terms of Bruening's (2012) Passive projection (Pass) on top of a basically active VoiceP lacking a specifier due to an unchecked D-feature.

Acknowledgements We would like to thank the editors of this volume and especially Norbert Hornstein for comments and discussion. The DFG Leibniz Prize (AL 554/8-1, Alexiadou) and a DFG grant to project B6 Underspecification in Voice Systems and the syntax morphology interface (Schäfer) of the Collaborative Research Center 732 at the University of Stuttgart are hereby acknowledged.

Bibliography

Alexiadou, Artemis, Elena Anagnostopoulou, and Florian Schäfer. 2015. *External arguments in transitivity alternations: a layering approach*. Oxford, UK: Oxford University Press.
Alexiadou, Artemis, and Edit Doron. 2012. The syntactic construction of two non-active Voices: passive and middle. *Journal of Linguistics* 48:1–34.
Baker, Mark. 1988. *Incorporation: A theory of grammatical function changing*. Chicago, IL: University of Chicago Press.
Baker, Mark. 1997. Thematic roles and syntactic structure. In *Elements of Grammar*, ed. Liliane Haegeman, 73–137. Dordrecht, The Netherlands: Kluwer Academic Publishers.
Baker, Mark, Kyle Johnson, and Ian Roberts. 1989. Passive arguments raised. *Linguistic Inquiry* 20:219–252.
Bhatt, Rajesh, and Roumyana Pancheva. 2006. Implicit arguments. In *The Blackwell Companion to Syntax*, ed. Martin Everaert and Henk van Riemsdijk, 554–584. Oxford, UK: Oxford University Press.
Borer, Hagit. 2005. *The normal course of events. Structuring sense: Volume II*. Oxford, UK: Oxford University Press.
Bruening, Benjamin. 2012. By-phrases in passives and nominals. *Syntax* 16:1–41.
Chomsky, Noam. 1957. *Syntactic Structures*. The Hague, The Netherlands: Mouton de Gruyter.
Chomsky, Noam. 1981. *Lectures on Government and Binding*. Dordrecht, The Netherlands: Foris.
Chomsky, Noam. 1986. *Knowledge of language: Its nature, origin, and use*. New York, NY: Praeger.
Chomsky, Noam. 1995. *The Minimalist Program*. Cambridge, MA: MIT Press.
Chomsky, Noam. 2000. Minimalist inquiries: The framework. In *Step by step: Essays on minimalist syntax in honor of Howard Lasnik*, ed. R. Martin, D. Michaels, and J. Uriagereka, 89–155. Cambridge, MA: MIT Press.
Chomsky, Noam. 2001. Derivation by phase. In *Ken Hale: A life in language*, ed. Michael Kenstowicz, 1–52. Cambridge, MA: MIT Press.
Collins, Chris. 2005. A smuggling approach to the passive in English. *Syntax* 8:81–120.

Embick, David. 2004. Unaccusative syntax and verbal alternations. In *The unaccusativity puzzle: explorations of the syntax-lexicon interface*, ed. Artemis Alexiadou, Elena Anagnostopoulou, and Martin Everaert, 137–158. Oxford, UK: Oxford University Press.

Harris, Zelig. 1957. Co-occurence and transformation in linguistic theory. *Language* 33:283–340.

Jaeggli, Oswaldo. 1986. Passive. *Linguistic Inquiry* 17:587–622.

Kastner, Itamar, and Vera Zu. 2014. The Syntax of Implicit Arguments. MS, New York University.

Kiparsky, Paul. 2013. Towards a null theory of the passive. *Lingua* 125:7–33.

Kratzer, Angelika. 1996. Severing the external argument from its verb. In *Phrase structure and the lexicon*, ed. Johan Rooryck and Laurie A. Zaring, 109–137. Dordrecht, The Netherlands: Kluwer.

Laks, Lior. 2009. The formation of Arabi passive verbs: lexical or syntactic? Proceedings of IATL 25.

Landau, Idan. 2010. The explicit syntax of implicit arguments. *Linguistic Inquiry* 41:357–388.

Lascaratou, Chryssoula, and Irene Philippaki-Warburton. 1984. Lexical versus transformational passives in Modern Greek. *Glossologia* 2-3:99–109.

Lees, Robert. 1960. *The Grammar of English Nominalizations*. The Hague, The Netherlands: Mouton.

Legate, Julie A. 2014. *Voice and v: Lessons from Acehnese*. Cambridge, MA: MIT Press.

Levin, Beth, and Malka Rappaport Hovav. 1995. *Unaccusativity: At the Syntax-Lexical Semantics Interface*. Cambridge, MA: MIT Press.

Lohndal, Terje. 2014. *Phrase structure and argument structure: A case study of the syntax-semantics interface*. Oxford, UK: Oxford University Press.

Marantz, Alec. 1991. Case and Licensing. *Proceedings of Escol* 234–53.

Marantz, Alec. 2001. Words and Things. Handout, MIT.

Müller, Gereon. 2016. The Short Life Cycle of External Arguments in German Passive Derivations. MS, Universität Leipzig.

Pitteroff, Marcel, and FLorian Schäfer. 2017. Implicit control crosslinguistically. MS, Universität Stuttgart & Humboldt-Universität Berlin.

Primus, Beatrice. 2011. Das unpersönliche Passiv: Ein Fall füïLr die Konstruktionsgrammatik? In *Sprachliches Wissen zwischen Lexikon und Grammatik*, ed. A. Engelberg, A. Holler, and K. Proost, 285–313. Berlin, Germany: de Gruyter.

Pylkkänen, Liina. 2008. *Introducing Arguments*. Cambridge, MA: MIT Press.

Ramchand, Gillian. 2008. *Verb meaning and the lexicon*. Cambridge, UK: Cambridge University Press.

Reinhart, Tanya, and Tal Siloni. 2005. The Lexicon-Syntax Parameter: Reflexivization snd other arity operations. *Linguistic Inquiry* 36:389–436.

Ruys, Eddy. 2010. Expletive selection and CP arguments in Dutch. *Journal of Comparative Germanic Linguistics* 13:141–178.

Schäfer, Florian. 2012. The passive of reflexive verbs and its implications for theories of binding and case. *Journal of Comparative Germanic Linguistics* 13:141–178.

Schäfer, Florian. 2017. Romance and Greek Medio-Passives and the Typology of Voice. In *The Verbal Domain*, ed. R. D'Alessandro, I. Franco, and Á Gallego. Oxford, UK: Oxford University Press.

Smirniotopoulos, Jane. 1992. *Lexical passives in Modern Greek*. New York, NY: Taylor & Francis.

Wasow, Tom. 1977. Transformations and the Lexicon. In *Formal Syntax*, ed. P.W. Culicover, T. Wasow, and J. Bresnan, 327–60. New York, NY: Academic Press.

Zaenen, Annie. 1993. Unaccusatives in Dutch and the syntax-semantics interface. In *Semantics and the Lexicon*, ed. J Pustejovsky, 129–161. Dordrecht, The Netherlands: Kluwer Academic Publishers.

Zombolou, Katerina. 2004. Verbal alternations in Greek: a semantic approach. Doctoral Dissertation, University of Reading.

Martina Wiltschko
Discovering syntactic variation

1 Introduction

Syntactic variation has not always been an object of investigation. In Chomsky's 1957 *Syntactic Structures* (henceforth SS), the object of investigation is English. However, it is assumed that the study of English—or any other language for that matter—allows us to draw conclusions about the nature of the system that underlies its grammar: "Linguists must be concerned with the problem of determining the fundamental underlying properties of successful grammars. The ultimate outcome of these investigations should be a theory of linguistic structure in which the descriptive devices utilized in particular grammars are presented and studied abstractly, with no specific reference to particular languages" (SS, 11). Eventually, this approach towards language has come to be known as *Universal Grammar* (henceforth UG).

While empirically syntactic variation is not considered in SS, as a framework, it makes predictions about the kinds of variation one would expect to find. Specifically, there are two radical innovations in SS which have changed the way we think about language and hence the way we think about language variation. The first innovation, illustrated in Figure 1, is the *decomposition of syntax* (one of the classic levels of linguistic description along with *phonology*, *morphology*, *lexicon*, and *semantics*). Specifically, syntax is decomposed into three distinct structures, which provide instruction formulas (F) for the analysis of the initial string (Σ), and which come with their own set of rules respectively: 1. *Phrase structure* (a set of rewrite rules that constructs terminal strings); 2. *Transformational structure* (a set of rules that rearranges, adds, or deletes terminal strings and creates word sequences); and 3. *Morphophonemics* (a set of rules that converts words into phonemes) (SS: 46 (35))

The second innovation concerns the ingredients of the syntactic structures illustrated in Figure 1. In the traditional model, syntax was viewed as the level of linguistic description which deals with the arrangements of *words* into *sentences*. This contrasts with the ingredients of SS. While the initial string of analysis (Σ) is also assumed to be the sentence, individual syntactic structures include ingredients other than words. For example, phrase structure rules not only contain words (in the form of terminal strings) but also affixes (*Af*) as in the rule for affix hopping

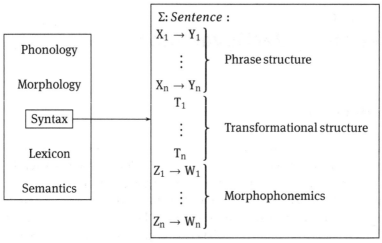

Fig. 1: Decomposing syntax into syntactic structures

in (1) where *Af* stands for any of the affixes *past, -s, 0, -en, -ing* and *v* stands for any modal, auxiliary, or verb.

(1) $Af + v \rightarrow v + Af \#$

SS: 39 (29ii)

In this way, syntactic rules can refer to elements below the word-level. Similarly, transformational rules (abbreviated with T) are labeled with subscripts that refer to different types of syntactic objects including words (such as T_{not}, T_{do}, T_{so}, T_{to}), morphemes (T_{ing}), categories (T_{aux}, T_{adj}), construction types ($T_{A(ffirmation)}$, $T_{q(uestion)}$, $T_{w(h\text{-}question)}$, $T_{passive}$) and even some prosodic concepts such as word boundary (cf. SS: 111ff.).

Within this model, the goal of the linguist then is to "develop and clarify the criteria for selecting the correct grammar for each language" (SS: 49). This foreshadows the concept of UG as SS poses "a condition of generality on grammars" (SS: 50). It requires that "the grammar of a given language be constructed in accordance with a specific theory of linguistic structure in which such terms as "phoneme" and "phrase" are defined independently of any particular language (SS: 50).

Generative linguists have, ever since, studied different languages in ways that have led to new discoveries, both empirically, as well as theoretically. We know much more now about the range and limits of variation than we did in 1957. The accumulation of knowledge went both ways: studying different languages is teaching us about the nature of UG; and studying languages from the point of view of

UG is teaching us about the characteristics of these languages, as already alluded to in SS: "The theory of linguistic structure must be distinguished clearly from a manual of helpful procedures for the discovery of grammars, although such a manual will no doubt draw upon the results of linguistic theory, and the attempt to develop such a manual will probably (as it has in the past) contribute substantially to the formation of linguistic theory." (SS: 106).

This chapter is intended as a celebration of the study of syntactic variation from a generative perspective. I will discuss the path towards the study of variation in the generative enterprise (section 2). In section 3, I discuss in detail the implications of the core innovations of SS: the decomposition of syntax into several layers, including transformations, as well as the introduction of ingredients other than words. In section 4, I discuss syntactic variation beyond language variation including dialectal and sociolectal variation. Throughout this essay, I will use some of the transformational rules introduced in SS as the basis for my empirical case studies. In section 5 I conclude.

2 What is syntactic variation?

The way we conceive of syntactic variation depends on one's theoretical framework. The main insight that syntax is to be decomposed and that its ingredients are not restricted to words is still upheld in current models; but the particular implementation of this idea has changed over the years (see section 3 for further discussion). The purpose of this section is to give an overview of the way syntactic variation has been approached since SS and how the innovations introduced in SS have helped to shape our understanding of linguistic variation.

2.1 Syntactic variation in the tradition of American Structuralism

Traditionally, syntax has been viewed as the domain of language responsible for the arrangement of words and phrases to create well-formed sentences. Practically, this translates into the study of word-order. Typically, word-order is described in terms of grammatical relations (S(ubject) and O(bject)) and how they are linearized relative to the verb (V). Thus, traditional typological descriptions will classify languages according to their dominant word order: SOV, SVO, VSO, VOS, OVS, or OSV (Dryer, 2013). This emphasis on word-order in research on syntactic variation can be gleaned from Greenberg's (1963) proposed language universals: virtually all of them are concerned with (linear) word order.

The exploration of languages in the tradition of American Structuralism (Bloomfield, 1933; Boas, 1911; Sapir, 1921) adopted this view of syntax. As a result, many of the descriptive grammars of the languages indigenous to the Americas had only a very short section on syntax. This is because, many of these languages are polysynthetic: the verb's arguments are marked on the verb via affixes or incorporated nouns; nominal arguments are often optional and display free word order. The description of these grammars then includes reference to the sound-system (phonemic inventories), the word-formation processes including (morphology), and a comparatively short section on word order (syntax). A striking feature of the American Structuralist tradition was the deliberate exclusion of semantics (which, notably, is echoed in SS). This was the result of the commitment to a description of language in purely distributional terms—it even affects the labelling of categories. For example, in the Algonquianist tradition, following Bloomfield (1927), the categories that make up a verb stem are labelled as *initial*, *medial*, and *final*—terms that are purely reflective of linear order. The rationale behind this research agenda is the aim to describe languages in their own terms (Boas, 1911). By sticking to distributional criteria for discovery the linguist—so the argument goes—will not be tempted to be influenced by the categories of the better studied languages. This methodological conviction led to the development of discovery procedures using purely distributional procedures. This is the linguistic landscape which serves as the backdrop for SS.

At the same time, research on language as a psychological phenomenon is dominated by behaviorism (Skinner, 1957) according to which the object of investigation (language acquisition) is fully explained by the stimulus-response schema. Whatever happens between the stimulus and the response is not observable and hence by hypothesis uninteresting. In this context, the comparison of languages to each other is only useful for historical reasons, i.e., to detect family relations and to reconstruct proto-languages.

Chomsky's enterprise was largely aimed against this behaviorist agenda: its focus is precisely to determine what happens in-between the stimulus and the response. The goal is to get a glimmer into the black box (Chomsky, 1959) and hence the rationale for exploring language variation becomes a very different one: it will serve to delimit the conditions of generality introduced in SS (50), which eventually led to the notion of UG.

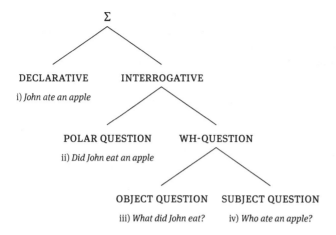

Fig. 2: Transformationally related sentences

2.2 Syntactic variation in SS: the role of transformations

To explore the conditions of generality (and ultimately to explore UG), we need to determine what aspects of language are universal, what varies, and how variation can come about in a principled way.

Trivially, languages differ in their inventory of terminal strings (i.e., simplex form-meaning correspondences). This follows from the classic Saussurian assumption that the relation between form and meaning is arbitrary hence it has to be acquired based on empirical evidence. But even after we set aside variation due to arbitrary inventories there is still a lot left that varies, at least by surface appearance.

One of the key insights into language explicitly introduced in SS is the assumption that seemingly different sentences may be related to each other via transformational rules (henceforth TR). This makes it possible for sentences to be compared to each other in ways that are reminiscent of comparison for the purpose of historical reconstruction. When comparing sentences within a language, the goal now is to "reconstruct" the underlying structure and the transformations that led to their surface form. And crucially, this assumption makes it possible to identify natural classes, where standard classification strategies would fail. Consider for example the relation between the sentences in Figure 2, which contain two basic sentence types: DECLARATIVES and INTERROGATIVES (both instances of Σ).

According to SS (90), it is difficult to find a formal basis for this classification: if they are classified based on their "normal intonation" declaratives and wh-questions would form a natural class: both are associated with falling intonation. If they are classified based on their word order, declaratives and subject questions would form a natural class: they are both SVO. Hence, these surface properties will not suffice to derive tha natural classes illustrated in Figure 2. Assuming, however, that these sentences are related via TR's (all are derived from the underlying terminal string in (2)) allows for a straightforward classification into DECLARATIVES and INTERROGATIVES. The DECLARATIVE sentence is derived by applying the obligatory number transformation (replacing C — *eat* with *eats*) while all INTERROGATIVES are derived by the (optional) question transformation T_q and wh-interrogatives are derived by the additional transformation T_w (which in turn comes in different guises depending on which phrase serves as the wh-constituent).

(2) John C — eat + an + apple
     SS:91 (116)

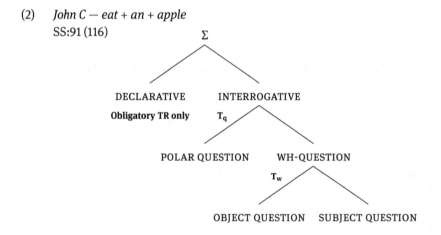

Regarding syntactic variation, the question that arises in this context is whether the same type of classification based on transformational relatedness is possible across all languages. The answer to this question will largely depend on whether different languages make use of the same TRs. That is, as can be gleaned from the list of TRs in SS (111–114), TRs are language- and construction-specific. Hence they are expected to vary, which in turn opens a new avenue of research into variation.

For example, not all languages have a TR to derive a passive construction like the one in (3). The language-specific characteristic of this TR is evident from the fact that there is reference to English terminal strings (*be, en, by*); and the construction-specific characteristic is evident from the label of the TR, which states *passive* (henceforth $T_{passive}$). Note in passing that the *format* of TRs always involves a *structural analysis* (a characterization of the input to the TR) and a description of the *structural change*.

(3) **Passive**
   Structural analysis
   $$NP - Aux - V - NP$$
   Structural Change:
   $$X_1 - X_2 - X_3 - X_4 \rightarrow X_4 - X_2+be+en - X_3 \text{ by } X_1$$
   adapted from SS: 112 (12)

Blackfoot (Algonquian) is a language which lacks a passive construction and hence arguably lacks a passive rule. Instead, Blackfoot has a system of *direct/inverse* marking, which is sometimes assumed to be the functional equivalent of an *active/passive* system. Specifically, the *direct/inverse* system orders arguments based on a person-hierarchy: roughly, if the subject of a predicate is higher on the person hierarchy the verb is marked as direct (4a); if it is lower on the person hierarchy, the verb is marked as *inverse* (4b).

(4) a. direct marking
   Nitsinóáwa
   nit-ino-**aa**-wa
   1-see.ta-**dir**-prox
   'I see him/her.'

   1/2 > 3
   | |
   subject object

   b. inverse marking
   Nitsinóóka
   nit-ino-**ok**-wa
   1-see.ta-**inv**-prox
   'S/he sees me.'

   1/2 > 3
    ✕
   object subject

The question that arises in this context is whether we should analyze the Blackfoot inverse as a separate rule $T_{inverse}$ found in Blackfoot but not in English (as illustrated in (5a)) or whether we should analyze it as a language-specific instance of $T_{passive}$ (illustrated in (5b)).

(5) a. 2 different TRs   b. 2 instances of the same TR

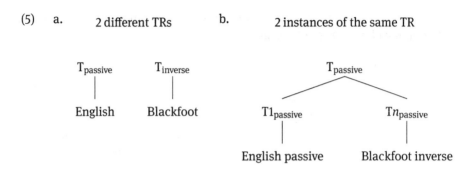

While current syntactic theories no longer include transformational rules, the same type of question is still relevant albeit in a different guise: for the case at hand we might ask whether both passive-morphology and inverse-morphology instantiate the same or a different kind of functional category. There are no clear criteria and diagnostics based on which we can decide whether or not two language-specific instances of a particular rule are instantiations of the same (universal) rule. This problem forms the basis of much ongoing research in the generative tradition.

2.3 From language-specific transformational rules to features and parameters

There are two key changes that define the transition from the (Extended) Standard Theory of the 60s and 70s to the Government and Binding Framework of the 80s (Chomsky 1981; henceforth GB) and the minimalist program initiated in the 90s (Chomsky, 1995):
i) syntactic constructions are no longer viewed as primitives
ii) language- and construction-specific rules are replaced by universal principles and language-specific parameters of variation.

These changes paved the way for a re-conceptualization of labelled TRs to current feature-based analyses of syntactic derivations (see e.g. Adger 2003; Adger and Svenonius 2011; but see Boeckx 2014 for a feature-free syntax).

Consider for example the history of the TR responsible for deriving polar questions (T_q). According to the Katz-Postal hypothesis (Katz and Postal, 1964), TRs cannot change meaning and hence T_q alone would not suffice to turn a declarative into a polar question. To solve this conundrum, Katz & Postal 1964 introduce a question feature [+q] which serves to type the sentence as a question before T_q applies (see also Baker 1970 among many others).[1] At least since Cheng's 1991/1997 clausal typing hypothesis, the [+q] feature (associated with the head of CP) is responsible for triggering movement in some languages (English (6)) and the insertion of dedicated question particles in other languages (Mandarin (7)). And finally, since some languages use rising intonation (↗) to derive polar questions (Atayal (8)), we might add the rising contour to the list of forms that can instantiate [+q].[2]

(6) English
    a. *She read the book.*
    b. *Did she read the book?*

(7) Mandarin
    a. Ta   du   guo   na   ben   shu
       she read ASP that CL   book
       'She read the book.'
    b. Ta   du   guo   na   ben   shu   **ma**
       she read ASP that CL   book PRT
       'Did she read the book?'

(8) Atayal
    a. *(b)lay ni'-un*↘
       good   eat-PV
       'It tastes good.'
    b. *(b)lay ni'-un*↗
       good   eat-PV
       'Does it taste good?'

On this view then, a feature [+q], rather than the label of the TR (e.g., T_q) will be the unifying ingredient of a particular construction. Assuming that the feature itself is a language universal (Watanabe, 1992) it is possible to define the cross-linguistic comparison set for question formation. This means that the surface variation we observe in the realization of [+q] boils down to the variation we have to trivially assume: the relation between form and meaning is arbitrary. The meaning [+q] is associated with different forms: inversion, particles, or intonational contours. And indeed, since Borer 1984 it is standardly assumed that variation always boils

---

[1] In this way, features may be viewed as descendents of (some of) the labels of TRs.
[2] The possibility of transformations affecting intonation is already alluded to in SS (71). Specifically, Chomsky suggests that the application of T_q in English converts a falling intonation to a rising one.

down to differences in *features* of lexical items (the Borer-Chomsky conjecture) which in turn serve as the triggers for derivations (the successors of TRs). According to this view, universal grammar may be viewed as a repository of features and discovering the limits of variation amounts to discovering the full inventory of features and a principled way of determining how these features may be realized.

The problem with this approach is, however, that it still leaves open the question as to how to determine whether a given form does indeed instantiate a particular (universal) feature. We need a language-independent heuristic for the discovery and comparison of such features (Wiltschko, 2014).

2.4 From discovery procedures to generative discovery heuristics

As outline in section 1, SS introduces the idea of a *condition of generality on grammars*, which eventually turned into the notion of UG. Crucially, both notions are to be stated independent of language-specific constructs. The question that arises in this context concerns the relation between UG and the language specific grammars we observe empirically. Before SS, it was assumed that a particular language corpus can be analyzed as instantiating a particular grammar by using *discovery procedures* as illustrated in Figure 3 (based on SS: 51 (36i))

Fig. 3: Discovery procedures

Discovery procedures are meant as a practical manual for the constructing of higher level-elements (e.g., morphemes) out of lower-level elements (e.g., phonemes). SS rejects this notion of discovery procedures in favor of a weaker requirement on the theory to provide an *evaluation procedure*, which takes as its input not just a corpus but also possible grammars associated with that corpus and determines which of these grammars is the simplest one.[3] This is illustrated in Figure 4 based on SS: 51 (36iii).

With this, however, comes a methodological problem: how do we construct the grammars that are to serve as the input for evaluation procedures (G_1 and G_2).

---

3 The notion of simplicity in SS (53) is replaced by conditions of *economy* in the current minimalist program (Chomsky 1995 and subsequent work).

(9)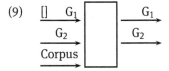

Fig. 4: Evaluation Procedure

The radical change in the conceptualization of language means that we cannot use structuralist procedures: SS has changed both the primitives of analysis (for example the inclusion of affixes in phrase-structure as well as transformational rules) as well as the architecture of the model (the decomposition of syntax). Thus, we need a discovery heuristic to be able to construct the grammar of languages in ways that are consistent with the conditions of generality (or later the restrictions imposed by UG). In other words, to evaluate grammars in generative terms, they have to be constructed in generative terms. And the same requirement holds for more current generative models (i.e., the minimalist program): we cannot use the output of a structuralist analysis as the input for a minimalist analysis (cf. Wiltschko 2014).

3 Discovering variation

The generative enterprise, in particular since its incarnation as a framework evolving around principles and parameters "led to an explosion of inquiry into a very broad range of typologically diverse languages, at a level of depth not previously envisioned" (Chomksy 2004:11). This suggests that generative assumptions made discoveries possible and I contend that it is the core innovations of SS that paved the way for these discoveries. Specifically, the decomposition of syntax into more abstract syntactic structures (3.1) and the introduction of transformations (3.2). For each of these innovations I give an overview of how it affected our exploration of language variation. I then move on to show that the change in the way we view the ingredients of syntactic analysis has led to a decomposition of words (3.3) at the lower end as well as the decomposition of sentences at the upper end (3.4)

3.1 The significance of syntactic structures

The most radical departure from classic linguistic theory in SS is arguably the introduction of abstract levels of representation. Instead of a simple syntactic structure, SS postulates three distinct syntactic structures: phrase-structure, transformational structure, and morphophonemics (see Figure 1 above). This allows for a fine-grained syntactic typology which would not be conceivable in a system that takes syntax to be the level of linguistic description for how words are combined into phrases and sentences. This is because it allows for the traditional primitives of syntactic description to be decomposed; and if they can be decomposed it follows that they can be composed in different ways within and across languages. I start with a discussion of the significance of the decomposition of syntax into a series of syntactic structures. I show that the decomposition of syntax allows for a decomposition of the classic notions of grammatical relations (*subject* and *object*), which in turn leads to a more fine-grained analysis of word-order typology than is possible under pre-SS assumptions.

The significance of SS's decomposition of syntax does not lie in the particular model of syntax that it assumes but rather in the fact that this decomposition was introduced in the first place. The model has changed significantly over the past 60 years, as I will now show, but what remains constant is the assumption that syntax is decomposed into a series of syntactic structures. Under the SS conceptualization of syntactic structures (Figure 1), transformational structure mediates between phrase structure and morphophonemics. When it became clear that the Katz-Postal postulate according to which TRs cannot change meaning was untenable the role of the underlying structure changed: it was no longer assumed to be the level of representation where sentence *meanings* are generated as in SS (Figure 5). Instead, both form and meaning are now assumed to be two separate levels of representation which—crucially—do not interact with each other. Hence no direct relation between form and meaning is postulated. Rather, it is syntax that mediates the form-meaning relation. Within GB, this assumption took the shape of the T-model (Figure 6) and within the Minimalist Program, this takes the shape of the Y-model (Figure 7). The latter differs in that there no longer are syntactic *levels* of representation (e.g., D-structure or S-structure). Rather syntactic computation is assumed to proceed without the need to "stop" the derivation at a particular level and check whether the derived representation is well-formed. For example, within the T-model, D-S is assumed to be the level of representation where thematic roles (AGENT, PATIENT, etc.) are assigned while structural case (nominative, accusative) is assigned at S-S.

In contrast, within the minimalist model in Figure 7, well-formedness conditions are assumed to be directly built into syntactic computation itself. The two levels (LF and PF) serve as the interface to our conceptual-intentional system (meaning) and the articulatory-perceptual system (sound).

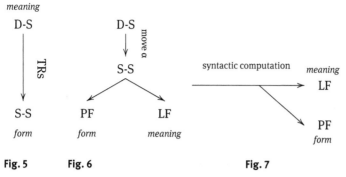

Fig. 5 **Fig. 6** **Fig. 7**

The reconceptualization of the architecture of syntactic structures depicted in Figures 5–7 went hand in hand with a reconceptualization of clausal architecture. Consider how. Within the (extended) standard theory initiated in SS, phrase structure rules generated sentences by rewriting S as a combination of NP and VP, with inflectional morphology (optionally hosted by auxiliaries) connecting the two phrases as in (9).

(10) Clauses in Standard Theory

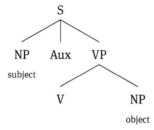

The introduction of X'-theory (Jackendoff, 1977) made the structure in (9) untenable. Specifically, all phrases are assumed to be endocentric: they contain one (and only one) head which determines their categorical identity (10).

(11) X'-theory

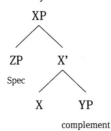

The structure in (9) is an exception to this generalization: the combination of NP, Aux and VP yields a phrase (S) without containing a head. This situation was rectified with generalized X'-theory (Chomsky, 1986) according to which the head of S was inflection (hence the label I(NFL)) projecting IP, as in (11).

(12) Extended X'-theory

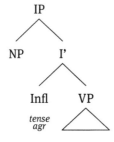

With the structure in (11), it becomes possible to assume two different structural positions for thematic roles and for case. Specifically, Koopman and Sportiche 1991 argue that subjects are introduced VP-internally where they receive their thematic role (e.g., AGENT) (see McCloskey 1997 for an overview of the VP-internal subject hypothesis). To receive nominative, case the VP-internal subject moves to SpecIP, hence INFL is functioning as a raising predicate. This is schematized in (12).

(13) VP-internal subjects

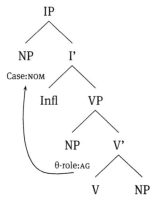

What is crucial for the present discussion is the fact that the complexity of syntactic structure allows for a decomposition of the traditional notion of SUBJECT. In particular, we can distinguish between *thematic subjects* (associated with SpecVP) and *grammatical subjects* (associated with SpecIP).[4] This has implications for our understanding of variation in word order. Recall that traditional typologies classify languages in terms of the order of subjects and objects relative to the verb. With the decomposition of subjects (and objects) into thematic and grammatical instantiations, we now have to ask whether a given order (e.g., SVO) refers to thematic or grammatical subjects. Hence this allows for a more fine-grained typology of word-order.

To see the effects of this, consider Modern Standard Arabic, which is classified as a VSO language in WALS.[5] According to Koopman and Sportiche (1991), the VSO order of Arabic is best analyzed, as in (13)a, where the verb moves to Infl but the subject remains in SpecVP. Note that the position where we would expect the grammatical subject to be realized (SpecIP) is occupied by a silent 3rd person pronoun (*pro*). Evidence for this analysis stems from the fact that in VSO sentences, verbs always display 3rd person singular agreement, independent of the phi-features of the subject (Koopman & Sportiche 1991: 221). Note further that Arabic also allows for SVO order. This can be derived by moving the VP-internal subject to SpecIP (as in (13)b) where it triggers full subject verb agreement.

---

[4] Objects have undergone a similar analysis such that the thematic position of objects has been distinguished form the position where they receive structural case (see for example Borer 1994)
[5] http://wals.info/feature/81A#2/18.0/152.9

(14) a. Arabic SVO   b. Arabic VSO

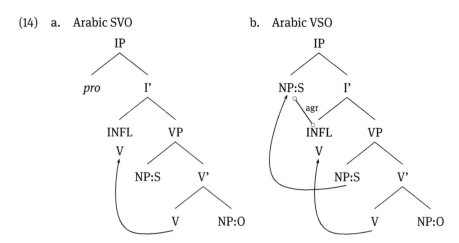

The possibility for the decomposition of the notion of subject (made possible by the decomposition of syntactic structures) allows for a fine-grained classification of word-order: it reveals the necessity to distinguish between thematic and grammatical subjects. Moreover, the structural analysis exemplified in (13) predicts a cluster of properties: whether a given "subject" is realized as the thematic subject (in SpecVP) or as the grammatical subject (in SpecIP) will correlate with a number of other properties (such as the agreement pattern of Arabic).

Note that the postulation of VP-internal subjects leads us to expect reflexes of this position in English as well. And indeed, despite the fact that in English the subject moves to SpecIP, we can still observe traces of its VP-internal position. Specifically, the quantifier in (14) can be analyzed as occupying the VP-internal subject position, having been stranded by the NP *the children*, which moved to SpecIP (Koopman & Sportiche 1991: 222; but see Dowty and Brodie 1984 for an analysis of floating quantifiers as VP-adverbs).

(15) **The children** are **all** playing.

Thus, the decomposition of syntactic structure enhances our understanding of syntactic variation in that it allows us to discover systematic patterns of variation, such as the correlation between word order and verb agreement in Arabic.

3.2 The significance of transformations

As discussed in section 2, one of the key analytical claims of SS is the assumption that the phrase-structure is mapped onto morphophonemics via the transformational rules (TR) of transformational structure. These rules include rules for adding, deleting, or reordering syntactic objects. While the particular implementation of this insight has changed over the years, what remained constant is the assumption that phrase-structure is not sufficient to adequately account for the data. The postulation of TRs requires heuristics to detect them and indeed generative syntactic theories have developed many diagnostics for different types of transformations. For example, to determine whether a given syntactic object has moved we need to establish whether it obeys restrictions on movement, such as island constraints for A'-movement (Ross, 1967). Investigating the empirical properties of insertion, deleting, and displacement operations has proven a fruitful research area since SS and has brought to light many generalizations about language and language variation that would not be conceivable without the assumption of a transformational structure (or whatever replaces it).

For example, movement of the verb to C in German (the so called V2 property) elegantly accounts for patterns of word-order: in matrix clauses the finite verb occupies the second position following one and only one constituent whereas in embedded clauses, the finite verb occupies sentence final position. This follows if we assume that the finite verb moves to C (via I), but if C is occupied by a complementizer, as it is in embedded clauses, V-to-C movement cannot take place.

(16) a. V2 b. V2 blocked

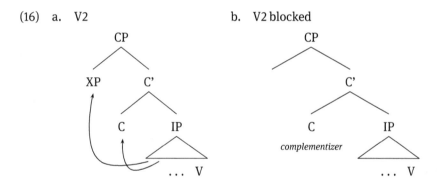

Without the assumption that different—seemingly unrelated—sentences are indeed related via TRs, German word order would appear to be quite erratic.

A second way in which the assumption of TRs has proven significant for the study of language variation has to do with the fact that properties of movement can be used as a heuristic for discovering the syntactic position of a given syntactic object. Take for example sentential negation, according to SS introduced by T_{neg} (16).

(17) T_{neg}

Structural analysis : $\begin{cases} NP-C-V\ldots \\ NP-C+M-\ldots \\ NP-C+\text{have}-\ldots \\ NP-C+\text{be}-\ldots \end{cases}$

Structural change: $X_1 - X_2 - X_3 \rightarrow X_1 - X_2 + n't - X_3$ SS: 112 (16)

Under more current conceptualizations of transformations, it will not suffice to specify the linear position for negation (i.e., following X_2) but instead we need to determine its structural position. As with any other syntactic object, there are two separate variables to consider: (i) how high in the syntactic structure it appears, and (ii) whether it functions as a head or as a modifier. It turns out that properties of movement may shed light on this question and hence movement can serve as a heuristic for syntactic position. In particular, the necessity for *do*-support in English negative clauses suggests that negation blocks the relation between INFL and the verb. Within SS, this relation was conceptualized as *affix hopping* introduced by the TR in (1), repeated below for convenience:

(18) [(1)] $Af + v \rightarrow v + Af$ #

SS: 39 (29ii)

In positive declaratives, the affix attaches to the verb (17)a (or an auxiliary if there is one (17)b). In contrast, in negative declaratives it can only attach to auxiliaries (18)a/b. Hence in the absence of negation, a dummy auxiliary *do* has to be inserted (18)c via T_{do} (19).

(19) a. *He sings*
 b. *He has sung*

(20) a. * *He not sings.*
 b. *He has not sung.*
 c. *He **does** not sing.*

(21) *do-Transformation*

 Structural Analysis: # — Af
 Structural Change: $X_1 - X_2 \rightarrow X_1 - do + X_2$

Under a structural analysis of this phenomenon, it can be analyzed as in (20). Assuming that the inflectional affix is hosted by INFL (20a), the fact that the presence of negation does not allow for affix hopping can be understood if we assume that heads have to stand in a local relation to each other, hence negation intervenes (20b)[6] and the dummy auxiliary *do* has to be inserted to host the affix (20c).

(22) A structural analysis for *do* support

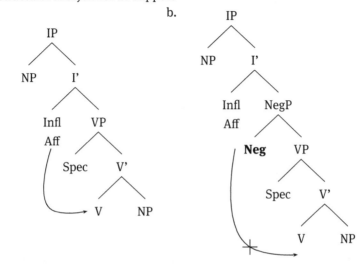

---

[6] The same generalization can be made within a lexicalist approach according to which verbs are inserted fully inflected but need to check their inflectional features in INFL. This would be an instance of head movement, which has to proceed strictly local (Travis, 1984).

c.

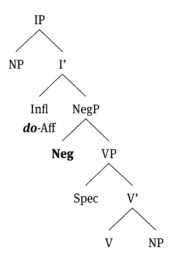

This analysis makes predictions about the interaction between negation and verb-movement. First, it is predicted that *do*-support is only necessary if negation is a head and that it intervenes between V and T. If either of these conditions does not hold, negation should not interfere for the marking of inflection on verbs. This prediction is borne out.

For example, in German, negation is not a head but a (phrasal) modifier (Haegeman, 1995; Wiltschko, 2006; Zanuttini, 1997, 2001; Zeijlstra, 2004) and therefore cannot disrupt the relation between V and T. As predicted *do*-support is not required.

(23)   a. *Sie kommen.*   b. *Sie kommen nicht.*
         they come   they come not
         'They are coming'   'They aren't coming.'

Second, there are languages (e.g., Spanish) where negation is generated above TP (Zanuttini, 2001) and hence cannot interrupt the relation between V and T either. As predicted, verbal inflection is not affected by negation (22).

(24)   a.
         Ellas pueden venir.   *Ellas **no** pueden venir.*
         they can come   they not can come
         'They can come.'   'They cannot come.'

b.
    Ellas vienen   Ellas **no** vienen
    they come   they not come
    'They are coming.'   'The are not coming'

Hence, generative assumptions have led us to discover correlations between the syntactic position of negation and the requirement for an auxiliary to support its use. Conversely, we correctly predict that if negation is a head between T and C it will block the relation between these two heads. For example, Spanish does not allow for a true negative imperative (Han, 2001; Zeijlstra, 2006). Instead the verb has to be inflected for subjunctive (23).

(25)   **Ven!**   *No ven!   **No** vengas!
      come.2sg.IMP   NEG come.2sg.IMP   NEG come.2sg.SUBJ.PRES
      'Come!'   'Don't come!'

This can be understood if we assume that Infl has to enter into a head-relation (via movement) with C, where imperative force is located. Hence, if negation is a head intervening between Infl and C, then we expect that this relation cannot be established.

(26)   A structural analysis for the ban on negative imperatives

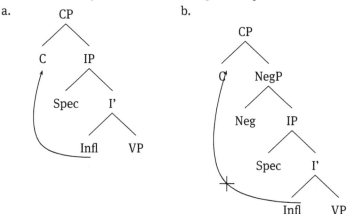

We have now seen that properties of movement can serve as a diagnostic for the structural analysis of negation (cf. Zanuttini 1997, 2001 a.o.). The way negation is integrated into syntactic structure (how high it is and whether it acts as a head or as an adjoined modifier) has significant ramifications for several, seemingly unrelated properties. In sum, the exploration of transformations has led to a series of discoveries of properties of the grammars of human languages and the language faculty that constructs them. Without the concept of transformational relations, the comparison of languages would have to remain focused on linear ordering alone missing certain clusters of properties.

3.3 The insignificance of words

We have now seen that one of the core assumptions of SS, namely the decomposition of syntax into various abstract levels, including a transformational level, has led to significant advances in our understanding of language variation. In this subsection, I turn to another major innovation introduced in SS, namely that the units of syntactic composition are not restricted to words. As we have seen, SS has laid the ground for syntactic analysis below the level of the lexical word. Specifically, it introduces into the set of possible building blocks inflectional affixes, passivization (a form of derivational morphology), and nominalization rules (also a form of derivation). This paved the way for the syntacticization of morphology more generally and indeed over the last 60 years, syntactic analyses for all types of morphology have been proposed. Recall again the TR for affix hopping repeated below.

(27) $[(1)] \; Af + v \rightarrow v + Af \; \#$

SS: 39 (29ii)

The inclusion of *Af* (for inflectional affix) in TRs blurs the boundary between syntax and morphology. The syntacticization of inflectional morphology is perhaps not surprising given that this type of morphology is sensitive to the syntactic context as evident from agreement morphology. Indeed, within generative syntactic theory the syntactic characteristic of inflectional morphology has played a major role for the analysis of the functional architecture associated with clause-structure. The first step towards this was the assumption that inflection is to be viewed as the head of the clause INFL (Chomsky, 1986), containing tense and agreement features, as illustrated in (25).

(28) INFL as the head of the clause

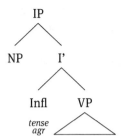

Eventually, INFL was decomposed and Pollock (1989) argues that each of the features associated with INFL are better analyzed as heading their own functional projection (TP and AgrP, respectively). Both, features as well as functional categories, have since been an arena for fruitful cross-linguistic research. It became possible to compare languages to each other independent of their morphological type: functional categories such as T and C can be occupied by different forms, including inflectional morphology, free morphemes, or abstract features triggering movement. Furthermore, since there are functional elements aside from tense, it is unsurprising that many categories, dedicated to hosting elements of specific semantic import have been proposed that may have sub-morphemic realizations. The most active research program to this effect is Cinque's 1999 *cartographic* approach to linguistic typology (see also the Starke's 2010 nanosyntax as well as Wiltschko's 2014 Universal Spine Hypothesis).

In sum, the postulation of the functional architecture responsible for gluing together lexical material has led to cross-linguistic comparison and typologies that go far beyond the classic structuralist typologies based on morphological type (analytic, synthetic, and poly-synthetic). The latter have long been known to be problematic (Anderson, 1985; Bauer, 1988; Spencer, 1991). By assuming functional architecture that can host language specific material we can compare languages to each other that are of different morphological type, but might share other properties in common. For example, Baker's 1996 polysynthesis parameter allows us to compare in interesting ways languages with rich morphology (Nichols' 1986 head-marking languages) but apparently optional arguments to those with less morphology but obligatory arguments. In particular, Baker 1996 argues that we should equate the arguments of a language like English to the agreement morphemes of a language like Mohawk; and conversely, we should compare dislocated (adjoined) material of the Romance-type to the optional arguments of Mohawk (see also Jelinek's 1984 pronominal argument hypothesis).

Baker's 1996 analysis of Mohawk (and other polysynthetic languages) has also contributed to the syntacticization of another phenomenon, traditionally thought of as falling into the domain of morphology, namely noun-incorporation (Baker, 1988). He argues that many properties of noun-incorporation follow if we assume that it is derived via movement of the head noun out of direct object position to head-adjoin to the selecting verb, as schematized in (26).

(29) The syntacticization of noun incorporation

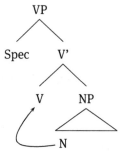

A movement analysis of noun-incorporation correctly predicts that noun-incorporation is restricted to objects and cannot apply to subjects—an instance of standard structurally conditioned subject-object asymmetries.

Assumptions have changed since Baker's analysis, with different mechanisms proposed for the derivation itself (see Barrie and Mathieu 2012 for recent discussion). However, the main claim, that it is syntactically derived has stood the test of time and has given rise to a fine-grained typology of noun-incorporation, one that would not have been possible under a morphological analysis (Wiltschko, 2009). For example, assuming that noun-incorporation correlates with particular semantic properties (e.g., the object cannot denote a specific referent), it has been proposed that even if the noun may not be overtly incorporated into the verb we can still maintain an incorporation analysis by postulating covert movement, which creates a semantic effect without any surface reflexes and hence is known as *pseudo-incorporation* (cf. Dayal 2011 for Hindi), which is also used to analyze OVS order in Niuean (Massam, 2001).

Without a syntactic analysis of incorporation, the parallelism between morphological noun-incorporation and semantic (pseudo-)incorporation would remain overlooked. Hence, the generative syntactic approach towards noun-incorporation extends the typological space considered and leads to discovery of variation.

Finally, let us consider the syntacticization of *derivational morphology*: it went hand in hand with the decomposition of lexical categories into (semi-)functional categories. For example, in the exoskeletal model (Borer, 2003, 2005) it is assumed that all grammatical properties of lexical items are introduced syntactically (via structure). This includes categorial information such as nounhood and verbhood introduced by *little n*, and *little v*, respectively (Marantz, 1997), as well as information about subcategories (such as the mass/count distinction or transitivity alternations). Hence, a seemingly simplex noun or verb is assumed to be composed of a series of (semi-)functional categories that introduce their systematic morphosyntactic and semantic properties. For example, a transitive verb may be decomposed into a verbalized root and a transitivizing *v*. This kind of decomposition receives evidence from languages that overtly encode transitivity. For example, in Basque, unergatives are formed with a bleached verb (*egin* 'do') and a nominal form roughly corresponding to English *do a cry/cough/laugh* (27). Similarly, in Halkomelem (Salish), unaccusative verbs are roots while all other verbs (unergatives, transitives, ditransitives) are derived by means of suffixation ((28); Gerdts 1988).

(30) a. *negar egin*   'cry'
     b. *eztul egin*   'cough'
     c. *barre egin*   'laugh'

Hale and Keyser 2002: 117 (22)

(31) a. *yéqw*   'burn'   *yeqw-**áls***   'perform burning'
     b. *íkw*   'lost'   *íkw'-**et***   'throw sthg. away'

Galloway 1993: 245–247

Strikingly, a decomposition of verbs according to their argument- or event-structure was independently proposed for English, a language which does not show any overt signs for this decomposition. Specifically, based on properties of double-object constructions Larson (1988) argues that verbs which take two objects are best analyzed by means of a VP-shell; and Hale and Keyser (1993) argue that unergative verbs in English are formed by means of incorporating a nominal root into an abstract verb.

This postulation of (semi-)functional categories in the composition of lexical categories allows for fruitful comparison across languages of very different types. This has led to a whole research program that seeks to understand universals and variation in argument-structure as well as event-structure (see Duguine et al. 2010; Hovav et al. 2010; Trueswell (forthcoming) for detailed discussion).

In sum, we have now seen that assumptions about the minimal ingredients of syntactic analysis have changed. Since SS, these ingredients are no longer assumed to be words. This is not surprising, given the fact that the notion of a "word" is elusive and escapes a clear definition (see Newell et al. 2017 for a recent overview). It would in fact be surprising if a problematic concept like the word were to serve as the primitive building block of syntax. Similarly, the classic notion of "morpheme" has been decomposed, arguably inspired by the decomposition of syntax introduced in SS. Specifically, on some current conceptualizations of this type of decomposition, syntax is no longer responsible for manipulating sound meaning-bundles (e.g., morphemes or words). Instead syntax is taken to manipulate abstract feature bundles; and form is inserted late, after the syntactic computation (Beard, 1995; Halle and Marantz, 1993). On this view, what appears to be a simplex morpheme, may be associated with a complex syntactic derivation.

Furthermore, as discussed in section 3.1, the postulation of a series of functional categories, is one way to implement the core insight of SS, namely that syntax is to be decomposed into a series of syntactic structures (cf. Williams 2003), including argument-structure sometimes also conceptualized as event-structure. In the next subsection, I consider the upper-bound of syntactic analysis: the notion of a sentence

4 The insignificance of the sentence

Following classic (structuralist) assumptions, the initial string of analysis in SS is assumed to be the sentence (Σ). However, the idea that syntax can be decomposed into a series of syntactic structures along with the assumption that different sentence types are related to each other via their transformational history (SS 91) has paved the way for the decomposition of the "sentence" as a primitive. Consider how. As we have seen in section 3.3, the syntactic structure of sentences is assumed to be made up of a series of functional categories. Crucially, there is no one-to-one correspondence between a particular functional category and what we may call a *sentence*. Rather, *clauses* can come in different sizes: under verbs of perception, a VP suffices; an IP is required for matrix declarative clauses; and certain verbs embed a CP. This is illustrated in (29).

(32)   Growing complexity of clause-structure

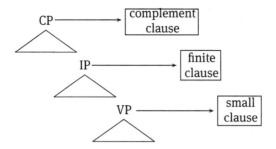

Accordingly, the notion of a sentence may best be defined contextually, such that it is perceived of as the highest functional category associated with a small clause (Wiltschko and Heim, 2016). Over the past twenty some years, the assumed size of clause-structure has grown even more. Specifically, the CP-domain (just as the IP and VP domain) has been articulated to include aspects of meaning that are considered to be discourse phenomena or part of the syntax-pragmatics interface. For example, based on properties of the left periphery, Rizzi 1997 decomposes the functional category C into several layers, including ForceP, TopicP, FocusP, and Fin(iteness)P. This is again in line with the general idea in SS according to which syntax is to be decomposed into a series of syntactic structures. The idea behind the articulation of the left periphery falls under the umbrella of adding another layer of syntactic structure, namely one that encodes *information structure* (see Féry and Ishihara 2016 for a recent overview including issues pertaining to language variation in this domain).

In a similar vein, the traditional domain of the sentence has been extended to include speech act structure, following an idea first introduced in the early 70s (Ross, 1970; Sadock, 1974). Current approaches towards the syntax of speech acts explore phenomena such as evidentials (Speas and Tenny, 2003), the relation between clause-types and speech acts (Speas and Tenny, 2003; Wiltschko and Heim, 2016), allocutive agreement (Miyagawa, 2017), discourse markers (Wiltschko, in press), discourse particles (Thoma, 2017), sentence final particles (Haegeman, 2014; Lam, 2014; Paul, 2014; Wiltschko and Heim, 2016), response markers (Krifka, 2013; Wiltschko, forthcoming), and vocatives (Hill, 2013), among others. Research on speech act structure and the syntax-pragmatic interface is currently growing but a systematic exploration of the range and limits of variation in this domain is still outstanding. But again, the core ideas introduced in SS (decomposition of syntax and the redefinition of syntactic atoms) are bound to play an important role.

5 Variation is variation is variation

The discovery of variation has been a major source of advancement in our understanding of UG, and conversely, the advancement in our understanding of the language faculty (largely triggered by some of the core assumptions introduced in SS) has led to new discoveries about language variation. In this way, Paul Postal's plea for the exploration of "exotic" languages through the lens of our knowledge about the language faculty (i.e., UG) rather than by following the American structuralist's dogma of describing languages in their own terms has come full circle.

> The well-founded pessimism which derives from the difficulties to be faced in studying languages not native to the linguist may, to an unknown extent, be mitigated by the (even at present far from nonexistent) advantages to be derived from approaching 'exotic' languages with a highly specific, substantively rich theory of language justified on the basis of the not insignificant range of distinct languages for which native linguists exist or can be expected to exist quite naturally. However, the possibilities so afforded will depend very much on overcoming the incredible harm done by that still dominant, extraordinarily exaggerated, habit of thought illustrated by the slogan 'describe each language in its own terms'. It will depend very much, that is, on the realization that the description of every aspect of a particular language must be partially determined by the knowledge we have of the nature of other languages, i.e., by the knowledge obtained about the nature of language itself. (Postal 1966: 93 Fn.4).

It is precisely through the decomposition of syntax as well as the deconstruction of the ingredients of language that it became possible to understand languages in their own terms and hence to understand language variation in a new way. I contend that the generative tradition should not only be viewed as a way to explore the human language faculty, it is also ideally suited to serve as a heuristic for discovery and comparison. Generative investigations of many understudied languages have led to advancement in our knowledge about their properties that go beyond the structuralist explorations that—while often very insightful—remain driven by surface phenomena. Given the fact that many of these languages are endangered, their in-depth investigation is no longer a matter of intellectual curiosity, but has to be viewed as an urgent matter. Indeed, many generative linguists are currently engaged in the documentation of these languages.

Similar considerations hold for the variation we observe within a language, namely work on dialectal as well as sociolectal variation. The inclusion of dialect variation in its empirical domain is a natural consequence of one of the core tenets of the generative enterprise: we are interested in a speaker's competence (what we know when we speak a language) rather than prescriptive rules about what we should know. Dialectal variation has been part of the generative agenda for decades now and includes work on dialects of Italian (Poletto 2000 a.o.), German (Bayer, 1984; Brandner, 2006; Weiß, 2005), Dutch (Barbiers, 2009; Bennis and MacLean, 2006; Van Craenenbroeck, 2010; Zwart, 1993), as well as English (Adger and Trousdale 2007; Henry 1995; Zanuttini and Horn 2014, a.o.).

Note that the often rather small-scale variation observed across dialects leads to the blurring of the boundaries between dialect, sociolect or idiolect such that socio-linguistic variation is no longer banned from generative analyses either. While generativists are typically not concerned with the sociological underpinnings of the observed variation, they are nevertheless interested in the range of variation (Adger, 2006). What we have learned over the years is that competence is not something that we need to explore within an idealized homogenous language community. It is our interest in language competence that legitimizes the exploration of the differences in competences of speakers.

6 Conclusion

SS has changed the way we think about language and therefore it also changed the way we think about how languages vary. It redefined the primitive building blocks of syntax such that we no longer think of syntax as the linguistic sub-discipline that deals with how words are arranged to create sentences. The introduction of transformational rules, which led to the postulation of features and functional categories, made it possible to compare languages to each other in ways that go beyond the comparison of linear ordering of words and constituents. Assuming that the building blocks of language are smaller, and much more abstract than words or morphemes makes it possible to discover patterns of variation that would have otherwise gone unnoticed. In a way, it allows us to view syntax as the system that mediates the relation between form and meaning. As such syntactic theory since SS transcends the traditional domains of linguistics, as already noted in SS: "there is little motivation for the objection to mixing levels, for the conception of higher-level elements as being literally constructed out of lower-level elements, or for the feeling that syntactic work is premature until all problems of phonemics or morphology are solved." (SS: 106).

This foreshadows the fact that much of current research in syntactic theory, and by extension much of the current explorations into language variation deal with interface issues.

Bibliography

Adger, David. 2003. *Core syntax: A minimalist approach*, volume 33. Oxford University Press Oxford.

Adger, David. 2006. Combinatorial variability. *Journal of Linguistics* 42:503–530.

Adger, David, and Peter Svenonius. 2011. Features in minimalist syntax. In *The Oxford handbook of linguistic minimalism*, ed. Cedric Boeckx, 27–51. Oxford: OUP.

Adger, David, and Graeme Trousdale. 2007. Variation in English Syntax: Theoretical Implications. *English Language and Linguistics* 11:261–278.

Anderson, Stephen R. 1985. Typological distinctions in word formation. In *Language typology and syntactic description*, ed. Timothy Shopen, volume 3, 3–56. Cambridge University Press Cambridge.

Baker, Carl L. 1970. Notes on the description of English questions: The role of an abstract question morpheme. *Foundations of language* 197–219.

Baker, Mark. 1988. *Incorporation: A theory of grammatical function changing*. Chicago, IL: University of Chicago Press.

Baker, Mark. 1996. *The polysynthesis parameter*. Oxford, UK: Oxford University Press.

Barbiers, Sjef. 2009. Locus and limits of syntactic microvariation. *Lingua* 119:1607–1623.

Barrie, Michael, and Éric Mathieu. 2012. Head movement and noun incorporation. *Linguistic Inquiry* 43:133–142.

Bauer, Laurie. 1988. *Introducing Linguistic Morphology*. Edinburgh, UK: Edinburgh University Press.

Bayer, Josef. 1984. COMP in Bavarian syntax. *The Linguistic Review* 3:209–274.

Beard, Robert. 1995. *Lexeme-morpheme base morphology: a general theory of inflection and word formation*. New York, NY: SUNY Press.

Bennis, Hans, and Alies MacLean. 2006. Variation in Verbal inflection in Dutch Dialects. *Morphology* 16:291–312.

Bloomfield, Leonard. 1927. On recent work in general linguistics. *Modern Philology* 25:211–230.

Bloomfield, Leonard. 1933. *Language*. New York, NY: Holt.

Boas, Franz. 1911. *Handbook of American Indian languages, vol. 1.*. Bureau of American Ethnology.

Boeckx, Cedric. 2014. *Elementary Syntactic STructures: Prospects of a Feature-free Syntax*. Cambridge, UK: Cambridge University Press.

Borer, Hagit. 1984. *Parametric Syntax*. Dordrecht: Foris.

Borer, Hagit. 1994. The projection of arguments. In *Functional projections*, ed. Elena Benedicto and Jeffrey Runner, number 17 in University of Massachusetts Occasional Papers in Linguistics, 19–47. Amherst, MA: GLSA.

Borer, Hagit. 2003. Exo-skeletal vs. endo-skeletal explanations: Syntactic projections and the lexicon. In *The Nature of Explanation in Linguistic Theory*, ed. John Moore and Maria Polinsky, 31–67. Standford, CA: CSLI Publications.

Borer, Hagit. 2005. *Structuring sense, vol. II: The normal course of events*. Oxford, UK: Oxford University Press.

Brandner, Ellen. 2006. Bare Infinitives in Alemannic and the Categorial Status of Infinitival Complements. *Linguistic Variation Yearbook* 6:203–268.

Cheng, Lisa Lai Shen. 1991. On the Typology of Wh-questions. Doctoral Dissertation, MIT, Cambridge, MA.
Cheng, Lisa Lai Shen. 1997. *On the typology of wh-questions*. New York, NY: Taylor & Francis.
Chomsky, Noam. 1957. *Syntactic Structures*. The Hague, The Netherlands: Mouton de Gruyter.
Chomsky, Noam. 1959. A review of B. F. Skinner's 'Verbal Behavior'. *Language* 35:26–58.
Chomsky, Noam. 1981. *Lectures on government and binding*. Dordrecht: Foris.
Chomsky, Noam. 1986. *Barriers*. Cambridge, MA: MIT Press.
Chomsky, Noam. 1995. *The Minimalist Program*. Cambridge, MA: MIT Press.
Chomsky, Noam. 2004. Beyond explanatory adequacy. In *Structures and Beyond*, ed. Adriana Belletti, number 3 in The Cartography of Syntactic Structures, 104–131. New York, NY: Oxford University Press.
Cinque, Guglielmo. 1999. *Adverbs and Functional Heads: A Crosslinguistic Perspective*. New York, NY: Oxford University Press.
Dayal, Veneeta. 2011. Hindi pseudo-incorporation. *Natural Language & Linguistic Theory* 29:123–167.
Dowty, David, and Belinda Brodie. 1984. The semantics of "floated" quantifiers in a transformationless grammar. In *Proceedings of the third West Coast Conference on Formal Linguistic*, 75–90. Stanford, CA: Stanford Linguistics Association.
Dryer, Matthew S. 2013. On the six-way word order typology, again. *Studies in Language. International Journal sponsored by the Foundation of Language* 37:267–301.
Duguine, Maia, Susana Huidobro, and Nerea Madariaga. 2010. *Argument structure and syntactic relations: a cross-linguistic perspective*, volume 158. London, UK: John Benjamins Publishing.
Féry, Caroline, and Shinichiro Ishihara. 2016. *The Oxford Handbook of Information Structure*. Oxford, UK: Oxford University Press.
Galloway, Brent Douglas. 1993. *A Grammar of Upriver Halkomelem*. Stanford, California: University of California Press.
Gerdts, Donna B. 1988. *Object and absolutive in Halkomelem Salish*. Outstanding dissertations in linguistics. New York, NY: Garland.
Greenberg, Joseph H. 1963. Some Universals of Grammar with Particular Reference to the Order of Meaningful Elements. In *Universals of Language*, ed. Joseph H. Greenberg, 73–113. Cambridge, MA: MIT Press. Reprinted as Greenberg 1990.
Greenberg, Joseph H. 1990. Some Universals of Grammar with Particular Reference to the Order of Meaningful Elements. In *On Language*, ed. Keith Denning and Suzanne Kemmer, 40–70. Stanford, CA: Stanford University Press.
Haegeman, Liliane. 1995. *The syntax of negation*, volume 75. Cambridge, UK: Cambridge University Press.
Haegeman, Liliane. 2014. West flemish verb-based discourse markers and the articulation of the speech act layer. *Studia Linguistica* 68:116–139.
Hale, Ken, and Samuel Jay Keyser. 2002. *Prolegomenon to a Theory of Argument Structure*. MIT Press.
Hale, Kenneth, and Samuel Jay Keyser. 1993. On argument structure and the lexical expression of syntactic relations. In *The view from Building 20: Essays in linguistics in honor of Sylvain Bromberger*, ed. Ken Hale and Samuel Jay Keyser, 53–109. Cambridge, MA: MIT Press.

Halle, Morris, and Alec Marantz. 1993. Distributed Morphology and the Pieces of Inflection. In *The view from Building 20: Essays in linguistics in honor of Sylvain Bromberger*, ed. Ken Hale and Samuel Jay Keyser, 111–176. Cambridge, MA: MIT Press.

Han, Chung-hye. 2001. Force, negation and imperatives. *Linguistic review* 18:289–326.

Henry, Alison. 1995. *Belfast English and Standard English: Dialect variation and parameter setting*. Oxford, UK: Oxford University Press.

Hill, Virginia. 2013. *Vocatives: How syntax meets with pragmatics*. Boston, MA: Brill.

Hovav, Malka Rappaport, Edit Doron, and Ivy Sichel, ed. 2010. *Lexical semantics, syntax, and event structure*. 27. Oxford, UK: Oxford University Press.

Jackendoff, Ray. 1977. *X-bar syntax: A study of phrase structure.*. Cambridge, MA: MIT Press.

Jelinek, Eloise. 1984. Empty categories, case, and configurationality. *Natural Language & Linguistic Theory* 2:39–76.

Katz, Jerrold J., and Paul M. Postal. 1964. *An Integrated Theory of Linguistic Descriptions*. Cambridge, MA: MIT Press.

Koopman, Hilda, and Dominique Sportiche. 1991. The position of subjects. *Lingua* 85:211–258.

Krifka, Manfred. 2013. Response particles as propositional anaphors. In *Semantics and Linguistic Theory*, ed. T Snider, volume 23, 1–18.

Lam, Zoe Wai-Man. 2014. A complex ForceP for speaker-and addressee-oriented discourse particles in Cantonese. *Studies in Chinese Linguistics* 35:61–80.

Larson, Richard K. 1988. On the double object construction. *Linguistic Inquiry* 21:589–632.

Marantz, Alec. 1997. No escape from syntax: Don't try morphological analysis in the privacy of your own lexicon. In *Proceedings of the 21st Penn Linguistics Colloquium (PLC 21)*, ed. Alexis Dimitriadis, Laura Siegen, Clarissa Surek-Clark, and Alexander Williams, volume 4 of *University of Pennsylvania Working Papers in Linguistics*, 201–225. Philadelphia, PA: Penn Linguistics Club.

Massam, Diane. 2001. Pseudo noun incorporation in Niuean. *Natural Language & Linguistic Theory* 19:153–197.

McCloskey, James. 1997. Subjecthood and subject positions. In *Elements of Grammar*, ed. Liliane Haegeman, 197–235. Dordrecht: Kluwer Academic Publishers.

Miyagawa, Shigeru. 2017. *Agreement beyond phi*. Cambridge, MA: MIT Press.

Newell, Heather, Maire Noonan, and Lisa Travis, ed. 2017. *The Structure of Words at the Interfaces*, volume 68. Oxford, UK: Oxford University Press.

Nichols, Johanna. 1986. Head-marking and dependent-marking grammar. *Language* 56–119.

Paul, Waltraud. 2014. Why particles are not particular: Sentence-final particles in Chinese as heads of a split CP. *Studia Linguistica* 68:77–115.

Poletto, Cecilia. 2000. *The higher functional field: Evidence from Northern Italian dialects*.

Pollock, Jean-Yves. 1989. Verb movement, Universal Grammar, and the structure of IP. *Linguistic inquiry* 20:365–424.

Rizzi, Luigi. 1997. The Fine Structure of the Left Periphery. In *Elements of Grammar*, ed. Liliane Haegeman, 281–337. Dordrecht: Kluwer Academic Publishers.

Ross, John R. 1967. Constraints on variables in syntax. Doctoral dissertation, MIT, Cambridge, MA.

Ross, John R. 1970. On Declarative Sentences. In *Readings in English transformational grammar*, ed. Roderick A. Jacobs and Peter S. Rosenbaum, 222–272. Washington, DC: Georgetown University Press.

Sadock, Jerrold M. 1974. *Toward a linguistic theory of speech acts*. New York, NY: Academic Press.

Sapir, Edward. 1921. An introduction to the study of speech. *Language* .
Skinner, Burrhus Frederic. 1957. *Verbal Behavior*. New York, NY: Appleton-Century-Crofts.
Speas, Margaret, and Carol Tenny. 2003. Configurational properties of point of view roles. In *Asymmetry in grammar*, ed. Anna Maria Di Sciullo, volume 1, 315–345. London, UK: John Benjamins.
Spencer, Andrew. 1991. *Morphological Theory*. Oxford, UK: Basil Blackwell.
Starke, Michal. 2010. Nanosyntax: A short primer to a new approach to language. *Nordlyd* 36:1–6.
Thoma, Sonja Christine. 2017. Discourse particles and the syntax of discourse-evidence from Miesbach Bavarian. Doctoral Dissertation, University of British Columbia.
Travis, Lisa DeMena. 1984. *Parameters and effects of word order variation*. Cambridge, MA: MIT Press.
Van Craenenbroeck, Jeroen. 2010. *The syntax of ellipsis: Evidence from Dutch dialects*. Oxford, UK: Oxford University Press.
Watanabe, Akira. 1992. Subjacency and S-structure movement of wh-in-situ. *Journal of East Asian Linguistics* 1:255–291.
Weiß, Helmut. 2005. Inflected complementizers in continental West Germanic dialects. *Zeitschrift für Dialektologie und Linguistik* 148–166.
Williams, Edwin. 2003. *Representation theory*. Cambridge, MA: MIT Press.
Wiltschko, Martina. 2006. C-selection is Unique. In *Proceedings of the 25th West Coast Conference on Formal Linguistics*, 444–452.
Wiltschko, Martina. 2009. $\sqrt{}$ Root incorporation: evidence from lexical suffixes in Halkomelem Salish. *Lingua* 119:199–223.
Wiltschko, Martina. 2014. *The universal structure of categories: Towards a formal typology*. Cambridge, UK: Cambridge University Press.
Wiltschko, Martina. forthcoming. Response particles beyond answering. In *Order and Structure in Syntax*, ed. L. Bailey and M. Sheehy. Language Science Press.
Wiltschko, Martina. in press. Ergative constellations in the structure of speech acts. In *The Oxford Handbook of Ergativity*, ed. Jessica Coon and Diane Massam. Oxford, UK: Oxford University Press.
Wiltschko, Martina, and Johannes Heim. 2016. The syntax of confirmationals. In *Outside the Clause: Form and function of extra-clausal constituents*, ed. Gunther Kaltenböck, Evelien Keizer, and Arne Lohmann, volume 178, 305. John Benjamins Publishing Company.
Zanuttini, Raffaella. 1997. *Negation and clausal structure: A comparative study of Romance languages*. Oxford, UK: Oxford University Press.
Zanuttini, Raffaella. 2001. Sentential Negation. In *The Handbook of Contemporary Syntactic Theory*, ed. Mark Baltin and Chris Collins, 511–535. Blackwell.
Zanuttini, Raffaella, and Laurence Horn, ed. 2014. *Micro-syntactic Variation in North American English*. Oxford, UK: Oxford University Press.
Zeijlstra, Hedde H. 2004. Sentential Negation and Negative Concord. Doctoral Dissertation, University of Amsterdam.
Zeijlstra, Hedde H. 2006. The ban on true negative imperatives. *Empirical issues in syntax and semantics* 6:405–424.
Zwart, Jan-Wouter. 1993. Clues from dialect syntax: Complementizer agreement. In *Dialektsyntax*, 246–270. Springer.